Systems Programming with C# and .NET

Building robust system solutions with C# 12 and .NET 8

Dennis Vroegop

‹packt›

Systems Programming with C# and .NET

Copyright © 2024 Packt Publishing

All rights reserved. No part of this book may be reproduced, stored in a retrieval system, or transmitted in any form or by any means, without the prior written permission of the publisher, except in the case of brief quotations embedded in critical articles or reviews.

Every effort has been made in the preparation of this book to ensure the accuracy of the information presented. However, the information contained in this book is sold without warranty, either express or implied. Neither the author, nor Packt Publishing or its dealers and distributors, will be held liable for any damages caused or alleged to have been caused directly or indirectly by this book.

Packt Publishing has endeavored to provide trademark information about all of the companies and products mentioned in this book by the appropriate use of capitals. However, Packt Publishing cannot guarantee the accuracy of this information.

Associate Group Product Manager: Kunal Sawant

Publishing Product Manager: Akash Sharma

Book Project Manager: Deeksha Thakkar

Senior Editor: Esha Banerjee

Technical Editor: Jubit Pincy

Copy Editor: Safis Editing

Proofreader: Esha Banerjee

Indexer: Hemangini Bari

Production Designer: Gokul Raj S.T

DevRel Marketing Coordinator: Sonia Chauhan

First published: July 2024

Production reference: 1120724

Published by Packt Publishing Ltd.

Grosvenor House

11 St Paul's Square

Birmingham

B3 1RB, UK

ISBN: 978-1-83508-268-3

www.packtpub.com

To my amazing daughter Emma and my wonderful wife Diana. They say books are written in solitary, but that is entirely untrue. I would not have been able to write this if it hadn't been for your support. This work is as much yours as it is mine. I would not have been the man I am today if it weren't for you. Thank you.

- Dennis

Contributors

About the author

Dennis Vroegop is a programmer, no matter what his business card states. He has been programming computers since the early 1980s and still gets a kick whenever he sees his software running. After graduating with a degree in Business Informatics, he has worked in many roles over the years while retaining his passion for developing great software. These days, he works as an interim IT manager or CTO, helping companies get their software development in shape and making the developers happy about their work again.

He has been awarded the Microsoft MVP Award every year since 2006. In that role, he has been working with the C# team in Redmond on design sessions and has helped shape the language (a little bit). Dennis is a sought-after international speaker and public figure who is always ready to teach new generations about programming. Apart from his computer-related activities, Dennis plays the guitar and sings in a classic rock cover band named "The Total Amateurs," which says all you need to know about their skills.

Dennis lives with his wife, Diana, and they have a wonderful daughter, Emma.

About the reviewers

Ankit Srivastava is a seasoned Senior Developer at Walmart; boasting seven years of extensive experience in software development. He specializes in .NET Development, Windows Development, WPF, WCF, REST API, .NET Core, .NET Standard, Python, and Linux. Ankit earned his Bachelor of Technology degree in Information Technology from Harcourt Butler Technological Institute and holds certifications in C#, C/C++, Python, Linux, Java, and SQL. Throughout his career, he has made significant contributions to diverse domains, including Semiconductors, Automotive, Storage, Chemical Heat Exchangers, and Health and Wellness.

Sarita Nag earned her master's degree in Computer Application from KIIT University, Orissa, India. She started her career as a Software Engineer at Thomson Reuters and since then she has worked for many multinational companies. She is currently working as a Senior Developer at Fiserv, New Jersey, USA.

Sarita has 10+ years of experience in the various phases of Software Development Life cycle (SDLC) and Agile methodologies. She has also worked in domains such as Tax and Accounting, Auditing, Financial, Communication, and Customer relationships.

She is passionate about taking on new challenges and learning new things. Besides Development and Coding, Sarita enjoys spending time with her family. Her hobbies include adventure sports and photography.

Table of Contents

Preface · xv

Overview of Systems Programming · 1

Let's define systems programming	1	What is .NET anyway?	12
When is a system user-facing and when is it not?	3	.NET, .NET Framework, .NET Standard – what is all this?	14
A better definition	7	Programming languages – a choice to make	15
Using C# and .NET in systems programming	8	Now what?	16
Higher-level languages for systems programming	8	Setting up your development environment	16
Kernel mode and user mode	9		
Why use .NET?	10		

1

The One with the Low-Level Secrets · 19

Technical requirements	20	Dealing with errors	34
What are low-level APIs, and how do they differ from higher-level abstractions?	20	Issues when debugging code with low-level APIs	39
		Error handling	39
Overview of .NET Core runtime components (CLR, BCL)	24	Interoperability	40
		Debugging tools	42
CLR	24	Compatibility and portability	43
BCL	27	Documentation and community support	43
Using P/Invoke to call low-level APIs	29	Next steps	43

2
The One Where Speed Matters — 45

Technical requirements	46	Arrays, Lists, and LinkedLists	58
Setting up the stage	46	Stacks and queues	59
Accessibility	46	HashSets and lists	60
Hosting costs	47	SortedList, SortedDictionary, and Dictionary	60
Planned obsolescence	47	Dictionary or last of tuples/objects	61
Energy usage	47	For versus ForEach	62
Which integer is the fastest?	47	**Strings**	**62**
The CTS	49	Use StringBuilder for concatenation	63
Value types and reference types	50	Interning strings	63
Classes and structs	50	Use String.Concat or String.Join	64
Floating-point numbers	51	Comparison	64
Where types live – the difference between value types and reference types	52	Preallocating StringBuilder	66
		Writing unsafe code	**66**
		Compiler optimizations	**68**
The stack and the heap	52	Aggressive optimization	68
Boxing and unboxing	54	The optimize flag	69
Hidden boxing and unboxing	56	**Next steps**	**70**
Choosing the right data structures and algorithms	58		

3
The One with the Memory Games — 71

Technical requirements	72	IDisposable	79
An overview of the GC	72	Memory-saving tips and tricks	87
GC and its generations	72	Unsafe code and pointers in C#	91
The LOH	77	Next steps	95
Finalizers	78		

4
The One with the Thread Tangles · 97

Technical requirements	97	Synchronizing threads	116
Concurrency and threading – the basics	98	Synchronization – how do we do that?	116
		Synchronization with async/await	119
The beginnings of concurrency – the IRQ	99	Canceling a thread	120
Cooperative and preemptive multitasking	99	Thread-safe programming techniques	124
Threads in C#	100	Lock()	125
Win32 threads	101	Records	126
.NET threads	105	Avoid static members and classes	126
Tasks and Parallel Library – the TPL	108	Using the volatile keyword	127
Async/await	110	Concurrent collections in .NET	127
Task.Wait() and Task.Result	115	Next steps	131

5
The One with the Filesystem Chronicles · 133

Technical requirements	134	Using CancellationTokens	153
File writing basics	134	BufferedStream	155
FileStream	135	File system security	156
Even faster – Win32	138	Encryption basics	156
File reading basics	140	Symmetric encryption and decryption	158
Reading binary data	141	Asymmetric encryption and decryption	160
Directory operations	142	File compression	162
The Path class	143	Compressing some data	162
The Directory class	144	Decompressing some data	163
The DirectoryInfo class	146	Serialization – JSON and Binary	164
File system monitoring	147	JSON serialization	164
Asynchronous I/O	152	Binary serialization	166
The naïve approach	152	Next steps	168

6

The One Where Processes Whisper — 169

Technical requirements	170	A TCP-based chat app	179
Overview of IPC and its importance in modern computing	170	UDP	183
		Using shared memory to exchange data between processes	184
Windows Messages	172		
A sample	173	Overview of RPCs and how to use them for IPC	186
Working with pipes for local IPC	174	JSON RPC	186
Named pipes	174		
Anonymous pipes	176	Overview of gRPC and how to use it for IPC	189
Using sockets to establish network-based IPC	178	Differences between JSON RPC and gRPC	193
Networking 101	178	Next steps	194

7

The One with the Operating System Tango — 195

Technical requirement	196	WMI	210
The Windows Registry	196	How to use WMI	211
What is the Windows Registry?	197	Reading the CPU temperature	212
How to access and store data with the Windows Registry	199	Reading the BIOS	213
		Controlling the Windows Update service	214
Comparing the Windows Registry to JSON settings files	202	Watching USB devices	215
Worker Services	203	Registry and WMI – risks and how to avoid them	217
Docker support	205	The Windows Registry	217
Dissecting the Worker Service	206	Potential risks when dealing with WMI	219
Controlling the lifetime of the service	208	Next steps	222
Wrapping up Worker Services	210		

8

The One with the Network Navigation — 223

Technical requirements	224	Making asynchronous calls	237
The fundamentals	224	**Networking performance**	**239**
A walk down the OSI layers	224	Connection pooling	239
Exploring the System.Net namespace	**226**	Caching	243
Understanding HTTP/HTTPS	226	Compression and serialization	244
FTP	227	Keep-alive connections	244
Email protocols	230	**Networking errors and time-outs**	**244**
Working with the		Using the HTTPClient wisely	244
System.Net.Sockets namespace	**232**	Implementing retries with Polly	246
Steps to take when using sockets	233	The circuit breaker pattern	248
IPv4 and IPv6	234	Validating network availability	248
Looking up time with sockets	235	Monitoring and logging	249
Async, non-blocking networking	**237**	**Next steps**	**249**

9

The One with the Hardware Handshakes — 251

Technical requirements	252	Receiving serial data with .NET	262
Connecting to serial ports	**252**	**Faking a serial device**	**271**
The path to the hardware	252	**Making it foolproof**	**273**
Why do we care?	254	Reasons things go haywire	273
A word about parity, data sizes, and stop bits	255	Hardening your code	274
Working with an Arduino	257	**Next steps**	**276**

10

The One with the Systems Check-Ups — 277

Technical requirements	278	Serilog	291
Available logging frameworks	**279**	Comparing the logging frameworks	294
Default logger in .NET	279	**Monitoring your applications**	**296**
NLog	285	Monitoring with Seq	296

11

The One with the Debugging Dances — 311

Technical requirements	311	Parallel Watch	327
Introducing debugging	312	Debugging deadlocks with Parallel Stacks and Thread windows	332
Debugging and profiling – an overview	312	Profiling application performance	336
Debugging	313	The prime application	337
Profiling	313	Profiling in Visual Studio	338
Debugging 101	314	Benchmarking different solutions	341
Debug builds versus Release builds	314	Other tools	344
Breakpoints	315	Debugging tools	345
Debug windows	321	Profiling tools	346
Diagnostic Tools	324	Next steps	347
Debugging multithreaded and asynchronous code	327		

12

The One with the Security Safeguards — 349

Technical requirements	350	Using environment variables	362
Security for system programmers	350	Using the right privilege level	364
What could happen if we have a vulnerability?	350	Admin-level scenarios	365
How to protect yourself	352	Impersonating as an admin	365
Working with strings	353	How to transmit network data securely	368
Protecting settings	353	How HTTPS works	368
Reading encrypted data	356	Certificates and certificate authorities	370
Where are the keys?	356	Creating a development certificate	372
Handling strings in memory	357	Securing TCP streams	373
Using key management	360	Next steps	378
Using the Azure Key Vault	360		

Performance counters 298
Prometheus 300
Other platforms for monitoring 305
What you should be monitoring or logging 306
Next steps 309

13

The One with the Deployment Dramas — 379

Technical requirements	380	Building a simple installer	397
From development to production	380	Writing a Custom Action	399
Publishing and file copy	381	Incorporating the custom action in the setup	402
Publish using Visual Studio	382	**Using Docker**	**404**
Publishing using the CLI	384	Adding Docker support to your background worker	404
Using Azure DevOps and GitHub	**386**	Deploying your Docker images	405
Deploying to Azure	386	Production-ready Docker repository	407
Enabling continuous integration in Azure DevOps	392	**Next steps**	**407**
Enabling CI from GitHub	395		
Building installers with Visual Studio	**396**		

14

The One with the Linux Leaps — 409

Technical requirements	410	Make your code cross-platform	427
An overview of Linux	411	How code can help you	428
A short history of Linux	412	**Writing services for Linux**	**430**
What is Linux?	413	The service description	430
A quick primer to use Linux	**416**	Installing the service	431
Basic commands	418	Uninstalling the service	432
Elevated privileges	420	Handling signals	433
Developing for Linux	**421**	**Summing up**	**435**
Installing .NET on Linux	421	Let's recap	435
Running a .NET background worker on Linux	424		

Index — 437

Other Books You May Enjoy — 450

Preface

Most people think of **graphical user interface** (**GUI**) applications when they think of software. Software is the code that the user interacts with. But these days, that's not true anymore. All modern applications, web servers, web applications, and mobile solutions mostly rely on hidden, unseen system software. This is the software that is built for other software. It is dormant until needed, then it does its job and goes back to sleep. These programs are the unsung heroes of our ecosystem, doing the work in the background. At the same time, GUI systems stand in the limelight. However, do not underestimate these hard-working systems: they must be extremely fast, reliable, and safe. Therefore, they are essential to good working systems and are hard to write. This book teaches you all you need to know to write these applications.

Who this book is for

People writing systems software are not junior developers. Ideally, you have a couple of years of experience developing software with C# and .NET. I will not explain what a variable is or how a while-loop differs from a for-loop. You know how to use NuGet. If I ask you to switch from Debug to Release mode in Visual Studio, you know what I am asking you to do.

But I do not expect you to know what instructions a CPU uses. I will explain those when we reach that point in the book. So there is no need to be on that low level just yet.

This book is for people who want to write system software. System software is software that is usually not visible to the regular user. However, it is essential to the good working of the complete software ecosystem running on your systems.

This means that you must have a passion for programs that run fast and are stable. This also means that the software we write is not the easiest to maintain: readability often decreases as performance increases. This is not for the faint-hearted: writing this kind of software is hard-core development. But if you are curious about how your programs really work deep inside the heart of the machine, this is the book for you.

The lessons learned here can, of course, be applied to all sorts of projects. Performance and stability can benefit all programs. So, if you are ready to take your C# and .NET skills to the next level, follow along!

What this book covers

Overview of Systems Programming sets the stage and explains what systems programming is all about.

Chapter 1, The One with the Low-Level Secrets, dives into the low-level APIs, the BCL and CLR, and how to use Win32 APIs.

Chapter 2, The One Where Speed Matters, examines how to make your software perform as fast as possible.

Chapter 3, The One with the Memory Games, talks about memory handling, the garbage collector, and how to be as memory efficient as possible.

Chapter 4, The One with the Thread Tangles, looks at threads and asynchronous programming.

Chapter 5, The One with the Filesystem Chronicles, teaches input/output, file handling, encryption, and compression of files.

Chapter 6, The One Where Processes Whisper, talks about how to make programs communicate on one machine or over a network.

Chapter 7, The One with the Operating System Tango, dives into the operating system's services and how to use them.

Chapter 8, The One with the Network Navigation, discusses everything we need to know about networking in your application, both as a server and a client.

Chapter 9, The One with the Hardware Handshakes, deals with connecting to outside hardware and communicating with other devices.

Chapter 10, The One with the Systems Check-Ups, talks about logging and monitoring your software.

Chapter 11, The One with the Debugging Dances, is all about debugging your software.

Chapter 12, The One with the Security Safeguards, talks about the security of your software.

Chapter 13, The One with the Deployment Dramas, teaches you how to deploy your software to the production machines.

Chapter 14, The One with the Linux Leaps, discusses the operating system that most of our software will run on: Linux.

To get the most out of this book

I use Visual Studio 2022 as the main software development tool in this book. It is advisable for you to have a working knowledge of this, including creating console applications, class libraries, and worker services. You do not need to know what a Worker Service is as long as you can create a default one.

Each chapter might have software that you may want to try out. You'll find the details explained in the *Technical requirements* section of the concerned chapter.

Software/hardware covered in the book	Operating system requirements
Visual Studio	Windows 10 or 11

If you are using the digital version of this book, we advise you to type the code yourself or access the code from the book's GitHub repository (a link is available in the next section). Doing so will help you avoid any potential errors related to the copying and pasting of code.

Download the example code files

You can download the example code files for this book from GitHub at https://github.com/PacktPublishing/Systems-Programming-with-C-Sharp-and-.NET. If there's an update to the code, it will be updated in the GitHub repository.

We also have other code bundles from our rich catalog of books and videos available at https://github.com/PacktPublishing/. Check them out!

Conventions used

There are a number of text conventions used throughout this book.

`Code in text`: Indicates code words in text, database table names, folder names, filenames, file extensions, pathnames, dummy URLs, user input, and Twitter handles. Here is an example: " One of them is the `Share` option. We have set it to `FileShare.Delete` "

A block of code is set as follows:

```
using var serialPort = new SerialPort(
    "COM3",
    9600,
    Parity.None,
    8,
    StopBits.One);
serialPort.Open();
try
{
    serialPort.Write([42],0, 1);
}
finally
{
    serialPort.Close();
}
```

Any command-line input or output is written as follows:

```
docker tag image13workerfordocker:dev localhost:5000/
image13workerfordocker:dev
```

Bold: Indicates a new term, an important word, or words that you see onscreen. For instance, words in menus or dialog boxes appear in **bold**. Here is an example: "**Compact object representations**: Sometimes, you can save some memory by smartly combining data into other data structures".

> **Tips or important notes**
> Appear like this.

Get in touch

Feedback from our readers is always welcome.

General feedback: If you have questions about any aspect of this book, email us at customercare@packtpub.com and mention the book title in the subject of your message.

Errata: Although we have taken every care to ensure the accuracy of our content, mistakes do happen. If you have found a mistake in this book, we would be grateful if you would report this to us. Please visit www.packtpub.com/support/errata and fill in the form.

Piracy: If you come across any illegal copies of our works in any form on the internet, we would be grateful if you would provide us with the location address or website name. Please contact us at copyright@packt.com with a link to the material.

If you are interested in becoming an author: If there is a topic that you have expertise in and you are interested in either writing or contributing to a book, please visit authors.packtpub.com.

Share Your Thoughts

Once you've read *Systems Programming with C# and .NET*, we'd love to hear your thoughts! Scan the QR code below to go straight to the Amazon review page for this book and share your feedback.

https://packt.link/r/1-835-08268-8

Your review is important to us and the tech community and will help us make sure we're delivering excellent quality content.

Download a free PDF copy of this book

Thanks for purchasing this book!

Do you like to read on the go but are unable to carry your print books everywhere?

Is your eBook purchase not compatible with the device of your choice?

Don't worry, now with every Packt book you get a DRM-free PDF version of that book at no cost.

Read anywhere, any place, on any device. Search, copy, and paste code from your favorite technical books directly into your application.

The perks don't stop there, you can get exclusive access to discounts, newsletters, and great free content in your inbox daily

Follow these simple steps to get the benefits:

1. Scan the QR code or visit the link below

    https://packt.link/free-ebook/978-1-83508-268-3

2. Submit your proof of purchase
3. That's it! We'll send your free PDF and other benefits to your email directly

Overview of Systems Programming

So, you want to learn about **systems programming** in .NET, using C#. At least, I assume you want to learn that; you probably read the title of this book and decided that this was a good match. Maybe you have dived into systems programming a bit and want to get better at it. Or, perhaps you haven't touched that subject and want to start. Or, maybe you picked the wrong book. If the latter is the case, I hope you still have your receipt so you can return this book and get something else. For all others: welcome!

Let's define systems programming

Before we go into the nitty gritty details of systems programming, we need to set the stage. We need to have a common understanding of a couple of things. For instance, what does the term "systems programming" even mean? What is it for? Who is it for?

Let me get started with a definition.

Systems programming is the programming of systems. That might technically be correct, but I don't think it helps us move forward.

Let us break it down: what is a *system*?

That one is easy. We have been building systems for ages, so we understand what we mean by a **system**.

Let me show you one definition:

A system is a set or arrangement of things that are related or connected so as to form a unity or organic whole. It is a collection of components or parts that interact with each other to function. This term is used in various fields such as physics, biology, computer science, and business management, each with slightly different connotations.

Great. But this definition is a bit broad. We might want to focus on computer science or software development. No problem; there are several definitions to choose from as well:

A system is a collection of software components that interact to perform a specific function or set of functions.

That is a lot better. If we dive into this a bit further, we can distinguish between different groups of systems:

- **Software systems**: This is an integrated set of software components that work together to carry out a specific function or set of functions. Those components can be a database server, microservices, and a frontend. Those components form the complete system, such as a CRM system, source control repository system, and others like that.

- **Operating systems (OSs)**: You probably know what an OS is. I think you have seen that term so often that there is a fair chance you didn't even realize it is a system. But it most definitely is an OS that contains many parts and components, such as drivers, tools, helpers, and logs. Together, they deliver a system you as a user can use to run your software on, independently of the hardware.

- **Distributed systems**: We often refer to loosely connected components on a network as a distributed system. Each part is isolated from the others, but they must collaborate to achieve something worthwhile. For example, Azure DevOps runs on many different servers in the Azure cloud. All the components run potentially on different servers and machines, and these components can even be running in different parts of the world. However, they work together to form a complete solution for the end user.

- **Embedded systems**: An embedded system is usually a combination of hardware and software. The components are tightly coupled with each other. Developers usually write the software to match specific specifications so it uses the hardware best. Think, for instance, about the systems in your car. If you have a reasonably recent car, you undoubtedly have an entertainment system on board. The word "system" in "entertainment system" is a bit of a giveaway: it consists of many distinct components. There is very likely a device that can collect electromagnetic waves from the air (we call that a radio). That device is connected to some software that interprets those waves and turns them into an electrical signal to feed the speakers. Next to that, a component shows you, as the user, what you are listening to. I am sure you can find a lot of other systems in your car and probably in your TV, your phone, or your refrigerator.

There are many more examples, but I hope you see that a system always consists of individual components that are not useful on their own but, when combined, deliver a solution to a problem.

But hold on. We are not done yet.

Given these definitions and examples, you might think that the art of systems programming is just the programming of these systems, and you would not be wrong. But that is, in general, not what systems programming means. It most certainly is not what I mean by that.

Very, very roughly, we can divide software into two types:

- **User-facing software**: This is software written to be used by people. It has a **user interface (UI)** with buttons, lists, labels, and more. People interact with the software by using various means of input modalities.

- **Software-facing software**: This is software designed to be used by other software. There are no UIs since we have no users. We could say other components are the users, but when I say users, I mean people. Software-facing software interacts with other components through APIs, RPC (Remote Procedure Calls) calls, file transfer, and many other ways. No humans are involved in this.

It is the second type we are most interested in here in this book – software meant to be used by other software.

When is a system user-facing and when is it not?

It is not always clear when people are the primary users of some code or when other processes are. We could be very rigorous and say that anything with a UI is user-oriented; anything else is systems-oriented. That will make life easier for us if we want a clear definition. However, in the real world, the boundaries tend to blur.

Let me give you an example. Have a look at this Visual Studio Solution:

```
Solution Explorer
Search Solution Explorer (Ctrl+;)
Solution 'MyAwesomeCalculator' (2 of 2 projects)
  ▲ MathFunctions
    ▷ Dependencies
    ▲ Simple
      ▲ Implementations
        ▷ Adder.cs
        ▷ Divider.cs
        ▷ Multiplier.cs
        ▷ Subtractor.cs
      ▷ IAdder.cs
      ▷ IDivider.cs
      ▷ IMultplier.cs
      ▷ ISubtractor.cs
    Statistical
  ▲ MyAwesomeCalculator
    ▷ Dependencies
    ▷ Program.cs
```

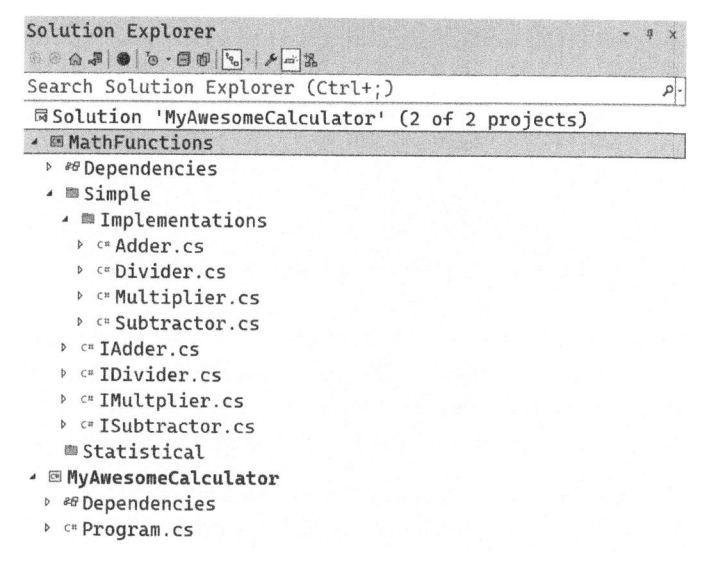

Figure 0.1: Solution Explorer with the Calculator project

We have a very, very simple solution here. It has a main program called `MyAwesomeCalculator` that contains the main code. This is the entry point of our app, using the console as the UI. All logic is in the `MathFunctions` class library. This is where the magic happens.

If we go back to our definition of Systems programming, we could say that writing the `MathFunctions` class library is part of Systems programming. After all, no user will ever interact with the classes and interfaces in that library. It is the code in `MyAwesomeCalculator` that actually uses it.

Great! This means writing the `MathFunctions` library is systems programming! Well, not so fast. We might come to another conclusion if we look at the sequence diagram that explains the flow. *Figure 0.2* shows this sequence diagram.

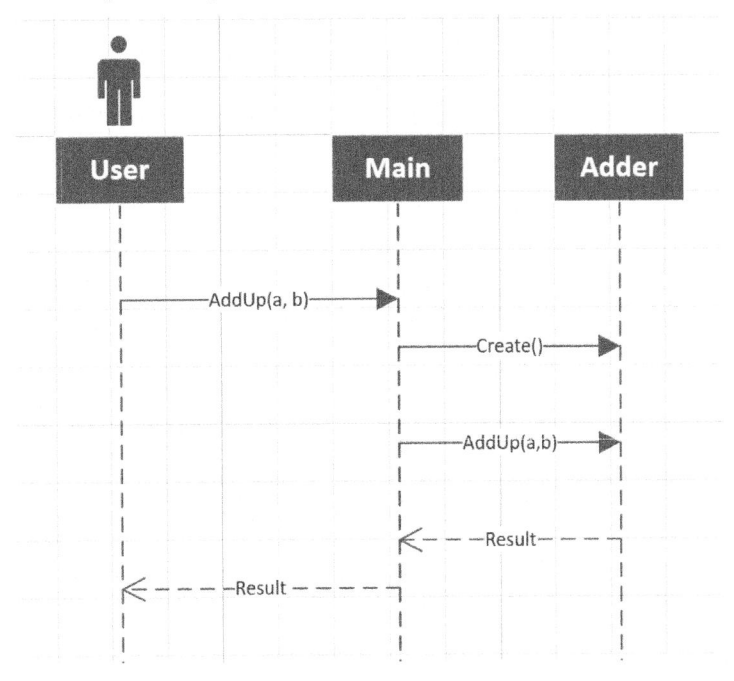

Figure 0.2: Sequence diagram for our calculations

As you can see in *Figure 0.2*, the user initiates an operation: they want to add up two numbers. They enter it in the UI of the `Main` class. The `Main` class then instantiates an instance of the `Adder` class. After that creation, the `Main` class calls the `AddUp(a,b)` method. The result is passed back to the `Main` class and shown to the user. After all this, we could discard the `Adder` instance.

Great. Where are the boundaries? If we look at it this way, we could say that the code in `Adder` and, thus, in the `MathFunctions` library is immediately tied to user actions. So, it is user-facing code instead of systems-facing code.

I still like to use the question of who is using the code to determine what kind of software we are writing. But apparently, this is not enough. We need to go a bit deeper.

The code in `MyAwesomeCalculator` and `MathFunctions` are in separate assemblies. The user interacts with one assembly; the other is accessed through code only. But they can still be seen as one. If we run the application, the runtime creates `AppDomain` for us.

`AppDomain` in .NET is different than `AppDomain` in .NET Framework. The latter had more ways to isolate code from each other. That was nice, but it was a typical Windows feature. That did not translate well to other platforms. So, to make .NET applications run on other platforms, they needed to redesign this. This results in `AppDomain` being less restrictive than it used to be. Still, `AppDomain` remains a logical boundary between different processes. Code runs in one app domain and cannot access other app domains directly.

Here, we have another clue: our `MyAwesomeCalculator` app and the associated `MathFunctions` assembly all run in the same `AppDomain`. To the OS, they are one. Since we decided that actual people use the `Main` method, the same applies to all other pieces of code in that particular `AppDomain`.

Let's rewrite our solution a bit. See the following screenshot.

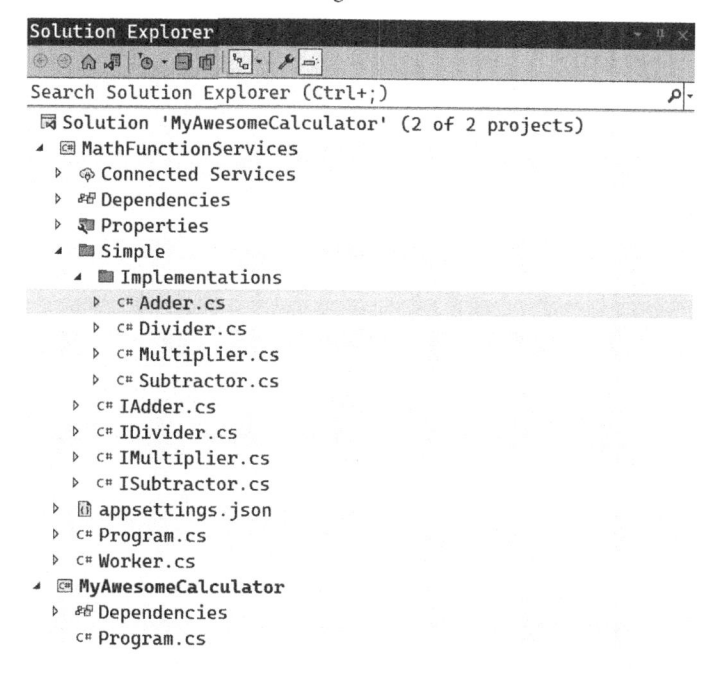

Figure 0.3: Our solution with a worker process

We removed the class library with the code that did all the work. Instead, we created a new project. That project is a **worker process**. Technically, I should have kept that class library and referenced that, but I wanted to keep things simple.

A worker process is a background process that runs all the time (not technically true, but for now, this is true enough). It just sits there doing nothing. Then, suddenly, something of interest happens, and it comes to life, does its job, and goes to idle mode again.

As shown in *Figure 0.4*, the sequence diagram in this case is also slightly different.

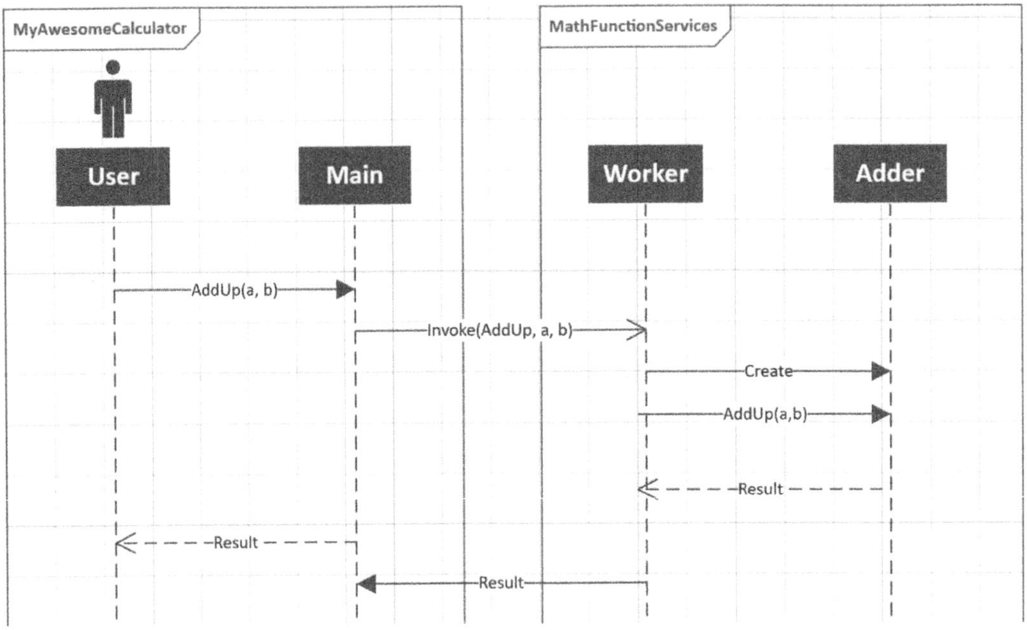

Figure 0.4: Sequence diagram for the new revised architecture

`MyAwesomeCalculator` and the `MathFunctionServices` worker are now independent of each other. They each run in their own `AppDomain`. When the user wants to perform the calculation, they enter this in the UI, which invokes the service. The `Worker` class picks up the command, creates an instance of the `Adder` class, calls the `AddUp` method, and then calls the `MyAwesomeCalculator` again with the results.

As you can see, the calls between all classes are synchronous (designated by a line with a solid arrowhead) except for the call between `Main` and `Worker`. That is asynchronous (designated by a line and an open arrowhead).

That makes sense; the calculator cannot know whether the command has arrived or the service is listening. It just does a fire-and-forget, crosses its digital fingers, and hopes for the best.

This is more like it. This is genuinely writing software used by other software (I am talking about `MathFunctionServices` here, not `MyAwesomeCalculator`).

I have not shown you how the code in `Main` calls `Worker` and how the result flows back from `Worker` to `Main`. After all, they are in separate app domains. So, they cannot share memory, right? That is correct. I did not show you that. But do not worry. I have a couple of chapters dedicated to this.

It is important to realize that `MathFunctionServices` does not have a UI in the ordinary sense of the word. No user ever touches this code. It lies there, dormant, until its services are required. If we compare that to the first example, we see the differences. That first example had all code loaded on the user's demand, and it somehow all responded to the users' actions.

A better definition

So, if we combine all of this, we can determine that systems programming is the art of writing components that can perform a function or a set of functions but interact only with other components.

That is what this book is all about. We will learn how to write software that is to be consumed by other software. That is a whole other way of looking at software, requirements, design considerations, and more compared to software meant for humans.

Writing software for software means other ways of thinking about communications, performance, memory usage, security, and so on. All those topics are covered here in this book. Now, you might say: "But wait a minute. Software written for users should also keep performance in mind!" You are right, but software communicating with software has unique needs.

Later chapters show how you can achieve the desired performance and explain why this is important. Let us agree that a component, potentially called thousands of times per second, could use more thought about performance than a screen with a button that a user might click once an hour. I am exaggerating here, but I am sure you get the point.

The same applies to memory consumption. I believe we should always write all software with memory consumption in mind. However, a component that gets used frequently by many other systems tends to be much more vulnerable to issues with memory than other software programs.

Performance and memory pressure are essential when we think about writing embedded systems. Embedded software usually runs on very limited hardware, so we have to try and take advantage of every trick in the book to get it running as fast as possible and using as little memory as possible.

As promised, we will spend much time looking at ways to communicate with these types of software.

To me, Systems programming is the purest form of software development. It is all about algorithms, tweaks, and trying out every trick in the book to get the most out of it. systems programming is the major league of software development. When you have this covered, all other software you write will also benefit from your newfound knowledge. What you learn when writing systems software will become second nature, and you will improve your overall software writing skills. Does this sound exciting? Then, let's get started!

Using C# and .NET in systems programming

We already run into a problem. You most likely are a C# developer. Maybe you are a VB.Net developer. But no matter what language, you are a .NET developer. After all, that is what this book is about.

Traditionally, Systems programming is done in Assembly, C, and C++. Systems programming has always been the realm of hardcore developers who know the systems they are working on inside out. In the early 50s of the last century, people wrote systems software using switches. A switch in the up position meant a 1, and a switch in the down position meant a 0. These early computers had 8, 16, or even more switches that pointed to the memory address to read or write. Then, 8 switches represented all the bits in a byte for that memory address. Above these switches, there were little lights (no, not LEDS: that invention happened later). Those little lights, if illuminated, meant a 1 in that byte (and a 0 if not illuminated). That way, you could read the contents of that memory address.

Do not worry; that kind of low-level programming is not the topic of this book. If you are interested, there are good remakes of the original Altair 8800 that started a company called Microsoft. You can program that computer in this way: use the switches and lights on the front panel to enter your software. That is how Bill Gates and Paul Allen wrote their first software. But we have other tools at our disposal.

Since systems software relies on efficient, fast, and memory-aware code, people often use programming languages close to the metal. That usually means using language such as machine code – such as the switches I mentioned earlier. Assembly language is another language used, especially in the seventies and eighties of the last century. C and later C++ are other examples of languages that can take advantage of the specifics of the hardware. Most parts of Windows, for instance, are written in C.

However, systems developers do not restrict themselves to low-level languages only. Let me give you an example.

Higher-level languages for systems programming

In 1965, IBM published a manual called *PL/I Language Specifications. C28-6571*. This relatively obscure title is a fascinating read: it outlines the specifications of the **PL/I programming language**. PL/I, a sort of abbreviation for **Programming Language One**, is a higher-level programming language. It contains block structures to allow for recursion, many different datatypes, exception handling, and many other features we take for granted today. It truly was a high-level language. However, they used it to write parts of the early OSs inside IBM. Remember, this was in the sixties when every microsecond counted. Machines were extremely slow compared to modern systems, so they had to utilize every trick in the book to make things work. Yet, a high-level language was considered appropriate. That means there is no reason not to use a high-level language today, especially considering memory profilers' compiler techniques and advantages.

Kernel mode and user mode

OSs and drivers are usually not built using .NET. The reason for this is that drivers and most parts of the OS run in kernel mode.

The CPU in your computer can run in two modes: **kernel** or **system mode and user mode**. User mode is where most of the applications run. The CPU shields the applications from using other memory or process spaces. The CPU protects the applications by placing them in a sandbox. That is precisely what you would want: it would be very undesirable for a program to snoop around in another application's memory. The processor handles this level of security.

Kernel mode, however, does not have those limitations. Software running in kernel mode is less restricted, controlled, and trusted. That makes sense: parts of an OS should be able to run in all parts of the system, including in the space of other applications.

However, to run in kernel, the compiled code needs to have certain flags set, and the layout of the binaries should be very specific. That is the problem we face. Our C# code relies heavily on the .NET Runtime, and that runtime is not built to be used in Kernel mode. So, even if we could compile our code so that the OS would accept it, it still would not work due to the app not loading the runtime.

There are ways around this. There are ways to pre-compile and include the runtime classes in your binary. Then, you can modify that binary to run in kernel mode. However, the results may vary, and the whole thing would be unreliable. Unreliable code is the exact opposite of what a device driver or OS part should be, so we will not get into this in this book. It's a hack, not a standard way of working.

Although this book does not deal with kernel-mode apps, I want to give you some insight. Especially since systems programming is usually programming "close to the metal," so to speak, we are interacting with systems that are running in kernel mode.

Kernel mode is a mode in the CPU. A system can request the CPU to turn on kernel mode. If the code requesting it has the proper privileges, the CPU will do so, thus unlocking parts of the memory previously unavailable. The code does what it needs to do, and then the CPU returns to user mode. Since the code is still in memory doing all sorts of things, it is quite wrong to say an app is a kernel or user-mode app. Some apps can switch the CPU into that state, but the app is almost always running in mixed mode: most of the time, it is in user mode, sometimes kernel mode. Oh, and when I say CPU, I mean **logical CPU**. This toggling happens on that level, not on the chip itself (but it can also do that).

I have Adobe Creative Cloud installed on my machine. We all know Photoshop, Illustrator, and Premiere, but these apps are meant to be accessed through the Creative Cloud app. This app monitors the system and launches any app you need when you need it. It also updates the background and keeps track of your fonts, files, colors, and other things like that.

Whenever you read something like "runs in the background," you might expect some systems programming going on, and indeed, there is.

For example, I get this image if I start **Performance Monitor** on my system and add the `% Privileged Time` and `% User Time` counters for the Adobe Desktop Service process.

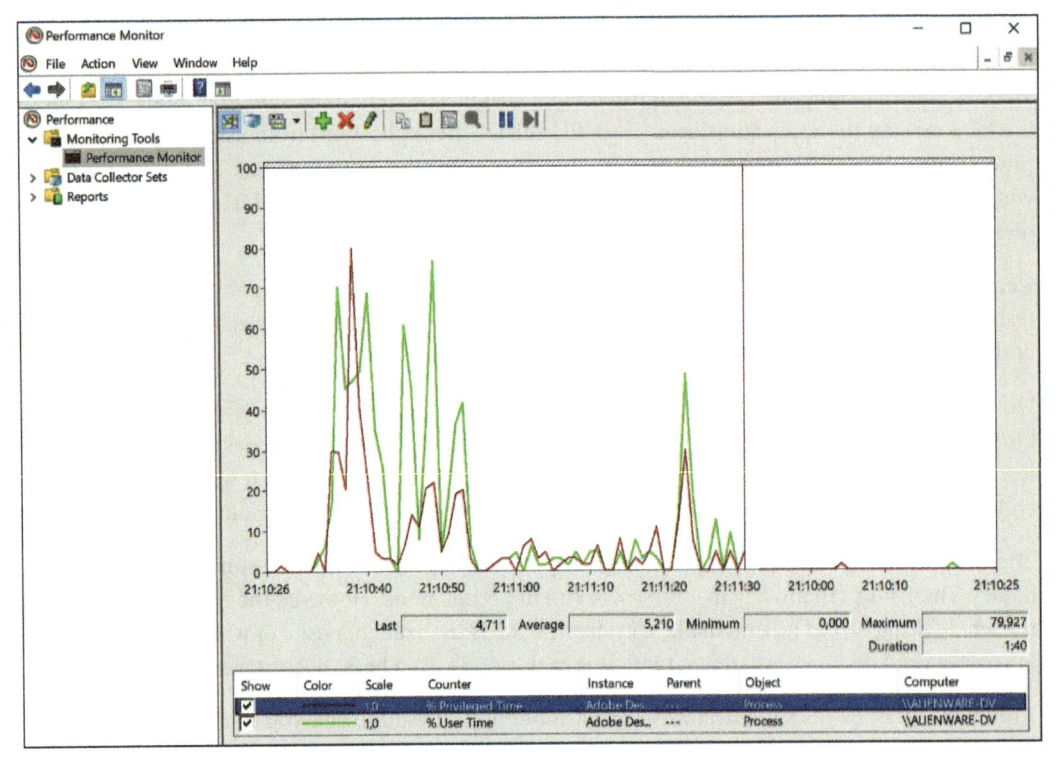

Figure 0.5: Performance Monitor showing kernel and user times

The red line in *Figure 0.5* shows how much time the Adobe Desktop Service spends in user time. The green line, however, shows how long the service is running in privileged time, and privileged time is just a fancy term for kernel time.

As you can see, this app is doing much work in the kernel time. Although I have to admit, I have no clue what it is doing there, but I am sure it is all for a good reason.

We will encounter kernel mode later in other chapters but we will not build apps that run in it.

Why use .NET?

So, we established that we cannot build an OS or a device driver in .NET. That might lead to the question: "Can we use .NET for systems programming?" The answer is a big yes. Otherwise, this would have been a very thin and short book.

Shall we have a look at our recently discovered definition of systems programming? "Writing software used by other software, as a part of a bigger system that works together to achieve a certain goal." I have shortened the definition, but it is all about this.

Looking at it this way, we can use .NET to write that software. Better yet: I bet .NET is one of the best choices to do so.

.NET offers many advantages over plain C or even C++ (not the managed kind of C++, that is still .NET.)

Back in the day, when we used .NET-Framework-based applications, it would have been a bad idea to use that for systems programming. However, with the introduction of the latest versions of .NET, many disadvantages have been taken care of. With many disadvantages out of the way, .NET-based systems are a viable choice for these kinds of systems.

C and C++ still are excellent languages for low-level systems code. However, C# and .NET Core have their advantages as well.

This table lays out the differences.

Topic	C# and .net core	C/C++
Performance	.NET Core has improved performance compared to .NET Framework, but there may still be overhead due to its runtime. This won't be an issue for most applications, but it could matter for highly performance-critical systems.	C/C++ provides direct control over hardware and, with careful optimization, can yield superior performance in performance-critical systems.
Memory management	.NET Core still provides automatic garbage collection, reducing the chance of memory leaks, but it gives less control to the developer. This is more suitable for application-level programming.	C/C++ gives developers direct control over memory allocation and deallocation, making it more suitable for systems programming that requires fine-grained memory management.
System-level programming	Some system-level programming tasks may still be more difficult in .NET Core due to its higher-level abstractions and safety features.	C/C++ is often used for system-level programming because it allows for direct hardware access and low-level system calls, which are essential for kernel development, device drivers, and so on.

Topic	C# and .net core	C/C++
Portability	.NET Core applications can run on multiple platforms without recompilation, but you must install the .NET Runtime on the target machine. This is an improvement over .NET Framework.	C and C++ code can be compiled and run on virtually any system but often requires careful management of platform-specific differences.
Runtime requirement	.NET Core applications still require the .NET Core Runtime to be installed on the target machine. This can limit its use on systems with limited resources.	C and C++ applications compile down to machine code and don't require a separate runtime. This can be beneficial for system-level applications or when working with resource-constrained systems.
Direct control	C# and .NET Core still provide many abstractions that can increase productivity, but these abstractions can limit direct control over the system and how code runs.	C/C++ provides more direct control over the system, allowing for finely tuned optimizations and precise control over how your code runs.
Community and support	.NET Core and C# have a growing community and plenty of support resources, including for cross-platform development.	C/C++ has a large, established community, many open-source projects, and a vast amount of existing system-level code.

Table 0.1: Comparison of C# and C/C++

As you can see, both options have advantages and disadvantages. However, most of the disadvantages of .NET Core can be removed using clever tricks and smart programming. Those are the topics of the rest of this book.

C# is a very mature and well-designed language. The capabilities far exceed what developers had when they used C to build, for example, the Unix OS.

What is .NET anyway?

.NET Core is the next version of the over two decades old framework that was meant to help developers get their work done quickly.

It all started with .NET Framework 1 back in 2002. Microsoft presented it as the end-all solution to many issues developers were facing. Fun fact: the project had the internal code name Project 42. You get bonus points if you know why they chose that name.

In the years following the introduction, we have seen many different functions of .NET Framework. Microsoft released the last version of .NET Framework on April 18, 2019.

Before that, Microsoft realized they needed to support other platforms as well. They wanted .NET to be available everywhere, including Linux, Macintosh, and most mobile devices. That meant they had to make fundamental changes to the runtime and the framework. Instead of having different runtime versions for each platform, they decided to have a unified version. That became .NET Core. Microsoft released this in June 2016.

.NET Standard was a set of specifications. The specifications told all developers which features of the runtime were available in which version of the runtime. Most developers did not understand the purpose of .NET Standard and assumed it was yet another version of the runtime. But once they got the idea behind this, it made a lot of sense. If you need a specific API, look it up in the documentation, see what version of .NET Standard it was supported, and then check whether your desired runtime supported that version of .NET Standard.

An example might be helpful here. Let's say you build an app that does some fancy drawing on the screen. You have worked with `System.Drawing.Bitmap` before, so you want to use that again. However, your new app should be running on .NET Core. Can you reuse your code? If you look up the documentation of the `System.Drawing.Bitmap` class, you see the following:

Product	Versions
.NET framework	1.1, 2.0, 3.0, 3.5, 4.0, 4.5, 4.5.1, 4.5.2, 4.6, 4.6.1, 4.6.2, 4.7, 4.7.1, 4.7.2, 4.8, 4.8.1
.NET platform extensions	2.1, 2.2, 3.0, 3.1, 5, 6, 7, 8
Windows desktop	3.0, 3.1, 5, 6, 7, 8

Table 0.2: Support for System.Drawing.Bitmap

Darn. This class is not part of .NET Standard. It is not available in all runtimes out there. You need to find another way to draw your images.

Your app also communicates with the outside world. It uses the `HttpClient` class, found in the `System.Net.Http` namespace. Can you move that to other platforms? Again, we need to look up the documentation of that class. There, we see this table:

Product	Versions
.NET	Core 1.0, core 1.1, core 2.0, core 2.1, core 2.2, core 3.0, core 3.1, 5, 6, 7, 8
.NET framework	4.5, 4.5.1, 4.5.2, 4.6, 4.6.1, 4.6.2, 4.7, 4.7.1, 4.7.2, 4.8, 4.8.1
.NET standard	1.1, 1.2, 1.3, 1.4, 1.6, 2.0, 2.1

Product	Versions
Uwp	10.0
Xamarin.ios	10.8
Xamarin.mac	3.0

Table 0.3: Support for Sstem.Net.Http.HttpClient

Now, that is more like it. `HttpClient` is part of the .NET Standard specification, which means that all runtimes that support the mentioned versions of .NET Standard implement this class. You are good to go!

.NET, .NET Framework, .NET Standard – what is all this?

Table 0.3 shows .NET Framework, .NET Standard, and .NET but not .NET Core. We do see .NET, though. What is this all about?

.NET Core was introduced to sit next to .NET Framework. Microsoft intended for .NET Framework to support Windows devices. However, as I explained, Microsoft later decided to support other devices, OSs, and other hardware architectures; hence the introduction of .NET Core. Then, they realized that this complicated things a lot. People lost track of what they could use and where they could use it. The solution to this was the introduction of the .NET Standard specifications, but that only worsened things – even the people who were not confused initially lost track of what was going on.

The version numbering was an issue as well. We have .NET Framework version 4.8.1 that matched .NET Standard 2.1. .NET Core 3.1 also supported .NET Standard 2.1. Many people had no idea what was happening. They could not understand why a .NET (Core) version of 3.0 was newer than .NET 4.5.

Microsoft saw this problem as well. They also had internal issues: they had to backport a lot of the code in the libraries so it would be available everywhere. To eliminate this mess once and for all, they announced that .NET Framework 4.8 would be the last version. .NET Core 3.1 would be the last version. From now on, it was all unified in something called .NET. Then, to prevent issues with the numbering, .NET started with the number 5.

They also made it easier to track when new versions would come out. Every single year, there will be a new version of .NET. So far, the odd numbers are under **Long Term Support** (**LTS**); the even numbers are under Standard Term Support (**STS**). STS is 18 months, and LTS is 3 years.

.NET 5 was an STS version, and since it was released in November 2020, the support ended in May 2022. .NET 6 was an LTS version. Released in November 2021, support ends November 2024. .NET 7 is again an STS, released in November 2022, with an end of life in May 2024.

By the time of writing this book, the preview versions of .NET 8 are out, and that will be an LTS version.

This is what I use in this book.

Now, the versioning is clear. The release cycle is understood. We can finally let that go. We can focus on building cool stuff instead of worrying about versions.

Programming languages – a choice to make

We are not done yet. We have figured out which version of the runtime we need. But the runtime is just that: a runtime. A set of libraries that we can use. Those libraries have a lot of tools and pre-built classes available, so we do not have to write that. That is awesome. However, we still have to write some code ourselves. We do that in a programming language, and then link to the libraries, compile the code, and have a binary we can deploy and run.

> **What language should we use?**
> Microsoft offers us three choices. Others have made their own .NET-compatible languages, but we ignore them. These days, the main languages to write .NET code are C#, F#, and Visual Basic.

F# is a language used for functional programming. This is a different approach to programming than most people are used to, but the financial domain and data-intensive systems use it a lot.

Visual Basic is an excellent language for people just getting started in development. Back in the nineties, at the end of the last century, it was one of the few options people had to build GUI systems rapidly. When .NET came along, Microsoft quickly ported Visual Basic to support this framework, so developers did not have as steep a learning curve. However, usage of Visual Basic is dwindling now that Microsoft stopped co-evolving it with C#.

C# is the language we use in this book.

Although not coupled with the available runtime, Microsoft seems to release a new version of the language around the same time they release a new version of .NET. Version 11 of the language came out in November 2022. Version 12 of C# is now in preview when writing this book.

Each new version of the language has improvements, but many are syntactic. That means that if you cannot use the latest language version, you can still use all the features in the runtime. They are officially decoupled. Sometimes, it is just a bit more typing work.

The .NET Runtime is an excellent foundation for building all sorts of systems. The ecosystem surrounding .NET is very extensive. Next, a huge group of people contributes to the framework daily. It is hard to think of a task that cannot be performed with .NET or one of the thousands of NuGet packages available.

Again, real Kernel mode systems, such as device drivers, are best built with non-managed languages. However, for all other purposes, .NET and C# are an excellent choice.

Now what?

Congratulations! You have made the first steps towards becoming a systems programmer. You now know what systems programming is and how it differs from the usual day-to-day programming you might be used to doing.

You know about the background of programming and the challenges our predecessors faced, and you know why .NET is such an awesome tool to build systems software in.

We are ready to take the next step. We will dive into the nitty-gritty details. However, before we do that, we will need to talk about APIs and .NET Framework, its upsides, and its downsides. So, let's go!

Setting up your development environment

I asked you to follow along. I requested that you open up your development environment and do what I do. However, to do that, you need to set up the right kind of development environment so that you can actually do what I do.

Let me help you with that.

I use **Visual Studio 2022 Enterprise**. There is no particular reason I use the Enterprise version besides having that on my machine. There are two other versions: The Professional and the free Community edition. All three versions are fine for the things we want to do. However, the Enterprise edition does have some debugging tools we might need when discussing debugging. When that time comes, I will pinpoint the differences and show you other ways of achieving your goals.

Alternatives such as JetBrains Rider and Visual Studio Code also work, but you might have to do more work yourself when we go into performance tuning and debugging. Again, I will tell you about these when we get there.

I have limited experience with Rider, so I cannot tell you precisely what you need to do, but I am sure that when you are an experienced developer, you can translate what I am showing you into the tools you know and love.

Use what you have and what you know. I am cool with that.

If you decide to go with Visual Studio, which I highly recommend, you should use version 2022 instead of 2019. The latest versions of .NET and C# offer a lot related to performance tuning and memory optimizations. Those versions are only available in the 2022 version of Visual Studio. So, make sure you have that one on your device.

Next to that, we will be doing a lot of console stuff. That means using PowerShell: gone are the days of using `cmd.exe`.

I highly recommend downloading Windows Terminal. With Terminal, you can have all sorts of consoles. We will use PowerShell most of the time, but when we talk about Linux, we will use the WSL feature to use our machines as Linux machines.

Setting up your development environment   17

Downloading and installing Terminal is a breeze: you can find it on the Microsoft Store.

Make sure to install Windows Subsystem for Linux as well. Instructions on how to do that are all over the internet; I will not repeat that here.

Once you have installed all of your favorite tools, you can select any one of them in your Terminal. Mine looks like this:

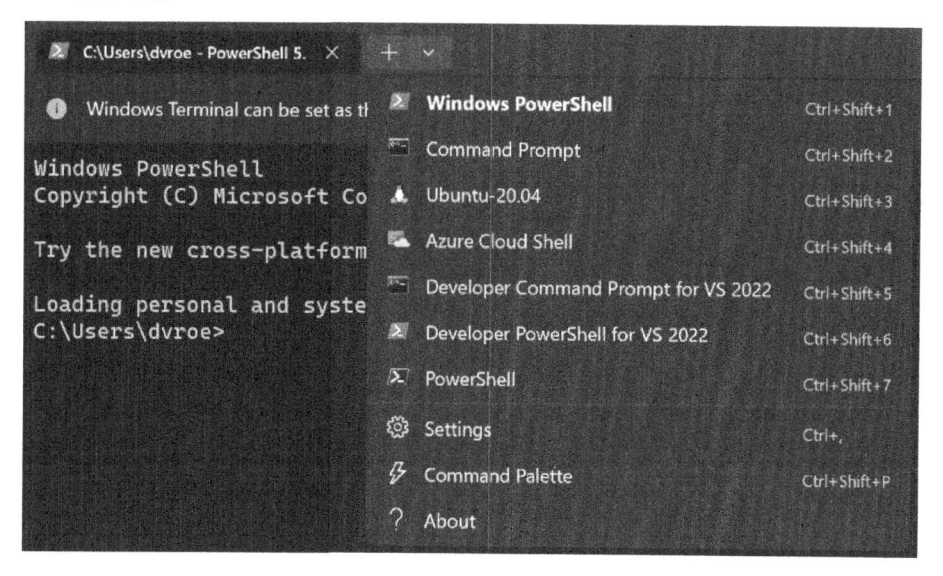

Figure 0.6: Windows Terminal with different shells

As you can see, I have **PowerShell**, **Command Prompt**, **Ubuntu**, **Azure Cloud Shell**, and some more installed. Selecting one of them is a matter of clicking.

Switching between Linux and Windows has never been easier!

Another tool we will be using later on is **WinDbg**. WinDbg is an extremely powerful external debugger. It can give you a lot of information about the processes you are interested in. It runs standalone, so you do not have to attach Visual Studio to the process. There are versions available for both X86 and ARM, so it is usable on many devices. You can find WinDbg on the Microsoft website at `https://learn.microsoft.com/en-us/windows-hardware/drivers/debugger/`. Download and install that. WinDbg might become one of your latest best friends.

Next, you might want to install **PerfView**. It is a free and open-source performance monitoring tool from Microsoft, specially built for analyzing performance on .NET applications.

You can find the source code at https://github.com/Microsoft/perfview. You can download the sources and build the tool yourself or grab one of the pre-build versions. Those are also on that same site. I would suggest building yourself and looking through the source code: there are some terrific examples of how to build software like this. I do not intend to describe how the tool works internally, but I will use it when discussing performance.

Now, all you need is a cup of your favorite beverage, and we are good to go!

1
The One with the Low-Level Secrets

Understanding low-level APIs

Writing software can be a daunting task. You need to consider many things when you try to convert your ideas into something that works on the machine. After all, there are so many things you need to tell the computer before it does something useful.

But we are in luck. Many of the instructions we need to give the CPU are encapsulated in frameworks, tools, packages, and other pieces of software. These building blocks allow us to focus on what we want to build instead of how the CPU might interpret our instructions. That makes life a lot easier!

This chapter looks into those building blocks, how they help us, and how we can best use them. This chapter also covers how .NET works and where it comes from. This is important: most developers take the advantages of .NET for granted. That is fine since the framework hides much complexity. However, when writing lower-level system software, it is essential to know why things in .NET work the way they do and how to use other solutions if needed. Also, it doesn't hurt to be reminded of some basic things occasionally, especially when you might have to deviate from the road user-facing software developers take.

So, we will cover the following topics:

- What are low-level APIs?
- How does the Base Class Library (BCL) help us .NET developers?
- What is the Common Language Runtime (CLR)?
- What are Win32 APIs and how do we call them?

All in all, we are going low here and getting all technical.

But before we dive into the building blocks the .NET ecosystem gives us, we need to chat about APIs – to be more precise, the difference between low-level and high-level APIs.

Technical requirements

You can visit the following link to view all the code in this chapter: `https://github.com/PacktPublishing/Systems-Programming-with-C-Sharp-and-.NET/tree/main/SystemsProgrammingWithCSharpAndNet/Chapter01`.

What are low-level APIs, and how do they differ from higher-level abstractions?

Well, maybe we are going a bit too fast. Before we can look at low-level and high-level APIs, we need to agree on what an API means.

API is an abbreviation for application programming interface. Although technically correct, it doesn't tell us much. We need a better definition of API.

What are interfaces?

Let's begin with the term **interface.** That alone can be defined entirely differently, depending on whom you ask.

An interface can be a **software interface**, which is the boundary between two pieces of software. For instance, a database such as SQL Server allows users to access data by accepting SQL queries. That is the main interface for that database system.

Another definition of an interface would be a **hardware interface**. The USB ports on your computer and the peripherals you connect to your machine using them are hardware interfaces.

Of course, in C#, we also have interfaces. Most object-oriented programming languages support interfaces in one way or another. For instance, C++ has the concept of pure virtual classes. Python supports abstract base classes, which serve the same purpose.

An API is the interface between a piece of software and other software meant for the programmer. This defines the boundaries of a given code set and how to interact with it.

So, it is possible to create a giant library filled with wondrous and highly complex code. As the library user, you get a list of methods, classes, interfaces (yes, the C# kind), enums, and other means of interacting with that library.

This is awesome since you can use that library without worrying about writing code yourself.

Low-level and high-level APIs

The level of an API is an arbitrary distinction to give you an idea of how close to the actual hardware an API is.

What are low-level APIs, and how do they differ from higher-level abstractions?   21

No metric tells us when something is a lower or higher-level API. It is all relative and open for debate. This, however, is something we are not going to do here.

Generally, a low-level API gives you more granular control over the hardware than a higher-level API. A higher-level API, however, is usually more portable and can be used to achieve goals much quicker.

If that all sounds a bit abstract, don't worry. Let me clarify this with some examples. For instance, imagine that you want to send some data across a network. Well, when I say network, I mean we send it to IP address 127.0.0.1. In other words, we send it to localhost; we are speaking to ourselves.

To do this, we need to call a lot of low-level APIs that the Windows SDK gives us. The code looks like this:

```
static void UseLowLevelAPI()
{
    WSAData wsaData;

    if (WSAStartup(0x0202, out wsaData) != 0)
    {
        Console.WriteLine("WSAStartup failed");
        return;
    }
    IntPtr sock = socket(2 /* AF_INET */, 1 /* SOCK_STREAM */, 0);
    if (sock == new IntPtr(-1))
    {
        Console.WriteLine("socket() failed");
        WSACleanup();
        return;
    }
    sockaddr_in sin = new sockaddr_in();
    sin.sin_family = 2; // AF_INET
    sin.sin_port =(ushort)IPAddress.HostToNetworkOrder((short)8000);
    // Port 8000
    sin.sin_addr = BitConverter.ToUInt32(IPAddress.Parse("127.0.0.1")
    .GetAddressBytes(), 0);

    if (connect(sock, ref sin, Marshal.SizeOf(typeof(
        sockaddr_in))) != 0)
    {
        Console.WriteLine("connect() failed");
        closesocket(sock);
        WSACleanup();
        return;
    }
    byte[] data = Encoding.ASCII.GetBytes("Hello, server!");
    if (send(sock, data, data.Length, 0) == -1)
```

```
    {
        Console.WriteLine("send() failed");
    }
    closesocket(sock);
    WSACleanup();
}
```

As you can see, many things must happen for such a relatively simple task. I have omitted all the code we need to access the APIs and the definition of the classes and structs, such as `WSAData`. I also simplified this sample and didn't use much error handling or memory management.

I won't go through what's happening in the preceding code as it isn't part of what I'm trying to show you. We will revisit this later in this book when we discuss networking. I provided this code to show you what a low-level API looks like. Here, I want you to pay attention to the calls to `WSAStartup()`, `WSACleanup()`, `socket()`, `connect()`, `send()`, and `closesocket()`. These are APIs that come from the Windows SDK. They are the parts of Windows that help us set up connections to network interfaces, translate addresses, open and close sockets, and send data.

> **Note**
> It is good to remember that the Windows SDK is a wrapper. The code inside the SDK, written mainly in C and a bit in C++, does the heavy lifting and calls the hardware. We don't have to worry about this: the people at Microsoft have already figured out how to do all this.

Like I said, low-level and high-level terms depend on how you look at them. It is all relative. You can consider Windows SDK APIs high-level APIs when you look at them from a C programmer's perspective, who has to do all the heavy lifting.

But we, as .NET developers, see this as rather low-level. This is because, as .NET developers, we have even easier tools to use. The preceding code isn't something most developers will write. Instead, they will write the following:

```
static void UseHighLevelAPI()
{
    try
    {
        // Connect to server at 127.0.0.1:8000
        using (TcpClient client = new TcpClient("127.0.0.1", 8000))
        using (NetworkStream stream = client.GetStream())
        {
            // Prepare the message
            byte[] data = Encoding.ASCII.GetBytes("Hello, server!");
            // Send the message
            stream.Write(data, 0, data.Length);
```

```
            Console.WriteLine("Sent: Hello, server!");
        }
    }
    catch (SocketException e)
    {
        Console.WriteLine($"SocketException: {e}");
    }
    catch (IOException e)
    {
        Console.WriteLine($"IOException: {e}");
    }
    catch (Exception e)
    {
        Console.WriteLine($"Exception: {e}");
    }
}
```

This code is much easier and a lot smaller. Most of the preceding code consists of catching exceptions.

The `TcpClient` class is doing the hard work. We instantiate an instance of it, give it the address we want to connect to, get a `NetworkStream` instance from it, and then write a bunch of bytes. Simple. It works brilliantly.

So, why would you care about the low-level stuff?

Although the low-level code is a lot more work and complicated, it gives you one significant advantage: more control.

We use TCP/IP here. But what if the device you want to communicate with doesn't have TCP? And before you say "Everything is IP-based these days," I'm pretty sure you have computers in your house that communicate over older technology. You might use devices that don't have TCP on board every day. I'm talking about remote controls for most television sets. They use infrared. Many devices still use infrared. It's cheap, well-understood, quick to install, and robust in terms of its use cases. It is also not supported by .NET.

But when it comes to low-level APIs, it is pretty simple. There are some differences in how to set up the connection: there is no IP address, so you have to use the device ID, but the connection itself is not that hard to use. Look at the line where we set up the call to `socket()`. We use 2 as the first parameter, which stands for `AF_INET`, which means TCP. Change that to `26 (AF_IRDA)`, and the underlying libraries switch to infrared devices.

This can't be done with the .NET libraries that are available.

The high-level APIs are amazing and help us write code that is easy to understand quickly. However, as systems programmers, we have to deal with hardware and other low-level systems. That's when we have to use the low-level APIs.

Before we dive into how to use these APIs, let's look at the .NET libraries themselves. While we're at it, we'll examine the CLR so that you have a clear picture of what .NET gives us.

Overview of .NET Core runtime components (CLR, BCL)

Previously, we examined the difference between low-level and high-level programming languages. Like the APIs, lower and higher mean how close to or far away you are from the actual machine. Programming in C means you are very close to the hardware; programming in C# means you are far away. Of course, being further away means you are working in abstractions. The advantage is that many things are simplified, as seen earlier in this chapter. Also, with many abstractions, moving your code to other platforms is more manageable.

The magic that makes this possible is the .NET runtime. Since the first version, the designers have always aimed to shield you from the low-level stuff as much as possible. This lets you write your code quickly and focus on functionality instead of boilerplate.

.NET is a complex topic. But in short, it comes down to a set of tools in many different forms that help you achieve your goal.

> **Fun fact**
> Before its initial launch, the project's code name was Project 42. 42 is the answer to life, the universe, and everything in the books, TV shows, and the major motion picture from science fiction author Douglas Adams: *The Hitchhikers Guide to the Galaxy*. Adams wrote that 42 was the answer to everything; hence, the .NET designers thought it appropriate to name the solution to all developer problems Project 42.

.NET does not solve all problems, but it makes life much easier. Let's see how it does that.

We can identify three major areas where .NET helps us:

- Development tools
- The CLR
- The BCL

I will not be spending time on development tools here. Instead, I want to discuss the CLR and the BCL. These two form the backbone of the .NET ecosystem. In later chapters, I will cover other essential parts of the .NET ecosystem, such as the **Common Type System** (**CTS**).

CLR

CLR is the runtime environment in which our code runs.

The compiler (covered later in this book) compiles the code we have written. For now, we can imagine that the compiler takes our human-readable text and changes it into something a computer can understand and use.

Well, not quite. I need to clarify things a bit here. Although what I wrote is technically correct when discussing compilers, this is only true for real compilers, such as those found using C or C++. This does not apply to the .NET-based world.

The .NET compilers compile while targeting a common runtime instead of the hardware we run on.

The compiler's output is not native to the hardware. Instead, it outputs something called Intermediate Language (IL). This is a sort of "in-between" form. It's not human-readable, but it is too abstract for computers to understand. It is in between those two forms.

Let me clarify that with an example.

I have written a .NET Console app with no top-level statements. In other words, this is the most simple piece of code we can write using .NET. The whole program consists of one single line:

```
Console.WriteLine("Hello, System Programmers!");
```

I don't need to explain what I'm doing here, right?

If we use Visual Studio to compile the code, it will take all of our files, give them to the compiler, and instruct it to build a binary. That looks like this:

```
.method private hidebysig static void  '<Main>$'(string[] args) cil managed
{
  .entrypoint
  // Code size       12 (0xc)
  .maxstack  8
  IL_0000:  ldstr      "Hello, System Programmers!"
  IL_0005:  call       void [System.Console]System.Console::WriteLine(string)
  IL_000a:  nop
  IL_000b:  ret
} // end of method Program::'<Main>$'
```

This is a bit harder to understand but not too hard. First, there's some code to set things up (.maxstack 8). We load the string with the call to the `ldstr` function and then call the `System.Console::WriteLine(string)` method, and we are done.

Again, this is not machine code. That looks a lot harder, and I'm not going to show you that. If compiled to something the CPU can understand and execute, this code is several pages long.

However, I will show you part of it to give you a taster:

```
00007FF9558C06B0    push        rbp
00007FF9558C06B1    push        rdi
00007FF9558C06B2    push        rsi
00007FF9558C06B3    sub         rsp,20h
00007FF9558C06B7    mov         rbp,rsp
00007FF9558C06BA    mov         qword ptr [rbp+40h],rcx
00007FF9558C06BE    cmp         dword ptr [7FF95597CFA8h],0
00007FF9558C06C5    je          Program.<Main>$(System.String[])+01Ch (07FF9558C06CCh)
00007FF9558C06C7    call        00007FF9B54D7A10
00007FF9558C06CC    mov         rcx,1A871002068h
00007FF9558C06D6    mov         rcx,qword ptr [rcx]
00007FF9558C06D9    call        qword ptr [CLRStub[MethodDescPrestub]@00007FF9559C17E0 (07FF9559C17E0h)]
00007FF9558C06DF    nop
00007FF9558C06E0    nop
00007FF9558C06E1    lea         rsp,[rbp+20h]
00007FF9558C06E5    pop         rsi
00007FF9558C06E6    pop         rdi
00007FF9558C06E7    pop         rbp
```

This tiny assembly code segment instructs the CPU to take a pointer to the memory where the string is and then calls the first part of the `WriteLine` method.

Again, the complete code would be several pages long.

I hope you are beginning to appreciate the brevity and simplicity of the .NET system. But I also want you to know what happens behind the scenes. When writing system software, we sometimes need to do things that aren't possible in .NET. Then, we have to rely on other ways to achieve our results. We won't write pure assembly in this book: that would be too much. But I do want you to know what's happening as that will benefit you enormously later on.

Okay. Between the IL code I showed you and the assembly code I showed you is the place where the CLR lives.

As stated in `https://learn.microsoft.com/en-us/dotnet/standard/clr`, the CLR offers us quite a lot of things:

- Performance improvements
- The ability to easily use components developed in other languages
- Extensible types provided by a class library
- Language features such as inheritance, interfaces, and overloading for object-oriented programming

- Support for explicit free threading that allows multithreaded and scalable applications to be created
- Support for structured exception handling
- Support for custom attributes
- Garbage collection

This information comes straight out of the documentation from Microsoft, so if you want to know more, I urge you to look it up and read more about it. Later chapters will discuss some of these items, such as threading, exception handling, and garbage collection. For now, it is enough to know that when we compile our code, we prepare it for the CLR to use and run it. The CLR will take care of the rest and make it work nicely on actual hardware.

The code that runs on the CLR is what we call managed code. All other code (thus code not under the CLR's control) is unmanaged. You will deal with managed code most of the time, but when writing system software, you'll encounter unmanaged code quite frequently. But don't worry: I will guide you through that!

BCL

One of the goals the designers of .NET had in mind was to eliminate something developers called DLL Hell.

The idea was that, when writing software, developers quickly realized that writing the same code repeatedly would be tiresome and a nightmare to maintain. Instead, they created libraries with functions they could reuse. These libraries would be loaded on demand and linked to the calling code. That is where the name **Dynamic Link Library** (**DLL**) originated.

Of course, developers, being developers, were not content with the DLLs they or someone else wrote earlier and made changes to them. These changes weren't always backward compatible. That meant that as a user of a DLL, you had to make sure you used the correct version. You couldn't easily upgrade without testing if that particular version of the DLL worked with your code.

There were two types of DLLs. One was proprietary to your code. You placed these DLLs in the same directory as your application, so all you needed to do was load the DLLs in your app directory. If a new application version came out, it came with its own set of DLLs.

Since most of the DLLs didn't change a lot (if they even changed at all) there were many repetitive and duplicate DLLs. So, instead of duplicating code, we were now duplicating DLLs.

Fortunately, a solution was available: you could place DLLs in a shared space. On Windows, that was the `C:\Windows\System32` directory. The runtime knew that if it needed to load a DLL and couldn't locate it in the `applications` directory, it could look at the `System32` directory and find it there.

When doing this, you needed to be sure you maintained backward compatibility.

Naturally, things went wrong. Updates would replace DLLs with newer, non-compatible versions. Sometimes, applications updated a DLL without realizing something else depended on it. Sometimes, an update would delete DLLs and thus break applications. In many cases, developers deployed the wrong versions. The list goes on and on. This caused many developers many frustrations and resulted in them calling this DLL Hell. Project 42 was set up to solve this. And in a way, it did.

A few decades ago, a `String` class was the first thing a new C++ programmer would write. C and C++ did not have such a thing: strings were not native to the language (they still aren't, but the helper classes containing them are part of the standard now). A string can be pretty simple: it is just a pointer to a place in memory where all subsequent bytes form one long string. The string ends when the system sees a byte with a value of 0 (zero, not the character o). That's it. A `String` class would contain the address of that array of bytes, some helper methods that allocate and clear the memory, and additional functions such as `Length()`. That's it.

Soon, everybody wrote different versions, which would all be slightly different. .NET solved that by having a `String` class available. That class was part of a DLL that got shipped with the framework. The system registered that DLL, along with its version number. So, all developers needed to do was tell the system which version of the framework it was using, and by magic, things such as Strings were available. I am oversimplifying things here, but that is basically how things work.

There is a vast library that you can use as a .NET developer. You can see it in `C:\Windows\assembly`. If you use Windows Explorer, you'll see a filtered view of the contents. You can see the actual contents using a terminal or command line.

These DLLs are part of the BCL. The BCL is a set of helper classes, functions, methods, and enums that help you do your work. Instead of figuring out all the code yourself, it is part of the installation and ready to use.

The classes and other code constructs in the DLLs that form the BCL are organized into namespaces. The BCL contains lots of helpful code some of which are as follows:

- **Core functionalities**: The `System` namespace, which contains classes such as `Object`, `String`, `Array`, and so on.
- **File I/O**: The `System.IO` namespace, for dealing with files, streams, and more.
- **Networking**: This has `System.Net` for dealing with networking.
- **Threading**: This has `System.Threading` for dealing with – you guessed it – multithreading.
- **Data access**: This has `System.Data` for dealing with data storage in databases and other ways of persisting data.
- **XML processing**: You can find `System.Xml` here, which you can use to handle XML files and data.

- **Diagnostics**: `System.Diagnostics` helps you identify issues in your code. We will be diving into this one later.
- **Security**: This contains the `System.Security` namespace, along with all things related to security and encryption.

There are many more namespaces, but these are some of the most used ones. We will revisit them later.

However, remember that these classes are there to help you. They wrap complicated and extensive code in good ways for most developers. However, If you find that the BCL code doesn't get you where you want to be, nothing is stopping you from writing the code yourself. As we saw earlier, the BCL code is awesome if you want to set up a TCP/IP connection, but if you want to use an infrared connection instead, you must do it yourself.

The good news is that you can mix and match. Use the BCL where you can and low-level APIs where you need to.

Using P/Invoke to call low-level APIs

We have established that .NET gives you many tools to develop something quickly. It also helps you out by shielding you from the low-level details of the underlying operating system. But it also allows you to use low-level APIs if you need to.

But how can we access those APIs? The answer is **Platform Invocation**, or (**P/Invoke**). We can use this tool to access the Win32 API directly. P/Invoke bridges the gap between the two platforms so that we can mix and match to our hearts' content.

> **Note**
> Win32 is the name of the SDK and the APIs made available. There is no such thing as a Win64 API. Our code is compiled against 64-bit Windows if you run that platform, yet we (and Microsoft) still call it the Win32 API.

How does P/Invoke work?

P/Invoke involves a couple of steps. These are the steps you must follow to use a Win32 API in a .NET application:

1. Find the API you want to use.
2. Find the DLL the API resides in.
3. Load that DLL in your assembly.
4. Declare a stub that tells your application how to call that API.
5. Convert the .NET data types into something the Win32 API can understand.
6. Use the API.

> **Warning!**
> You are out of the loving and caring hands of .NET Framework and the CLR. You are no longer protected against mistakes. You are in an unmanaged world now. In the old days, they probably would have marked this part of the documentation with the warning "Here be dragons." You are now responsible for many more things than you might be used to, such as memory management and error handling. You have more power over the system now, but remember: great power comes with great responsibility!

Let me start with an example. This showcases the power of .NET Framework, but it also shows how the aforementioned steps work in practice. We are going to do a simple "Hello World."

To make sure we're on the same page, let me show you the .NET version of this program:

```
Console.WriteLine("Hello, System Programmers!");
```

Yes, this is the same sample we saw earlier. Hey, we have to start somewhere, right?

Now, `Console` is a class from the BCL. It has a static method, `WriteLine`, that outputs that string to the output. But what if we assume we don't want to use that class? How should we go about this then? To frame this question another way, how does `WriteLine` work internally? After all, there has to be a point somewhere during execution where the code has to call the Win32 API. That can be done by the CLR or by us, but something or someone has to call it.

Let's rewrite the code using P/Invoke. I will show you the entire program first, then dissect it and explain how it works line by line:

```
01: using System.Runtime.InteropServices;
02:
03: [DllImport("kernel32.dll", CharSet = CharSet.Auto, SetLastError = true)]
04: static extern bool WriteConsole(
05:     IntPtr hConsoleOutput,
06:     string lpBuffer,
07:     uint nNumberOfCharsToWrite,
08:     out uint lpNumberOfCharsWritten,
09:     IntPtr lpReserved);
10:
11: [DllImport("kernel32.dll", SetLastError = true)]
12: static extern IntPtr GetStdHandle(int nStdHandle);
13:
14: const int STD_OUTPUT_HANDLE = -11;
15:
16: IntPtr stdHandle = GetStdHandle(STD_OUTPUT_HANDLE);
17: if (stdHandle == IntPtr.Zero)
18: {
```

```
19:         Console.WriteLine("Could not retrieve standard output
                handle.");
20:         return;
21: }
22:
23: string output = "Hello, System Programmers!";
24: uint charsWritten;
25:
26: if (!WriteConsole(
27:     stdHandle,
28:     output,
29:     (uint)output.Length,
30:     out charsWritten,
31:     IntPtr.Zero))
32: {
33:     Console.WriteLine("Failed to write using Win32 API.");
34: }
```

That's a lot of code, but let's go through it.

In *line 1*, we import the namespace that allows us to use P/Invoke. .NET uses the name `InteropServices` for this, so it makes sense to import that.

In *line 3*, we see the magic happening. Remember the steps we have to take? *Step 1* is to "Find the API you want to use." Since we want to print something on the screen, the `WriteConsole` API sounds like a good fit.

The official documentation from Microsoft states that the `WriteConsole` API *"Writes a character string to a console screen buffer beginning at the current cursor location."* That sounds good to me.

The documentation then gives us the signature of this API:

```
BOOL WINAPI WriteConsole(
  _In_              HANDLE    hConsoleOutput,
  _In_        const VOID      *lpBuffer,
  _In_              DWORD     nNumberOfCharsToWrite,
  _Out_opt_         LPDWORD   lpNumberOfCharsWritten,
  _Reserved_        LPVOID    lpReserved
);
```

If you're a .NET developer, this might look weird. A lot is going on that we don't know about or understand. We need to translate those types into something the CLR understands. Luckily, somebody has already figured that out for us. To make life even easier, they did *Steps 2* (find the DLL) and *4* (declare the stub) for us as well. Given the correct parameters, the CLR takes care of *Step 3* (load the DLL).

That "someone who figured this out" is the people behind `https://pinvoke.net`. You can search for APIs and learn how to use them there.

The official documentation has a part called **Requirements**, and in that section, you'll learn that the API lives in `Kernel32.dll` (`Pinvoke.Net` also gives you that information).

Line 3 is what tells `InteropServices` to load the DLL. Let's dive into that:

```
[DllImport("kernel32.dll", CharSet = CharSet.Auto, SetLastError = true)]
```

This line tells the CLR to load `kernel32.dll`. It then specifies how to handle characters. Characters and strings can be complicated. There are several different ways to represent a single character. It can be an ASCII character, it can be Unicode, or it can be ANSI. They all have a different representation in memory. Here, we say we want to use `Auto`. When doing that, the system looks at the complete string we use, finds out which set it can use to represent the complete string, and uses the first one it can find. Since it starts by trying to fit it in an ASCII string and then "moves up" toward more complicated, slower, and more memory-intensive ways, this guarantees we get the best way to represent this string.

Next, we can see `SetLastError = true`. This instructs the system to inform us whenever something goes wrong. In case of an error, it calls the `GetLastError` API to get the error and return it to us. We will use this a lot later. For now, I advise you to always set `SetLastError` to `true`.

Our runtime now knows to load `kernel32.dll`. But we must tell it what specific API we want to use. That happens in the following line. The function's signature must always follow that `DllImport` directly: they always belong together. If you want to load multiple functions from the same Dll, you must still use `DllImport` for each.

The following line is the stub for the function:

```
static extern bool WriteConsole(
    IntPtr hConsoleOutput,
    string lpBuffer,
    uint nNumberOfCharsToWrite,
    out uint lpNumberOfCharsWritten,
    IntPtr lpReserved);
```

This looks like the code we saw from the official documentation, but now, the types have been translated into their .NET equivalents. Again, `Pinvoke.Net` is your friend here!

The parameters are more or less self-explanatory, except for the first one. Let's skip that one and look at the others:

String lpBuffer	The string we want to print
nNumberOfCharsToWrite	The number of characters we want to print from the given string
lpNumberOfCharsWritten	How many characters were written to the system
lpReserved	This isn't used, so it can be ignored

Table 1.1: Parameters for WriteConsole

One thing to notice here is that Win32 APIs use the Hungarian notation for their parameters. This style says you have to prefix every parameter with an abbreviation of the type so that when you read the code later, you know what type this stands for. In the days before the current modern and fast IDEs, this helped a lot: you couldn't hover your mouse over a variable to see what type it was; you had to scroll through the code to find the declaration. By prefixing it, you could see it immediately. These days, we don't need to do that anymore, but C and C++ developers still use this standard.

So, as you can see, the string to print is a long pointer (lp), and the number of characters to write is a number (n).

But let's have a look at `hConsoleOutput`. It is a handle (it starts with h), which translates it into `IntPtr` in .NET.

A pointer is just an address of something in memory. In our case, this memory belongs to the place where the console is. But how do we get that? Where is the code that controls `Console`, which is located in memory?

The answer is that we don't know. There is no fixed place; this can and will change every time you restart your program. So, we need to look for it.

Luckily, that isn't that hard to do as there's an API we can use to do so. This API is called `GetStdHandle` and it lives in `kernel32.dll`. We know how to import that, and we can see it in our code on *lines 11* and *12*:

```
[DllImport("kernel32.dll", SetLastError = true)]
static extern IntPtr GetStdHandle(int nStdHandle);
```

There are no strings, so we don't need to set `CharSet`. However, we do need to set `SetLastError`.

The method to find the address is called `GetStdHandle`, and it takes one parameter: `nStdHandle`. This tells this API what type of Console we are looking for. There are three types available: `STD_INPUT_HANDLE`, `STD_OUTPUT_HANDLE`, and `STD_ERROR_HANDLE`. These three constants have -10, -11, and -12 as values, respectively. You're right if you think it's strange that they're negative values. It's weird. However, in Win32, these values are unsigned. They are the end of the integer range, so they don't get in the way of any other types of console you might define yourself. Casting a high value of an unsigned int to a signed int results in a negative value.

On *line 14*, we define the `STD_OUTPUT_HANDLE` constant and give it a value of `-11`. This sort of thing is common: the Win32 API is a mess with magic numbers and constants.

On *line 16*, we use `GetStdHandle` to get the pointer to `Console` in memory, giving it `STD_OUTPUT_HANDLE`. If that goes wrong, we get a 0 (zero) back. But since .NET is strongly typed, we cannot use that number. Instead, we have to use the `IntPtr.Zero` constant, which is the same thing but in the correct type.

Every time you get a 0 back from a Win32 API, you have an error situation going on. We need to deal with that, but that is a topic for later.

Assuming all goes well, we can define our string, and the `out` variable tells us how many characters are written (*lines 23* and *24*).

Then, on *line 26*, we call the actual API:

```
if (!WriteConsole(
    stdHandle,
    output,
    (uint)output.Length,
    out charsWritten,
    IntPtr.Zero))
{
    Console.WriteLine("Failed to write using Win32 API.");
}
```

This should be clear now. We call the API, give it the correct parameters, and check if the result is 0 (`IntPtr.Zero`).

The CLR converts the complex .NET `String` type into a simple array of bytes with a 0 at the end. We don't have to worry about that. We can give this API a C# string and everything will work out fine.

And that's it. We have written something to the console using Win32 APIs!

Dealing with errors

In the previous examples, we did a little bit of error checking. If we couldn't get the handle, we showed a message. We did the same thing if we couldn't write to the console. I realize it's funny to write to the console that the system cannot write to it (look at *line 33*, for instance), but you get what I mean here.

But this isn't good enough if you want to know what's going on for real. We need a more thorough way of handling errors.

In .NET, we are used to getting exceptions whenever things go wrong. We know how to deal with that. In the low-level world, things are different. When something goes wrong, we get 0 back, and we're left to deal with it. We could continue with the code without being bothered by the error. We could even ignore the results of a call to an API. However, that would lead to disaster. You should always check and deal with the results of an API call. How to deal with that is something we discuss in this section.

There is a low-level API called `GetLastError` that can help us out here. The signature for P/Invoke is as follows:

```
[DllImport("kernel32.dll")]
static extern uint GetLastError();
```

It seems pretty straightforward. There are no parameters to worry about, and we don't have to set that `SetLastError` value here. Since `SetLastError` ensures that any error is saved in the registry so that `GetLastError` can read it, there's no value in having that here. If there would be, and we set it to false, then how does `GetLastError` work?

This function returns an unsigned integer. This number corresponds with an error; you can look up what that number means in the documentation.

But there's an issue: it doesn't work. Well, it does, but there are no guarantees regarding the result.

The BCL and the `CLR` work with the low-level Win32 APIs constantly. That is obvious: the BCL is a wrapper around the Win32 API, and the CLR uses that wrapper to call into the core system of the operating system. We can call the APIs ourselves, as we have just done, but the CLR also calls it. Sometimes, it does it in the same thread. Other times, it calls it on another thread. Things can also go wrong during the CLR calls to the APIs. That results in `GetLastError` possibly returning no errors or the wrong errors. Well, technically, they aren't the wrong errors, but they might not have to do anything with what we're doing.

Luckily, the designers of .NET have thought about that and have added a class called `Marshal` to the `System.Runtime.InteropServices` namespace. That class is used to marshal between managed and unmanaged code – or, to put it in the context of what we are doing here, between Win32 APIs and our C# .NET code.

Let's assume we made a mistake. I know that's hard to imagine but bear with me here. Instead of assigning `-11` to `STD_OUTPUT_HANDLE`, we set it to `11`. We all make mistakes, right?

We then call `GetStdHandle` with `11`. That isn't correct; we know that. The documentation says that the function returns 0 (or `IntPtr.Zero` in C#) if anything goes wrong. But in our case, it returns something else: `0xffffffffffffffff`. This is the unsigned version of the signed value, `-1`. In other words, the call to the API returns `-1`, which is not a valid handle.

However, we don't check that. We only check for the 0 value. This makes sense if you think about it. After all, 0 indicates something went wrong when calling that function. That didn't happen: the function worked flawlessly. It just didn't find anything matching the ID we gave it (`11` instead of `-11`). So, as far as the API is concerned, there are no errors.

But then we get to the point where we call `WriteConsole`. We give it the handle of the console – or rather, we think we do. Instead, we give it a value of `-1` (`0xffffffffffffffff`). That is not a valid handle that `WriteConsole` can work with.

In .NET you would get an exception, but that doesn't happen here. The code continues happily without complaining. It just doesn't output anything.

These errors can be a pain to find and solve. In this case, it is quite straightforward, but imagine a situation where you try to set up a connection to an infrared receiver and something goes wrong. However, we keep going since we don't check for that result. By the time we are ready to send data, nothing happens – or worse, the system crashes. We start to look at the code that does the actual sending, but nothing is wrong there. It takes much time and careful debugging to see that the error happens when we set up the connection. Let me repeat something I said earlier: you should always check the results of all API calls. That burden is on you. The .NET runtime generates exceptions in these cases, but if you are in unmanaged land, you are responsible for doing so.

Let's improve our code a bit.

First, we'll wrap our call to `WriteConsole` in a `try-catch` block and just catch `Exception`, although that is generally a bad idea. However, here, this is good enough.

If `WriteConsole` returns `IntPtr.Zero`, we have a problem and something goes wrong. In an unmanaged environment, you would call `GetLastError` to see what happens, but that doesn't work here. Instead, we use that `Marshal` class I spoke about earlier:

```
if(!WriteConsole(stdHandle, output, (uint)output.Length, out
charsWritten, IntPtr.Zero))
{
    var lastError = Marshal.GetLastWin32Error();
    Console.WriteLine($ something went wrong. Error code:
        {lastError}");
}
```

When running this with `STD_OUTPUT_HANDLE` set to `11`, the system reports that something went wrong. It even tells us that the error code is 6.

Looking this up in the official documentation results in the following information:

ERROR_INVALID_HANDLE

6 (0x6)

The handle is invalid.

This is precisely what's going on.

"Wait a minute," I can almost hear you say. "I can't ask my users to look up the official documentation to see what an error message means every time something goes wrong!"

Well, you've got a point there. And the .NET design team agrees. They've added some ways to get that error message. There are two ways to get it, and you can choose which one you want.

First, if you want to have that error message, you can get it with the following code:

```
if(!WriteConsole(stdHandle, output, (uint)output.Length, out
charsWritten, IntPtr.Zero))
{
    var lastError = Marshal.GetLastWin32Error();
    var errorMessage = Marshal.GetPInvokeErrorMessage(lastError);
    Console.WriteLine($"Something went wrong. Error message:
        {errorMessage}");
}
```

Again, we start by getting the error code. We always have to do this, and we should do it as quickly as possible before another error somewhere else messes things up.

Then, we call the `Marshal.GetPInvokeErrorMessage` method and give it that `lastError` code. It returns a string telling us `The handle is invalid`.

Nice. But what if this error is so impactful that we cannot continue? .NET tells us to use exceptions in those cases. Good practice teaches us never to throw an exception but to use a specialized derived exception. We have just the right thing for that: `Win32Exception`.

We could throw that and set the message to the message we got from `GetPInvokeErrorMessage`, but since that is such a common scenario, .NET Framework gives us a shortcut to do just so. Look at the following code:

```
try
{
    if(!WriteConsole(stdHandle, output, (uint)output.Length, out
        charsWritten, IntPtr.Zero))
    {
        var lastError = Marshal.GetLastWin32Error();
        throw new Win32Exception(lastError);
    }
}
catch(Win32Exception e)
{
    Console.WriteLine($"Error: {e.Message}");
};
```

This looks a lot better. This code results in a message on our screen stating `Error: The handle is invalid`. Okay, since this is just a simple example, I fail to properly deal with the issue (a rethrow would be a good idea here). How you continue after such an error depends on your coding style, your use case, and what you want to achieve.

There is one other way to get the error message. This one is quite nice but not as straightforward as the others we've discussed: `FormatMessage`.

The `FormatMessage` function comes from the Win32 API. Its declaration is as follows:

```
[DllImport("kernel32.dll")]
static extern uint FormatMessage(
    uint dwFlags,
    IntPtr lpSource,
    uint dwMessageId,
    uint dwLanguageId,
    [Out] StringBuilder lpBuffer,
    uint nSize,
    IntPtr Arguments);
```

If we have an error code, we can use it as follows:

```
var lastError = Marshal.GetLastWin32Error();
int bufferSize = 256;
var errorBuffer = new StringBuilder(bufferSize);
var res = FormatMessage(
    0x00001000,
    IntPtr.Zero,
    (uint)lastError,
    0,
    errorBuffer,
    (uint)bufferSize,
    IntPtr.Zero);
if(res != IntPtr.Zero)
{
    var formattedError = errorBuffer.ToString();
    Console.WriteLine(formattedError);
}
```

First, we create `StringBuilder`. The API uses this to build up the string with the error message. We give it a size of `256` characters. This size should be enough for most, if not all, errors. We need to give this size since in C and C++, you need to allocate a buffer beforehand; it cannot expand dynamically (well, it could, but you wouldn't do that if you want high performance). We call `FormatMessage` with the 0x00001000 flag. This flag means "use the error code provided." We can use other flags, but this one is used most of the time. We don't have a message we want to format, so the second parameter is `IntPtr.Zero`. Then, we give it `lastError`, 0 for the language (that is, the system default, usually English), the buffer, the size of the buffer, and another `IntPtr.Zero` parameter. This last one means we don't use arguments. Here, arguments are the same as what we have in C# when we want to format a string:

```
Console.WriteLine("Hello {0}", 42);
```

Here, `42` is the argument.

We get that same "The handle is invalid" message when we run this.

You might want to use this API because it can do some nice tricks. For instance, replace `languageId` code 0 with the code 0x0413. This `languageId` is the Windows language ID for Dutch (please use whatever language you want.)

The result is `De ingang is ongeldig`, which is more or less a good translation of the original error.

This way, you can have nicely formatted, translated error messages!

There's one last thing to cover here: many samples online use the following code:

```
if(!WriteConsole(stdHandle, output, (uint)output.Length, out
charsWritten, IntPtr.Zero))
{
    var lastError = Marshal.GetLastWin32Error();
    var errorMessage = new Win32Exception(lastError).Message;
    Console.WriteLine($"Error: {errorMessage}");
}
```

Technically, there's nothing wrong with this. But this isn't why exceptions are there. Creating one just to get the message is wrong. However, I have seen this so many times that I thought I should warn you against it. If you don't want to throw an exception, don't create one. In that case, call `Marshal.GetPInvokeErrorMessage` instead. You will do yourself and those maintaining your code a huge favor.

Issues when debugging code with low-level APIs

Working with low-level APIs such as the Win32 API opens up a treasure trove of new and powerful tools. However, it comes with a couple of downsides. Debugging your code suddenly gets a lot harder, and it also becomes more critical.

There are a couple of areas you need to be aware of when you want to debug your code using low-level APIs:

- Error handling
- Interoperability
- Debugging tools
- Compatibility and portability
- Documentation and community support

Each of these can pose a challenge, requiring you to think about your debugging strategy before you start coding. Let's go through the potential issues.

Error handling

As mentioned previously, you're responsible for error handling when using low-level APIs. You don't get exceptions from the functions you call when something goes wrong. You always have to be careful to check the return code of the calling code to see if it is 0. And even then, there is no guarantee that things work out as you expected. For instance, the call to `GetStdHandle` worked fine when we gave it an invalid type of `ConsoleId`, but the result was still not what we expected. You have to be very careful with these kinds of calls. Ideally, we would have caught that problem immediately and informed the system that something went wrong.

Even if you catch all the error codes, that doesn't mean you can identify what went wrong. Sometimes, the error messages are so cryptic that you must read the documentation to see what's happening.

There is a method in the API called `CoCreateInstance`. It deals with creating COM objects, which you use to connect to other systems, such as Word or Excel. To make that connection, give it the ID of the object you want to connect to. Those IDs are in the form of GUIDs, and you have to type them in. If there ever were a situation where it is easy to get things wrong, this would be it.

Using a non-existing `ClassID` returns an error code of `0x80004005`. If we use the methods described previously to get the error message, you would expect to read something like `Invalid ClassId` or `COM Object not found`. Unfortunately, what you get is `E_FAIL: Unspecified error`.

Sigh.

That isn't helpful at all, is it? It failed. Okay, we got that. But why? What failed? We don't know. The system doesn't help you here at all. You have to know what you're doing and what the system expects and go through every single line of the code to spot the error. That's not easy.

Interoperability

As we've discussed, one of the steps you must take when calling Win32 APIs is to translate the types used in C# into their Win32 equivalents and vice versa. Sometimes, that's easy; sometimes, it can be pretty challenging.

The framework designers did a lot to help us: when the Win32 API expects a string, you can usually give it a C# string, and the CLR marshals the type back and forth without you even knowing it. But still, there is some marshaling going on. A C-style string is a pointer to a place in memory where a character sits. The next character is next to it, and so on, until the system finds a value of 0. That is the end-of-string marker. This is entirely different from the `String` class we have in C# (internally, the `String` class still has that list of characters ending with 0 somewhere, but we never see that, so we can pretend it isn't there at all).

Most types in C# have a sibling in Win32. Here's a list of the most used types:

C# Type	Win32 Type	Description
byte	BYTE	8-bit unsigned integer.
sbyte	CHAR	8-bit signed integer, typically used for ASCII characters.
short	SHORT	16-bit signed integer.
ushort	WORD	16-bit unsigned integer.
int	INT or LONG	32-bit signed integer
uint	UINT or DWORD	32-bit unsigned integer. Also used for flags and enumerations.

C# Type	Win32 Type	Description
`long`	LONGLONG	64-bit signed integer.
`ulong`	ULONGLONG	64-bit unsigned integer.
`float`	FLOAT	32-bit floating-point number.
`double`	DOUBLE	64-bit floating-point number.
`char`	WCHAR or TCHAR	16-bit Unicode character in C#, whereas WCHAR/TCHAR varies in Win32.
`bool`	BOOL	Boolean type. `True` or `False` in C#, and typically TRUE or FALSE in Win32. Here, FALSE is defined as 0, whereas TRUE is defined as NOT FALSE, meaning any other value, but usually, it is 1.
`IntPtr`	HANDLE, HINSTANCE, HWND, and so on	Represents a pointer or a handle. The type varies on context.
`UIntPtr`	Rarely used in Win32	An unsigned pointer or handle.
`T[]`	T* or SAFEARRAY	An array of the T type. Its representation depends on the context in Win32.
`DateTime`	FILETIME or SYSTEMTIME	Represents Date and Time. Representation varies in Win32.
`Guid`	GUID or UUID	GUID. 128-bit number. (GUID is usually tied to Windows platforms, while UUID is found on other platforms. They are basically the same, though.)
`TimeSpan`	Typically represented by a combination of DWORDs	A time interval. This is not available on Win32.

Table 1.2: C# and Win32 types

As you can see, most types can easily be translated between the platforms. When we dive into the more complex types, things get a bit more complicated since a lot of them are dependent on context or implementation. This makes marshaling types between the platforms a challenge.

Another thing to consider is something called calling convention. A calling convention defines how to handle parameters when calling a function. The two most common types are `stdcall` and `cdecl`. Win32 APIs usually use `stdcall`, while most other C libraries expect `cdecl`.

I won't dive too deep into these two calling conventions. However, let's summarize the most important differences:

- `stdcall`: The callee cleans the stack. It has a fixed number of arguments and it is commonly used in the Windows API. Here, function names usually get decorated.
- `cdecl`: The caller cleans the stack and allows variable-length argument lists. It is commonly used in the C standard library. Here, function names aren't decorated.

As you can see, knowing how to call a function is essential. The wrong convention can mess up the stack, and the arguments are passed to the function or return the wrong results. You could even mess up the memory, which is almost unheard of when writing managed code.

When you don't specify the calling convention, `stdcall` is assumed. You should give the correct calling convention if you need to call another library.

Maybe an example would help here. We used `WriteConsole` to write to the console earlier, but there is a much easier way: the `printf` function. This function is part of the C runtime in the Microsoft `msvcrt.dll` library. If you want to use this function, import it with the now well-known `DllImport` declaration:

```
[DllImport("msvcrt.dll", CallingConvention = CallingConvention.Cdecl)]
static extern int printf(string format, int i, double d);
printf("Hello, System Programmers!\n", 1, 2.0);
```

Since this function is not part of the Win32 API but instead resides in a separate DLL, you must be careful and specify the correct calling convention. Here, we need to use `cdecl`, which we can specify by setting `CallingConvention = CallingConvention.Cdecl`.

Other types include `WinAPI`, `StdCall` (they are basically the same), `ThisCall`, and `FastCall`. You will hardly ever encounter the last two, but at least you have heard of them now.

When you call an API and get weird errors or unexpected behavior, you might want to look into how to marshal the types or the calling conventions. The system doesn't help you here by giving you good error messages.

Debugging tools

Visual Studio Debugger is awesome. However, when mixing managed with unmanaged code, things might get tricky. If something goes wrong, the system might halt and show you a breakpoint. But since the code that's being called is not C#, the debugger might not show you what you need to see. It tries its best, so it will probably disassemble the code and show you the assembly code that is at fault.

I showed you some assembly code at the beginning of this chapter. That isn't something you might want to see if you want to find errors in your code. Well, I don't know if that applies to you, but I certainly don't want to see that.

If that happens, you might want to use other debuggers, such as WinDbg. Later in this book, when we cover debugging, we take a closer look at this tool. But trust me, debugging mixed code is no walk in the park.

Compatibility and portability

Windows changes. Sometimes, it changes a lot; sometimes, the changes are subtle. Although Microsoft is known for trying to keep things backward compatible as much as possible, sometimes, APIs change. The signature might change, or the behavior might change. And you only find out about that when things go horribly wrong. Again, you see very few exceptions or error messages, so you're left to debug the code and step through it.

As soon as you start using Win32 APIs, you are tying yourself to a limited set of devices and platforms you can use.

And don't even think about deploying the preceding code to a Linux platform. Sure, .NET runs fine on Linux, but not when you start using P/Invoke. And it might be that your code runs fine on one edition of Windows but breaks horribly on the next one that comes out of Redmond. We could call that "job security" since it will require us to update our code now and then, but I wouldn't go as far as calling it fun.

Documentation and community support

The primary audience for the documentation of the Win32 API is C and C++ developers. As a C# developer, it is hard to find the information needed. Sites such as `https://pinvoke.net` help, but only if you know how they work.

The documentation of third-party DLLs you might want to use as a .NET developer is even harder to find. Sometimes, you must inspect a DLL, see how it works internally, and then translate it into the proper DLL import statement. If you do that, ensure you have the correct calling convention and types!

Community support when mixing managed and unmanaged code is also a challenge. Most developers fall into one of two camps: they work in the unmanaged world or they work in the managed world. Doing both is very rare.

Good developers who can do both are scarce. The good news is that by reading this book, you are on the right path to becoming one of that very elite group!

Next steps

This chapter looked at the difference between low-level and high-level APIs. We dove into the foundations of .NET by examining the BCL and CLR. Then, we examined how to call into low-level APIs such as the Win32 API. We did that by reimplementing the ubiquitous `Console.WriteLine` into code that the Windows operating system can run without using the BCL. That led us to discuss error discovery and error handling, and how to best go about them.

We also discussed the issues you might encounter when you start doing that sort of coding. We mentioned the differences in type systems and the issues you might have when dealing with debuggers.

I hope this chapter has made you appreciate the .NET Framework and the hard work the BCL and CLR do for you as a developer. But I also hope you realize the power you get when using the Win32 API or other third-party libraries written in C or C++.

System programming relies heavily on these techniques. Although using these APIs ties you to the operating system you're developing for or even a specific version of that system, this is often the only way to achieve your results. And to be honest, I think working with these APIs is fun. It is all about getting back to the basics.

Working with low-level APIs can be challenging. They can lead to a lot of hard-to-solve errors. But when used correctly, they can lead to better performance in your code. When writing system software, that is very important. As discussed previously, system software should not get in the way of the user or the systems the user directly interacts with. Instead, it should be as fast as possible. So, using the correct APIs might give you just that extra performance you need. I think this is so important that I wrote a complete chapter on performance, which happens to be the next chapter. We were born to run, so let's run as fast as possible to the next part!

2
The One Where Speed Matters

Writing for performance

Most users agree that applications can never be fast enough. Anytime you talk to people about what annoys them in a piece of software, performance, or lack thereof, it is the one thing that gets to the top of the list.

And that makes sense: we are all busy, and we certainly don't want to spend time waiting for a piece of machinery to catch up with us. It has to be the other way around!

But if you think about it, you'll realize it is a miracle that computers can do anything at all within a reasonable time. If you think you're busy, just look at everything computers need to do! You can do the following experiment:

1. Reboot your computer.
2. Log in.
3. Start (if you're using Windows) Task Manager (hint: use the *Ctrl* + *Shift* + *Esc* combination).
4. Look at how much stuff is going on in the section background processes.

All of those processes are examples of system programming. They are all there to help the system do its job or to help the user-facing software get things done. And there are a lot of them. These processes all take up a bit of CPU time, a bit of networking, and some memory. Most are dormant and just waiting for something interesting to happen, but they are still there. They take away resources from the user-facing software.

I guess it is pretty clear that system software needs to be as small and as fast as possible so that there are enough resources left for the rest of the system – that is, the part the user cares about. The next chapter deals with making it small (or as memory-efficient as possible).

In this chapter, we will cover the following topics

- Why does speed matter?
- What is the **Common Type System (CTS)**?
- What is the difference between value types and reference types?
- What has boxing got to do with performance, and what is it anyway?
- How to choose the right data structures and algorithms to be as fast as possible
- How do strings work and how can we make them faster?
- What is unsafe code and how can we deal with it safely?
- Some compiler flags that help speed things up

To summarize, this chapter will show you how to make your systems as fast as possible. So, buckle up; we are about to go fast!

Technical requirements

You will find all the code in this chapter in the following link: `https://github.com/PacktPublishing/Systems-Programming-with-C-Sharp-and-.NET/tree/main/SystemsProgrammingWithCSharpAndNet/Chapter02`.

Setting up the stage

So far, we've established that we need as much performance as possible to allow the other systems to do their things. But there are other reasons you might want to optimize your code:

- Accessibility
- Hosting costs
- Planned obsolescence
- Energy usage

Let's examine these one by one.

Accessibility

Whenever I mention accessibility to software developers, they usually think about making software useable for people with physical challenges. I like to think a bit broader. Not everybody can afford the latest and fastest hardware. Many people need to make do with older, slower machines. Suppose your code slows that already sluggish machine down. In that case, you might be responsible for these people not being able to use the device anymore.

Other people use shared devices. Often found in institutions, more than one person uses these devices, and everybody adds their software. If your software slows the machine down, it affects everybody.

Hosting costs

More software these days runs in the cloud, in which case you have to pay per usage. If your software requires a lot of horsepower to run, it might increase costs. When added up, every bit of performance loss impacts the monthly cloud provider bill.

Planned obsolescence

Machines have a fiscal lifetime and an economic lifetime. These lifetimes determine when the company decides to replace the device. The fiscal lifetime is easy to calculate: when the organization buys a machine, the accountants tell you in how many years the value is too low to keep it around. They take the purchase price, calculate the depreciation for each year, and make notes of that in their spreadsheets. I'm oversimplifying things here, but I'm not an accountant.

The economic lifetime is harder to calculate. This lifetime is usually when a machine becomes so unusable that it is no longer worth upgrading or investing in. A computer that becomes too slow to be used should be replaced, even if the fiscal lifetime hasn't expired.

Your software could lead to that happening. If your performance is too low, the organization could write off the machine earlier than desired. And that leads to much e-waste: perfectly good computers get replaced simply because the software was written less-than-perfectly.

Energy usage

Using more CPU power means using more electrical power. You might think it might not be such a big difference, but in the end, all those machines use a lot of energy worldwide. Writing your code as efficiently as possible saves power usage and helps the environment. It's as simple as that.

Performance can be gained in a lot of places, even in pieces of your code where you deal with the humble integer. Let's discuss that!

Which integer is the fastest?

Choosing the right type of integer to use can have an impact on the performance of your system. I wouldn't worry too much about this: the CLR is pretty good at optimizing your code, and the **just-in-time (JIT)** compiler also applies many optimizations. Let's consider an example. Imagine that we have a `for` loop that iterates over a piece of code. If we have less than 255 iterations, we might be tempted to use a byte. After all, a byte is just 1 byte. If you use an integer, it will be 4 bytes. That is more memory and probably takes longer to process, right?

Wrong!

Don't try to outsmart the compiler. It knows the system a lot better than you do.

Let me show you.

We have the following four lines of C# code:

```
var a = byte.MaxValue;
var b = UInt16.MaxValue;
var c = UInt32.MaxValue;
var d = UInt64.MaxValue;
```

We set four variables to some values. The following table describes the specifics of each type:

C# Type	Short Name	Description	MaxValue (Hexadecimal)
System.Byte	byte	A byte	0xFF
System.UInt16	ushort	Unsigned 16-bit integer	0xFFFF
System.UInt32	uint	Unsigned 32-bit integer	0xFFFFFFFF
System.UInt64	ulong	Unsigned 64-bit integer	0xFFFFFFFFFFFFFFFF

Table 2.1: Numeric types with their maximum values

Let's examine what the compiler makes out of it. If you want to see this for yourself, create a new C# console program in Visual Studio (using .NET 7 or .NET 8), use top-level statements, and copy those four lines. Then, set a breakpoint on the first line and run it. As soon as you hit the breakpoint, press *Ctrl + K, G*. Doing that opens the disassembler.

You'll get something like this (I've cut some of the code that isn't that useful to us here):

```
01: # var a = byte.MaxValue;
02: 00007FFF956076EE   mov        dword ptr [rbp+3Ch],0FFh
03: # var b = UInt16.MaxValue;
04: 00007FFF956076F5   mov        dword ptr [rbp+38h],0FFFFh
05: # var c = UInt32.MaxValue;
06: 00007FFF956076FC   mov        dword ptr [rbp+34h],0FFFFFFFFh
07: # var d = UInt64.MaxValue;
08: 00007FFF95607703   mov        eax,0FFFFFFFFh
09: 00007FFF95607708   cdqe
10: 00007FFF9560770A   mov        qword ptr [rbp+28h],rax
```

I know I promised we wouldn't be doing assembly programming, but you need to know what's happening if you want your code to run as fast as possible. Let me talk you through it.

Lines 1, 3, 5, and 7 are comment lines that show the C# code that resulted in this assembly.

On line 2, we can see the code the CPU handles when we want it to set the value to a variable. The actual command is MOV, which means move. It then takes two parameters. The first is the target of the MOV, and the second is the value. There are several types of MOV commands; this particular one moves a DWORD. In Win32, DWORD stands for Double Word, which we know as an unsigned 32-bit integer. We are moving the hardcoded value, 0FFh (255 in decimal), to [rbp+3Ch]. In case you're wondering, rbp is the stack pointer. So, we're moving our value, 0xFF, to position 3C on our stack.

Great. We should know that value types go on the stack instead of the heap. Don't worry if you didn't realize that. The next chapter is all about memory. For now, just accept that we have two types of memory: a small but fast stack and a slow but huge heap. This byte goes to the stack.

Line 4 moves 0xFFFF to [rbp+38h]. Again, we are moving a DWORD here.

Line 6 does more or less the same: we move 0xFFFFFFFF to the stack. Again, it is a DWORD.

When compiled, a byte, a UInt16, and a UInt32 are considered a DWORD. There is no difference between them. If you look at the assembly code, there's no way of knowing what type the C# intended to use. That means there is no difference in performance here when using an 8-bit byte or a 32-bit unsigned integer. And in case you're wondering, the signed 32-bit integer looks the same, with the difference that Int32.MaxValue is half the value of UInt32.MaValue. However, the compiled code is the same.

Look at the code to copy the 64-bit integer to the stack. That works quite differently. On line 8, we move 0xFFFFFFFF to a register (a register is a special piece of memory inside the CPU that holds temporary variables). Then, we call CDQE. That copies whatever is in the EAX register (which can hold 32 bits) into the RAX register, which can hold 64 bits. Then, on line 10, it copies the first 32 bits of the contents to the stack.

As you can see, setting a variable to Int64.MaxValue involves a lot more work than the other three variants. It is considerably slower: the CPU has to do a lot more.

However – and this is important – this might not always be the case. This is what happens on my modern, beefy 64-bit Windows 11 machine. Things might be completely different on a low-powered Raspberry PI running Linux on an ARM processor. And that is one of the challenges of system programming: you must know how types behave to have the highest possible performance.

I think it's time to discuss the CTS.

The CTS

The CTS is a set of rules describing the types that are used in a .NET program. That's it. Nothing binary is going on; it is just a set of rules – a standard that compilers, languages, and the runtime must adhere to.

There are several different languages available on .NET Framework. Microsoft has C#, VB.Net, and F#. They also offer J#, a Java variant running on the CLR. You can also write .NET programs in C or C++. Other vendors also provide languages and tools you can choose from. Think of IronPython or Delphi.NET, for instance.

All these languages must stick to the rules. The compiler must emit IL code (again, IL looks like assembly but isn't). The JIT compiler then takes the IL to create machine code the CPU can understand and run.

There is a subset of the rules in the CTS that are called the **Common Language Specification** (**CLS**). These are the rules you, as a language designer, must follow to ensure your code and components can be used by other languages. However, you can choose not to follow those rules. That means other languages cannot easily use your code. That usually isn't a big problem, but it might be something to be aware of when you're designing a new .NET language. For instance, the CLS says the publicly available types cannot be unsigned integers. You will get a warning if you write code with a Uint16 as a public property and mark your code with the `[assembly: CLSCompliant(true)]` attribute.

Our aim here is not to design languages, so we aren't going to dive deeper into this.

All types used in .NET languages must adhere to the CTS rules. This book is not about learning to program in .NET. Still, knowing about the inner workings is crucial if you're a system programmer. We will cover just the highlights of the CTS here.

Value types and reference types

Later in this chapter, I'll discuss value and reference types in a lot more detail. Here, I will simply say that value types hold their values directly. In contrast, reference types are pointers that point to a value somewhere else in memory.

Classes and structs

.NET-based languages are supposed to be object-oriented. From this, it follows that the languages should support classes. These classes also have to have specific characteristics.

Classes should have visibility. They can be public, internal, protected, or private. We all know what those classifiers mean.

Classes have methods, properties, fields, delegates, and so on. These items can be private, protected, or public. You probably already know all of this; I don't have to explain what this all is.

However, a lot of developers struggle with **structs**. To the casual observer, they are more or less the same. And yes, they are indeed similar. They can both have methods, properties, fields, and so on. They can both implement interfaces. And they can both have static members.

The differences between classes and structs are more interesting. First, a class instance lives on the heap, and you will get a pointer that you store in the stack. However, a struct lives on the stack.

Since the variable that "holds" the class is the pointer to the heap memory where the data is stored, that variable can be null. In that case, it points to nothing; it is just a placeholder for a future instance of that class.

A struct cannot be null. There is an edge case: nullable types such as MyStruct? can be null, but that is the whole point of nullable types. Structs cannot inherit from each other. They can implement interfaces, though, just like classes can. That also means you cannot have an "abstract" or "sealed" struct. Those two modifiers are meant for classes that must be inherited. Since we cannot inherit from structs, this doesn't make sense.

Looking at this, you might think that a class is a better choice: there are only a few downsides and a lot of upsides in using them over structs. And you're not wrong. But structs have one significant advantage over classes: they are initialized on the stack, not the heap. And as I said previously, the stack is way faster than the heap. Since we aim for maximum performance, structs are used much more in our applications than in others.

Floating-point numbers

We already saw that it doesn't matter what kind of integer you use for most cases. UInt64, Int64, UInt128, and Int128 are generally slower than the other types, so only use them when you have thought it through and decided you need them.

Things are a bit different for floating-point numbers, however. We have three floating-point types in the CLS and, thus, in C#. Please look at the following table to see which ones they are:

Type	C# Type	Description
float	System.Single	32-bit single-precision floating-point
double	System.Double	64-bit double-precision floating-point
decimal	System.Decimal	The 128-bit decimal type is more precise but has a smaller range than a double

Table 2.2: Floating-point types

Which type you choose depends on your scenarios. You must select a decimal over a float if you need more precision. That would be obvious. But things are slightly more complicated if you don't need the 128-bit precision a decimal gives you.

On a 64-bit machine, the double (System.Double) is the fastest floating-point number. The CPU can understand this natively, so no conversions are needed. Performance-wise, this is your best choice. However, a float (System.Single) is more memory efficient. However, this is only true on a 64-bit machine. If you're targeting other platforms, the results might be different. For instance, if you want to run your code on an ARM-based device such as a Raspberry Pi, you will find that the CPU is optimized for the float type. So, you would be better off using a single-precision variety if you care about performance. Again, if your use case needs a higher precision, please use one of the other types. They are here for a reason, after all.

Where types live – the difference between value types and reference types

Types in the CTS can be either a value type or a reference type. It is essential to know the difference between these two options. Value types operate on the stack, while reference types live on the heap. Stuff residing on the stack is usually much faster than what happens on the heap.

From this, you would think using value types on the stack is the best way to get your desired sweet performance. Unfortunately, that is not how things work. The reference types are there for a reason, and they can give you significant performance improvements if used correctly!

The stack and the heap

Before discussing the difference between value types and reference types, we need to quickly look at the difference between the stack and the heap. I have already mentioned that the stack is faster than the heap but smaller. This is true, but there's a bit more to this.

The following table shows the differences between the two types of memory:

Feature	Stack	Heap
Allocation/Deallocation	Fast, compile time	Slow, runtime
Lifespan	Limited to scope	Beyond scope
Size Limitation	Smaller, fixed-size	Larger, dynamic size
Data Types	Value types (usually)	Reference types
Behavior	Deterministic	Non-deterministic
Fragmentation	No	Possible
Thread	Thread-specific	Shared between threads

Table 2.3: Differences between stack and heap memory

The memory allocation for stack variables is done at compile time, and the memory is pushed on and popped off the stack. This makes allocation and deallocation extremely fast. For heap variables, the memory is allocated dynamically at runtime.

However, the lifespan of variables on the stack is limited to the function's scope or the block of code. Once your code no longer needs that variable, such as because you reached the end of a `for` loop, the memory for this variable is automatically freed. For the heap, it is up to you or the garbage collector to get rid of the memory when it's unnecessary.

The stack is smaller, and you are much more likely to run out of stack memory than heap memory. Heap memory can be huge, especially compared to stack memory.

If you're wondering how big that stack is, the answer is, "It depends." You can even specify it yourself. Since the stack is tied to a thread, you can set the stack size when working with new threads:

```
// Create a new thread with a stack size of 1 MB
var thread = new Thread(new ThreadStart(ThreadMethod), 1024 * 1024);
thread.Start();
```

Here, we created a new thread and gave it a 1 MB stack. It's easy to determine this! If you want to limit the amount of memory a thread uses, you can estimate how much you need and allocate it that way.

On a side note, most developers know of `https://StackOverflow.com`. Strangely enough, I have met many developers who have no idea where that name comes from.

When you create a thread with a given stack size but try to use more memory than available, you get a `StackOverflowException` error. That is where that name comes from.

Let me show you. Oh – and don't use this in production code. This sample is just for illustrative purposes:

```
try
{
    Recur();
}
catch (StackOverflowException e)
{
    Console.WriteLine($"Oh oh.. {e.Message}");
}
return;
static void Recur()
{
    Recur();
}
```

The preceding code calls a recursive function that does one thing: it calls itself. When you call a function or a method, the system stores the address to return to when the function ends. The system stores this return address on the stack. After all, this is short-lived and needs to be fast. You want to continue with your regular flow after the function call.

But this code does nothing except call a function repeatedly and never returns from it. Thus, the return address gets added to the stack thousands of times until the memory runs out, and you get that famous `StackOverflowException` error.

If you want to experiment with this, run the preceding code in a separate thread and give it different stack sizes. Doing this will give you an idea of how significant an impact having the correct stack size has.

Boxing and unboxing

So far, things look pretty straightforward. Value types live in the stack; reference types live on the heap. An integer is a value type; thus, you have it on the stack. A class you define is on the heap since that is a reference type. If you want your class to be faster, you can turn it into a struct and have it available quicker since it goes on the stack. You might be thinking this is easy, but you'd be wrong. Things can be a lot more complicated than that.

Let's look at our good friend, the integer. An integer is a whole number, so it has no decimal point. As we saw earlier, we have a couple of variations of the integer. We have the 16-bit, the 32-bit, the 64-bit, and even a 128-bit version. And we have them in signed and unsigned versions. We even have a byte: this is technically not an integer, but since it compiles to a DWORD, we can have it in the same category. An integer is a value type, so it lives on the stack. However, if you look at *Table 2.1*, you'll see that the official name of an integer is `System.Int32`. I don't know about you, but that looks like a class or a struct name.

A struct still lives on the stack, but it is less performant than you might expect compared to a simple integer. Luckily, the compiler helps us with this. As we saw earlier, the compiler turns our integers into DWORDs, so there is no performance penalty. But sometimes, things work differently. So, we need to talk about boxing and unboxing.

C# is a genuine object-oriented language. That means everything is an object, and all descend from a base class. At the top level, one base class is the ancestor of all other classes. That is `System.Object`. Our integer is no different: the `System.Int32` struct derives from the `System.ValueType` class, which, in turn, is a descendant of `System.Object`. So, we still follow the rules of object orientation. Still, there seems to be a mix of classes and structs here. Don't worry; these are semantics, and the compiler deals with them when needed.

"Dealing with" sometimes means that the runtime converts value types into reference types or vice versa. That is what we call boxing and unboxing.

Boxing happens when the system converts a value type into a reference type. Converting a reference type into a value type is known as unboxing. Think of it as putting our value type in a box, in the shape of a class, or getting it out again if you go the other way:

```
int i = 42;
object o = i; // Boxing
int j = (int)o; // Unboxing
```

The first line declares a simple 32-bit integer, and we give it a value. We saw this previously; this is a relatively simple and fast instruction. In assembly, we move a hardcoded value into a DWORD position on the stack.

We want to make a copy of it, but this time, we use an object instead of an integer. Since `System.Int32` is derived from `System.Object` (with `System.ValueType` in between), you wouldn't expect this to be that much work. In the end, we still have an integer. But things are more complicated. Again, let's have a look at the assembly code. To be clear, you don't need to know assembly, but it is easier to understand how to get the most performance if you know what happens under the hood.

Here, `object o = i` translates to quite a lot of code:

```
1: object o = i; // Boxing
2: 00007FF9625E76F1    mov     rcx,7FF96254E8D0h
3: 00007FF9625E76FB    call    CORINFO_HELP_NEWSFAST
(07FF9C20D0960h)
4: 00007FF9625E7700    mov     qword ptr [rbp+20h],rax
5: 00007FF9625E7704    mov     rdx,qword ptr [rbp+20h]
6: 00007FF9625E7708    mov     ecx,dword ptr [rbp+3Ch]
7: 00007FF9625E770B    mov     dword ptr [rdx+8],ecx
8: 00007FF9625E770E    mov     rdx,qword ptr [rbp+20h]
9: 00007FF9625E7712    mov     qword ptr [rbp+30h],rdx
```

I won't explain everything that's happening here, but there are a lot of moving parts here. Line 3, however, is the important one: `CORINFO_HELP_NEWFAST` is a method in the CLR that allocates memory on the heap. Yes, the heap. Not the stack. This is what we call a very expensive operation: it takes a relatively long amount of time. After that, much copying occurs, all of which takes time.

Compare this with copying that integer variable to another integer without going through boxing:

```
1: int j = i;
2: 00007FF9625B7716    mov     eax,dword ptr [rbp+3Ch]
3: 00007FF9625B7719    mov     dword ptr [rbp+2Ch],eax
```

This assembly code takes the value of what's in the `i` variable (in the `[rbp+0x3C]` memory location) and moves it to the eax register. Then, it transfers that register to `[rbp+0x2C]`, where the new variable, `j`, is.

This was just two quick move calls, from the stack to the register (blazingly fast) and from the register back to the stack. That hardly takes time.

Going from the heap to the stack seems to be quicker since less coding is going on. Here, `int j = (int)o` leads to unboxing. The assembly for that code looks like this:

```
1: int j = (int)o; // Unboxing
2: 00007FF9625F7726    mov     rdx,qword ptr [rbp+30h]
3: 00007FF9625F772A    mov     rcx,7FF96255E8D0h
4: 00007FF9625F7734    call    qword ptr
[CLRStub[MethodDescPrestub]@00007FF9625EB8D0 (07FF9625EB8D0h)]
5: 00007FF9625F773A    mov     eax,dword ptr [rax]
6: 00007FF9625F773C    mov     dword ptr [rbp+2Ch],eax
```

This assembly code doesn't have that very expensive call to allocate memory. This makes sense: the stack doesn't require this. The stack has a fixed amount of memory, so you can use it if needed. If you run out of it, you get the `StackOverflow` exception we looked at earlier. The rest is just moving data about. There's still much more code here than what we saw when we copied two integers. Still, it doesn't look that bad, does it?

Don't be fooled: if we decide to use the j variable from now and not use o anymore, it can be removed from the heap. The garbage collector takes care of that, so you don't have to worry about it. But the garbage collector also comes with a lot of performance loss. The garbage collector is the topic of another chapter but be assured it can be a huge performance drain. This isn't obvious from this bit of code. There are hidden costs involved.

Hidden boxing and unboxing

Copying a value type, such as an integer, to a reference type leads to boxing. If you can avoid that, you should do so. But sometimes, boxing and unboxing happen when you don't expect it. Look at the following code:

```
internal void DoSomething()
{
    int i = 42;
    DoSomethingElse(i);
}
internal void DoSomethingElse(object o)
{
    Console.WriteLine(o.ToString());
}
```

Here, we declare an integer, i, in `DoSomething()`. Then, we call `DoSomethingElse()` with that integer. The original author of `DoSomethingElse` was trying to write the code so it could be reused. So, they decided to accept `System.Object` as a parameter. Since everything is, in the end, derived from that, this seems like a good idea. But it isn't. Here, i will be boxed before being passed to `DoSomethingElse`, along with the performance penalty that happens when boxing.

It would be better if the developer wrote the method like this:

```
internal void DoSomething()
{
    int i = 42;
    DoSomethingElse(i);
}
internal void DoSomethingElse<T>(T o)
{
    Console.WriteLine(o.ToString());
}
```

Here, instead of accepting an object, we take a generic type. Since we pass it as an integer, the compiler understands that this is a value type and doesn't convert it into an object. No boxing is happening here. This code is a lot faster than the previous version.

How about this line of code?

```
int i = 42;
string message = "Hello Integer " + i;
```

It looks pretty simple. But again, boxing is happening here. Before string concatenation can happen, the `i` variable is first boxed to the reference type.

The next one is nice as well:

```
var list = new ArrayList();
list.Add(i); // boxing!
int j = (int)list[0]; // unboxing!
```

Value types are part of reference types that usually live on the heap. So, they need to be boxed. Getting the values back will then lead to unboxing.

Moving value types to reference types leads to this behavior. Take a look at the following code:

```
IComparable i = 42;
```

This is safe, right? We aren't converting; we're just declaring that we are interested in part of the integer that belongs to the `IComparable` interface. The `System.Int32` struct implements a lot of interfaces, and this happens to be one of them. Still, it is a struct, so all should be good.

Let's have a quick look at the associated assembly for that simple line of C# code:

```
1: IComparable i = 42;
2: 00007FF9625E76F1    mov        rcx,7FF96254E8D0h
3: 00007FF9625E76FB    call       CORINFO_HELP_NEWSFAST
   (07FF9C20D0960h)
4: 00007FF9625E7700    mov        qword ptr [rbp+20h],rax
5: 00007FF9625E7704    mov        rax,qword ptr [rbp+20h]
6: 00007FF9625E7708    mov        dword ptr [rax+8],2Ah
7: 00007FF9625E770F    mov        rax,qword ptr [rbp+20h]
8: 00007FF9625E7713    mov        qword ptr [rbp+30h],rax
```

You should recognize this by now, especially the call to CORINFO_HELP_NEWSFAST. This is boxing in action. The same happens when using the `IEquatable<int> = 42` line. Although we now use a generic, we still get boxing.

Let's look at one more example. This one is a bit silly:

```
object myString = "some string";
var stuff = true ? 42 : myString;
```

Here, we have a string that we appoint to an object, `myString` (that is not the silly part). Then, we assign something to `stuff`, depending on `true` being true (which it always is; this is the silly part). If `true` is true, we assign 42 to stuff. If not, we copy `myString` to `var`. At first glance, you might expect `stuff` to be of the `int` type since `true` is always true. But that is not how a static-typed language works. It needs to know what type `stuff` is at compile time. The conditional operator, `? :`, expects both sides to be equivalent types. Thus, it decides that one part is an object and can cast the integer literal to an object. Therefore, it boxes that 42 into an object instance, and `stuff` here is another object instance. And there you have it: more boxing.

Boxing and unboxing allow you to mix and match value and reference types. It would be tough to write reusable code otherwise. But be aware of this, and be mindful of the costs associated with boxing and unboxing. It happens in places you might not be aware of. And that results in less-than-stellar performance.

Choosing the right data structures and algorithms

Object orientation is all about having the data and the operations on that data together in a cohesive and loosely coupled structure. That is what classes and structs do: they combine the two. This way, you can define your data structures in a way that makes sense concerning the system's functionality.

But when speaking about performance, other factors come into play. Having static classes is usually a code smell that you must avoid. However, they're fast. You don't need to instantiate something, resulting in that costly call to allocate heap memory. And that memory doesn't need to be cleaned by the garbage collector later.

Of course, if you have member variables for that class, you might as well instantiate it. Ultimately, all that happens is that those variables end up on the heap (with a little bit of housekeeping). The methods themselves are part of your application code and are stored differently.

The BCL also has many classes and data structures you can use to store data. Some of them are better suited for high performance than others. Which one you choose depends on your use case, but I think writing a bit more code is worth it if that means you can use a more efficient class.

Arrays, Lists, and LinkedLists

Arrays, **Lists**, and **LinkedLists** are all structures you can use to store data sequentially. That data is stored in the heap as well. Yes, you read that correctly. Look at the following two lines of code:

```
int i = 42;
int[] r = { 42 };
```

The first line is a simple assignment. The system copies the hard-coded value of 42 (0x2A in hex) to a DWORD and stores it on the stack. The second line creates a new array, allocates memory for that on the heap, initializes the array, and then copies 42 into the first position.

Read that again and try to see if you can guess if there's any boxing going on.

You might expect that there is, but there's no boxing here. The array holds a pointer to a place in the heap that contains individual DWORD values. It knows how long each value is (32 bits, to be precise), so it can move the values directly without changing anything. Also, no unboxing occurs when taking an element from the array and storing it in a local variable. The system copies the DWORD value and leaves it at that.

A list is the same as an array. Internally, the data is stored in an array. However, a list offers the option to resize it dynamically. Next to that, it has some nice methods such as `Add()`, `Remove()`, and `IndexOf()` that can be very helpful. But nothing comes for free: the methods take time to perform, and dynamic reallocation is very expensive in terms of performance. You must judge if you need those extra methods and dynamic reallocation. If you do, use a list. If you can go without, use an array.

There is an in-between solution: you can use `List<T>` and initialize it with an appropriate size. After all, you must do the same for an array: you need to know how big it is. Doing that causes the `List` class to initialize the array it uses internally to that exact size, and no reallocations happen – unless, of course, you find out you need more room. But that's great; you don't run out of memory. Yes, you get the performance penalty in that case, but that's okay. If you pre-initialize the `List` class, the performance is almost identical to the pure, basic array.

The `LinkedList` class has some nice features. It is a double-linked list of items, which means each item is accompanied by a pointer to the next and the previous object. This means more data is needed to store things: we cannot just store the items themselves, but the system must also add those pointers. This results in slower behavior: those pointers must also be calculated and copied. So, you might think `LinkedList` is wrong when considering performance.

However, `LinkedList` might be a great choice if your use case requires insertions and removals. Inserting an item simply means storing the object and adjusting some pointers. In an array or list, inserting would mean moving everything up one place in the internal array when you want something to sit in the middle.

Again, use your judgment. If you can, use arrays (or pre-initialized lists), go for the uninitialized list, and only then look at `LinkedLists`.

Stacks and queues

Stacks and **queues** look very similar. They are more or less similar performance-wise, with one big difference: a stack is fast if you need to access the latest added items, whereas a queue is very fast when you need quick access to the items in the order they were entered. In other words, a stack is optimized for **last in, first out** (**LIFO**) scenarios, while a queue is better in **first in, first out** (**FIFO**) scenarios.

However, your code runs faster if you can think of a way to use a stack instead of a queue. A stack is slightly more efficient than a queue in handling its work, at least enough to make it worth rewriting your code.

HashSets and lists

A **HashSet** and a list are different types with different behaviors, but there are cases when you might want to swap your list for a `HashSet`. A `HashSet` can be efficient when you're adding, removing, or looking up items.

A `HashSet` has one significant advantage over a list concerning performance: a HashSet has a constant-time average complexity for add, delete, and search operations. A list, however, has a linear-time search complexity. In everyday English, a HashSet always takes the same time to look up items, no matter how many elements it contains. A list needs more search time when more items are added to it.

But beware: a constant time means the time doesn't change. This doesn't imply a `HashSet` is faster! Quite the contrary: a `HashSet` can be pretty slow. And that makes sense: before an item is added to the `HashSet`, it needs to calculate the unique hash for that item. That hash is the key that's used to store the object's position. And then, it has to check if an object with that hash has already been added.

Of course, once this has been done, looking up an item is very quick: it needs to have the hash, and then it can find it easily. Also, when you have one of these two collections and need to add an item, the HashSet is faster than the list in many cases.

As with most of these cases, look at your requirements and try to do a couple of benchmark tests to see what you can use best.

SortedList, SortedDictionary, and Dictionary

SortedList, **SortedDictionary**, and **Dictionary** all store their data as key-value pairs. You need something to identify the item and store the key separately from the object. This way of working looks like working with the `HashSet`, but the big difference is that you can retrieve the items by its key in a `Dictionary`. You can retrieve the data in the `HashSet`, but you must use a `foreach` statement to get them all or a `Linq` statement such as `Where()`.

The keys in the `SortedList`, `SortedDictionary`, and `Dictionary` must be unique. If your use case allows for that, these collections can do wonders, but only if you choose the right one. The following table compares these three types in terms of their performance:

Property	Dictionary <TKey, TValue>	SortedList <TKey, TValue>	SortedDictionary <TKey,TValue>
Underlying data structure	Hash table.	Array for keys, array for values. Keys are sorted.	Balanced binary search tree.

Property	Dictionary <TKey, TValue>	SortedList <TKey, TValue>	SortedDictionary <TKey,TValue>
Ordering	No ordering of elements.	Elements are sorted by key.	Elements are sorted by key.
Insertion	$O(1)$ average time complexity.	$O(n)$ time complexity since it might need to shift elements to maintain order.	$O(\log n)$ time complexity.
Deletion	$O(1)$ average time complexity.	$O(n)$ time complexity, for the same reason as insertion.	$O(\log n)$ time complexity.
Lookup	$O(1)$ average time complexity.	$O(\log n)$ time complexity.	$O(\log n)$ time complexity.
Memory	Generally less memory efficient than SortedList, but better than SortedDictionary.	More memory efficient than SortedDictionary since it uses arrays for the keys.	Generally less memory-efficient.
Use-case	When you don't want ordering but want fast insertions, deletions, and lookups.	When you have a relatively small dataset that you want to keep sorted and you will be doing lots of lookups.	When you have a larger dataset that you want to keep sorted, and you need faster insertions and deletions than SortedList offers.

Table 2.4: Key-based collections

Again, check your requirements and benchmarks to see what works best for you.

Dictionary or last of tuples/objects

A **List<Tuple>** and a **Dictionary** are different things, but with some rewrites, you could use both to achieve your goal.

The lookup speed in the `Dictionary` is very fast. Since you look for the key instead of the actual item, you can achieve a much better performance than with the list, where you have to iterate through the whole list to find what you need. Also, insertion and deletion are fast and constant when using a Dictionary.

However, with a `Dictionary`, the keys need to be unique. With a list, this is not necessary. Again, with some rewrites, you might be able to use a `Dictionary` instead of a list and benefit from some highly-needed performance gains.

For versus ForEach

ForEach is amazing. It helps us write our code so much faster. However, it can also slow down our code.

`ForEach` is so helpful that the people who built the compiler added all sorts of optimizations. ForEach does lots of work: it gets the enumerator and then enumerates through the collection using methods such as `MoveNext()`. They all take time, and you would think that it is much slower than using a `for` loop. However, these optimizations make the difference negligible when using For or ForEach on an array or `List<T>`.

But suppose you use your own collection where you have implemented `IEnumerable<T>` and `IEnumerator<T>`. In that case, chances are the C# team did not optimize for that in the compiler. That might result in a slower loop than a regular `for` loop.

As always, benchmark whether using the much more readable ForEach is better than a regular `for` loop.

Strings

In the old days, strings used to be simple. You identified the length needed to store a sentence, allocated memory, and copied each character's ASCII values in a single row. Then, you put a 0 (zero) at the end, and you were done. Easy. But then you realized you needed something more dynamic as you were unsure how long the string would be. So, you wrote code to change the buffer required to store it. You also realized that you needed to have some operations on those characters. For instance, you might have wanted to know how long the string was and not have to count the characters every time, or maybe you wanted to convert all characters into uppercase. So, you wrote code for that as well. At that point, you had some data in the form of characters (with the zero at the end) and some methods on that data. That is the definition of a class, so in C++, you write a `String` class.

Things got even more complicated when you realized that other cultures used other characters. Luckily, others also realized this, so they created the **Unicode standard**. But now, instead of storing a single byte per character, you must store a Unicode character. And that can be anything from 8 bits (in UTF-8) to 4 bytes. Then, you learned that although a single character can take 32 bits, that is technically incorrect: that applies to code points. A code point usually *is* the character, but sometimes, it isn't. In those situations, the character you want to display has multiple code points in the string. That's when most people give up.

The good news is that you no longer have to worry about that since we have the `System.String` class in .NET. It takes care of all of those details, and they look deceivingly simple. Assigning a sentence to an instance of that `String` class is as simple as the following code:

```
string someMessage = "Hello, World!";
string theSameEmoji = "\U0001F600";
string someEmoji = "😀";
```

The first line assigns "Hello, World!" to the someMessage variable. When we do this, the compiler generates all the code necessary to create an instance of the System.String class and initializes it with the correct text.

The following two lines contain the same Unicode characters: a friendly smiley. The first uses the Unicode character, while the second uses the actual character. Yes, this is valid C#!

Strings are reference types, so they live on the heap. We learned that the heap is slower than the stack earlier, but we have no choice in this case. The pointer is copied when we copy a reference type to a new variable. This means we have two variables pointing to the same data structure. This also happens when we copy a string: a new pointer is made and points to that class's same instance.

Strings are immutable. You cannot change the contents of a string. If you do that, the CLR creates a new string, and the old one is ready to be garbage collected. Again, this might lead to unwanted performance issues.

There are some other things we must consider when talking about string performance. Let's go through them.

Use StringBuilder for concatenation

When talking about string performance, this one gets the most attention. And for good reason: this simple "trick" can help get your application faster. The idea is that when you're in a loop, do not concatenate strings. Create a StringBuilder object and use that. The difference in performance is enormous. And that makes sense: changing a string is impossible, so each time you add to one, a new one is created, the content is copied with the added string on top of it, and the old one is discarded.

Use StringBuilders in loops. You can go ahead and just do it.

Interning strings

Strings are interned. If you have a string in your code and the actual text is known at compile time, any other string with the same content will point to the same class. Have a look at this code:

```
string str1 = "Hello Systems Programmers";
string str2 = "Hello Systems Programmers";
// Reference equality test
if (Object.ReferenceEquals(str1, str2))
    Console.WriteLine("Both strings point to the same
        memory location.");
else
    Console.WriteLine("Strings do not point to the same
        memory location.");
```

When you run this code, you will get a message stating that both strings point to the same memory location.

But if you read the contents of both strings from the console, use `Console.ReadLine()`. If you enter the same string twice, they will not be interned. This is because interning happens at compile time.

You could call `String.Intern` yourself. This checks to see if the string you wish to intern is already there, and if so, it makes it point to that instead of having its own copy. This could save a lot of memory, but it has a performance penalty. So, use it wisely.

Use String.Concat or String.Join

I said that you should use `StringBuilder` when joining strings in a loop. But creating a `StringBuilder` object is a bit overkill if you're outside a loop and only want to add to a string once. In that case, you should use `String.Concat` or `String.Join`.

Just to be clear here: if you are looping, use `StringBuilder`. The `StringBuilder` object is the fastest way to concatenate strings. But creating an instance of a `StringBuilder` class takes time (it is a class, thus on the heap). If you only want to add one or two strings to an existing one, `String.Concat` is faster overall than having a `StringBuilder` object.

That looks like this:

```
var startString = "Welcome to System ";
var longString = startString.Concat("Programmers!");
```

The `String.Join` object is another good way to build up strings. You can use this one when you want to combine a collection of items into one string. The list of items can be anything since the CLR calls `ToString()` on them. Here, `ToString()` needs to make sense; otherwise, you'll get a long list of class names.

It looks like this:

```
string[] myElements = {"C#", "VB.Net", "F#", "Delphi.Net"};
string result = string.Join(",", myElements);
```

Printing `result` will show `C#,VB.Net,F#,Delphi.Net` on your screen.

Be careful what you use as the list of elements. If those are `ValueTypes`, a lot of boxing happens. That negates our performance gain when using the suitable string methods.

Comparison

Chances are that you have to compare strings in your code. There are several ways to improve your performance when doing that. For instance, taking into account a culture takes a lot longer compared to not doing that. If you don't need a culture-specific check, you should specify that. The same goes for the casing: if you don't care about the casing when comparing, please don't use one of the comparisons that take care of that.

There are several ways to compare strings. The most obvious one is the equality operator:

```
string a = "my string";
string b = "my string";
var areTheyEqual = a == b; // true
```

In this case, there's no comparison at all. Since the compiler interns the strings, the pointers point to the same data. The equality checks for that and returns `true`.

You could also do it like this:

```
string a = "my string";
string b = "my string";
var areTheyEqual = a.Equals(b); // true
```

This code does the same thing, with the same caveat concerning the interning. Here, `operator ==` calls `Equals()`, so it shouldn't be surprising that the results are the same, with the same performance.

Now, look at this code:

```
string a = "my string";
string b = "my string";
var areTheyEqual = a.Equals(b,
    StringComparison.InvariantCultureIgnoreCase); // true
```

This way of comparing is significantly slower than the previous examples. The CLR now has to compare the strings in all their different appearances: in all sorts of cultures and all casings.

This way works brilliantly if you need it, but if you don't, please omit the options!

I see many people writing this sort of code:

```
string a = "my string";
string b = "my string";
var areTheyEqual = a.ToUpper() == b.ToUpper(); // true
```

This way of comparing is the worst way of doing this. Calling `ToUpper()` doesn't convert a string into all uppercase. Instead, it creates a new string with all uppercase characters. Again, strings are immutable, so the runtime creates a new one whenever you change something. Here, we are doing that twice so that we can compare them.

Using `StringComparison.IgnoreCase` is about five times as fast compared to calling `ToUpper()` (or `ToLower()` for that matter).

Preallocating StringBuilder

One final tip: knowing the length of the resulting string when using `StringBuilder` helps tremendously if you tell that class about that. Preallocating helps optimize the code and reduces many allocations, resulting in better performance.

Writing unsafe code

A word of warning before we start talking about unsafe code. There is a reason it is called "unsafe." You could be in for much trouble when you leave safe code.

The CLR checks many things for you when you run your code. For instance, it ensures type safety and ensures you are not playing around with spaces in memory that are not yours to play with.

In the "old" days, when using C++ or C in Windows development, this was the primary source of program crashes. Developers made a slight mistake in their pointer arithmetic and ended up reading or writing memory they had no access to. The operating system immediately killed your process, and you got that dreaded `AccessViolationException` error. This is the ultimate slap on the wrist: the operating system telling you to stay out of someone else's memory. Sometimes, it would be worse: the operating system might not have caught it, and you messed up the operating system or another program. That could lead to even worse situations: the whole machine could crash.

The safe environment of the CLR in .NET has practically removed that completely. The CLR governs everything you do and ensures you stay in the areas where you are allowed to stay.

You've probably realized that this is nice, but checking what's happening always has a performance hit. Nothing comes for free. We give up some performance in exchange for a stable system.

If you want that performance back, you could tell the CLR to stay out of your way. The CLR will obey and hand over the reins to you. Again, you are on your own and responsible for not messing things up. But things run a bit faster now!

Let's consider an example.

An array is a pointer to a consecutive list of items. So, `int [1000]` is just a pointer to a long list of a thousand integers, all nicely lined up.

You can access these items in the list by giving the array the index of the item you want. First, the CLR checks if the array has been initialized and not pointing to some weird random place in memory. Then, it checks if your index falls in the range that the CLR allocated for the array. If that checks out, it gets and returns the item for you. Nice.

The following code example iterates through the array and adds up all the values:

```
long sum = 0;
for (int i = 0; i < array.Length; ++i)
{
    sum += array[i];
}
```

This piece of code works nicely, but it can be faster. All those checks take time, and we might decide we don't need them. We tell the CLR to take a break and leave it all to us!

The following snippet shows how to do this:

```
unsafe
{
    long sum = 0;
    fixed (int* pArray = array)
    {
        int* pEnd = pArray + array.Length;
        for (int* p = pArray; p < pEnd; p++)
        {
            sum += *p;
        }
    }
}
```

We declare the block we want to optimize with the `unsafe` keyword. Everything in that block is now no longer checked.

Then, we retrieve the pointer to the array. We mark it as `fixed`. This keyword means the garbage collector doesn't move the array until we are done with it. It would be disastrous if the garbage collector moved the array to another place in memory when we accessed it. The `fixed` keyword prevents that.

Then, we get the pointer to the end of the array in memory so that we know when to end. In the `for` loop, we get the pointer to the elements, read the data at that memory position, and add the `sum` variable.

This piece of code works fine. It is also faster than the safe version. But just for fun, mess around a bit with the pointers. Instead of letting it end at the end of the array, let it end at that position plus `0xFFFF`. Now, there is no way to tell what's going to happen. It might continue reading past the end of the array, getting all those byes and adding them to `sum`. That would mean you are getting the wrong result. It is more likely that you get the `AccessViolationException` error, followed by your program being terminated.

We use unsafe code to improve performance, such as in the preceding example, but also when we need to interact with native libraries written in C/C++. But if you can avoid it without sacrificing performance too much, please do.

Compiler optimizations

I have said it before and will repeat it here: don't try to outsmart the compiler. The C# compiler is a fantastic piece of software that can do tricks we can't even think of. But sometimes, we can help the compiler make choices that affect performance in a good way.

Aggressive optimization

Look at the following method:

```
private int AddUp(int a, int b)
{
    return a + b;
}
```

I am sure you agree that this is not an exciting method. Calling this, however, does take a lot of time: the calling method has to store the return address, move all parameters (the integer values, a and b) to the right place, jump to the method, retrieve the parameters, do the actual work, store the return value in the right place, retrieve the return address, jump to that return address, and assign the result to the variable in the calling method.

The compiler knows this. So, in this particular case, it will probably optimize it and "inline" it. But if you think the compiler doesn't know about this, you can instruct it to take a closer look at the code and be a bit more aggressive about it. You do that like so:

```
[MethodImpl(MethodImplOptions.AggressiveOptimization)]
private int AddUp(int a, int b)
{
    return a + b;
}
```

This tells the compiler to be aggressive when optimizing the code. This is a hint to the compiler: there is no guarantee it will do what you ask. But in this case, it will probably honor your request (again, it would likely have done it already) and inline the method.

Inlining means it takes the method's body and injects it into the calling method directly. So, instead of all this copying and moving I described previously, it will now execute the code inline, as if it is part of the original method.

This is way faster, of course. It also means your original method gets bigger: it now contains that extra bit of code, as do all the other methods that use this AddUp() method. It gets copied all over the place.

It is a matter of choice: more performance over less efficient memory usage.

The optimize flag

The compiler can optimize your code. But it doesn't always do that. You can add the `optimize` flag to the compiler to force optimization.

There are several ways to do that. First, you can add it to the command line if you use that to build your code:

```
dotnet build -c Release -property:Optimize=true
```

Alternatively, you can use `MSBuild`:

```
msbuild /p:Configuration=Release /p:Optimize=true
```

They both achieve the same result.

You could also set it as an option in your `CSProj` file. The best way to do that is to add it to the project properties:

- Build
  - General
  - Errors and warnings
  - Output
  - Events
  - Strong naming
  - Advanced

Unsafe code
[✓] Allow code that uses the 'unsafe' keyword to compile.

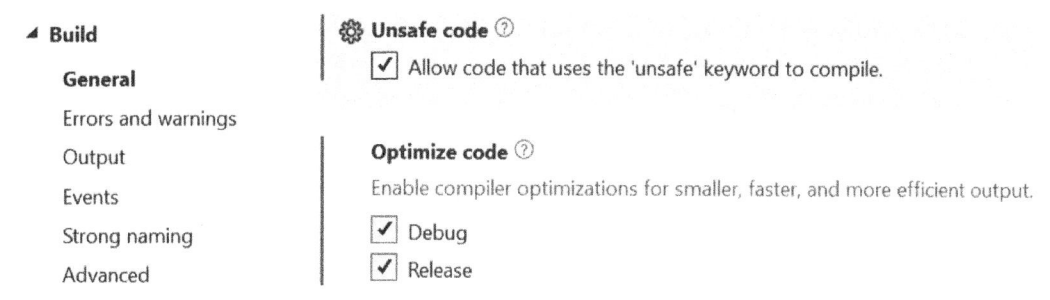

Optimize code
Enable compiler optimizations for smaller, faster, and more efficient output.
[✓] Debug
[✓] Release

Figure 2.1: The project properties showing the Optimize code option

As you can see, you can set **Optimize code** for **Debug** and **Release**.

This will add or change the following setting to your `.csproj` file:

```
<PropertyGroup>
  <Optimize>True</Optimize>
</PropertyGroup>
```

It's good to know that by default, programs compiled in the **Debug** configuration have optimizations turned off. In contrast, programs compiled in the **Release** configuration have it turned on.

When debugging, you are better off using non-optimized code. When releasing, the opposite applies.

Next steps

Performance – that was what this chapter was all about. We learned why it is crucial, especially for system programming, to write software that is as fast and efficient as possible.

First, we looked at the BCL and the CLR and saw how the different data types can affect performance, but also that things don't always behave as expected.

Then, we examined the types in the CTS and identified which types give us the best-performing systems and what to avoid. We spent quite some time in the `Strings` class. We also learned how to rewrite our code so that it uses the best tools this class gives us to make it behave faster.

After, we dove into the dark underworld of unsafe types and saw that they could give us even more performance but with the downside of the possibility of crashing our application, or even our system, in the most spectacular way.

Finally, we looked at ways to help the compiler make our systems even faster. Here, we learned that the compiler is smart enough to make those changes. It's worth repeating that you shouldn't try to outsmart the system. You really should only use the unsafe code and compiler tricks if benchmarking shows that you have an issue. Otherwise, leave those two alone. However, they are good tricks to understand if you do need them.

However, better performance often leads to less efficient memory usage. It is a trade-off. Sometimes, it is better to have a more memory-efficient system than it is to have a fast system. Sometimes, you have to mix and match. In the next chapter, we'll consider memory and cover these aspects in greater detail.

3
The One with the Memory Games

Efficient Memory Management

Performance is critical for system programming. We discussed this in the previous chapter and outlined why it is crucial. Memory consumption is just as important, however. The trouble is that better performance often leads to worse memory usage. And trying to optimize for memory usage often leads to worse performance. As in all things in life, it is a matter of compromising.

That being said, you might also encounter situations where you get both simultaneously – for instance, using the stack instead of the heap (or value types instead of reference types) results in faster code using less memory.

However, you usually don't get one item for free while pursuing the other. You have to make informed decisions and the correct choices. And that is what this chapter is all about. I hope you remember most of it once we reach the end of this chapter!

In this chapter, we'll cover the following topics:

- An overview of memory management
- An overview of the **garbage collector** (**GC**)
- How to correctly use `IDisposable`
- A long list of tips and tricks on how to save memory
- Unsafe code and pointers

Technical requirements

Everything in this chapter can be done in a plain installation of C#. The only thing you might need extra if you're following along is the NuGet `MessagePack` package. You can install that through Visual Studio Code or using the following CLI command:

```
dotnet add package MessagePack
```

An overview of the GC

.NET is a managed system. As discussed earlier, many issues developers had to deal with are now handled by the **Common Language Runtime** (**CLR**). The CLR abstracts away most of the tedious tasks a developer faces so that they can focus on functionality instead.

Memory management is a tricky thing to do right, but also very important. Doing this wrong usually leads to memory leakage or instability in the software. Although no software should have that, system programming needs to avoid this. It might lead to unstable systems, making the whole computer unusable. Therefore, it is good that .NET developers don't have to worry about this. The GC manages much of the memory and deals with those intricate details.

Learning how the GC works is worth it so that your code is much more memory efficient. That means knowing how memory allocation functions in .NET.

We already discussed the difference between the stack and the heap. But just as a reminder, the stack is the short-term, smaller, but faster piece of memory that's used for value types, while the heap is longer-term and much more extensive but also slower.

If you declare an integer in a code block, the CLR puts it on the stack. That memory is released at the end of that block's scope. The heap works differently. Since items on the heap can live much longer, we need another way of handling this memory. That's where GC comes in.

The GC process can run on a separate thread or in the main or user thread. For now, it is easiest to assume that the GC runs on a background thread. We will deal with the real-world situation a bit later.

GC and its generations

GC is a generational system. This means it works with generations. Does that help? I guess not. Okay, let me elaborate.

Look at the following code snippet:

```
1: {
2:     object a = new object();
3: }
4: {
5:     object b = new object();
6: }
```

This snippet is not our most exciting piece of code, but we must start somewhere. The curly braces are necessary here, though.

The preceding code snippet results in less activity than expected, especially if you come from a C or C++ background.

The following figures will help you make sense of what's going on when we run the preceding code snippet:

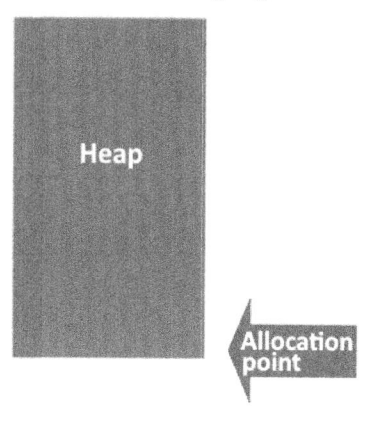

Figure 3.1: The empty, allocated heap

During the program's startup, the CLR allocates a continuous memory block. This block isn't very big but big enough to house all the startup objects, plus anything else it can determine is needed. At that point, a pointer is created that points to the first area available for the project to use.

On line 1, we begin a code block. Then, on line 2, we create an instance of the `Object` type and store that in the `a` variable. The memory of all data that belongs to that object lives on the heap. The runtime initializes, calculates how big that memory for `a` should be, and moves the allocation pointer up to the next available piece of memory in the block. A pointer is created on the stack (we call it `a`), and that pointer points to the memory block on the heap where its data lives:

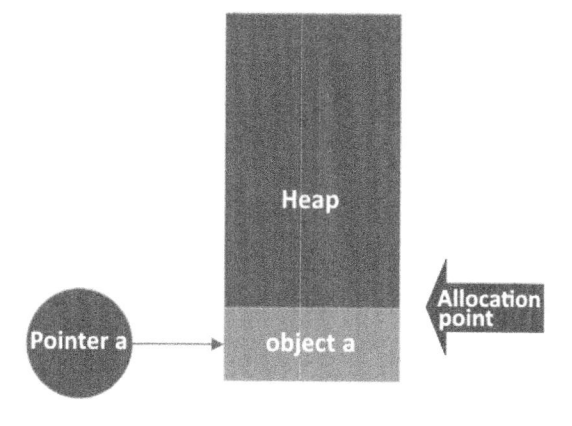

Figure 3.2: The heap after creating object a

On line 3, we end the scope of that variable. As we have learned, variables on the stack live only as long as the scope they belong to. Thus, a pointer is cleared, and its occupied memory is released. But on the heap, nothing happens. The data for a is still there, and the allocation pointer still points to the same place:

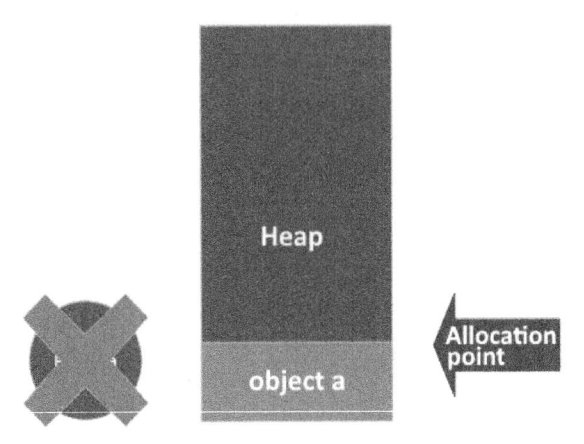

Figure 3.3: The heap after a goes out of scope

Then, on line 4, we create a new scope block; on line 5, we create a new instance of Object and call it b. The whole circus starts all over again, but the data for b is now stored on top of a. Nobody knows about this; the data for a has become unreachable. But it is still there!

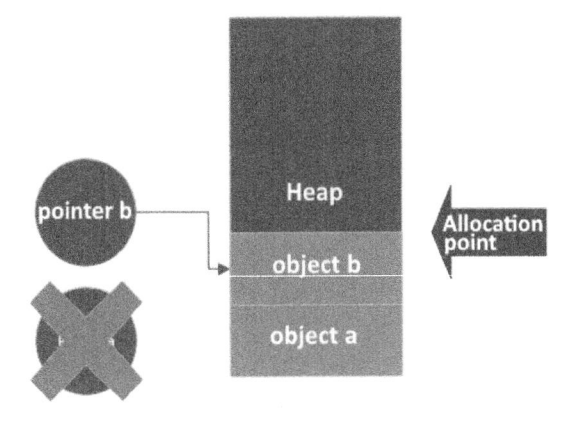

Figure 3.4: The heap when we allocate object b

And, of course, on line 6, the scope ends, so the stack variable, b, is removed again. Again, nothing happens to the heap:

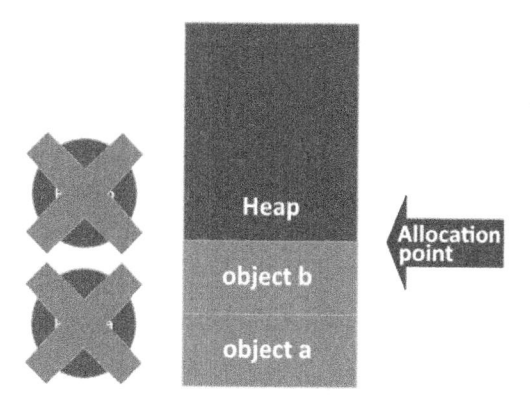

Figure3.5: The heap after b also goes out of scope

As you can see, we don't allocate or deallocate memory on the heap. Here, a pointer moves up whenever we need a new object. Moving a pointer is much faster than allocating and freeing memory. Allocating and deallocating, or freeing memory, are very expensive performance-wise. Avoiding these operations as much as possible is one of the reasons applications in .NET can run so fast.

However, you have probably seen a potential problem. What happens when we run out of space on the heap? The allocation pointer cannot move beyond the end of that block, so what happens then?

I'm glad you asked. That's when the GC comes into play. The moment we run out of memory in the block we allocated initially, the GC will have a look at all the items in that block.

First, it goes through all objects in the heap and sees which still have active pointers pointing to them. In our example, we have none, but imagine that we have some other objects allocated that are still in scope.

The GC marks all those orphaned memory locations to know it can reclaim that memory. But what about the items that the GC cannot remove?

The answer to that question concerns the GC being "generational." The CLR places each object in a particular part of the heap marked with a generation number. All new objects are in generation 0.

When the GC does its trick, it moves all objects still alive and in scope to the next generation. They are now in the generation 1 heap.

> **A bit more detail**
>
> In reality, there are only two heaps: one for all generations and one for the **large object heap** (**LOH**) (we'll cover this in more detail later). The heap is divided into sections, one for each generation. However, we can think of each generation as having its own heap. Although this isn't technically correct, thinking about the layout like this makes it a bit easier to understand what's going on.

Now, all objects that survived the garbage collection process are in the generation 1 heap; all objects that can no longer be reached are ready to be cleaned up. The GC clears out the memory and sets the allocation pointer back to the beginning of the heap. Now, the whole thing can start all over again.

That's pretty neat, isn't it? But there's another problem. What happens if our generation 1 heap fills up?

In that case, we see a similar behavior. Everything in generation 1 that is no longer reachable (and that includes not being reachable from objects that are in other generations) is marked for deletion; the GC promotes all others to generation 2.

Okay; let's continue. What happens when generation 2 fills up? You would be wrong if you guessed that all reachable items move to generation 3. There's no generation 3. If we fill up generation 2, the runtime allocates a new block that's big enough to hold the current heap and sufficient to add more objects. Then, it moves all objects to the new heap and returns the old heap to the operating system.

Sometimes, the CLR asks for more memory for the heap and gets a slap on the wrist from the operating system. There's no more memory available. In that case, we see the dreaded `OutOfMemoryException` error.

> **Handling OutOfMemoryException errors**
>
> The rule with handling exceptions is that you should only catch exceptions you know how to handle so that you can bring the system back into a stable state. With `OutOfMemory`, you have no way of doing that. The `OutOfMemoryException` error is one of the exceptions you'd better just let go. You can't do much here to help.

The LOH

You can probably imagine that moving data in memory takes a lot of time and will hinder your performance. And that is correct: performance takes a huge hit when the GC runs.

The GC is optimized to prevent that as much as possible, but memory operations are inherently expensive. Reallocating memory and moving the bytes around to all the different locations in particular take a lot of time to perform.

One of the things the CLR designers did to alleviate that problem a little bit was to declare a special heap called the LOH.

As the name implies, it is a heap for large objects. Currently, it deals with large objects – that is, objects bigger than 85,000 bytes.

Objects of that size or bigger do not go to the regular heap. They are not subject to the generational behavior of the rest of the system.

The GC does help with keeping the LOH clean, but it runs far less frequently. Also, it doesn't have generations for the LOH.

When the GC clears objects from the LOH, the memory gets fragmented. What this means is that after a while, our block of memory looks a bit like Swiss cheese: there are holes everywhere. Areas of the memory that were once occupied by objects, which have been reclaimed, are now empty. After a while, the memory consists of valid objects and empty space. That means that although technically there is enough memory to allocate new objects, the system cannot find one continuous block of memory. If that happens, the GC will compact the LOH to make the memory contiguous again. But that only happens on very rare occasions. This way of working means the LOH is much slower than the other heaps.

Also, the LOH doesn't have a predefined size. It grows if needed. Again, this is a costly and slow operation.

The good news is that these large objects are out of your way in the usual heaps, so they don't slow down the GC there.

Be mindful when creating large objects. They can bring your application to a grinding halt.

Finalizers

You may have been programming in .NET for over a decade and have never seen or used a finalizer. If that is the case, good job. We don't need them. Well, we mostly don't. There are some edge cases when we do; one is when you use the `IDisposable` pattern. This pattern has a whole section dedicated to it later in this chapter.

I want to show you what happens with the GC if you add a finalizer to your classes.

> **Fun fact!**
>
> Finalizers are often mistaken for destructors. That makes sense: if we have a constructor at the start of the lifetime of an object, why not have destructors at the end of that? C++ has them, after all. But we don't. So, never call finalizers as destructors. They don't destroy. They are pacifists who just want to clean up after them.

Let me briefly explain what a finalizer is. A **finalizer** is a method in a C# class that the runtime calls just before the object is cleaned up and removed. Just like a constructor, it has a special name. The following code block provides an example of a finalizer:

```
class MyClass
 {
     public MyClass()
     {
         // Initialize everything here...
     }

     ~MyClass()
     {
         // Clean up here
         // (well, don't. Use IDisposable for that).
     }
 }
```

This class, `MyClass`, has both a constructor and a finalizer. The constructor has the name of the class, an access modifier (`public`, in this case), no return type (since it is not a method), and it might have some parameters. I have no parameters here, but I could have added them if needed.

This constructor is called after the CLR has allocated the memory. You can think of it as being called as part of a "new" operation. You know when it is called: as soon as you create an instance, the CLR invokes the constructor. Simple enough, right?

So, an instance of a class can be created like so:

```
var myClass = new MyClass();
```

The finalizer is a bit different. It has no access modifier, no return type, and no parameters. It is the name of the class that is preceded by a tilde (~). You never call this code. The CLR does. You cannot set any parameters here.

The question is, of course, when is it called? And the answer is that we don't know.

Let's go back to the GC run. Generation 0 is getting full, so the GC must clean up. It looks for all objects that are out of scope to remove that memory. Let's assume `myClass` is also out of scope.

I explained how the GC cleans up memory previously but left out two steps the GC also takes.

The first extra step is that after it finds all the locations in memory without active variables pointing to them, it looks for objects in those areas with a finalizer. If it finds one, it will place a pointer to that memory structure in a special queue called `FReachableQueue` (the F stands for finalizer). Then, it leaves it alone. The memory on the heap for that object is not reclaimed. It is also not moved to another generation. It just survives the cleaning up. Now, it just sits there once more.

Well, only until the GC runs again. That's where the second step comes into play. Just before it cleans up the generation, it goes through `FReachableQueue`. For all objects in that queue, the CG calls the finalizers. Then, it removes the pointer from `FReachableQueue`, and the object is now finally ready to be garbage collected.

This has some profound implications:

- Objects with finalizers survive an extra round of garbage collection. They stick around longer, adding to the memory pressure.
- Objects with finalizers will have their finalizers called, but we have no idea when. We don't know when the GC runs, after all.
- Moving the pointers around is an extra step for the GC, making things even slower.

Finalizers are a huge performance drain. They are better not used at all. Unless, of course, you use the `IDisposable` pattern to clean up. We'll discuss this next.

IDisposable

.NET is a managed environment. I have said that before, and I will mention it again. I keep repeating this because many think "managed" means "I don't have to take care of stuff." And as we have seen, that is simply not true. Yes, the CLR takes away a lot of the pain other developers suffer, but still, there's a lot that you have to do yourself – especially if you are, like we are, writing system software.

One of the things the CLR does is clean up resources after us. Value types are on the stack and don't need to be cleaned up. Reference types need to be cleaned up, but the GC takes care of that. However, as we have seen, cleaning up doesn't always happen when we expect it to happen.

And there is another problem: the GC doesn't clean up all used resources. The CLR only cleans up managed objects. Non-managed objects are yours to clean up and dispose of. Most examples that explain this behavior mention classes such as files and database connections. And to be honest, for most developers, those are the only real-life occurrences they will find when dealing with unmanaged resources. For us, this is a bit different. When writing system software, we, more often than usual, encounter things from low-level APIs, external hardware, interfacing with third-party software, attaching our code to external debuggers, and so on. We will see examples of these later in this book when we talk about the filesystem, networking, and interfacing with other hardware.

So, you must understand how to clean up if the GC doesn't do this for you. And that is where `IDisposable` comes into play.

The `IDisposable` interface is very simple. This is what it looks like:

```
public interface IDisposable
{
    void Dispose();
}
```

Classes that implement this interface must ensure they have a `void` method without parameters called `Dispose`.

It is an interface, so it doesn't do anything. If you add it to a class, nothing happens. The CLR ignores it. This statement is important. I will repeat it: the CLR does nothing with classes that implement this interface.

The `IDisposable` interface is more like a contract. We add it to classes that deal with unmanaged resources. Other developers see that interface in the class declaration and assume they must handle unmanaged resources.

And that is it.

So, how do we implement it? Let's have a look at the following sample:

```
class ResourceUser
{
    private readonly IntPtr _ptr;

    public ResourceUser()
    {
        // Allocate an 8 KB block of memory
        _ptr = Marshal.AllocHGlobal(8 * 1024);//
    }

    ~ResourceUser()
    {
        Marshal.FreeHGlobal(_ptr);
    }
}
```

In the constructor, we allocate a block of memory of 8 KB. We store the pointer to that block in `ptr;`.

This block of memory is unmanaged. So, it is up to us to clean it up as well. We decided to do that in the finalizer. After all, it is guaranteed to run, so we are good here!

But we have already established that we aren't sure when this will happen. And we don't want a block of perfectly fine memory just being allocated until the GC decides to run (twice, since it is in a finalizer!). That's just wasting memory and a lot of CPU cycles.

We need another way to clean up. Let's rewrite the code:

```
class ResourceUser
{
    private IntPtr _ptr;
    public ResourceUser()
```

```
    {
        // Allocate an 8 KB block of memory
        _ptr = Marshal.AllocHGlobal(8 * 1024);//
    }
    ~ResourceUser()
    {
        //nothing to do here!
    }
    public void Cleanup()
    {
        if (_ptr == IntPtr.Zero) return;
        Marshal.FreeHGlobal(_ptr);
        _ptr = IntPtr.Zero;
    }
}
```

This code moves the cleanup code to a new method called `Cleanup`. If we want to use this class, we can simply create an instance and then make sure we always call `Cleanup()`. We can ensure that by using a `try-finally` block. Let's do this:

```
var myClass = new ResourceUser();
try
{
    // Do something with myClass
}
finally
{
    myClass.Cleanup();
}
```

This is pretty simple, right? And to be honest, that is all there is to it for the `IDispose` interface. The most significant difference is that instead of having a method called `Cleanup()`, we have a method called `Dispose()`. And we mark our class with the correct interface, just as a courtesy to other developers. That way, they know they must clean up after using our class. Let's do this using the following code block:

```
class ResourceUser : IDisposable
{
    private IntPtr _ptr;

    public ResourceUser()
    {
        // Allocate an 8 KB block of memory
        _ptr = Marshal.AllocHGlobal(8 * 1024);//
```

```
    }

    ~ResourceUser()
    {}
    public void Dispose()
    {
        if (_ptr == IntPtr.Zero) return;
        Marshal.FreeHGlobal(_ptr);
        _ptr = IntPtr.Zero;
    }
}
```

And that's all we need to do. In our calling code, we should call `Dispose()` instead of `Cleanup()` so that our code compiles. Let's do that. I won't show you that code here as I'm sure you know how to do that. However, I will show you the **Intermediate Language** (IL) code. As a reminder, IL is a language that is not quite C# but also not machine code. It sits in between. But it does give us a nice indication of what the compiler makes of our code before it turns it into actual machine code. The IL code looks like this:

```
01: .method private hidebysig static void  '<Main>$'(string[] args) cil managed
02: {
03:    .entrypoint
04:    // Code size       21 (0x15)
05:    .maxstack  1
06:    .locals init (class ConsoleApp1.ResourceUser V_0)
07:    IL_0000:  newobj     instance void ConsoleApp1.ResourceUser::.ctor()
08:    IL_0005:  stloc.0
09:    .try
10:    {
11:      IL_0006:  nop
12:      IL_0007:  nop
13:      IL_0008:  leave.s    IL_0014
14:    } // end .try
15:    finally
16:    {
17:      IL_000a:  nop
18:      IL_000b:  ldloc.0
19:      IL_000c:  callvirt   instance void ConsoleApp1.ResourceUser::Dispose()
20:      IL_0011:  nop
```

```
21:        IL_0012:  nop
22:        IL_0013:  endfinally
23:        }  // end handler
24:    IL_0014:  ret
25: } // end of method Program::'<Main>$'
```

The IL code looks almost identical to our C# code. The critical part for us is on lines 15 through 23. This is the `finally` block, containing the call to the `Dispose()` method. We now know that, no matter what, our resources will be cleaned up.

This is brilliant. It's so useful (and important) that the people behind the C# language gave us a new construct that helps us in doing so: they gave us the `using` statement.

Using that statement means that `Dispose()` is called when you don't need the resource anymore. That calling can be done in two ways: as a block statement or as an inline statement.

The block statement looks like this:

```
using (var myClass = new ResourceUser())
{
    // Do something with myClass
}
```

Here, `using` starts a new scoping block. The resource can be deallocated and cleaned up at the end of the scope.

The inline variant is even easier:

```
using var myClass = new ResourceUser();
// Do something with myClass
```

The compiler will detect when `myClass` goes out of scope automatically. As soon as that happens, the typical workflow of the `using` statement resumes.

"But," I can almost hear you say, "you just told me that the CLR does nothing with that IDisposable interface, yet here it understands what to do with it!"

That's a smart observation, but the knowledge about `IDisposable` is not in the CLR here. The compiler is the one who's that smart. If we take the inline version of `using`, build our program, and inspect the IL, we'll see the following code:

```
.method private hidebysig static void  '<Main>$'(string[] args) cil managed
{
   .entrypoint
```

```
    // Code size       20 (0x14)
    .maxstack  1
    .locals init (class ConsoleApp1.ResourceUser V_0)
    IL_0000:  newobj     instance void ConsoleApp1.ResourceUser::.ctor()
    IL_0005:  stloc.0
    .try
    {
      IL_0006:  leave.s    IL_0013
    }  // end .try
    finally
    {
      IL_0008:  ldloc.0
      IL_0009:  brfalse.s  IL_0012
      IL_000b:  ldloc.0
      IL_000c:  callvirt   instance void [System.Runtime]System.IDisposable::Dispose()
      IL_0011:  nop
      IL_0012:  endfinally
    }  // end handler
    IL_0013:  ret
  }  // end of method Program::'<Main>$'
```

There are tiny differences between this code and the one where we called `Dispose()` ourselves, but these differences are not important. What's important is that the compiler looked at our code and translated that into a `try-finally` block with the `Dispose()` method being called in that `finally` part. In other words, it does precisely the same thing.

So, `using` is just a convenient shorthand to instruct the compiler. If we had used `Cleanup()` instead of `Dispose()`, the compiler would not have understood it. But in the end, the code that gets run on the processor is the same. There's no difference. There's no magic involved in using `IDisposable()`.

The IDisposable pattern

Unfortunately, we aren't done yet. The preceding code works. It cleans up and does this when we don't need the resources anymore. But we rely on the user of our `ResourceUser` class to do the right thing: they have to use `Dispose()` or a `using` statement. If they don't, we might have a memory leak. And don't forget that the developer who fails to do that is probably you, 6 months after you have forgotten what you did.

We need a better way to do this.

The `IDisposable` pattern is a recipe to make sure the resources get cleaned up, no matter what.

For instance, what happens if the user of our class doesn't call `Dispose()`, either directly or through the `using` statement? We need to clean up no matter what. Fortunately, we can do that. We have the finalizer. This always runs, although it might not run at the best time. But at least we can be sure that our resources get cleaned up eventually.

We could copy the cleaning-up code to our finalizer. However, we don't want to clean up twice. The preferred way to ensure our resources are disposed of is to write an overloaded version of `Dispose`. The whole implementation looks like this:

```
01: class ResourceUser : IDisposable
02: {
03:     private IntPtr _ptr;
04:     private IDisposable? _someOtherDisposableClass;
05:     private bool _isDisposed;
06:     public ResourceUser()
07:     {
08:         // Allocate an 8 KB block of Memory
09:         _ptr = Marshal.AllocHGlobal(8 * 1024); //
10:     }
11:     public void Dispose()
12:     {
13:         Dispose(true);
14:         GC.SuppressFinalize(this);
15:     }
16:     ~ResourceUser()
17:     {
18:         Dispose(false);
19:     }
20:     private void Dispose(bool isDisposing)
21:     {
22:         if (_isDisposed)
23:             return;
24:         if (isDisposing)
25:         {
26:             _someOtherDisposableClass?.Dispose();
27:         }
28:         if (_ptr != IntPtr.Zero)
29:         {
30:             Marshal.FreeHGlobal(_ptr);
```

```
31:                _ptr = IntPtr.Zero;
32:            }
33:            _isDisposed = true;
34:        }
35: }
```

Let's see what happens here.

On line 3, we have the pointer to our unmanaged memory block. On line 4, I added a new field for another class that implements IDisposable. This field could be anything, such as a file or a database. What it is isn't important here. All we need to know here is that it is a managed class we must clean up after use. On line 5, I added a Boolean that we use to see if the instance of this class has already been disposed of.

Lines 6 through 10 comprise the constructor's body in which we allocate our 8K memory block.

On line 11, we have our Dispose method. In that, I first call an overloaded method of Dispose and give it a true parameter. We use this parameter to keep track of who calls the overloaded Dispose. What this parameter does is something I explain in a couple of lines below, but before I do that, I have to explain the GC.SuppressFinalize(this) line. This is the magic line. It tells the GC not to move this instance to FReachableQueue when it's doing its magic. Effectively, this removes the finalizer code from our class so that when the GC runs, it can clear away the memory on the stack immediately instead of waiting for another run.

After this, we have the finalizer. The finalizer only gets called if the class user forgets to call Dispose (or using) due to the GC.SuppressFinalize(this) call. This time, we call Dispose(false).

Let's discuss the parameter I added to the Dispose() method and that I promised to explain. On line 20, we have the actual code for the cleanup. By now, I hope that you understand what the isDisposing flag does. If that flag is set to true, we got here because the user of the class called Dispose(). If the flag is false, the developer didn't use Dispose() and left it to the finalizer.

Of course, we first check if we didn't already clean up by checking the _isDisposed variable on line 22.

Line 24 is essential. Our class has a managed resource that we need to clean up. But if we came from the finalizer, we have no idea when this code will run. It might be the case that the GC already cleaned up the memory allocated by _someOtherDisposableClass. There's no way of knowing. If it had already been deallocated, calling Dispose() on it would result in a severe error and potentially crash our system. So, we must ensure we only call Dispose on that member if we are sure it is still around. If we got in this method via the finalizer, we cannot be sure. The order in which things are destroyed is non-deterministic. The only time we can be sure is when we got here through the call to Dispose().

The memory block, however, is something else. That block is unmanaged, so we know that the GC didn't clean it up already. It can't. That's why we call it unmanaged. So, we clean it up here on lines 28 through 32, no matter what.

And that is it. Things get a little bit more complicated if you have a derived class that stems from this class but isn't so complex that you can't figure it out yourself (hint: make `void Dispose(bool isDisposing)` protected virtual),

The `IDisposable` interface is very important if you want your code to use memory as efficiently as possible. Here, you learned how to implement it properly and how to code in such a way as to remove memory leaks. Again, since we as system programmers are more likely to have to deal with unmanaged code compared to other developers, this is crucial knowledge.

But knowing about `IDisposable` is not enough. There are many more tips and tricks I want to share with you about saving memory in your app.

Memory-saving tips and tricks

System programmers need to be aware of the memory that's used by the systems they write on. So, I want to share tips that will help you reduce **memory pressure**. Memory pressure is a fancy word to indicate how much memory is used compared to the amount of memory available. Again, some of these tips will make your system slower. As a system programmer, you must make informed choices and trade-offs between fast and memory-efficient code writing. Sometimes, you get lucky, and you get both. Other times, you must look at the options and pick the lesser of two evils. The following will cover specific things you can do to reduce memory pressure on your system.

- **Use value types over reference types**: Values types on the stack are usually smaller than reference types. The overhead of the pointer to the class and the pointers in the heap themselves can be a reason to move to value types, such as structs, instead of using reference types, such as classes. However, you'll probably notice a performance hit if your structs get too big. Value types are copied by value when used as parameters, and copying big structures takes much longer.

- **Pool objects**: Sometimes, it is a feasible option to pool objects. Pooling means an instance of an `ObjectPool<T>` class holds a pool of objects you can use and return when you're done with them. Instead of creating an instance of your class and waiting for the GC to clean it up, you can make a couple and store them in the pool. Initially, this might increase memory pressure, but depending on your scenario, it might save you some memory usage.

- **Use arrays over collections**: An array of items is smaller and much more memory efficient than collections such as `List<T>`. The list does offer a lot of functionality. It can be very flexible but comes with a higher memory consumption.

- **Optimize data structures**: Speaking of `List<T>`, sometimes, it is tempting to use it to store some items. The same applies to `Dictionary<TKey, TValue>`. But you don't always need it. If you know what you want to store in your classes, it might be more efficient to declare simpler variables for this and use those instead.

I have seen people using `Dictionary<TKey, TValue>` to store a username and an email address. Using two fixed strings for that would have been much easier, faster, and memory efficient. Be a smart developer!

- **Use Span<T> and Memory <T>**: Assume you have an array of integers. Nothing special, just something like this:

    ```
    int[] myBuffer = new int[100];
    ```

Arrays are reference types, so this allocates a memory block on the heap. There's nothing wrong with that. You want to split the array into two parts for some reason. There are multiple ways of doing that, but the simplest (although not the fastest) is using Linq, as shown here:

```
int[] firstHalf = myBuffer.Take(50).ToArray();
int[] secondHalf = myBuffer.Skip(50).ToArray();
```

Now, we have three arrays on the heap. One is the original, and the others are the two new ones. That uses a lot of memory. That's without me even mentioning the performance hit we get by copying all that data.

Maybe you need a copy. If so, then this is a good approach. However, you should use `Span<T>` if you just need to split. This class is a view on the memory you give it. It isn't copying; it's just a window on the original data.

That code looks like this:

```
var firstHalf = new Span<int>(myBuffer, 0, 50);
var secondHalf = new Span<int>(myBuffer, 50, 50);
```

This code sample doesn't copy the data or allocate a new array. It just gives you a view of the data.

Of course, if the original array is garbage collected, the span points to invalid memory.

Here, `Memory<T>` is more or less the same, but it's better when you're using async operations. Next to that, a span always lives on the stack. So, you cannot have a span as a field in a class (remember, classes are reference types, so all their data is stored on the heap). In contrast, `Memory<T>` can be used on the heap so that you can use them as fields in classes.

- **Avoid boxing**: Value types are fast and memory-efficient, so long as they stay value types. As we discussed previously, value types suddenly have the annoying habit of turning into reference types. We call this process **boxing**. Boxing takes a lot more memory than the simple value type. So, try to be aware of those situations and avoid them if possible.

- **Use lazy initialization**: If you create an instance of a complicated class, you might not need to initialize all fields in the constructor. Sometimes, it's better to do that only when needed. This way of working is called **lazy initialization**: try to postpone that initialization for as long as possible.

- **Compress data**: You can compress classes with a lot of data you don't frequently use to save memory. Of course, compressing data takes a lot of CPU time, but if the classes need to stay around but you only use them occasionally, compressing might be worth it. There is a whole namespace dedicated to this: `System.IO.Compression`. This contains many classes that help you compress and deflate your data.
- **Unload unnecessary data**: You could choose to remove data you don't need lying around all the time. Then, when you need it, you can reload it on demand. The overhead of doing this might be worth it if you have large datasets and don't always need them.
- **Use weak references**: As we learned earlier, the GC cleans up all resources that are no longer reachable. All objects with no pointer to them are cleaned up when the generation doesn't have enough space for more objects.

  If you have an object you don't need, you can create a `WeakReference<T>` reference. This means you tell the GC to remove the object if needed. Let me show you what I mean:

  ```
  var myObject = new object();
  var myObjectReference = new
  WeakReference<object>(myObject);

  // Much further in the code, we might need myObject

  if (myObjectReference.TryGetTarget(out var retrievedObject))
  {
      // Do something with retrievedObject
  }
  else
  {
      // We need to recreate myObject
      myObject = new object();
      myObjectReference.SetTarget(myObject);
  }
  ```

  First, we create an instance of an object, called `myObject`. Then, we get a weak reference to it. Let's assume that later in our code, we need `myObject` again. First, we ask `WeakReference` if the object is still available or if the GC has collected it. If it is available, we can use it. Otherwise, we recreate it and store the new pointer in `WeakReference`. Pretty neat.

- **Compact object representations**: Sometimes, you can save some memory by smartly combining data into other data structures. Let me show you. We can express three states a customer can have in the following manner:

  ```
  bool customerHasPayed= false;
  bool customerHasCredit = true;
  bool customerPaymentIsLate = true;
  ```

  Here, `bool` is usually internally represented by a byte. So, this takes 3 bytes.

We could rewrite this as follows. First, we create a new enum value:

```
[Flags]
enum CustomerPaymentStatus : byte
{
    CustomerHasPayed = 1 << 0,
    CustomerHasCredit = 1 << 1,
    CustomerPaymentIsLate = 1 << 2
};
```

The notation I have used to assign the values reminds me where I am in the sequence: by doing a left shift, I can easily number the items (0, 1, and 2).

> **Shifting bits**
>
> In system programming, we work with bits and bytes a lot. So, you should be aware of this kind of notation.
>
> The << operator takes all the bits in a byte and moves them one step to the left, effectively multiplying the value by 2. So, 1 << 0 moves nothing, 1 << 1 moves all bits 1 step and results in the value 2, while 1 << 2 moves the bits 2 steps, resulting in 4. In binary, the results are 00000001, 00000010, and 00000100.

We can set a variable as follows:

```
CustomerPaymentStatus customerStatus =
    CustomerPaymentStatus.CustomerHasCredit &
    CustomerPaymentStatus.CustomerPaymentIsLate;
```

We have the same information as we had in the first example, but this time, we're only using one byte. That's a 66% reduction in memory usage!

- **Set large collections and objects to null**: This tip should be obvious now, but setting large collections and objects to null allows them to be cleaned up. Since the CLR stores large objects on the much less frequently cleaned-up LOH, setting them to null enables the GC to clean them up there.

- **Consider using static classes**: Instance classes have many pointers going back and forth between the members and their data. These pointers and the member data can take up extra memory. Using static classes eliminates this overhead. The savings can be pretty significant.

At this point, I want to reiterate that for system developers, it is very important to be as memory-efficient as we can. The tips and tricks I just shared with you should be part of your development style. Saving memory frees up time from the GC and it makes your programs faster to load and usually also to execute. It helps in getting a better experience for the user. Of course, these tips and tricks can be applied to all sorts of C# programming. Every program could use better memory management.

The same thing, however, cannot be said about unsafe code and pointers. Those are topics that most developers will rarely encounter. However, we, as system programmers, probably cannot avoid them. So, I think we should spend some time looking at them.

Unsafe code and pointers in C#

If you're concerned about the memory, you could take over from the CLR and the GC and do it all yourself. I wouldn't recommend this, but sometimes, you have no choice. Although the compiler, the CLR, and the GC do amazing things, they cannot always predict what you are trying to achieve or what your limitations are. Especially for system developers, this can sometimes hinder you in achieving your goals. In those cases, you might have to resort to managing memory yourself. I think an example is in order here.

Let's start with a simple class:

```
[MessagePackObject]
public class SimpleClass
{
    [Key(0)]
    public int X { get; set; }
    [Key(1)]
    public string Y { get; set; }
}
```

The `MessagePackObject` and `Key` attributes come from the `MessagePack` NuGet library.

The `MessagePack` library is a tool that enables you to serialize and deserialize instances of classes into a binary representation. Another popular serializer format is JSON, which is far less efficient regarding memory. That is why we're using binary formatting here.

I have written two methods: one to serialize and one to deserialize. The serializer comes first:

```
public static byte[] SerializeToByteArray(SimpleClass simpleClass)
{
    byte[] data = MessagePackSerializer.Serialize(simpleClass);
    return data;
}
```

This is pretty simple. We get an object and give it to the `Serialize` method of the `MessagePackSerializer` static class. That will return a `byte[]` value that we return to the caller of this method.

Of course, this also needs deserialization:

```
public static SimpleClass DeserializeFromByteArray(IntPtr ptr, int length)
{
    byte[] data = new byte[length];
    Marshal.Copy(ptr, data, 0, length);
    var simpleClass = MessagePackSerializer.
        Deserialize<SimpleClass>(data);
    return simpleClass;
}
```

This method is slightly more complicated: we get a pointer to a piece of memory and the length of our data. We create a `byte[]` value of the correct size. Then, we copy the memory from the heap into the byte array so that we can deserialize it with the `MessagePackSerializer` class. The object we get is then returned.

We can use these methods as follows:

```
var simpleClass = new SimpleClass()
{
    X = 42,
    Y = "Systems Programming Rules!"
};
var memory = IntPtr.Zero;
try
{
    byte[] serializedData =
        MemoryHandler.SerializeToByteArray(simpleClass);
    memory = Marshal.AllocHGlobal(serializedData.Length);
    Marshal.Copy(serializedData, 0, memory,
        serializedData.Length);
    SimpleClass deserializedSimpleClass =
        MemoryHandler.DeserializeFromByteArray(
            memory,
            serializedData.Length);
}
finally
{
    Marshal.FreeHGlobal(memory);
}
```

Here, we create an instance of `SimpleClass` and give it some data.

Then, we serialize that object using our new `SerializeToByteArray` method we discussed. This gives us a `byte[]` value with the raw data. Then, we allocate the memory on the heap where we want to store that data. We copy the data. Then, we can discard the `simpleClass` instance: it can be garbage collected.

Note that the GC will never clean up the memory we just allocated. Our data is stored in our memory.

If we want to use it, we need to deserialize it again, which is something we can do by calling `DeserializeFromByteArray`. We give the pointer to the allocated memory and the size we occupy.

And, of course, we need to free the memory when we're done with it. The GC doesn't do that for us. We are responsible for this.

In this example, we only used 29 bytes to store the data, which isn't a lot. We can allocate that memory if needed and deallocate it when we decide. This is a very fast and efficient way of handling the memory of our system.

> **Warning**
> Don't use `BinaryFormatter` to do this. Although using `BinaryFormatter` is much simpler, it is inherently unsafe. You are better off using `MessagePack`, as I showed here, or using a JSON-based serializer and deserializer. For more information, please read https://aka.ms/binaryformatter.

We can go a bit further with this. Using pointer arithmetic, we can manually copy all the data into our memory block. Since pointer arithmetic is unsafe, we need to tell the compiler we want to do this by using the `unsafe` keyword and setting the project options to `allow unsafe`, as we discussed at the end of the previous chapter.

The serialization remains the same. Deserialization is simpler. The code to store the bits in our memory is slightly different. The whole code, however, is faster and more memory efficient. Here it is:

```
var pointer = IntPtr.Zero;
try
{
    byte[] serializedData = MemoryHandler.
        SerializeToByteArray(simpleClass);
    pointer = Marshal.AllocHGlobal(serializedData.Length);

    unsafe
    {
        // copy the data using pointer arithmetic
        byte* pByte = (byte*)pointer;
        for (int i = 0; i < serializedData.Length; i++)
```

```
            {
                *pByte = serializedData[i];
                pByte++;
            }
            //deserialization is done here
            byte[] deserializeData = new byte[serializedData.Length];
            pByte = (byte*)pointer;
            for (int i = 0; i < serializedData.Length; i++)
            {
                deserializeData[i] = *pByte;
                pByte++;
            }
            var deserializedObject = MessagePackSerializer.
            Deserialize<SimpleClass>(deserializeData);
        }
    }
}
finally
{
    Marshal.FreeHGlobal(pointer);
}
```

We start similarly by using `MessagePack` to get a binary representation of our object. But instead of using `Marshal.Copy()`, we copy the bytes ourselves. We have a pointer to the beginning of the data; we take the first byte, copy it into the memory block we allocated, increase the pointer, and repeat this until we copy the whole thing.

Deserialization works in the same way. We get the pointer to the block of memory we allocated, which now contains our data. We read the first byte, copy it into the array, and repeat until we finish.

Then, we deserialize it by calling the `MessagePackSerializer.Deserialize()` method, which takes a type, and we give it the array with all bytes.

Again, this is a speedy and efficient way to handle memory, but it does come with many risks. Remember, making a small mistake will mess up your day.

Unsafe code and using pointers in your code can speed things up a lot. But I want to make sure you understand the implications: you're taking over all control from the CLR. You're responsible for making sure your program runs fine and safe. Make sure you know what you're doing when going this route. If you do this, there are a lot of benefits when it comes to speed and memory efficiency!

Next steps

I hope you remember most of the things we discussed, but just in case you forgot, we will go through the most essential points again.

First, we discussed how the CLR and GC work together to remove the pain of memory management. We looked into how the GC works, what the generations mean, and what the LOH does.

We also talked about finalizers and why they can kill your performance. We also saw that they have a place when you use the `IDisposable` pattern (so long as you don't forget to call `GC.SupressFinalize(this)` to remove the finalizer if it is unnecessary).

Then, I shared a couple of techniques you can use to optimize your memory usage if you need the least amount of memory usage in your system.

I want to reiterate a crucial point about memory optimization. In 99 of 100 cases, the CLR and the GC do an outstanding job. Trying to outsmart them doesn't always result in better systems. The team behind these tools is good at what they do, and they use all the tricks in the book (and some that are not in that book!) to help you reduce memory pressure.

As a system programmer, you will run into situations where the GC and the CLR are just not doing a good enough job, and that is when the topics discussed here can help. But please be very careful. Managing memory can lead to weird and even catastrophic results when done wrong.

You should test and benchmark your code before tweaking memory usage. But if you follow my tips and advice, you can get exceptional results! However, things get much more complicated once you have multiple threads in your system. We need to talk about threads. A lot. And that is precisely what we are going to do in the next chapter!

4
The One with the Thread Tangles

Concurrency and threading

Threading and **concurrency** are things that most developers think they know all about. The theory sounds so simple, yet in practice, threading is where a lot of mistakes are made and where all those frustrating bugs originate. Threading can be quite complex, but the people of the BCL and CLR teams have done their best to help us as much as they can to make things simpler.

Once you get the hang of it, threading is a great addition to your skills and can make a major difference in your systems.

We will look at the following topics in this chapter:

- What is concurrency and threading?
- How do threads work internally in .NET and Windows?
- How does the CLR help us?
- What is async/await?
- How do we synchronize threads and make them work together?
- How can I make sure my code behaves nicely when working with threads?
- How can I use collections over threads?

Let's look into this fascinating topic!

Technical requirements

All the source code and samples in this chapter can be downloaded from this book's GitHub repository at `https://github.com/PacktPublishing/Systems-Programming-with-C-Sharp-and-.NET/tree/main/SystemsProgrammingWithCSharpAndNet/Chapter04`.

Concurrency and threading – the basics

This morning, I woke up as I do every day. I got out of bed, took a shower, and got dressed. Then I walked the dog for 30 minutes (it's a Sunday today). I returned home, made some coffee, and then sat down to write this.

I am sure that your day looks the same in general. You do something, then you do the next thing. Things are done in order. Sometimes, I make a phone call to people in other time zones when I walk the dog, but most of the time, I do the things I do one at a time. It is more efficient that way. If I were to sit down to write this chapter but stop to walk the dog a bit after five minutes, then leave him standing near a tree while I run back to the house to write for five more minutes, followed by me running back to the dog to walk another 500 meters, things would never get done. I would get a workout with all the running back and forth, but it would be inefficient.

That is a silly way to lead your life (no judgment; if this is what you do, I am okay with it, it just doesn't work for me).

However, in the case of computers, we tend to assume that this way of working enables work to get done quicker. Why do we think that?

Computers cannot do two things at the same time. No, wait. Let me rephrase that. CPU cores cannot do two things at the same time. In the old days, before AMD released the **Athlon 64 X2 processor** in 2005 and before Intel released the Pentium D in the same year, regular computers were all single-core. That means that computers, before 2005, could generally only do one thing at a time.

These days, most devices have multiple cores. Your computer, laptop, and phone all have a multi-core processor. However, as a system programmer, you might encounter devices with only one core. Think of IoT devices: they need to be cheap and very low in power consumption. Those systems often have a single core. Systems programmers run into single-core devices more often than people writing other software.

However, in the end, that doesn't really matter. My primary development machine has 16 cores. That sounds like a lot. However, if I look at my Task Manager, I can see many things running simultaneously, much more than those 16 cores can handle. So, even in a multi-core environment, machines must do something to enable all those tasks. As systems programmers, we have to be aware of how to write our software to get the most benefit out of those cores.

We are thus dealing with two separate topics here. One is concurrency; the other is threading.

Concurrency is the concept whereby the system executes several sequences of operations in overlapping periods. It is not really simultaneous execution; that is called parallelism. It is all about tasks running at what seems to be the same time without waiting for other tasks. It is a concept, not a programming technique.

Threads, on the other hand, are a programmer's construct. Threading is one of the ways to achieve concurrency.

> **Nice to know**
>
> Threads can be hardware threads or software threads. The CPU handles the first type; the second is handled in our software. The **Operating System** (**OS**) can assign threads to actual hardware threads, but as a developer, you are almost always going to be working with software threads. I will mostly be talking about software threads here, but I will point it out when I mean hardware threads instead.

The beginnings of concurrency – the IRQ

For now, let us ignore the fact that computers cannot multitask aside from spreading the load across the physical cores a CPU might have. To make life easier, we will assume that a computer can do two things at once.

This has not always been the case. In the early days, a computer did one thing at a time. That meant that if you wrote some software for a computer, you had complete control over all available hardware. Everything was yours and yours alone.

Well, when I say that it was yours, I mean that it was mainly yours. Sometimes, something would happen that would need the attention of the CPU. In those days, we had something called an **Interrupt Request** (**IRQ**). An IRQ is a hardware feature that is usually tied to other hardware. An external device, such as a floppy disk drive or a modem, could signal the CPU (by putting a voltage on a particular connection to the CPU). When this happened, the CPU finished the instruction it was doing, stored all of its state in memory, looked up the address belonging to that IRQ (there could be more than one), and started the code in that address. When that function finished, the whole thing would be reversed: the CPU would load the previous stored state and continue executing the original code as if nothing had happened.

This mechanism worked reasonably well, but there were a lot of potential issues. For instance, there were only a handful of IRQ lines available. If your code overwrote the registration of another piece of code attached to some hardware, that hardware would fail to work.

To make things worse, if you made a silly mistake and your code never returned from the IRQ, you could bring the whole machine to a halt. It would simply never return from your code and the running program would be on hold indefinitely. So you had to be very careful to ensure that you had no such bugs in your code!

IRQs are still used today, especially in low-power devices such as Raspberry Pi. We will encounter those later in this book.

Cooperative and preemptive multitasking

IRQs work okay, but they should be used by hardware devices. Since there aren't that many IRQs, and since they have the potential to kill running processes, we have moved away from using them in normal software.

However, having a computer and only being able to do one thing at a time with it seemed like a waste of resources. Computers became more and more powerful. They could soon do more things than we asked them to do. That was when multitasking OSs came into play.

For instance, the versions of Windows before Windows 95, such as Windows 3.1, used something called **cooperative multitasking**. The principle was reasonably straightforward. A piece of code would do something, and when it thought it could use a break, it would just tell the OS: "Hey, I am on a break; if you need me to do something, just let me know." It would then halt execution. This meant that the OS could allocate CPU time to another process.

We called this cooperative multitasking because we expected the software to cooperate and share the resources fairly.

Of course, if a program misbehaved, it could still claim all the CPU time, thus stopping other software from running as intended.

A better way was needed. Windows NT 3.1 and later Windows 95 did much better: they introduced **preemptive multitasking**.

The idea is straightforward: allocate some time for a process to run, and when that time is out, store the state of that process, park it somewhere, and move on to the next process. When the time comes for the original process to do something again, the OS loads the program back into memory and restores the state, then the process can continue. The process was utterly oblivious to the time it had been dormant unless it kept track of the clock.

Processes could no longer claim all of the available CPU time. The OS would pause the process if its time had run out.

Preemptive multitasking is still the way modern OSs work today.

However, all of this deals with multiple processes on a computer running simultaneously. How can we have one process doing multiple things at the same time? Well, one solution would be to use threads.

Threads in C#

Threads are a concept that allows computers to seem to be doing more than one thing at once in your program. Just as an OS allows multiple programs to run simultaneously, threads allow your program to run multiple flows in your application concurrently. A thread is nothing more than an **execution flow** in your program. You always have at least one thread: the one that got started when the program began its execution. We call this the main thread. The runtime manages this thread and you have little control over it. All the other threads, however, are yours, and you can do whatever you want with them.

Threads are nothing magical. The basic principle is quite easy:

1. Create a method, function, or any other piece of code you want to run.
2. Create a thread, giving it the address of the method.

3. Start the thread.
4. The OS or runtime executes that method or function while running the main thread simultaneously.
5. You can monitor the progress of that thread. You can wait for it to end, or you can use a fire-and-forget strategy by just letting it do its work.

How you do these steps depends on which version you want to use. Do you choose the .NET way or go down the rabbit hole we know as the Win32 API?

In .NET, threads are represented by an actual class (or, more precisely, an instance of a class). In Win32, they are just something created by the Win32 API.

Win32 threads

In Win32, you use the `CreateThread` API to create a thread. I want to show you how this works, but I must be honest: you will probably never do this in your code. There are better ways to create threads than using the Win32 API. Still, there might be circumstances when having complete control of the Win32 threads might be necessary.

Let me show you how to do this in the Win32 API.

We will begin by declaring a `delegate`. This `delegate` is the form of the function that contains the work that the thread executes:

```
public delegate uint ThreadProc(IntPtr lpParameter);
```

Since we are calling Win32 APIs, we need to import them:

```
[DllImport("kernel32.dll", SetLastError = true)]
public static extern IntPtr CreateThread(
    IntPtr lpThreadAttributes,
    uint dwStackSize,
    ThreadProc lpStartAddress,
    IntPtr lpParameter,
    uint dwCreationFlags,
    out uint lpThreadId
);
[DllImport("kernel32.dll", SetLastError = true)]
public static extern bool CloseHandle(IntPtr hObject);

[DllImport("kernel32.dll", SetLastError = true)]
public static extern uint WaitForSingleObject(IntPtr
hHandle, uint dwMilliseconds);
```

We will import three APIs: `CreateThread`, `CloseHandle`, and `WaitForSingleObject`.

Before we can use these APIs, we have to write the code that does something useful. In this case, it is not really useful, but this is the code that will be executed in the thread:

```
public uint MyThreadFunction(IntPtr lpParameter)
{
    for (int i = 0; i < 1000; i++)
        Console.WriteLine("Unmanaged thread");

    return 0;
}
```

This `MyThreadFunction` function matches the delegate that we defined earlier.

With all of that out of our way, we can create the threads and have our program do something. Or rather, it can do lots of somethings simultaneously. Here we go:

```
public void DoWork()
{
    uint threadId;
    var threadHandle = CreateThread(
        IntPtr.Zero,
        0,
        MyThreadFunction,
        IntPtr.Zero,
        0,
        out threadId
    );

    // Wait for the thread to be finished
    WaitForSingleObject(threadHandle, 1000);
    // Clean up
    CloseHandle(threadHandle);
}
```

The `DoWork()` method creates a thread by calling the `CreateThread` Win32 API. This API has some parameters. Let me explain what they do with the help of *Table 4.1*:

Parameter	Description
IntPtr lpThreadAttributes	A pointer to the security attributes struct
uint dwStackSize	The size of the stack required for this thread
ThreadProc lpStartAddress	A pointer to the function that the thread runs

Parameter	Description
IntPtr lpParameter	A pointer to a variable that is passed to the thread
uint dwCreationFlags	Additional flags determining how the thread is created
out uint lpThreadId	An out parameter with the ID of the thread

Table 4.1: Parameters for the CreateThread Win32 API

The security attributes define who or what has access to the thread and what this thread can use. The security attributes are rather complex. I will not be diving into them here, mainly because with threads they are not often used. Here, we have set the security attribute to `IntPtr.Zero`.

The `dwStackSize` parameter defines the stack size that the thread uses. As discussed before, each thread gets its own stack, where it can store its value types. This stack is reclaimed when the thread is done.

Then, we get the function pointer that the thread will execute as soon as that thread starts. In C#, we can pass the method's name and let the compiler do the hard work of figuring out the memory address.

After supplying the start address of the method, we get something more interesting: we can pass data into the thread method. The `lpParameter` parameter is a pointer to the memory where that data is located. To get data into the thread is quite a lot of work unless you want to use a simple `Int32`. After all, an `IntPtr` is a 32-bit value, so you can take an int and cast it back and forth to get that data in the thread function. I am not passing anything here, but will I show you how to do that a little later in this chapter.

Next are the flags that define how the system creates the thread. There are two flags that we can use, not counting the default 0, which means "do nothing special." These flags are explained in *Table 4.2*.

Flag	Value	Meaning
0	0x00000000	Do nothing special
CREATE_SUSPENDED	0x00000004	Create the thread, but suspend it immediately instead of starting it.
STACK_SIZE_PARAM_IS_A_RESERVATION	0x00010000	If this is set, the stack size is a reservation. If not, the stack size is committed.

Table 4.2: Thread creation options

`CREATE_SUSPENDED` creates the thread but puts it in a suspended state when it is created. The default behavior is to run the code that `lpStartAddress` points to immediately.

`STACK_SIZE_PARAM_IS_A_RESERVATION` is an interesting one. This flag is one of the main reasons you might want to use the Win32 version of creating threads instead of the .NET one. Each thread has its own stack. You can specify how big that stack should be, but when you do that, all that happens is that the system reserves that memory. This reserving is a quick operation. Reservation only tells the system that you want to use this amount of memory at some point. You will get an error if the system doesn't have enough memory to fulfill your request.

However, the memory is not yet committed. Committed means that the OS reserves the memory you requested and marks it as being used by a process. Reservation is just telling it that you want the memory to be available later.

> **Page faults**
>
> When your application requests memory or tries to access memory from the system, certain things can happen.
>
> The first instance happens when the memory is available in your stack or heap. You get the pointer to that memory; it's all yours now.
>
> The next happens if the memory is *not* in your stack or heap yet but it is available on the system. This results in a soft page fault. The system will add the new memory to the current stack or heap.
>
> Next, it's possible that the memory you want to reach is not in your computer's memory chips. In this case, it has probably been swapped to disk. This is a hard page fault. The OS will load the memory from the disk and add it to your working set.
>
> Page faults are great for adding flexibility to the system. However, they come with a big performance hit.

A page fault might occur when you reserve memory and want to access it. When this happens, your application's performance will degrade.

If you commit memory, it is guaranteed to be available when it is needed. This makes your memory footprint larger and faster since you will not get a page fault.

You must choose here: which of the two scenarios do you prefer? You can control that for the stack with the STACK_SIZE_PARAM_IS_A_RESERVATION flag.

The code sample ends with two statements: WaitForSingleObject() and CloseHandle(). The *Synchronizing threads* section in this chapter explains WaitForSingleObject() in much more detail. Still, the short description is as follows: wait for the thread to finish before continuing on the main thread.

CloseHandle clears up all used resources. Yes, this is an unmanaged resource. This would be a great place to use the IDisposable pattern.

.NET threads

Threads in the .NET BCL are much simpler to use. Of course, when something is simplified, you usually sacrifice flexibility as a result.

The following sample shows how to do the same work as we did with the Win32 thread using the .NET constructs.

We will begin with the thread function, which runs on the new thread. It is almost the same as the Win32 sample. The following snippet shows the code that we want to run inside the thread:

```
void MyThreadFunction()
{
    for (var i = 0; i < 1000; i++)
        Console.WriteLine("Managed thread");
}
```

In the main body of our code, we create the thread, give it the function to run, and start it:

```
var myManagedThread = new Thread(MyThreadFunction);
myManagedThread.Start();
myManagedThread.Join();
```

We create a new instance of the `Thread` class and pass the method we want to use in the constructor. Then we start it. Then, we use `Join()` to wait for it, effectively pausing the main thread until our new thread is done doing whatever it is doing.

That's it. If you compare this with the Win32 version, I am sure that you will appreciate this simplicity.

However, do not be fooled: this simplicity does not mean that you cannot control your threads. You can control them and you can do much more than what I have just shown you. For instance, you can also specify the stack size you want to use for your thread:

```
var myHugeStackSize = 8 * 1024 * 1024; // 8 MB
var myManagedThread = new Thread(MyThreadFunction, myHugeStackSize);
```

Here, we allocate 8 MB for the stack for our new thread.

> **Nice to know**
>
> The default stack size for a 32-bit application is 1 MB; for a 64-bit application, it is 4 MB. You will rarely need more than that. Requesting a big stack should only be done if you have tested your application and found that you really need it.

In the Win32 sample, we had to explicitly state that we wanted to create a thread in a suspended state. If we did not do that, it would have started immediately. In .NET, things work differently. A newly created thread in .NET is considered *unstarted*. This means that it will not be starting immediately. It is also not yet suspended; there is quite a difference in behavior.

A suspended thread is fully formed and placed on the OS's scheduler list. Its stack is allocated and all resources are present.

An **unstarted thread** is just an instance of the Thread class. The stack is not yet allocated and it has not yet been given to the OS, so it is not yet on the scheduler, and so on.

When we call Start() on that .NET thread, the runtime does all that work. Creating a thread is much faster than the CreateThread() call in Win32, but that performance gain is lost when you start the thread. Think of it as lazy initialization.

The designers of the CLR took advantage of this. If it is relatively cheap to create threads and only becomes expensive when we use them, why not move that burden of creation to the beginning of the program? Starting an application takes time; if we extend that a bit, it does not matter. However, that would mean that we have a faster system when it is in use. We can have a pool of threads available when we need one or two. That is precisely what they did.

An example will probably make this clearer. However, before I can show you that, we must make some modifications. We want to create many threads that run simultaneously. To distinguish the output from each thread, we need to pass some data to that thread so that it can display it. Thus, we need to have something to store data in.

We need immutable data for reasons that will become clear when we discuss thread safety later in this chapter. The record, which was added to C# 9, is a great way to do this::

```
internal record ThreadData(int LoopCounter);
```

We can now work on our method that executes in that thread:

```
void MyThreadFunction(object? myObjectData)
{
    // Verify that we have a ThreadData object
    if (myObjectData is not ThreadData myData)
        throw new ArgumentException("Parameter is not a
                ThreadData object");
    // Get the thread ID
    var currentThreadId = Thread.CurrentThread.ManagedThreadId;
    // Write the data to the Console
    Console.WriteLine(
        $"Managed thread in Thread {currentThreadId} " +
        $"with loop counter {myData.LoopCounter}");
}
```

The thread gets a parameter of the `Nullable<object>` type. We cannot declare it as any other type, as this is what the runtime expects.

To use this data, we need to cast it to the right type.

Then, we will get the ID of the current thread. Each thread has a unique ID, so we can interact with it, although we will only display it here.

Let us create some threads:

```
for (int i = 0; i < 100; i++)
{
    ThreadData threadData = new(i);
    var newThread = new Thread(MyThreadFunction);
    newThread.Start(threadData);
}
Console.ReadKey();
```

We will create one hundred threads and start them immediately after creation. We will give them some data to see where in the loop we are.

After the loop, I added the `Console.ReadKey()` so the program does not exit before all threads are done. The main thread that starts when running your program is special: if that ends, the CLR ends the whole program and unloads all memory. So, keeping your main thread alive is crucial until you are sure that all work is done. In a real-world scenario, you wouldn't use `Console.ReadLine()` for this, but for this demo, it works just fine.

If you run this, you will probably see the thread ID increasing in line with the loop counter. They are not equal. The CLR already created a dozen or so threads before you ran your loop.

If you increase the loop to do a much higher number of iterations, you will eventually see the same thread ID now and then. The CLR reuses threads to avoid thread starvation.

However, I promised to show you the thread pool. Replace the part of the code where we had the for-loop with the following code:

```
for (int i = 0; i < 100; i++)
{
    ThreadData threadData = new(i);
    ThreadPool.QueueUserWorkItem(MyThreadFunction, threadData);
}
Console.ReadKey();
```

We will use the thread pool here to pull threads out of the pool when needed. If you run this, you repeatedly see the same thread IDs. Threads are pulled out of the pool and started with the correct data. When the thread is done, it is winded down, its resources are de-allocated, and it is placed back in the pool, ready to be used again if needed.

The overhead is minimal and the advantages are enormous. Systems using this are much more efficient.

`ThreadPool` hides many more secrets and tricks that you can use, but its usage has largely been replaced by the **Task Parallel Library** (**TPL**), which handles most of this for you. Let us have a look.

Tasks and Parallel Library – the TPL

The TPL has been around for quite some time. It was introduced back in 2010 with the release of .NET 4.0.

The TPL simplifies many of the things we used to do with threads. Threads still have their place, especially when dealing with third-party libraries. However, in most cases, we can let the TPL figure things out.

In the TPL, the `Task` class is the main class to work with. `Task` is a class that handles the instantiation of threads when needed. It does much more, but we will deal with that later.

I said "when needed" because it is smart enough to determine when a new thread is needed.

Let us begin with a straightforward example and then work from there:

```
Task myTask = Task.Run(() => { Console.WriteLine("Hello from the task."); });

Console.WriteLine("Main thread is done.");
Console.ReadKey();
```

`Task` is just another C# class that handles much of the concurrency for us. In this case, we call static method `Run()`, which takes a delegate that it performs.

We can rewrite this as follows:

```
Task myTask = Task.Run(DoWork);
Console.WriteLine("Main thread is done.");
Console.ReadKey();
return 0;
void DoWork()
{
    Console.WriteLine("Hello from the task.");
}
```

This code snippet does the same, but we call the method instead of using the lambda expression.

We can more or less do the same thing in a slightly different way:

```
Task myTask = new Task(DoWork);
myTask.Start();
```

I have omitted the `Console` stuff and the actual method; they will remain the same (until I say that I have changed them).

This code does more or less the same thing as the previous sample. The difference is that the `Task` does not start unless we explicitly call `Start()`.

The second example gives you more control over the `Task`. You can set properties and change the task's behavior before starting it. `Task.Run()` is mostly designed for fire-and-forget scenarios. `Start()` is more flexible; it allows us to change the scheduling and, for instance, tell it to run on a specific thread. You can also specify the priority of the `Task` this way.

This example is not very exciting. Let us try to make it a bit more exhilarating. We can change our method to the following:

```
void DoWork(int id)
{
    Console.WriteLine($"call Id {id}.");
}
```

We will add a parameter to our method to identify who calls the method. Since we now have a parameter, we must also change how we pass this to the `Task` constructor. Let's not stop there. Imagine that we want to chain method calls. After the `Task` has finished with `DoWork` with `Id 1`, we want it to call that method again but with `Id 2` this time. In real life, you would probably chain two completely different methods, but the way of working is the same.

The code looks like this:

```
Task myTask = new Task(() => DoWork(1));
myTask.ContinueWith((prevTask) => DoWork(2));
myTask.Start();
```

We have changed the parameter in the constructor so that we can pass that 1 integer to the method. The following line is more interesting. It says: "When you finish the first step, call `DoWork` again, but this time with `Id 2`." The `prevTask` parameter is the previous `Task` that has finished its work. This triggered the start of the second `Task`.

If you run this, you will see the lines printed to the console in the correct order.

Let us rewrite the method that gets called one more time:

```
void DoWork(int id)
{
    Console.WriteLine($"call Id {id}, " +
                      $"running on thread " +
                      $"{Thread.CurrentThread.ManagedThreadId}.");
}
```

We added the `id` of the thread this method runs on to the output. I also want to see that `id` thread before we start the tasks. Our calling code now looks like this:

```
Console.WriteLine($"Our main thread id = 
{Thread.CurrentThread.ManagedThreadId}.");

Task myTask = new Task(() => DoWork(1));
myTask.ContinueWith((prevTask) => DoWork(2));
myTask.Start();
```

If you run this, you will probably see that the tasks run on a different thread rather than the main one. If you repeat this a few times, it might even happen that the second task runs on a different thread from the first one. It is impossible to predict when this will happen; the scheduler picks whatever works best given the current conditions. We do not have to worry about this. It just works. Neat, isn't it?

Another nice class that is available in the TPL is the `Parallel` class. It allows us to do stuff in parallel. Let's see that

```
Console.WriteLine($"Our main thread id = 
{Thread.CurrentThread.ManagedThreadId}.");

int[] myIds = {1, 2, 3, 4, 5, 6, 7, 8, 9, 10};
Parallel.ForEach(myIds, (i) => DoWork(i));
```

First, we will print the `id` of the current thread. Then we will create an array of integers from 1 to 10; nothing special here. After that, we will call the static `ForEach` method on the `Parallel` class and give it the array and the lambda to call. The method iterates through the array and calls the lambda with the correct parameter. It does that in parallel, not sequentially, as with a standard `ForEach` loop.

When you run this, you will see some exciting results. The order in which the program prints the IDs is entirely random. You will see that the runtime uses multiple threads, but sometimes it reuses some of these threads.

Again, the TPL determines the best way to do this and handles all the threads' creation and scheduling for you.

TPL is extremely powerful. It is also the backbone of the async await pattern. This is a pattern that simplifies working with concurrency so much that most users do not realize what is happening behind the scenes. With your newfound knowledge, you should have no problem following what is happening. So, let's have a look at async/await.

Async/await

Software hardly ever runs in isolation. Most software needs to reach outside of its boundaries and access something that is not part of the code block at some point. Examples include reading and writing files, reading data from a network, sending something to a printer, and so on. Suppose that a typical machine can access a byte in memory in about 10 nanoseconds. Reading that same byte from an SSD takes approximately 1,000,000 nanoseconds or even longer. Reading data from external devices is usually about 100,000 to 1,000,0000 times slower than reading local data from memory. Think about that when you try to optimize your code if you know that your software transfers data to and from external hardware.

Let's take this one step further. Let us assume that you have a decent machine that can quickly process data. You need to read data from an external website. Your program must wait very long before that data is available. It can take milliseconds before that data reaches us. For us mere humans, that is pretty fast, but the computer could have done a million other tasks in the meantime. That seems like a colossal waste of our expensive resources, right?

Threading can help, of course. You can create a thread to call the external website and wait for that to finish, doing other things in the meantime. However, as we have seen, threads can be quite cumbersome. The TPL helps, but still, things can get complicated. Reading data from external sources or writing data to external targets is so common that the CLR designers decided to help us by introducing async/await.

The top-down approach is simple: anything that takes more time than simple operations should be done asynchronously. However, we do not want to deal with the threads themselves. Async/await, which uses the TPL internally, is a pattern that can help.

What it does is this: as soon as you have code that needs to be run asynchronously, the compiler injects code that wraps our code into a state machine. This state machine tracks the threads and the progress of our code and switches back and forth between the blocks of code that need attention.

Does that sound complicated? Well, it is. The usage, however, is straightforward. However, before I show it to you, I want to introduce a little piece of helper code I often use when discussing async/await. This code is just an extension method on the `string` class and outputs a `string` to the console and adds the `ManagedThreadId`. It even allows for coloring the output, making it easier to distinguish between the different threads. If you want to use this, go ahead. If you would rather use `Console.WriteLine()` everywhere yourself instead, be my guest. However, using this makes the critical part of the code more readable. Here is my extension method:

```
using static System.Threading.Thread;
namespace ExtensionLibrary;

public static class StringExtensions
{
    public static string Dump(this string message,
        ConsoleColor printColor = ConsoleColor.Cyan)
    {
        var oldColor = Console.ForegroundColor;
        Console.ForegroundColor = printColor;
```

```
        Console.WriteLine($"({CurrentThread.ManagedThreadId})\t : 
          {message}");
        Console.ForegroundColor = oldColor;
        return message;
    }
}
```

You can also find this code in the GitHub repository.

First, I want to show you the most simple example:

```
using ExtensionLibrary;

DoWork();
// The program is paused until DoWork is finished.
// This is a waste of CPU!
"Just before calling the long-running DoWork()"
    .Dump(ConsoleColor.DarkBlue);
"Program has finished".Dump(ConsoleColor.DarkBlue);
Console.ReadKey();

void DoWork()
{
    "We are doing important stuff!".Dump(ConsoleColor.DarkYellow);
    // Do something useful, then wait a bit.
    Thread.Sleep(1000);
}
```

Imagine that we want do something that takes a long time, such as reading a file from storage, in our `DoWork()` method. I have simulated that here by pausing the current thread for a second. Our entire program is paused while we call this in our main method. Our costly and powerful CPU is left to do nothing (at least not for our program). That seems wasteful! We've seen that we can use threads or the TPL to improve that. However, that code is also wrapped in the async/await pattern, so why not use this?

To do this, I replaced `Thread.Sleep()` with a call to `Task.Delay()`. That more or less does the same thing but allows us to improve on our code. Remember: this `Thread.Sleep()` and the new `Task.Delay()` method are just a stand-in for the real work your application should be doing. Having a `Sleep()` or `Delay()` method in your code is usually a bad idea.

If you have to call an async method, you must wait for it. So, we will add the `await` keyword before the call to `Task.Delay()`.

Once we have done that replacement, I will also prefix our method with the `async` keyword. This keyword tells the compiler that it should wrap this method in the state machine I mentioned earlier. However, any async method should never return void for reasons that will become clear later. We need to return a `Task` or a `Task<>` if you actually return something. So, we changed our void to `Task`. Again, any async method needs to be called with the `await` keyword. So, the result looks like this:

```
using ExtensionLibrary;

"Just before calling the long-running DoWork()"
    .Dump(ConsoleColor.DarkBlue);
await DoWork();
// The program is no longer paused until DoWork is finished.
// This allows the CPU to keep working!
"Program has finished".Dump(ConsoleColor.DarkBlue);
Console.ReadKey();

async Task DoWork()
{
    "We are doing important stuff!".Dump(ConsoleColor.DarkYellow);

    // Do something useful, then wait a bit.
    await Task.Delay(1000);
}
```

Run this and see what happens.

You will probably see that the program starts on one thread and then carries out the `DoWork()` method on that same thread, but that it switches to a new thread when that is done. That is because the compiler sees our `Task.Delay()` await and decides to free up the CPU to do other things. The runtime puts our current thread on hold and stores its state in memory, leaving our main code free to do other things. Only when `Task.Delay()` finishes is our main thread revived. However, since the main thread is no longer associated with our code here, we need a new thread. That one is pulled from the `ThreadPool` (remember: that is fast since the threads there were created at startup) and populated with the state we had. Then the system can continue on that thread. The program ends on that new thread as well!

I mentioned that all async methods need the async modifier and should return a `Task` instead of a void. There is a simple reason for this. If you do not do this, your code will work but not as expected. The **Async all the way to the top** rule is simple but very important.

> **Async all the way to the top!**
>
> If you have a method containing an `await` keyword, the method needs to be async and return a `Task`. However, since you will probably call that method yourself somewhere, the calling code must also be async and return some form of `Task` or `Task<>`. Since that method is also called… well, you get the idea. The rule is: async all the way to the top! Every method in that chain needs to have that async!

Another rule, which is not as strict as the "Async all the way to the top" rule, is that all async methods should be named as such. Our `DoWork()` method should be renamed to `DoWorkAsync()`.

However, before we do that, let us see what happens if we are sloppy and do not return a `Task`. Try it yourself: replace the `Task` return type with a void and remove the await before `DoWork()` (you cannot await a void, so you will get an error if you do not remove that).

Run it. It works just fine, right? Okay, there is no new thread created, but who cares? The software does what it needs to do.

Now, let's change our `DoWork()` method a bit:

```
using ExtensionLibrary;

"Just before calling the long-running DoWork()"
    .Dump(ConsoleColor.DarkBlue);
DoWork();

"Program has finished".Dump(ConsoleColor.DarkBlue);
//Console.ReadKey();

async void DoWork()
{
    "We are doing important stuff!"
        .Dump(ConsoleColor.DarkYellow);

    await Task.Delay(1000);
    throw new Exception(
        "Something went terribly wrong."
    );

    "We're done with the hard work."
        .Dump(ConsoleColor.DarkYellow);
}
```

I also temporarily removed the `ReadLine()` to make the program more lifelike. The main thread finishes when everything is done.

Run it. See that we do not get the "We're done with the hard work" message. That makes sense; there is an exception in front of it. However, please notice that we also do not see that exception.

Why is this? It's complicated, but the simplified explanation is that the state machine is still created since DoWork is still an async method. The exception is raised on a different thread (after the `Task.Delay()` await). However, since the state machine is not configured to wait for all results (because we omitted the `await` keywords), it just ignores that thread. If you move that "We're done with the hard work" `Dump()` line to the line before the exception, you will see that it is not called. In reality, it *is* called; you just don't see it. This thread has become a fire-and-forget thread. You lost all control over it.

Can you imagine a complex piece of software where something goes wrong deep in the bowels of your code? Can you imagine not getting the exception? Can you imagine the horror of debugging that?

You will get that exception if you use async/await all the way up.

Oh, before I forget: the reason that I removed the `Console.ReadKey()` line is that by doing so, I forced the main thread to quit as soon as possible, resulting in unloading the application from memory. If you restore that line, you will see the exception, since the main thread is paused there. Now other things will be allowed to happen.

However, that is not really a solution to our problem. You do not want to wait for the main thread to become idle before you get exceptions. It could take ages for that to happen.

Please restore the async/await keywords, replace the void in `DoWork()` with `Task`, and run it. The exception is thrown precisely where you would expect it to be.

This is really important, so I like to repeat it once more: async all the way to the top!

Task.Wait() and Task.Result

There are many blog posts and articles about why you should not use `Task.Wait()` or `Task.Result`. The reason for this is pretty simple: these calls block the current thread. Using them removes the scheduler's ability to resume work on the calling thread and return to the execution flow when the `Task` is done. If you do this, why use async/await in the first place? Async/await also allows for thread synchronization, so there is no need to use `Wait()` and `Result`.

Hold on. There are some situations where you might decide to use them anyway:

- You may want to use them if you are working on legacy code that you are modernizing. The rule is "Async all the way to the top," which might require extensive code refactoring. That is not always feasible. In those cases, you might use `Wait()` and `Result` instead.

- In unit tests, you can mock or stub async methods. However, sometimes it might be better for the unit test to use `Wait()` and `Result`.

- You might not care about the main thread staying responsive in systems programming. There is no user interface, after all. So, blocking the main thread may not be a big problem. I still think that it is bad form not to use async/await, but in these cases, you can get away with using `Wait()` and `Result`.

As with all rules in software development, be vigilant about these rules and apply them as much as possible, only breaking them if you have a good reason and have thought about it well. Also, please do your future self a favor and document why you chose to deviate from the usual way of working in the source code.

So, now you know how to use async/await. Although they do not always result in multiple threads, they are a great way to balance the load in your application. They help tremendously in keeping your code organized. You are relieved of the burden to do all synchronization between threads. However, that doesn't mean that you never have to care about synchronization at all. There is no avoiding that, so I think we should talk about it right now.

Synchronizing threads

The async/await pattern has made life easier for us developers. If you have a long-running task (and remember: anything that uses devices outside the CPU is long-running), you can call that method asynchronously. Then you can sit back and wait for it to finish without blocking the execution of your app in other places. The TPL takes care of the thread management.

However, sometimes you may want to have a bit more control. You might have a situation where you must wait for a method to finish before you can continue. Imagine that you have your main thread and call the `A()` method. That method is long-running, so you make it async (rename it to something ending with 'async') and change the return type to `Task` or `Task<>`. Now you can wait for it. However, another thread might have to wait until your `Aasync()` method is finished. How do you do that?

Welcome to the wonderful world of thread synchronization.

Synchronization – how do we do that?

In the old days, when we still used threads and the `ThreadPool`, synchronization could be a hassle. However, with `Task` and async/await, things have become much easier without having real downsides. Before I show you that, I want to show you how to synchronize threads instead of tasks.

Let me start with the base program:

```
using ExtensionLibrary;

"In the main part of the app.".Dump(ConsoleColor.White);
ThreadPool.QueueUserWorkItem(DoSomethingForTwoSeconds);
ThreadPool.QueueUserWorkItem(DoSomethingForOneSecond);
"Main app is done.\nPress any key to
stop.".Dump(ConsoleColor.White);
Console.ReadKey();
return 0;

void DoSomethingForOneSecond(object? notUsed)
{
    $"Doing something for one second.".Dump(ConsoleColor.Yellow);
    Thread.Sleep(1000);
    $"Finished something for one second".Dump(ConsoleColor.Yellow);
```

```
}

void DoSomethingForTwoSeconds(object? notUsed)
{
    "Doing something for two
        seconds.".Dump(ConsoleColor.DarkYellow);
    Thread.Sleep(2900);
    "Done doing something for two
        seconds.".Dump(ConsoleColor.DarkYellow)
}
```

This sample should be obvious now. I have two methods that do something that takes a long time to finish. I pull some threads out of the `ThreadPool` and run all of this simultaneously.

If you run this, the **Main app is done** message is printed first. The only reason why we see the other messages is because we have the `Console.ReadKey()` in place. What could we do if we want to wait for the two methods to be finished before we move on?

The answer is to use a synchronization mechanism. This means that we have an object that we can use to flag certain states. We can write it ourselves, but we must take care of a lot of synchronization and thread safety. Luckily, we do not have to. The Win32 API provides tools that are neatly wrapped in BCL classes.

One of these is the `CountdownEvent` class. As the name suggests, it allows us to count down events.

Change your main method to look like this:

```
"In the main part of the app.".Dump(ConsoleColor.White);
// Tell the system we want to wait for 2 threads to finish.
CountdownEvent countdown = new(2);
ThreadPool.QueueUserWorkItem(DoSomethingForOneSecond);
ThreadPool.QueueUserWorkItem(DoSomethingForTwoSeconds);
// Do the actual waiting.
countdown.Wait();
"Main app is done.\nPress any key to stop.".Dump(ConsoleColor.White);
Console.ReadKey();
return 0;
```

We will create a new instance of the `CountdownEvent` class and initialize it to 2.

Then, we will get the threads and allow them to do their work.

In the code in the methods, I have added one line:

```
void DoSomethingForOneSecond(object? notUsed)
{
    $"Doing something for one second.".Dump(ConsoleColor.Yellow);
```

```
    Thread.Sleep(1000);
    $"Finished something for one second".Dump(ConsoleColor.Yellow);
    countdown.Signal();
}
```

At the bottom of the method, you will see the `.Signal()` countdown. Since that instance is reachable in this method, I can use it. `Signal()` tells the countdown to decrease the number of events to wait for.

I did the same to the `DoSomethingForTwoSeconds()` method.

That means that when both methods are done, they call `Signal()` on the countdown. In the main method, I added `countdown.Wait()` after the `ThreadPool` code, telling the main thread to pause until the countdown reaches zero.

If you run this, you will see it works wonderfully and that the rest of the main thread is perfectly synchronized with the threads.

However, what if I want the `DoSomethingForTwoSeconds` method to start when `DoSomethingForOneSecond` is finished?

That is almost as easy. We can use one of the other synchronization classes to help us out. Let me show you how to do this using the `ManualResetEvent`. This class does more or less the same as the `CountdownEvent`. The difference is that the `ManualResetEvent` class does not count; it just waits for a signal.

In the main method, before calling the `ThreadPool`, I have added this line:

```
ManualResetEvent mre = new(false);
```

I have set it in the initial `False` state. Doing so results in any thread waiting for the event to be set.

In `DoSomethingForOneSecond()`, I have added one line right at the end:

```
// Tell the second thread it can start
mre.Set();
```

The call to `Set` tells the `ManalResetEvent` that any waiting thread can continue.

In `DoSomethingForTwoSeconds()`, I have added the following to the beginning of the method:

```
// Wait for the first thread to finish.
mre.WaitOne();
```

`WaitOne()` tells the code to pause the thread until the `mre` gets a signal (which happens at the end of `DoSomethingForOneSecond()`).

If you run your program now, you will notice that everything is nicely synchronized and waiting for other stuff to finish.

Of course, you might have achieved precisely the same result by not using threads. We have basically removed all multitasking from our application. If you need to synchronize threads, now you know how. However, be careful: you might introduce weird errors if you make mistakes. Trust me: debugging multithreaded applications is no walk in the park.

Synchronization with async/await

You might have guessed by now that using async/await dramatically reduces the complexity of working with threads and synchronizing between them.

Let us return to our example of the `DoSomethingForOneSecond` and `DoSomethingForTwoSeconds` methods. This time, we will rewrite them to use async/await.

Your `DoSomethingForOneSecond` should be like this:

```
async Task DoSomethingForOneSecondAsync()
{
    $"Doing something for one second.".Dump(ConsoleColor.Yellow);
    await Task.Delay(1000);
    $"Finished something for one second".Dump(ConsoleColor.Yellow);
}
```

I renamed the function to end with async, as I should have done much earlier.

The `DoSomethingForTwoSecondsAsync()` should get the same treatment.

Calling the methods in the main method now looks like this:

```
"In the main part of the app.".Dump(ConsoleColor.White);

await DoSomethingForOneSecondAsync();
await DoSomethingForTwoSecondsAsync();
"Main app is done.\nPress any key to stop.".Dump(ConsoleColor.White);
Console.ReadKey();
return 0;
```

The results are identical to those from the example where we did all the synchronization ourselves, with the only difference being that we have no blocking threads anymore. So this is not only easier to do but it is also much better.

However, what happens if we do not want to do the methods sequentially? What if we want them to run simultaneously?

Well, that is easy enough. Since our methods return a `Task`, we can work with that. Instead of waiting for them individually, we can simultaneously wait for them. Let me show you:

```
var task1 = DoSomethingForOneSecondAsync();
var task2 = DoSomethingForTwoSecondsAsync();
// Wait for all tasks to be finished
Task.WaitAll(task1, task2);
"Main app is done.\nPress any key to stop.".Dump(ConsoleColor.White);
Console.ReadKey();
return 0;
```

We will take advantage of the fact that we get tasks back. The `Task` class has a static method called `WaitAll()` that only returns when all tasks are finished.

There are other methods, such as `WaitAny` (only continue when any of the tasks finish), `WhenAll` (do something when they are all done), and `WhenAny` (you can figure this out by yourself).

The difference between `WaitAll` or `WaitAny` and `WhenAll` or `WhenAny` is that `WaitXXX` is a blocking call. It blocks the current thread until the condition has been met. `WhenXXX` returns a Task itself that you can await and thus does not block the thread.

However, there is a bigger difference: `WhenAll` allows you to capture the return result. If any tasks that you want to wait for return a result, you can get that with `WhenAll`. `WhenAll` returns the results to you in an array. You can get at them, which is something you cannot do with `WaitAll` or `WaitAny`.

In case you were wondering, `WhenAny` returns a `Task<T>`. That `Task<T>` has a property called `Result`; you can read that property to get access to the result of that Task. This is one example when using `Result` is actually a good thing!

Canceling a thread

Sometimes, you want to stop a thread from running. There might be several good reasons to do this, but whatever your reason, be sure to clean up after yourself. Threads are expensive to use and leaving them in an unknown state is a horrible practice: you shoot yourself in the foot one day.

In the days of .NET Framework, the `Thread` class had a method called `Abort()`. However, it turned out that the method did more harm than good, so the BCL and CLR people decided to get rid of it. If you try to abort a thread, you will get a `PlatformNotSupportedException`. I guess they really do not want us to use that anymore.

The best way to stop a running thread is the same way you should stop a running `Task`: using something we call **cooperative cancellation**. A calling thread can request another thread to stop. It is up to that second thread to honor that request – or not. There is no guarantee.

The standard way of doing this is by using a `CancellationToken`. A `CancellationToken` is an object we use to signal that we want to cancel something.

Of course, you can write this class yourself. There is not much going on besides some thread safety. However, having a `CancellationToken` in your threads or tasks makes it clear to the user that it can be canceled.

I am going to rewrite our `DoSomethingForOneSecondAsyncMethod()` a bit:

```
async Task DoSomethingForOneSecondAsync()
{
    $"Doing something for one second.".Dump(ConsoleColor.Yellow);
    for(int i=0;i<1000;i++)
        await Task.Delay(1);
    $"Finished something for one second".Dump(ConsoleColor.Yellow);
}
```

Instead of having the `Task.Delay(1000)` call, I do `1000` await `Task.Delay1)`. In theory, that would result in a one-second delay. However, when you run this, it takes considerably longer. The await call itself takes up some time as well.

I could measure how long it takes and then recalculate the number of iterations, or I could simply rename the method to `DoSomethingForSomeUnderterminedAmountOfTimeAsync()`. I will leave that decision up to you.

Assume that we get bored after 500 milliseconds after waiting in our main method and decide to stop this thread. How would we achieve that?

This is where the `CancellationToken` steps in. Again, a `CancellationToken` is a simple class. You can create one if you want to, but it is better to use a specialized class. This `CancellationTokenSource` class is created specifically for this and works in all sorts of weird conditions. It is inherently thread-safe.

Let us create one right at the beginning of the main method:

```
using ExtensionLibrary;

"In the main part of the app.".Dump(ConsoleColor.White);
using var cts = new CancellationTokenSource();
var task1 = DoSomethingForOneSecondAsync();
Task.WaitAny(task1);
"Main app is done.\nPress any key to stop.".Dump(ConsoleColor.White);
Console.ReadKey();
return 0;
```

I use `WaitAny` here because we want to cancel that task after the moment when we create it and before it has finished. Also, note the `using` statement. `CancellationTokenSource` implements `IDisposable`, so we must honor that.

Canceling is simple. Between the `var task1` and `Task.WaitAny()` lines, add the following:

```
await Task.Delay(500);
"We got bored. Let's cancel.".Dump(ConsoleColor.White);
cts.Cancel();
```

We will wait a bit, then get bored and call `cts.Cancel()`.

However, if you run this, nothing will happen. That's not entirely true; many things will happen. To be precise, the entire loop in DoSomethingForOneSecondAsync happens.

CancellationToken is not a magic way to cancel running tasks. You have to check for that token yourself.

We have to add a parameter to our method of the CancellationToken type. The method signature will now look like this:

```
async Task DoSomethingForOneSecondAsync(CancellationToken
cancellationToken)
```

We have to pass in that token when we call it. In our main method, change the line calling this method to this:

```
var task1 = DoSomethingForOneSecondAsync(cts.Token);
```

We will take our CancellationTokenSource and get its token. That is what we will pass on to our method.

Inside our method, we must check to see whether we need to cancel. Yes, that is why I added the loop around the Delay. The full method will now look like this:

```
async Task DoSomethingForOneSecondAsync(CancellationToken
cancellationToken)
{
    $"Doing something for one second.".Dump(ConsoleColor.Yellow);
    bool hasBeenCancelled = false;
    int i = 0;
    for (i = 0; i < 1000; i++)
    {
        if (cancellationToken.IsCancellationRequested)
        {
            hasBeenCancelled = true;
            break;
        }

        await Task.Delay(1);
```

```
    }

    if(hasBeenCancelled)
    {
        $"We got interrupted after {i} iterations.".Dump(ConsoleColor.
            Yellow);
    }
    else
    {
        $"Finished something for one second".Dump(ConsoleColor.
            Yellow);
    }
}
```

If someone calls `Cancel` on the `CancellationTokenSource`, the `IsCancellationRequested` flag on the token will be set to `True`. We have to honor that. I do that by breaking out of the `for` loop. I have also set a `hasBeenCancelled` variable to `True` so I can inform our users that we have canceled this loop and tell them after how many iterations it was canceled.

We could have skipped this boolean and used `IsCancellationRequested` again. However, there might have been a risk of the request coming in right after the loop was done but before the printing of the message. In that case, the loop was not interrupted. But we said it was anyway, which is incorrect. This way we avoid printing the wrong message.

Run it and see what happens. On my machine, I get about 40 iterations before it cancels.

There is one bug in this code. It is good practice to pass on the `CancellationToken` to any method that accepts it. In our case, that would be `Task.Delay()`. There is an overload that accepts a `CancellationToken`.

I deliberately left that out here. Since the code would be in that line almost 100% of the time, awaiting the Delay, we would cancel that and never see any printed messages. However, let's now add it:

```
await Task.Delay(1, cancellationToken);
```

Rerun it and see what happens.

You might notice that we are missing a lot of screen output. The reason is simple. `Task.Delay()` throws an `OperationCancelledException` when it is canceled. However, we are not using `await` on our `Task` in the main method, so we will miss the exception. Remember when I said it was all too easy to miss exceptions when not everything is done right?

Synchronization helps to prevent errors from happening. However, there are a lot of techniques to make sure our code is thread-safe. Let's dive into those now.

Thread-safe programming techniques

Look at this piece of code. Run it and see what happens:

```
using ExtensionLibrary;
int iterationCount = 100;
ThreadPool.QueueUserWorkItem(async (state) =>
{
    await Task.Delay(500);
    iterationCount = 0;
    $"We are stopping it...".Dump(ConsoleColor.Red);
});

await WaitAWhile();
$"In the main part of the app.".Dump(ConsoleColor.White);
"Main app is done.\nPress any key to stop.".Dump(ConsoleColor.White);
Console.ReadKey();
return 0;
async Task WaitAWhile()
{
    do
    {
        $"In the loop at iterations {iterationCount}".
            Dump(ConsoleColor.Yellow);
        await Task.Delay(1);
    }while (--iterationCount > 0) ;
}
```

We have a `Task` that counts down from 100 to 0. Since we `await` this, the main part of the code waits nicely for this to finish before continuing. However, we also have a second thread that waits for 500 milliseconds and then sets the counter to 0. The result is that the loop finishes prematurely.

What we see here is easy to debug. Every line of code is one screen, so I imagine that you will be able to spot the bug quite easily.

However, what if the integer used here is a member of a class? As you know, instances of classes are reference types. Reference types get passed on by reference, not by value. So if the Task has access to that instance, it can alter the members in that instance. However, every other task, thread, or piece of code sees the effects of that.

Thread safety is all about avoiding these kinds of things.

Value types are inherently safe. You will have no issues if you pass a value type such as integer to your `Task`. The value of the integer is copied and you are not changing the original value.

However, if you need to access more complex types, you will need to think about this. The good news is that the runtime offers us several tools to mitigate this issue.

One of the tools you get is the Lock() keyword.

Lock()

The simplest way to safeguard your data is to have a lock around it. A lock is an object that more or less works as a moat around a piece of code. A lock ensures that only one thread can simultaneously be in that code block. The syntax is straightforward:

```
lock (new object())
{
    iterationCount--;
}
```

The lock takes one argument. It uses this to identify the area to lock. It doesn't do anything with this object; this is just something to hook the lock to. So, having a new object() will suffice.

Any code in this code block is safe, meaning that only one thread can decrement the iterationCount simultaneously. When another thread tries to do the same thing simultaneously, it blocks as soon as it reaches the lock statement. That thread remains blocked until the previous threat exits the code block.

Yes, this means that if the other thread crashes in that code (not very likely in this example: crashing on a -- operator happens very infrequently), the rest of the system can never enter that code block.

Lock() is syntactic sugar around a monitor object. The compiler actually uses Monitors. So, the following code results in the same IL (Intermediate language):

```
var lockObject = new object();
Monitor.Enter(lockObject);
try
{
    iterationCount--;
}
finally
{
    Monitor.Exit(lockObject);
    lockObject = null;
}
```

I do not know about you, but the lock() statement looks much more effortless to me.

Records

The best way to ensure that data is not accidentally overridden is to ensure that the data cannot be altered. Immutable types are designed to do just that.

Let me create a record first:

```
record Counter(int InitialValue);
```

A record is a reference type, so its memory is allocated on the heap. However, records are meant to be immutable. You can create records that are not immutable, but that does not help us here.

Right now, I have a record with one member, `InitialValue`. I have to set the value for that when constructing the `Counter`, but I can never change it after that. So, no thread can come along and mess with that value anymore.

However, since I cannot change it anywhere, I also have to change the code in the `Task`. It will now look like this:

```
async Task WaitAWhile()
{
    var actualCounter = myCounter.InitialValue;
    do
    {
        $"In the loop at iterations {actualCounter}".
            Dump(ConsoleColor.Yellow);
        await Task.Delay(1);
    } while (--actualCounter > 0);
}
```

I have made a copy of the value to decrement that in the loop. If you are a bit like me, you might say, "Wait a minute. Why didn't I just copy that original `iterationCount` to a local variable and use that instead of this record?"

I see many people doing that. However, that is not guaranteed to work. What if a separate thread changes the value of `iterationCount` before you can make a copy? You would start with the wrong initial value.

Immutable records guarantee that the values inside it do not change, ever. Period. You are safe.

Avoid static members and classes

I know that it can be a nuisance to create instances of classes. Sometimes, it seems easier to create a static class filled with static members and use those instead. They certainly do have some use cases. However, remember this: static classes are not thread-safe out of the box. Static members are shared across threads so that anybody can change them.

Using the volatile keyword

Sometimes, code seems straightforward, but it might not be. Look at this line:

```
int a=42;
```

We know how this works. This integer is on the stack. If we change the value, the value at that memory address changes. Simple, right? Wrong. The compiler does all sorts of tricks to optimize our code, especially when you build it in Release mode. Building in Release mode means that the compiler might cache the value of even a simple integer to speed things up. It might even decide to move that line to another place in the code if it thinks it will not make a difference in the execution.

That is not a problem until multiple threads or tasks deal with that code. The compiler might make mistakes. It cannot determine which tasks can access that variable simultaneously.

Yes, even simple writing to an integer can go wrong in a multithreaded system.

If we use `lock()`, we can guarantee that only one thread can access that code block, but that still does not mitigate the issue of the compiler optimizations.

To solve this problem, we can use the `volatile` keyword. It looks like this:

```
private static volatile int _initialValue = 100;
```

Instead of using a cached value, the compiler ensures that we always go directly to the memory address and stored value. That means that all threads will go to the same place and work with the same integer, thus eliminating the risk of working on old, stale, or cached data.

You might be tempted to add that `volatile` keyword everywhere, but I suggest that you refrain. It does mess with the compiler's optimization techniques. You should only use it if you suspect that there might be an issue with that particular piece of code.

So, now you know how to be more safe when dealing with threads. This is very important: if you mess things up you can get horrible and hard-to-debug bugs in your code. This is especially true if you are dealing with collections in multiple threads. How do you keep them synchronized? We're in luck though; the BCL has got us covered there. Let's talk about concurrent collections.

Concurrent collections in .NET

Collections are the backbone of many programs. Arrays, lists, dictionaries – we use them all the time. However, are they thread-safe? Let us find out:

```
using ExtensionLibrary;
var allLines = new List<string>();
for(int i = 0; i < 1000; i++)
{
    allLines.Add($"Line {i:000}");
```

```
}
ThreadPool.QueueUserWorkItem((_) =>
{
    Thread.Sleep(1000);
    allLines.Clear();
});
await DumpArray(allLines);

"Main app is done.\nPress any key to stop.".Dump(ConsoleColor.White);
Console.ReadKey();
return 0;
async Task DumpArray(List<string> someData)
{
    foreach(var data in someData)
    {
        data.Dump(ConsoleColor.Yellow);
        await Task.Delay(100);
    }
}
```

We have a `List<string>`. Then we added 1000 strings to that list We have a task that iterates through them, displays them on the screen, and waits a bit.

We also have a separate thread that clears the list after waiting for a second.

If you have read the previous section in this chapter, you might expect the loop in the task to abort prematurely. It should not print all items, since the list is suddenly empty and thus the `ForEach()` stops.

However, if you run it, you will see a different result. You will get a nice `InvalidOperationException` telling you that the collection was modified, which messed up the `ForEach` code.

Collections in the BCL are not thread-safe. If one thread works with them and another decides it needs to deal with that collection, things go wrong.

The following collections are not thread-safe and should be avoided when working with tasks:

- `List<T>`
- `Dictionary<TKey and TValue>`
- `Queue<T>`
- `Stack<T>`
- `HashSet<T>`
- `ArrayList`
- `HashTable`
- `SortedList<TKey, TValue>`, and `TSortedList`

Do not use these in multiple threads or tasks simultaneously.

Some collections are thread-safe. This is what they are and what they do:

Collection name	Description
`ConcurrentDictionary<TKey, TValue>`	A thread-safe collection of key-value pairs. It allows for concurrent adds, updates, and removals.
`ConcurrentQueue<T>`	A thread-safe version of a First-in, First-out (FIFO) collection.
`ConcurrentStack<T>`	A thread-safe version of a Last-in, First-out (LIFO) collection.
`ConcurrentBag<T>`	A thread-safe, unordered collection of objects. It is suitable for scenarios where the order is not important.
`BlockingCollection<T>`	Represents a thread-safe collection that can be bounded in size. It provides blocking and non-blocking `add` and `take` operations.

Table 4.3: Thread-safe collections

The first four collections are just thread-safe versions of the collections that we already know. Most people, however, would not recognize the last one: the `BlockingCollection<T>` collection.

This collection is, first of all, thread-safe. It also allows for blocking. Let me give you an example:

```
using ExtensionLibrary;
using System.Collections.Concurrent;
// We have a collection that blocks as soon as
// 5 items have been added. Before this thread
// can continue, one has to be taken away first.
var allLines = new BlockingCollection<string>(boundedCapacity:5);
ThreadPool.QueueUserWorkItem((_) => {
    for (int i = 0; i < 10; i++)
    {
        allLines.Add($"Line {i:000}");
        Thread.Sleep(1000);
    }
    allLines.CompleteAdding();
});
// Give the first thread some time to add items before
// we take them away again.
Thread.Sleep(6000);
// Read all items by taking them away
```

```
ThreadPool.QueueUserWorkItem((_) => {
    while (!allLines.IsCompleted)
    {
        try
        {
            var item = allLines.Take();
            item.Dump(ConsoleColor.Yellow);
            Thread.Sleep(10);
        }
        catch (InvalidOperationException)
        {
            // This can happen if
            // CompleteAdding has been called
            // but the collection is already empty
            // in our case: this thread finished before the
            // first one
        }
    }
});
"Main app is done.\nPress any key to stop.".Dump(ConsoleColor.White);
Console.ReadKey();
return 0;
```

A lot is happening here, so let me walk you through it.

First, we created an instance of the `BlockingCollection`. This class has a nice overloaded constructor that only allows this number of items to be added. If there are more, block the thread. I do not need that functionality here, but I found adding it funny.

Then we spun up a new thread that adds items to this collection. We can try to add 10, but again, it only allows five items. So, when the fifth item is added, this thread blocks until we have removed one of those items.

At the end of the loop, we told the collection that we had nothing left to add. We did this by calling `CompleteAdding()`.

Before we read the data in the second thread, we waited for a few seconds so the first one had time to fill the collection.

The second thread (third if you also count the main thread) took that collection and took an item from it. It is a FIFO collection, so the first item we could take was the first item added to the list. We displayed what we took and waited a bit. We needed to catch the `InvalidOperationException`. If the `CompleteAdding` was called due to timings by the time we had already taken all the items from the collection, an exception would have occurred. We need to catch that.

Due to our timings and `Thread.Sleep()` calls, we will see a fascinating effect. The first thread fills up the collection with five items. Then it waits. This operation takes five seconds in total. Six seconds after the start of the program, we will start taking items. Since there are plenty of them (five to be exact), the program will print these items on the screen quickly. When we take one item, the first thread gets permission to add a new item. However, since it takes a second to add an item, the second thread has to wait until it has been added. `Take()` will also block if there is nothing to take yet.

Only when the first thread calls the `CompleteAdding()` method does the second thread know it is done (since we checked the `IsCompleted` property). Then, we can exit the threads.

There is much synchronization behind the scenes, but it works amazingly well. This is undoubtedly an excellent addition to your toolbox!

Next steps

That was quite a ride. Threading can be complicated, but we got through it all right.

We looked at many different things in this chapter. We described what multitasking is, starting with old-fashioned IRQs, walking through cooperative multitasking, and arriving at the modern style of pre-emptive multitasking.

Then, we investigated Win32 threads and their .NET counterparts. We saw how to create threads but quickly found that the `Threadpool` offers a better way of doing so in most cases. However, we learned that most of that is moot, since the TPL handles many details for us.

In particular, we learned that async/await hides much complexity and makes writing multithreaded code a breeze. As with all tools, we learned that async/await comes with risks. You have to know what happens and where bad things can happen. Luckily, we covered those situations as well.

We looked at collections and how to make your code thread-safe. We also learned something fundamental regarding async/await: async all the way to the top!

Asynchronous programming is imperative when dealing with devices outside the CPU. One of the areas where we need to use these techniques extensively is in the file system. However, file systems have a lot of other things that you need to know about. So, it's great that the next chapter deals with that topic!

5
The One with the Filesystem Chronicles

File Systems and IO

Computers are incredible machines, but they have one downside. If the power goes off, they forget everything. If we do not want to lose our work, we must store it elsewhere. We can print data, put it on the network, or store it in permanent storage. This is the most common option. Of course, we need to have a way to get data into the CPU. We can read data from a file or a network. We can even use the keyboard to enter data. This is something that both you (a programmer) and I (a writer) are very familiar with.

When we are programming software, we refer to the concept of **streams**. A stream represents a sequence of data elements made available over time. This sequence can be stored on a disk, it can be data flowing over network wires, or it can be the state of a memory chip. Data must flow back and forth no matter what physical medium we use. This chapter handles that topic, covering streams, files, and other ways of **Input and Output** (**IO**).

One thing that we will not dive into in this chapter is the topic of networking. Networking is such a different concept that a separate chapter will deal with this topic. You can find all the low-level networking details in *Chapter 8*. However, the concepts of data handling over that network are the same for files and other media. So, the principles laid out here still apply.

In this chapter, we cover the following topics:

- How to work with files using .NET
- How to use Win32 APIs to work with the filesystem
- How to work with Directory and Path

- Why and how we should use asynchronous IO
- How to use encryption and compression

We have a lot of ground to cover, so let's dive in!

Technical requirements

To view all the code in this chapter, you can visit the following link: https://github.com/PacktPublishing/Systems-Programming-with-C-Sharp-and-.NET/tree/main/SystemsProgrammingWithCSharpAndNet/Chapter05.

File writing basics

There cannot be anything more straightforward than writing to a file, right? That's why I think that that is a good starting point. Here is the code to do so:

```
var path = System.IO.Path.GetTempPath();
var fileName = "WriteLines.txt";
var fullPath = Path.Combine(path, fileName);
File.WriteAllText(fullPath, "Hello, System Programmers");
```

The first line gets the system `temp` path. Then we specify the filename, add that to the `temp` path, and write a line of text to that file.

This example is simple enough, but it already shows something useful. First, we can get to the `temp` folder quickly; we don't have to specify where that is in our code. Second, we can combine the filename and the path without worrying about the path separator. On Windows, the parts of the path are separated by a backslash, while on Linux, this is a forward slash. The CLR figures out what it should use and uses the correct one.

The `File.WriteAllText` then takes that data and creates a file, opens it, writes the string, and closes the file. If the file is already there, the system overwrites it.

If we wanted to have a temporary filename instead of `WriteLines.Text`, the code could have been even easier:

```
var path = System.IO.Path.GetTempFileName();
File.WriteAllText(path, "Hello, System Programmers");
```

The system looks up the path for `temp` files, generates a new file with a unique filename, and uses that to write the string. The downside is that we now have no idea which file it is. We have to log that somewhere; otherwise, our `temp` folder will fill up quickly with unused files (most operating systems clean up the `temp` folder though, so no real worries there).

You can obviously use any folder you want. However, if you want to use some of the special folders, such as the `Documents` folder on Windows, the system can help you get to those as well. Have a look at the following code snippet:

```
var path = Environment.GetFolderPath(Environment.SpecialFolder.
MyDocuments);
var fileName = "WriteLines.txt";
var fullPath = Path.Combine(path, fileName);
File.WriteAllText(fullPath, "Hello, System Programmers");
```

This code looks up the location of `My Documents` on my machine and returns that so that I can write the file to that location. You can choose from a long list of special locations, all of which are part of the `SpecialFolder` enum. I will not list all of them; you can find them here: https://learn.microsoft.com/en-us/dotnet/api/system.environment.specialfolder?view=net-8.0.

This way of writing files is effortless. However, as we have seen many times before, ease comes with less control. As systems programmers, we want all the control we can get. Let's take back some control.

FileStream

The static `File` class is easy to use and very convenient if you quickly want to write something to, or read something from, a file. However, it is not the fastest way. At least, it is not the fastest if we are referring to execution time. As systems programmers, we are very interested in speed, even if it means giving up on ease of coding.

The following example is about 20% faster than the previous one, but it does the same things. It just needs a few more lines:

```
var fileName = Path.GetTempFileName();
var info = new UTF8Encoding(true).GetBytes("Hello, System 
Developers!");
using FileStream? fs = File.Create(fileName, info.Length);
try
{
    fs.Write(info, 0, info.Length);
}
finally
{
    fs.Close();
}
```

This sample uses the `FileStream` that `File.Create()` returns. We can, of course, create one ourselves. Replace the line where we created the `FileStream` through `File` with the following:

```
using var fs = new FileStream(
    path: fileName,
    mode: FileMode.Create,
    access: FileAccess.Write,
    share: FileShare.None,
    bufferSize:0x1000,
    options: FileOptions.Asynchronous);
```

I have used the most extensive overload here to show you some of the options that you can use. Most are self-explanatory, but I want to highlight two parameters: **share** and **options**.

`Share` is a flag that tells the operating system how to share the file while we use it. It has the following options:

Flag	Value	Description
`None`	0	No sharing is allowed. Any other process trying to access the file will fail to do so.
`Read`	1	Other processes can read the file while we are still using it.
`Write`	2	Other processes might write to the file at the same time.
`ReadWrite`	3	This combines the `Read` and `Write` flags.
`Delete`	4	This allows requests for deletion of the file while we are using it.
`Inheritable`	16	The file handle is inheritable by child processes. However, this does not work on Win32 applications.

Table 5.1: Share options for files

Although specifying a flag from this list might indicate that other processes can do things with our files while we use them, there is no guarantee that these other processes can actually do so. Usually, they need other permissions as well.

`Delete` is a nice flag. It allows for deletion while we are still working with the file. That could lead to weird situations. If we create a file and specify that we allow deletion, we might write to the file while another process has already deleted it. The system does not complain and continues running. However, you will end up without that file, which means losing your data forever. Let me show you what I mean:

```
using System.Text;
var fileName = Path.GetTempFileName();
var info = new UTF8Encoding(true).GetBytes("Hello fellow System
```

```
    Developers!");
using (var fs = new FileStream(
    path: fileName,
    mode: FileMode.Create,
    access: FileAccess.Write,
    share: FileShare.Delete, // We allow other processes to delete the
                             //file.
    bufferSize: 0x1000,
    options: FileOptions.Asynchronous))
{
    try
    {
        fs.Write(info, 0, info.Length);
        Console.WriteLine($"Wrote to the file. Now try to delete it.
            You can find it here:\n{fileName}");
        Console.ReadKey();
        fs.Write(info);
        Console.WriteLine("Done with all the writing");
        Console.ReadKey();
    }
    finally
    {
        fs.Close();
    }
}

Console.WriteLine("Done.");
Console.ReadKey();
```

This example is straightforward. We will first get a temporary filename. Then, we will get the bytes that form our payload. After that, we will create an instance of the `FileStream`, setting a couple of properties as we do so.

One of them is the `Share` option. We have set it to `FileShare.Delete`.

We will write some data to the file and then pause the program. If you run it, this is the moment to take the output that tells you the name and location of the file and delete it. You should notice that you can do that. Then continue the program. As you can see, the following line writes the same data again to the file we just deleted. Nothing happens. Really, nothing happens. There are no errors, but no data is written anywhere either.

In most cases, this is a behavior you would want to avoid. However, maybe your use case calls for just this kind of behavior. In that case, now you know how to do this.

Even faster – Win32

There is a faster way to write files. If we remove the overhead of the CLR, we can write files about 20% faster. A 20% increase in speed can mean the difference between a sluggish application and one that seems lightning-fast. As usual, this comes with a price. All the good things the CLR provides us with are now in our own hands. We have to do a lot more work. However, if you are looking for the fastest way to write data to a file, the Win32 approach is, again, the best way to do this.

We will begin by declaring some constants:

```
private const uint GENERIC_WRITE = 0x40000000;
private const uint CREATE_ALWAYS = 0x00000002;
private const uint FILE_APPEND_DATA = 0x00000004;
```

GENERIC_WRITE tells the system that we want to write to a file. CREATE_ALWAYS specifies that we want to create a new file every time we call this. FILE_APPEND_DATA means that we want to add to the current file (which doesn't make much sense, since we just created the file).

It is time to import the Win32 APIs:

```
[DllImport("kernel32.dll", SetLastError = true)]
private static extern SafeFileHandle CreateFile(
    string lpFileName,
    uint dwDesiredAccess,
    uint dwShareMode,
    IntPtr lpSecurityAttributes,
    uint dwCreationDisposition,
    uint dwFlagsAndAttributes,
    IntPtr hTemplateFile);

[DllImport("kernel32.dll", SetLastError = true)]
[return: MarshalAs(UnmanagedType.Bool)]
private static extern bool WriteFile(
    SafeFileHandle hFile,
    byte[] lpBuffer,
    uint nNumberOfBytesToWrite,
    out uint lpNumberOfBytesWritten,
    IntPtr lpOverlapped);
[DllImport("kernel32.dll", SetLastError = true)]
[return: MarshalAs(UnmanagedType.Bool)]
private static extern bool CloseHandle(SafeFileHandle hObject);
```

We will import three methods from `kernel32.dll`. `CreateFile` creates a file, `WriteFile` writes to that file, and `CloseHandle` closes handles and, in our case, the handle to the file.

That is all we need to write. Let me show you how that works:

```
public void WriteToFile(string fileName, string textToWrite)
{
    var fileHandle = CreateFile(
        fileName,
        GENERIC_WRITE,
        0,
        IntPtr.Zero,
        CREATE_ALWAYS,
        FILE_APPEND_DATA,
        IntPtr.Zero);

    if (!fileHandle.IsInvalid)
        try
        {
            var bytes = Encoding.ASCII.GetBytes(textToWrite);
            var writeResult = WriteFile(
                fileHandle,
                bytes,
                (uint)bytes.Length,
                out var bytesWritten,
                IntPtr.Zero);
        }
        finally
        {
            // Always close the handle once you are done
            CloseHandle(fileHandle);
        }
    else
        Console.WriteLine("Failed to open file.");
}
```

With the knowledge you have right now, you should be able to follow along. We will first create a file with the correct parameters. If that works, we will get the bytes we want to write and then use `WriteFile` to do the actual writing. After that, we will close the handle. We do that in the `finally` block; handles are expensive and they lock access to the file. We want to close it so other processes can access the file.

You are partially correct if you think that this does not look too bad. This was very simple. However, I omitted a lot of things, such as error checking. Do you remember what I told you about performance? I said in the previous chapters that file IO takes forever compared to normal CPU operations. Thus, we must use the asynchronous approach as much as we can. You can do that with Win32, but that is pretty complex. I will not show you how to do that here, but if you do a quick search on the Win32

API, `CreateFile`, and `FILE_FLAG_OVERLAPPED`, you can find out how it all works. In short, you will have to check everything yourself. My advice is to stick to the CLR functions. We will discuss asynchronous I/O later in this chapter.

We have learned how to write to files and all that goes with doing that. However, that is only one part of the story. Let's move to the other half of the equation: reading a file.

File reading basics

Great. We have written a file. Now we should be able to read it as well, right? Okay, let's dive into that. We will start with a simple example: a file with some lines of text that we want to read into a string:

```
public string ReadFromFile(string fileName)
{
    var text = File.ReadAllText(fileName);
    return text;
}
```

I can't make it simpler than this. We have the static `ReadAllText` method, which takes a filename and reads all text into the string. Then we return that. Keep in mind that not all files contain text. I even dare to say that *most* files do not contain text. They are binary. Now, technically, a `text` file is also a `binary` file. So, let's read the file again, but now by reading the actual bytes. I use the `FileStream` this time, so we have a bit more control over what is happening:

```
public string ReadWithStream(string fileName)
{
    byte[] fileContent;
    using (FileStream fs = File.OpenRead(fileName))
    {
        fileContent = new byte[fs.Length];
        fs.Read(fileContent, 0, (int)fs.Length);
        fs.Close();
    }

    return Encoding.ASCII.GetString(fileContent);
}
```

The nice thing about the `FileStream` is that it knows the length of the stream. That means that we can allocate enough space for our array to contain all the data.

We will read all data through one call to `fs.Read()`, giving it the byte array, the start position `0`, and the total number of bytes to read. Again, we will close the stream when we are done with it.

Last, we will convert the file to a string, assuming the contents are ASCII characters.

This way of reading works fine if you have a relatively small file. In that case, you can read it all in one go. However, if the file is too big, you must read it in chunks.

For that, the `Read()` method helps you by telling you how much data it has read. You can create a loop and iterate through the complete file.

We can rewrite the part where we read the file like this:

```
fileContent = new byte[fs.Length];
int i = 0;
int bytesRead=0;
do
{
    var myBuffer = new byte[1];
    bytesRead = fs.Read(myBuffer, 0, 1);
    if(bytesRead > 0)
        fileContent[i++] = myBuffer[0];
}while(bytesRead > 0);
fs.Close();
```

This is a silly way to do this, but it illustrates my point. We will keep reading the file until we have all the data, in which case `fs.Read()` returns `0`.

Reading binary data

If you have a `binary` file that you know the structure of, you can use a `BinaryReader` to help.

Binary data is usually much more memory-efficient than text data. Since we, as systems programmers, are always searching for more efficient code, this is worth looking into.

Let's assume that I have the following class. This doesn't mean anything special; it is just a data collection:

```
class MyData
{
    public int Id { get; set; }
    public double SomeMagicNumber { get; set; }
    public bool IsThisAGoodDataSet { get; set; }
    public MyFlags SomeFlags { get; set; }
    public string? SomeText { get; set; }
}
[Flags]
public enum MyFlags
{
    FlagOne,
    FlagTwo,
    FlagThree
}
```

Let us assume that I have created an instance of this class with the properties `42`, `3.1415`, `True`, `MyFlags.One | MyFlags.Three` and `Hello, Systems Programmers`. I can write it to a file using JSON serialization. That results in a file of 114 bytes. If I use a binary format, I can shrink it down to 44 bytes. That is a considerable saving, especially when putting that data on a network.

Reading that file is straightforward using the `BinaryReader` class. Let me show you:

```
public MyData Read(string fileName)
{
    var myData = new MyData();

    using var fs = File.OpenRead(fileName);
    try
    {
        using BinaryReader br = new(fs);
        myData.Id = br.ReadInt32();
        myData.IsThisAGoodDataSet = br.ReadBoolean();
        myData.SomeMagicNumber = br.ReadDouble();
        myData.SomeFlags = (MyFlags)br.ReadInt32();
        myData.SomeText = br.ReadString();
    }
    finally
    {
        fs.Close();
    }
    return myData;
}
```

Doing it this way means that you have to be very careful. You have to know the structure of the file precisely. You are responsible for getting all data in the correct order and knowing each field's type exactly. However, doing it this way ensures efficiency and can save you many CPU cycles.

We now know all about how to read and write files. However, files are not the only things we can find in file systems. We need a way to organize all those files. That brings us to the next topic in IO: directories!

Directory operations

Imagine having a file system with one root folder. All files on your drive are stored there. You would have a tough time finding all your files. Luckily, operating systems all support the notion of folders or directories. The CLR helps us by giving us two classes to work with paths, folders, and directories: **Path** and **Directory**.

The Path class

`Path` is a class that has helper methods for dealing with paths. With `Path`, I mean the string that denotes the name of a directory. You should use the `Directory` class when dealing with the actual directory and files.

We have already seen the `Path` class in previous samples. I used it to get a temporary filename and the name of the `Documents` folder. I also used it to combine a path and a filename to avoid dealing with path separators myself.

There are quite a few handy methods and properties in the `Path` class. You can see some of the most-used ones in the following table.

Method	Description
Path.Combine	Combines two or more strings into a path
ath.GetFileName	Returns the filename and extension of the specified path string
Path.GetFileNameWithoutExtension	Returns the filename of the specified path string without the extension
Path.GetExtension	Gets the extension (including the period) of the specified path string
Path.GetDirectoryName	Gets the directory information for the specified path string
Path.GetFullPath	Converts a relative path to an absolute path
Path.GetTempPath	Returns the path to the system's temporary folder
Path.GetRandomFileName	Returns a random filename that is not already in use
Path.GetInvalidFileNameChars	Returns an array of characters that are not allowed in filenames on the current platform
Path.GetInvalidPathChars	Returns an array of characters that are not allowed in path strings on the current platform
Path.ChangeExtension	Changes the extension of a file path
Path.HasExtension	Determines whether a path includes a filename extension
Path.IsPathRooted	Gets a value indicating whether the specified path string contains a root
Path.DirectorySeparatorChar	A platform-specific separator character that is used in path strings

Table 5.2: The Path class and its methods and properties

As you can see, the `Path` class has a set of nice and convenient helpers. We will encounter them again when we investigate other platforms, but for now, please remember to use them as much as possible.

The Directory class

The `Directory` class deals with the actual directory in your filesystem. This class works closely with the `Path` class. If you need to specify the directory's name (and thus its location), you would use the `Path` class.

Let's assume that we want to list all images in our `Pictures` folder on our Windows machine. You would do that like this:

```
var imagesPath =
Environment.GetFolderPath(Environment.SpecialFolder.MyPictures);
string[] allFiles =
    Directory.GetFiles(
        path: imagesPath,
        searchPattern: "*.jPg",
        searchOption: SearchOption.AllDirectories);

foreach (string file in allFiles)
{
    Console.WriteLine(file);
}
```

I use `Environment.SpecialFolder.MyPictures` here to identify the folder that has all my pictures. The actual path depends on your operating system, the username, and how you have set up your machine. That means there are a lot of possible variations, but we need not bother much about that. Let the operating system figure that out, as long as we get the correct folder.

I used the `Directory.GetFiles()` method to iterate through that folder. I want all the JPEG images I have collected in all subfolders. Notice how I spelled the extension in the `searchPattern` variable: `*.jPg`. On Windows, filenames are not case-sensitive. On Linux, they are. So, on a Linux-based machine, this would not work. Okay, it will work, but it does not return all the files you might expect to get. Unfortunately, `GetFiles()` cannot set up a filter for case insensitivity. If you want to get all JPG images, no matter what their extensions look like, you have to do this another way:

```
var regex = new Regex(@"\.jpe?g$", RegexOptions.IgnoreCase);
var allFiles =
    Directory.EnumerateFiles(imagesPath)
        .Where(file => regex.IsMatch(file));
```

I have created a regular expression here, saying I want to filter on strings that end in `.jpg` or `jpeg` and ignore the case. Then I use `Directory.EnumerateFiles()` and apply the `Where()` LINQ operator to apply the `regex` filter.

This method works fine on all platforms. You could have avoided the `regex` filter by using the following code, which is more verbose but, I assume, more readable to many people:

```
var files = Directory.EnumerateFiles(imagesPath)
    .Where(file => file.EndsWith(".jpg",
StringComparison.OrdinalIgnoreCase) ||
                file.EndsWith(".jpeg",
StringComparison.OrdinalIgnoreCase));
```

I have collected the most-used methods and properties of the `Directory` class for you in the following table:

Method or property	Description
`Directory.CreateDirectory`	Creates all directories and subdirectories in the specified path unless they already exist
`Directory. Delete`	Deletes the specified directory and, optionally, any subdirectories and files in the directory
`Directory.Exists`	Determines whether the given path refers to an existing directory on the disk
`Directory.GetCurrentDirectory`	Gets the current working directory of the application
`Directory.GetDirectories`	Gets the names of subdirectories (including their paths) in the specified directory
`Directory.GetFiles`	Returns the names of files (including their paths) in the specified directory
`Directory.GetFileSystemEntries`	Returns the names of all the files and subdirectories in a specified directory
`Directory.GetLastAccessTime`	Returns the date and time when the specified file or directory was last accessed
`Directory.GetLastWriteTime`	Returns the date and time when the specified file or directory was last written to
`Directory.GetParent`	Retrieves the parent directory of the specified path, including both absolute and relative paths
`Directory.Move`	Moves a file or a directory and its contents to a new location
`Directory.SetCreationTime`	Sets the creation date and time for the specified file or directory
`Directory.SetCurrentDirectory`	Sets the application's current working directory to the specified directory

Method or property	Description
`Directory.SetLastAccessTime`	Sets the date and time when the specified file or directory was last accessed
`Directory.SetLastWriteTime`	Sets the date and time when the specified file or directory was last written to

Table 5.3: The methods and properties of the Directory class

The `Directory` has some nice helpers and properties. You could figure out all of these properties yourself, but why bother if the CLR is friendly enough to help you? These properties will also be beneficial when we move to other platforms later on.

The DirectoryInfo class

There is one more class I want to discuss: the `DirectoryInfo` class. The difference between `Directory` and `DirectoryInfo` is that the former uses static methods, whereas the latter is used as an instance. `Directory` returns information about directories as strings. `DirectoryInfo` returns objects with much more information. Let me give you an example:

```
var imagesPath = Environment.GetFolderPath(
    Environment.SpecialFolder.MyPictures);
var directoryInfo = new DirectoryInfo(imagesPath);
Console.WriteLine(directoryInfo.FullName);
Console.WriteLine(directoryInfo.CreationTime);
Console.WriteLine(directoryInfo.Attributes);
```

I created an instance of the `DirectoryInfo` class and gave it the path to our `images` folder. This instance has a lot of valuable properties, such as the full name, time of creation, attributes, and many more. I have listed the most-used properties and methods in the following table.

Method or property	Description
`DirectoryInfo.Create`	Creates a directory
`DirectoryInfo.Delete`	Deletes this instance of a `DirectoryInfo`, specifying whether to delete subdirectories and files
`DirectoryInfo.Exists`	Gets a value indicating whether the directory exists
`DirectoryInfo.Extension`	Gets the string representing the extension part of the directory
`DirectoryInfo.FullName`	Gets the full path of the directory or file
`DirectoryInfo.Name`	Gets the name of this `DirectoryInfo` instance

Method or property	Description
`DirectoryInfo.Parent`	Gets the parent directory of a specified subdirectory
`DirectoryInfo.Root`	Gets the root portion of a path
`DirectoryInfo.GetFiles`	Returns a file list from the current directory
`DirectoryInfo.GetDirectories`	Returns the subdirectories of the current directory
`DirectoryInfo.GetFileSystemInfos`	Retrieves an array of `FileSystemInfo` objects representing the files and subdirectories of the current directory
`DirectoryInfo.MoveTo`	Moves a `DirectoryInfo` instance and its contents to a new path
`DirectoryInfo.Refresh`	Refreshes the state of the object
`DirectoryInfo.EnumerateFiles`	Returns an enumerable collection of file information in the current directory
`DirectoryInfo.EnumerateDirectories`	Returns an enumerable collection of directory information in the current directory
`DirectoryInfo.EnumerateFileSystemInfos`	Returns an enumerable collection of file system information in the current directory

Table 5.4: DirectoryInfo properties and methods

As you can see, `Path`, `Directory`, and `DirectoryInfo` can greatly help when dealing with files.

File system monitoring

As systems programmers, we must find ways to communicate with our apps. After all, there is no user interface wherein the user can indicate their desired actions.

Most apps in that category listen to network ports or have other ways for systems to communicate with them. One of those ways is to wait for changes in files or directories.

Keeping an eye on files or folders is a fairly common scenario. For instance, we could build a system that processes the files that we get through an email system. As soon as a file is delivered as an attachment, the mail client places it in a directory and our system picks it up.

This means that we need to have a way to keep an eye on that folder. Luckily, that is not too hard to do. It does require some explanation, so let me walk you through it.

We will begin with the class that other classes interact with:

```
internal class MyFolderWatcher : Idisposable
{
    protected virtual void Dispose(bool disposing)
    {
        if (disposing)
        {
            // Dispose managed state (managed objects).
        }
    }

    ~MyFolderWatcher()
    {
        Dispose(false);
    }
    public void Dispose()
    {
        Dispose(true);
        GC.SuppressFinalize(this);
    }
}
```

We will need to clean up some resources later, so I have implemented the `IDisposable` interface here. The class that we need to clean up is an instance of the `FileSystemWatcher` type. This class, when instantiated, keeps an eye on a folder and, optionally, a filter for the filenames. If something of interest happens there, the `FileSystemWatcher` notifies us. It is up to us to define what "something of interest" means.

Let's set it up as a private member of our class:

```
private FileSystemWatcher? _watcher;
```

We could change our `Dispose(bool disposing)` method to clean this up, but I will hold on to that for now. We need to do more than just dispose of the `FileSystemWatcher`.

A `FileSystemWatcher` is resource-intensive. Keeping an eye on a folder can lead to much CPU pressure. Therefore, we must be sure to only enable it when we need it.

Then, we will add a method that enables the watcher and set some settings:

```
public void SetupWatcher(string pathToWatch)
{
    if(_watcher != null)
        throw new InvalidOperationException(
            "The watcher has already been set up");
    if(!Path.Exists(pathToWatch))
```

```
            throw new ArgumentOutOfRangeException(
                nameof(pathToWatch),
                "The path does not exist");
    // Set the folder to keep an eye on
    _watcher = new FileSystemWatcher(pathToWatch);
    // We only want notifications when a file is created or
    // when it has changed.
    _watcher.NotifyFilter =
        NotifyFilters.FileName |
        NotifyFilters.LastWrite;
    // Set the callbacks
    _watcher.Created += WatcherCallback;
    _watcher.Changed += WatcherCallback;
    // Start watching
    _watcher.EnableRaisingEvents = true;
}
```

We will start with two checks. First, we will see whether the watcher has not already been created. If it has, we will throw an error. The second is to check whether the supplied path exists or not.

If those two checks both pass, we will create an instance of the `FileSystemWatcher` class and give it the path we want to monitor.

You can specify what you want to monitor. This is controlled by the `NotifyFilter` property. This property takes an enum or a combination of the `NotifyFilter` enums. You can see what your options are in the following table.

NotifyFilters enum	Description
`Attributes`	Watches for changes in the attributes of the file or folder
`CreationTime`	Monitors changes to the creation times of files and directories
`DirectoryName`	Watches for changes in the names of directories
`FileName`	Watches for changes in the names of files
`LastAccess`	Monitors changes to the last access times of files and directories
`LastWrite`	Watches for changes to the last write times of files and directories
`Security`	Monitors changes in the security settings of files and directories
`Size`	Watches for changes in the sizes of files and directories

Table 5.5: NotifyFilters options

I am only interested in new or changed files in our folder. So, I have given it the `NotifyFilters.FileName | NotifyFilters.LastWrite` value. The `FileName` of a file changes, of course, when you first create the file. I could also have chosen `CreationTime`, which hardly ever changes. I will also keep a watch on `LastWrite`, which tells me when a file has changed.

After this, I will give the `_watcher` a callback to call when either of the two events I care about are raised. Since all events share the same signature, I can get away with just one method. That method is what we will look at next. However, before we do that, we need to start the watcher by setting `_watcher.EnableRaisingEvents` to `True`. The next piece of code contains the body of the eventhandler:

```
private void WatcherCallback(object sender, FileSystemEventArgs e)
{
    switch (e.ChangeType)
    {
        case WatcherChangeTypes.Created:
            FileAdded?.Invoke(this, new FileCreatedEventArgs
                (e.FullPath));
            break;
        case WatcherChangeTypes.Changed:
            FileChanged?.Invoke(this, new
                FileChangedEventArgs(e.FullPath));
            break;
    }
}
```

When the watcher calls this callback, we get an instance of the `FileSystemEventArgs` class. This class contains a field called `ChangeType` that indicates what type of change triggered this call. It also contains the full path and name of the file affected in the `FullPath` property.

We will switch on that `ChangeType` field and call one of the two event handlers for our class. Those two event handlers that are part of our class look like this:

```
public event EventHandler<FileCreatedEventArgs>? FileAdded;
public event EventHandler<FileChangedEventArgs>? FileChanged;
```

The `FileCreatedEventArgs` and `FileChangedEventArgs` types for the `EventHandler` are straightforward as well. I could have used only one type. However, for future uses, I decided to give them distinct classes that I might extend at some point with more information. They look like this:

```
public class FileCreatedEventArgs : EventArgs
{
    public FileCreatedEventArgs(string filePath)
    {
        FilePath = filePath;
    }

    public string FilePath { get; }
```

```
}

public class FileChangedEventArgs : EventArgs
{
    public FileChangedEventArgs(string filePath)
    {
        FilePath = filePath;
    }
    public string FilePath { get; }
}
```

`FileSystemWatcher` implements `IDisposable`. So, we must dispose of it when we no longer use it. We need to rewrite our own `Dispose(bool disposing)` method to look like this:

```
protected virtual void Dispose(bool disposing)
{
    if (!disposing) return;

    if (_watcher == null)
        return;

    // Stop raising events
    _watcher.EnableRaisingEvents = false;
    // Clean whoever has subscribed to us
    // to prevent memory leaks
    FileAdded = null;
    FileChanged = null;
    _watcher.Dispose();
    _watcher = null;
}
```

After doing some checks, we will stop the system from receiving any events. Then we will clear the events. If we do not do this, other objects might hold a reference to our class and thus prevent this class from being freed from memory.

When that is done, we dispose of `_watcher` and set it to null.

That's it. If you run it from your program, give it a folder, and attach some `eventhandlers` to it, you will be able to see what happens when you add or change files in that folder.

It is almost perfect. Almost – but not quite.

If you add a file, you will get multiple events. If you think about that, it makes sense. After all, a file is created on the file system and then it is changed immediately. If you wanted to, you could change our class to consider that. It is not hard to do, so I will leave that up to you.

Asynchronous I/O

I have said it before, but this is so important that I have to repeat it here: IO is slow. Every piece of code that works with IO should be done asynchronously. Luckily, most of the classes in the `System.IO` namespace have asynchronous members that we can use with async/await.

I would be happy if Microsoft decided to mark all non-asynchronous methods in `System.IO` as obsolete.

The naïve approach

Most of the methods you know in `System.IO` have an asynchronous version. So, just add the async postfix to the method name and await it. Simple!

On second thought, no. It is not that simple.

Let me show you an example:

```
public async Task CreateBigFileNaively(string fileName)
{
    var stream = File.CreateText(fileName);
    for (int i = 0; i < Int32.MaxValue; i++)
    {
            var value = $"This is line {i}";
            Console.Writeline(value);
            await stream.WriteLineAsync(value);
                await Task.Delay(10);

    }

    Console.WriteLine("Closing the stream");
    stream.Close();
    await stream.DisposeAsync();
}
```

This method creates a file and then writes a string line to it. Once finished, it closes the file and nicely disposes of it. It does that asynchronously. So this is the way things should be, right?

Let's use this method:

```
var asyncSample = new AsyncSample();
await asyncSample.CreateBigFileNaively(@"c:\temp\bigFile.txt");
```

Add these two lines to your main Console application. Run it and let it run for a few seconds. Note what line is written to the file on the screen (it should say something to the effect of *This is the line n*, where n is the number of the line). Then press *Ctrl + C* to cancel the operation. The program will stop. Now, please open the file and see how far it got. There is a big chance that you will see that the last line written on the file is not the number that you saw on the screen.

Why is that, you might wonder? The CLR ensures that performance is as high as possible for our code. So, all data written to a file system is buffered into a cache before it is sent to the SSD or other media. After all, writing to storage is slow. However, since we killed the process, the CLR did not have time to flush the cache.

Using CancellationTokens

Of course, this would not happen often in the real world. However, you might want to cancel a long-running IO process, and then you might encounter this.

There is a solution to this. Remember the chapter where we talked about threads? Remember that I said that there was this thing called a `CancellationToken`? That is the one that we need.

Let's rewrite the code that writes the file. Let's remove the naïve from the method name; we know better now:

```
public async Task CreateBigFile(string fileName, CancellationToken 
cancellationToken)
{
    var stream = File.CreateText(fileName);
    for (int i = 0; i < Int32.MaxValue; i++)
    {
        if (cancellationToken.IsCancellationRequested)
        {
            Console.WriteLine("We are being cancelled");
            break;
        }
        else
        {
            var value = $"This is line {i}";
            Console.WriteLine(value);
            await stream.WriteLineAsync(value);
            try
            {
                await Task.Delay(10, cancellationToken);
            }
            catch (TaskCanceledException)
            {
                Console.WriteLine("We are being cancelled");
                break;
            }
        }
```

```
    }

        Console.WriteLine("Closing the stream");
        stream.Close();
        await stream.DisposeAsync();
    }
```

We have added quite a bit of code here. Let me walk you through it. First, we added a parameter of the `CancellationToken` type to the method. We will constantly check to see whether `Cancel` has been requested in our loop. If so, we will print the message on the screen and graciously exit the loop.

In the `Task.Delay()`, we also passed the `CancellationToken`. After all, while the system waits for this delay, the cancellation can also be requested. However, when that happens during a `Task.Delay()`, the CLR will throw an exception of the `TaskCanceledException` type. We have to catch that to prevent our program from crashing and stopping. That's why we have the `try..catch` block here. We need that `try..catch` block to prevent the exception from bubbling up the call stack.

We have to mimic breaking up the loop from the outside. Change the code that calls this method into the following:

```
var cancellationTokenSource = new
CancellationTokenSource();
ThreadPool.QueueUserWorkItem((_) =>
{
    Thread.Sleep(10000);
    Console.WriteLine("About to cancel the operation");
    cancellationTokenSource.Cancel();
});
var asyncSample = new AsyncSample();
await asyncSample.CreateBigFile(
    @"c:\temp\bigFile.txt",
    cancellationTokenSource.Token);
```

First, we will create a new `CancellationtokenSource`. Then, we will pull a thread from the `ThreadPool` and give it something to do. After waiting for 10 seconds, it will request a cancellation.

The call to `CreateBigFile` now has a `CancellationTokenSource`.

Run it and see that it stops after 10 seconds. Notice which line it stopped on and check the actual file to see whether that was the last line written to it. On my machine, this works nicely.

Remember: when dealing with asynchronous file handling, no matter what you do, try to use a `CancellationSourceToken`. Also, be sure that you deal with any side effects. Be sure to clean up after the cancellation has been requested so that the CLR can properly flush the cache and clean up its resources.

BufferedStream

The CLR is pretty good at maximizing performance for your I/O operations. As we saw, it can cache data before writing to external devices. This caching speeds up our code since we no longer have to wait for the slow write operations to finish. However, the CLR makes an educated guess about those caches. Sometimes it gets it wrong. If we know the size of the data we want to write, we can use that knowledge to get even more performance out of our application.

Let's say that we have a system that writes the following record to the I/O:

```
internal readonly record struct DataRecord
{
    public int Id { get; init; }
    public DateTime LogDate { get; init; }
    public double Price { get; init; }
}
```

This block is 24 bytes long. We can quickly determine that by adding up the sizes of `int`, `DateTime`, and `double`.

If we write that to a file, the CLR will cache it until the systems find a suitable moment to do the actual writing of the data to the storage. However, we can improve that. We can use the `BufferedStream` class to write this data to a buffer first. Then the CLR can flush that buffer to the underlying storage when it thinks it is the best time. The advantage here is that we control the size of that buffer or cache. If we specify the size just right, we will not waste memory. However, we are also not making it too small so that it flushes too often. It is just right for us.

The code to do that looks like this:

```
public async Task WriteBufferedData(string fileName)
{
    var data = new DataRecord
    {
        Id = 42,
        LogDate = DateTime.UtcNow,
        Price = 12.34
    };
    await using FileStream stream = new(fileName, FileMode.CreateNew,
    FileAccess.Write);
    await using BufferedStream bufferedStream = new(stream,
    Marshal.SizeOf<DataRecord>());
    await using BinaryWriter writer = new(bufferedStream);
    writer.Write(data.Id);
    writer.Write(data.LogDate.ToBinary());
    writer.Write(data.Price);
}
```

First, we will create a `FileStream`. This `FileStream` is the actual handle to the file we are writing to. Then, we will create a `BufferedStream` and give it the `FileStream` and the size of the record that we want to write. After that, we will create a `BinaryWriter` to take our data and write it to the buffer as efficiently as possible.

When that has all been set up, we will do the writing.

> **A word of warning**
>
> If you are not sure of the size of the data, having a `BufferedStream` might work against you. `BufferedStream` works best if you are doing a lot of smaller, frequent writes of data that you know the size of. Otherwise, the cache management is best left to the CLR.

File system security

Files are where we store things. Those things might not be for everybody to see. Sometimes, we must hide data or ensure that only programs that we trust can access it. OSs can help. Every OS has a way of handling access to files and directories. You can generally allow or disallow read- or write access to them.

However, what happens when you want to share files? Let us assume that you want to transfer data over a wire or store it on another drive such as a removable USB drive. In that case, ensuring that level of security is quite challenging. This means that you might have to encrypt data to prevent it from being abused.

> **Security – a topic of its own**
>
> I am only covering the basics of security and encryption here. This is not a complete guide to this complicated and extensive topic. There have been hundreds of books written on this topic alone. I want you to know that you can do security and encryption. However, if you want to take this seriously, I suggest that you go out and find a few good resources on those topics and learn from there.

Encryption basics

Basically, we have two encryption flavors: **symmetric** and **asymmetric** algorithms. Although there are many similarities between them, one big difference is in how they handle keys.

Let's discuss an elementary sample. We'll say that you have a message and want to transmit it to someone else. Since the contents of the message are sensitive, you do not want anyone else to be able to read it, so you decided to encrypt it. That means that you will change the contents of your message so that nobody can make any sense of it. The recipient then decrypts it to change your text into something intelligible. We call the text that people can actually read and understand **cleartext**. In contrast, the encrypted, unreadable text is something we call **ciphertext**. People read cleartext; ciphertext needs decrypting.

This way of protecting information is not new. Julius Caesar did such a thing over 2,000 years ago. He used a straightforward substitution algorithm. All he did was take a piece of text he wanted to send to his commanders in the field and then shift all characters left or right by a certain number of positions. The number here is what we call his key.

So, if Ceasar chose a key of 3, all As in his message would become Ds. The character B would become an E, and so on.

If you knew the key, you could take his ciphertext and reverse the operation to get back to the cleartext.

The problem here is to transmit the actual number to use. Both parties need to know the key, or things never work out. You need a secure way of telling the other person which key to use so that they can decrypt your ciphertext into cleartext.

If you know the other person, sharing this key is not hard. You can walk up to them, give them the key on a piece of paper in a sealed envelope, and tell them to open it only when they receive the encrypted message. These days, however, that is a lot harder to do. Computers do not know the other computer they want to talk to. It is hard to exchange keys safely.

A possible solution for this is asymmetric encryption and decryption. This solution is complicated, but the basis is this: you have two keys. One key is used to encrypt the data and another is used to decrypt the data. One of the keys is kept private and the other is made public. The private key is yours and yours alone. You use it to encrypt a file. Anyone with the public key can then decrypt it. Of course, if you want the message to only be read by one other party, you can reverse this. You can request that the other party share their public key with you. You would then take that key and encrypt the message. Now, only the other party can decrypt it again with their private key.

Symmetric algorithms are much faster than asymmetric ones. However, they face the issue of key sharing. This issue is why most algorithms combine the two methods. They use an asymmetric algorithm to encrypt a key, which can be used for symmetric encryption. The key is relatively tiny, so encrypting and decrypting can be done reasonably quickly. Then that symmetric key is used to encrypt the complete message. This way, the symmetric key can be part of the message. It is encrypted itself, so only the intended recipient can decrypt the key and, thus, the rest of the message.

If this sounds complicated, I have some good news: the CLR has many classes to help us do this. They are pretty simple to use as well.

Symmetric encryption and decryption

Let's see whether we can encrypt and decrypt a simple message in C# code:

```
public static void EncryptFileSymmetric(string inputFile, string
outputFile, string key)
{
    using (FileStream inputFileStream = new
    FileStream(inputFile, FileMode.Open, FileAccess.Read))
    using (FileStream outputFileStream = new FileStream(outputFile,
    FileMode.Create, FileAccess.Write))
    {
        byte[] keyBytes = Encoding.UTF8.GetBytes(key);
        using (Aes aesAlg = Aes.Create())
        {
            aesAlg.Key = keyBytes;
            aesAlg.GenerateIV();
            byte[] ivBytes = aesAlg.IV;
            outputFileStream.Write(ivBytes, 0, ivBytes.Length);
            using (CryptoStream csEncrypt = new
                CryptoStream(outputFileStream,
                aesAlg.CreateEncryptor(),
                    CryptoStreamMode.Write))
            {
                byte[] buffer = new byte[4096];
                int bytesRead;
                while ((bytesRead =
                    inputFileStream.Read(buffer,
                    0, buffer.Length)) > 0)
                {
                    csEncrypt.Write(buffer, 0, bytesRead);
                }
            }
        }
    }
}
```

This method takes the names of an input file, an output file, and a key. Then, it opens the input file, reads its contents, encrypts it, and writes the cyphertext to the output file.

The way this works is pretty straightforward.

First, we will create the two streams. Then we will take the key and generate its byte array. The key must be a 128-bit, 192-bit, or 256-bit array. In other words, it has to be 16, 24, or 32 bytes long. The longer the key, the harder it is to hack. However, a long key also slows down the encryption and decryption processes. The choice is yours.

We will create an instance of the Aes class. **Advanced Encryption Standard** (**AES**) is widely considered a good and safe encryption algorithm. To make things even safer, the key we will use is augmented with an **Initialization Vector** (**IV**). You can think of this as something we add to the key to make it less readable. We will write that IV as the first thing in our file.

Then, we will create an instance of the CryptoStream class. This class helps us write encrypted data, as you can see in the ensuing code block. We will take arrays of bytes and write them to the CryptoStream class. Since we initialized the CryptoStream class with our AES class (well, the result of the call to CreateEncryptor of that class, to be more precise), it uses our key to encrypt data.

Decrypting is also simple. It works along the same principle: get the files from the key, read the IV from the file, then decrypt the rest and store it in a new file. That looks like this:

```
public static void DecryptFileSymmetric(string inputFile, string
outputFile, string key)
{
    using (FileStream inputFileStream = new FileStream(inputFile,
    FileMode.Open, FileAccess.Read))
    using (FileStream outputFileStream = new FileStream(outputFile,
    FileMode.Create, FileAccess.Write))
    {
        byte[] keyBytes = Encoding.UTF8.GetBytes(key);
        using (Aes aesAlg = Aes.Create())
        {
            byte[] ivBytes = new byte[aesAlg.BlockSize / 8];
            inputFileStream.Read(ivBytes, 0,
               ivBytes.Length);
            aesAlg.Key = keyBytes;
            aesAlg.IV = ivBytes;
            using (CryptoStream csDecrypt =
                   new CryptoStream(outputFileStream,
                   aesAlg.CreateDecryptor(), CryptoStreamMode.Write))
            {
                byte[] buffer = new byte[4096];
                int bytesRead;
                while ((bytesRead =
                inputFileStream.Read(buffer, 0, buffer.Length)) > 0)
                {
                    csDecrypt.Write(buffer, 0, bytesRead);
                }
            }
        }
    }
}
```

Instead of getting an `Encryptor` from the `CryptoStream`, we now get a `Decryptor`. The rest should be self-explanatory by now.

Asymmetric encryption and decryption

In the previous example, we generated a simple 128-bit, 192-bit, or 256-bit key. For instance, you can pass it a string such as `SystemSoftware42` and get the bytes. The same key is used for encrypting and decrypting.

For asymmetric encryption, keys are a bit harder to get. However, there are helper classes for that, so it's not hard to do in practice. Here is the code:

```
public static (string, string) GenerateKeyPair()
{
    using RSA rsa = RSA.Create();

    byte[] publicKeyBytes = rsa.ExportRSAPublicKey();
    byte[] privateKeyBytes = rsa.ExportRSAPrivateKey();

    string publicKeyBase64 = Convert.ToBase64String(publicKeyBytes);
    string privateKeyBase64 = Convert.ToBase64String(privateKeyBytes);

    return (publicKeyBase64, privateKeyBase64);
}
```

I used the RSA class to generate the key pair. The **Rivest, Shamir, and Adleman (RSA)** class was named after the three cryptographers who invented this algorithm.

We will create an instance of RSA by calling `Create()`. Then, we will call `ExportRSAPublicKey()` and `ExportRSAPrivateKey()` to get the generated keys out of it.

Since the keys are byte arrays, we will use `ToBase64String()` to make them more or less readable. That makes it easier to share the keys.

Now that we have a key pair, we can use it to encrypt a message. Of course, we can also decrypt it again. That code looks like this:

```
public static byte[] EncryptWithPublicKey(
    byte[] data,
    byte[] publicKeyBytes)
{
    using RSA rsa = RSA.Create();
    rsa.ImportRSAPublicKey(publicKeyBytes, out _);
    return rsa.Encrypt(data, RSAEncryptionPadding.OaepSHA256);
}
```

```
public static byte[] DecryptWithPrivateKey(
    byte[] encryptedData,
    byte[] privateKeyBytes)
{
    using RSA rsa = RSA.Create();
    rsa.ImportRSAPrivateKey(privateKeyBytes, out _);
    return rsa.Decrypt(encryptedData, RSAEncryptionPadding.
      OaepSHA256);
}
```

This code is simple enough. I only want to point out the last parameter in the `rsa.Encrypt()` and `rsa.Decrypt()` methods. We will use padding here to add extra data to the results (and we will remove it again when decrypting). This padding makes it harder for attackers to try to hack our message.

You can use the three methods combined like this:

```
(string, string) keyPair = Encryption.GenerateKeyPair();
keyPair.Item1.Dump();
keyPair.Item2.Dump();
var publicKey = Convert.FromBase64String(keyPair.Item1);
var privateKey = Convert.FromBase64String(keyPair.Item2);
string message = "This is the text that we, as System Programmers,
    want to secure.";

byte[] messageBytes = Encoding.UTF8.GetBytes(message);
byte[] encryptedBytes = Encryption.EncryptWithPublicKey(messageBytes,
    publicKey);
string encrypted = Encoding.UTF8.GetString(encryptedBytes);
encrypted.Dump(ConsoleColor.DarkYellow);
byte[] decryptedBytes = Encryption.
    DecryptWithPrivateKey(encryptedBytes, privateKey);
string decrypted = Encoding.UTF8.GetString(decryptedBytes);
decrypted.Dump(ConsoleColor.DarkYellow);
```

First, we will create a key pair. Our method returns that pair as strings so we can print them (I am again using our handy `Dump()` extension method). However, the keys need to be in a binary format, so I am reverting them to byte arrays.

I will define the message I want to encrypt, get the bytes of that message, and encrypt it. Then, I will print the encrypted message. If you do this, I think you will agree that it is hard to see the actual message. It is a mess of characters.

Then, we will reverse it by calling `DecryptWithPrivateKey()`. This method returns our string.

If we send the `Base64` version of our public key to someone and then transmit the encoded message, they can decode it with that public key. They would be sure that we sent that message; no one, other than us, can generate a message that can be decrypted by that public key but us. After all, private and public keys are a pair. You need one to encrypt so the second can decrypt.

Julius Caesar would be proud of us!

However, we have one more thing to talk about. We need to lose weight. Well, not us personally, but the payload in our files could benefit from this. Let's talk about file compression.

File compression

Files can get quite large. As we have already discussed, file IO and network IO take a long time, especially compared to CPUs' speeds. Anything we can do to minimize the time it takes to read from or write to IO could be worth it. This is even true if it means that we must make the CPU do a lot more. Of course, you need to measure this and see whether that also applies in your situation, but sometimes, sacrificing CPU time to speed up IO can make a huge difference.

One of the ways to do this is by limiting the amount of data we write in a file or a network stream. That can be done using compression.

In the CLR, you have a choice. You can use `DeflateStream` or `GZipStream` to do this. `GZipStream` uses `DeflateStream` internally, so `DeflateStream` is obviously faster. `GZipStream`, however, produces compressed files that can be read by external software. GZip is a standardized compression algorithm.

Compressing some data

Let's compress a string using `GZipStream`:

```
public async Task<byte[]> CompressString(string input,
    CancellationToken cancellationToken)
{
    // Get the payload as bytes
    byte[] data =
    System.Text.Encoding.UTF8.GetBytes(input);

    // Compress to a MemoryStream
    await using var ms = new MemoryStream();
    await using var compressionStream = new GZipStream(ms,
    CompressionMode.Compress);
    await compressionStream.WriteAsync(data, 0,
    data.Length, cancellationToken);
    await compressionStream.FlushAsync(cancellationToken);
    // Get the compressed data.
    byte[] compressedData = ms.ToArray();
    return compressedData;
}
```

Since compression and decompression might take a long time to finish, we really should use the `Async/Await` pattern here.

We will take some strings that we want to compress and pass them to the input variable. I use a `MemoryStream` in this example, but you could use any stream you like. Most real-world examples use a `FileStream` of some sort.

I will create an instance of the `GZipStream` class and give it the `MemoryStream` instance. This memory stream is where it writes the data. I will also tell the class that I want to compress data.

Then I just write data to it, flush the buffers, and get the bytes out of it.

That's it! I have just compressed a string.

Decompressing some data

Decompressing is just as easy. Look at the following code sample:

```
public async Task<string> DecompressString(byte[] input,
    CancellationToken cancellationToken)
{
    // Write the data into a memory stream
    await using var ms = new MemoryStream();
    await ms.WriteAsync(input, cancellationToken);
    await ms.FlushAsync(cancellationToken);
    ms.Position = 0;

    // Decompress
    await using var decompressionStream = new GZipStream(ms,
    CompressionMode.Decompress);
    await using var resultStream = new MemoryStream();
    await decompressionStream.CopyToAsync(resultStream,
    cancellationToken);

    // Convert to readable text.
    byte[] decompressedData = resultStream.ToArray();
    string decompressedString =
    System.Text.Encoding.UTF8.GetString(decompressedData);
    return decompressedString;
}
```

Here, I used two instances of the `MemoryStream` class. I used one as the source of the data and one as the destination of the uncompressed data. Again, please use any stream you want.

You can use these methods as follows:

```
var cts = new CancellationTokenSource();
var myText = "This is some text that I want to compress.";
var compression = new Compression();
var compressed = await compression.CompressString(myText, cts.Token);
var decompressed = await
    compression.DecompressString(compressed, cts.Token);
decompressed.Dump(ConsoleColor.DarkYellow);
```

That was not too hard, was it?

However, we are not done yet. The data that we want to store or read needs to be in a certain format. If you have a C# class with data in it, you cannot simply write that to a file. We need to translate that somehow. That's where serialization comes in.

Serialization – JSON and Binary

Earlier in this chapter, we saw how to write binary data to a stream. We can call all the `write` methods to write all sorts of types to a file. However, that can be pretty hard and also quite error-prone. You have to keep track of the format of the data. One simple mistake will make your files unreadable.

A better way would be to serialize your data in a format that the streams can understand. There are two ways to do that: **JSON** and **Binary**.

JSON is simple: most programming languages and platforms understand it. JSON has become the de facto standard for displaying a structure in text. In most places, JSON has replaced XML. JSON is smaller and more lightweight.

However, it can be even more lightweight. You can also serialize your data as a binary stream. That requires more coding but usually results in much smaller files and data streams. Again, that might be precisely what we, as system programmers, are looking for.

JSON serialization

To serialize an object to the JSON format, people used to turn to `NewtonSoft.JSON` by default. `NewtonSoft.JSON` was the library of choice. It was easy to use (and still is) and offered many features that people liked, such as custom converters. However, Microsoft has since released `System.Text.Json`, which does the same but is much more efficient. As system programmers, we care about memory efficiency and speed, so I will focus on that one here.

Before we can serialize something, we need something to serialize. The advantage of `System.Text.Json` is that I do not need to change my classes with attributes. The framework is smart enough to figure out what is needed and does that.

I will use the same data class we saw earlier in this chapter in these examples. However, to save you from flipping through pages, I present it to you here once again:

```
class MyData
{
    public int Id { get; set; }
    public double SomeMagicNumber { get; set; }
    public bool IsThisAGoodDataSet { get; set; }
    public MyFlags SomeFlags { get; set; }
    public string? SomeText { get; set; }
}
[Flags]
public enum MyFlags
{
    FlagOne,
    FlagTwo,
    FlagThree
}
```

If we want to serialize this to JSON to store it as text and later reread it, we will use the following code:

```
public string SerializeToJSon(MyData myData)
{
    var options = new JsonSerializerOptions
    {
        WriteIndented = true,
        PropertyNamingPolicy = JsonNamingPolicy.CamelCase
    };

    var result =
    System.Text.Json.JsonSerializer.Serialize(myData,options );

    return result;
}
```

The code presented here is pretty straightforward. We will take the `MyData` class and give it to the static `Serialize` method, `System.Text.Json.JsonSerializer`. There are a couple of overloads for this method. I will use the one that takes an instance of the `JsonSerializerOptions` class. This way, I can format the output. I will set the `WriteIdented` property to `True`. I would get the whole string on one line if I had not done that. Granted, that would have saved me a couple of newline and tab characters, but for readability, I prefer this.

We will get the following result if we run this with some values in our class:

```
{
  "id": 42,
  "someMagicNumber": 3.1415,
  "isThisAGoodDataSet": true,
  "someFlags": 2,
  "someText": "This is some text that we want to serialize"
}
```

Deserializing, thereby reversing the process, is just as simple:

```
public MyData DeserializeFromJSon(string json)
{
    var options = new JsonSerializerOptions
    {
        WriteIndented = true,
        PropertyNamingPolicy = JsonNamingPolicy.CamelCase
    };

    var result = System.Text.Json.JsonSerializer.
        Deserialize<MyData>(json, options);
    return result!;
}
```

As you can see, the process is simple enough.

Binary serialization

It is not the most efficient way to encode an object so you can store it in a file. It is relatively fast, but the actual data is also pretty large. Binary formatting is more work and the result is not human-readable, but it does lead to smaller files. That means that the time spent reading and writing data to a slow storage medium is significantly reduced. Of course, the tradeoff is that the CPU gets a bit busier, but that might be worth it. As always, measure and then decide whether this applies to your situation.

In .NET Framework, before the days of .NET Core and .NET, we had a class named `BinaryFormatter`. That class, however, is now marked as obsolete. There are serious security concerns associated with that class, so Microsoft decided to get rid of it.

There are third-party packages you can use to achieve the same goal. However, if you do not want to use those, you can always do it yourself. We already discussed the `BinaryWriter` class and its methods. There is nothing wrong with using that class, but the downside is that you must write all the code, writing and reading each field or property. The `BinaryFormatter` class did that. That was quite handy, to be honest.

The best package these days to achieve the same thing is `protobuf-net`. This package is available on NuGet, making it easy to install in your project. If you want to use `protobuf-net`, you must annotate your classes before you can serialize them. Using our `MyData` class again, it would look like this:

```
[ProtoContract]
public class MyData
{
    [ProtoMember(1)]
    public int Id { get; set; }
    [ProtoMember(2)]
    public double SomeMagicNumber { get; set; }
    [ProtoMember(3)]
    public bool IsThisAGoodDataSet { get; set; }
    [ProtoMember(4)]
    public MyFlags SomeFlags { get; set; }
    [ProtoMember(5)]
    public string? SomeText { get; set; }
}
```

We have decorated the class with the `ProtoContract` attribute. Then, we decorated the properties with the `ProtoMember` attribute. This attribute can have associated data, but the first one is mandatory. This is the tag and it defines where the field is stored in the file. There is no hard rule on the numbering or the order aside from one: you cannot start with 0. Yes. Indeed. I heard you gasp there. This is the only example I can think of in programming where starting with 0 is forbidden. If you want to start with 42, you can do that. However, the number has to be a positive integer, and 0 is not a positive integer.

Serializing and deserializing are simple. You have to ensure that the data is available in a memory stream or can be written to a memory stream, but that is the only slightly complicated thing. This is the code:

```
public async Task<byte[]> SerializeToBinary(MyData myData)
{
    await using var stream = new MemoryStream();
    ProtoBuf.Serializer.Serialize(stream, myData);
    return stream.ToArray();
}

public async Task<MyData> DeserializeFromBinary(byte[] payLoad)
{
    await using var stream = new MemoryStream(payLoad);
    var myData =
        ProtoBuf.Serializer.Deserialize<MyData>(stream);
    return myData;
}
```

That is it. I promised you that it would be simple, didn't I?

If I take the same data as in the JSON serialization and compare the sizes, I can see that the binary version is much smaller. Even if I use the option not to write intended files, thus saving on newlines and tabs, the JSON version is 131 bytes. In comparison, the binary version is only 60 bytes long. That is a big difference!

Next steps

I/O is essential for all software. No software runs in isolation, especially software written for systems. After all, these applications do not have a traditional user interface; they are meant to be used by other software. The only way to communicate with that software is by exchanging data in one way or another.

This chapter has looked at ways to serialize and deserialize data to and from storage. We saw that JSON is simple and produces human-readable data. However, the data can be pretty big. In contrast, the binary version results in much smaller data, but that data is not human-readable anymore. Additionally, it requires a third-party package. What is the best solution? That depends on your use cases! It doesn't matter whether you use files or a network connection; they are all approaches of I/O. In this chapter, you saw how to do that efficiently, quickly, and safely.

However, one way that is much more efficient for systems software to communicate is through direct communication over **Interprocess Communications** (**IPC**). IPC is a perfect way for systems software to establish an interface layer that other software can talk to or listen to. It is also the topic of the next chapter.

6
The One Where Processes Whisper

Interprocess Communication (IPC)

In the previous chapter, we talked about input/output. Most of our attention was on files. Files are one of the first things that spring to mind when people think about sharing data with other systems. Another often-used method is networking. However, there are other ways systems can communicate with one another. Files are great if you want to keep data around for a more extended time. Network connections are an excellent way to connect more directly between systems on different machines. But files and networking are more about the underlying technology to transmit data. We also must decide how to connect to systems using those methods. That is what **interprocess communication** (**IPC**) in short, is all about. How can we have two systems talk to each other?

In this chapter, we will cover the following topics:

- What is IPC?
- What considerations do we have to worry about when designing IPC?
- Windows Messages – a Windows-native way of messaging
- Pipes – both named and anonymous
- Sockets – a network-based messaging system
- Shared memory – a quick and simple local messaging system
- **Remote procedure call** (**RPC**) – controlling other machines
- **Google remote procedure call** (**gRPC**) – the newest kid on the block

Welcome to the beautiful world of whispering systems!

Technical requirements

You will find all the code in this chapter in the following link: `https://github.com/PacktPublishing/Systems-Programming-with-C-Sharp-and-.NET/tree/main/SystemsProgrammingWithCSharpAndNet/Chapter06`.

Overview of IPC and its importance in modern computing

Most software has a user interface. After all, that is how the user should interact with the application. The user clicks buttons, enters text, and reads the response on the screen. The screen is how data, the user, and the application exchange data and instructions.

People do not use systems software. Other software does. So, it needs a different way to interact. I suppose it would technically be possible to write a regular user interface and use tricks to read or enter data, but that is not really efficient.

Applications communicate differently when they are talking amongst themselves. They have their own language and their own protocols. This is what IPC is all about – the communication between processes.

Given the nature of systems, we must consider several key points when designing the interface between systems. We make different choices when designing this interface than if we were designing a user interface meant for people. There are many factors to consider here. Let's go through them.

- **Choose your language wisely:** Systems can use many different ways to talk to one another, and, just like human conversations, it helps tremendously if all parties involved speak the same language. This chapter describes how we can make the systems talk to each other, but there are many more. Some ways are better suited for a particular environment or use case than others, so you must think it through. Do not pick the one you feel most comfortable with because you know that solution. Think of all the use case scenarios and then pick the proper protocol.

- **Security**: Security is a huge topic, especially in systems programming. We are dealing with data, and the systems are hidden deep in our computers. Most people do not know that multiple processes are running on their machines, so they are not very likely to inspect them and assess their level of security.

- **Data format and serialization**: You must consider the best way to transform your data as it moves from one system to another. The data must be part of a package, envelope, or other transmitting method. There are many different formats and ways to serialize, but which one you choose depends on many factors. For instance, if you use a direct memory connection between two 64-bit processes on the same Windows machine, you can use a very efficient, lightweight binary representation. However, suppose you have to talk to a machine running a different operating system on the other side of the globe. In that case, you must devise a serialization mechanism both systems understand.

- **Error handling and robustness**: Software can go wrong. We all know that. The problems with bugs and availability scale up exponentially if you are talking about multiple independent systems. So, you must be mindful of that. You also have to consider what your requirements are. Do you need guaranteed delivery? Do you need error recovery? Those two things might be handy, but they come with a price. Nothing comes for free, after all. You need to think about those scenarios. Usually, you must devise a solution you can get away with and not go overboard on error correction schemes.

- **Performance and scalability**: Transferring blocks of memory inside a process is pretty quick. Moving data between processes can be really slow or even unimaginably slow. Moving a block of bits to another machine over a **Transmission Control Protocol** (**TCP**) connection is thousands of times slower than doing that in memory. Writing data to a disk, even a speedy SSD, is even slower than that.

- That means you must ensure optimal IO strategy for those use cases. Setting up a connection or creating a file is slow, but you have to do that only once for each transfer. Once you have that, you can write the data. If you have lots of tiny packets, you might want to bundle them so you only have to initiate it once. As we have stated before, it might be a good idea to compress data before transmitting. Yes, compression takes CPU cycles, but it might be worth it since transferring that data to another system is orders of magnitude slower.

- **Synchronization and deadlocks**: Once your data leaves your system, you no longer know what is happening to it. Other processes might also be asking for the recipient's attention, or the recipient might be out of data. You have to be very careful to ensure the data is synchronized. Or not. It depends on your use case, of course. Also, deadlocks can occur. You might wait for an operation to finish on the recipient's side, but if that one waits for your system, you have a problem. Be mindful of those problem areas.

- **Documentation and maintainability**: Sharing data with other systems means sharing your data structures with other developers. Do not forget that "other developers" could be yourself in six months when you look at what you did and wonder what you were thinking. Documenting your work, your thoughts, and the structures of your data saves you and your peers a lot of headaches further down the road. Do yourself a favor and document your data and its structure, what you did to satisfy all the constraints, and your assumptions. That makes your code much more maintainable. Of course, this applies to data-sharing scenarios and all software development, but it is so much more important when you need to share data with other systems. Do not skip on this!

- **Platform and environment constraints**: You might not always be aware of the kind of hardware your data will be shared with. If you do not know this, you must consider all available options. Assume the worst and plan for that. For instance, if you transmit data packets of a couple of gigabytes, encrypted and wrapped in a compression algorithm, you might get complaints that the recipient is a very low-end IOT device with limited memory and CPU power.

Not all platforms support all of the strategies I outline in this chapter. For instance, Windows Messages, which we discuss next, is only available on Windows. The name sort of gives it away, doesn't it? Be aware of the platform and environment constraints and design your data sharing around those.

So, now that you know the considerations to take when choosing a communication method, let's look at what methods we have available. We start with a classic: Windows Messages.

Windows Messages

Windows Messages are the oldest type of IPC in Windows. They may not be the best choice when writing systems software, but they can be helpful. More importantly, they are extremely fast and lightweight. However, as the name suggests, they are a Windows-only feature.

Messages work with windows. I do not mean the operating system; I am talking about the screens on your monitor. Almost everything on the GUI in Windows is a window. The windows obviously are, but so are buttons, edit boxes, text boxes, sliders, and so on. The operating system communicates with your application by sending messages to a window. Your application has at least one main window, which then distributes the message to the *subwindows* or handles the messages for those subwindows. However, each window can have its own message-handling logic.

Since messages work with graphical screen elements, such as buttons, labels, and list boxes, you might think they cannot be used on console applications or Windows services. That is technically correct, but we can get around that. We can create a hidden window that can receive the messages.

A message is straightforward. It is nothing but a structure containing four numeric parameters. This is what the parameters are and what they are used for.

Name	Type / C# Type	Description
hWnd	HWND / IntPtr	The unique handle of the window that is to receive the message
Msg	UINT / uint	The ID of the message
wParam	WPARAM / IntPtr	An additional parameter, or pointer to a data structure
lParam	LPARAM / IntPtr	An additional parameter, or pointer to a data structure

Table 6.1: Parameters in a Windows Message

That is all that a message has. The wParam and lParam pointers point to some memory containing the payload. They can also be just a number if that is all you want to send. In 16-bit Windows, wParam was 16 bits, and lParam was 32. In 32-bit versions of Windows, they are both 32-bit long, and in 64-bit versions, they are both 64-bit long. So, there is no real difference between wParam and lParam anymore regarding length.

These messages are all communications from the operating system to your application. If the user moves the mouse over your window, you get notified. Well, in the case of the mouse movement, you get hundreds of notifications. If the user presses a key, you get a message. If the user resizes the window, you get another message. Anything that happens on the operating system that might be interesting for your application is sent to you as a message. There are hundreds, if not thousands, of messages sent to your application all the time. Your application is required to listen to those messages. We shall see how that works shortly.

The message identifier can be predefined; it can be a number you choose, or the operating system can generate it.

Let me explain what I mean by that.

If Windows sends a message, it is one of the predefined ones. For instance, if the mouse has moved, you get the `WM_MOUSEMOVE` message. `WM_MOUSEMOVE` is a constant with the `0x0200` value. `wParam` contains information about the state of the mouse buttons and keys, such as the *Ctrl* key on your keyboard. You can decode these flags to see whether a button is pressed while the mouse moves. `lParam` contains both the *X* and the *Y* position of the mouse relative to the upper-left corner of the window that receives the message (the first half of `lParam` contains the *Y* coordinate, and the second half contains the *X* coordinate).

An interesting message is `WM_CLOSE`. This has the `0x0010` value. If a window receives that message, the user wants to close it. If that happens on your main window, the application ends.

You can also define your own message. There is a constant called `WM_USER` (with a value of `0x0400`). You can freely use any of the values between `WM_USER` and `0x7FFF` in your application to define your message. One caveat: you can only use them if you send those messages to your application's other windows. You cannot use them to communicate with other applications. The reason is simple: you have no idea who uses those values outside your system.

If you want to send messages to other applications, you need to register that with Windows. You can call an API to reserve a unique and reserved number as long as the computer stays on. If two applications reserve the same message name, they get the same ID. This is something you can use to communicate between processes, and that is precisely what we will be doing now.

A sample

To work with messages, we need to use a lot of Win32 APIs. The logic is not complex, but this sample requires a lot of setup.

We can break it down as follows:

1. **Register a Window class**: Since the operating system sends all messages to a window, we must create a window first. But before you can do that, you need to create a definition of that window. That is the `Window` class. It's just like object-oriented programming: you define a class first and then create instances. Windows are just like that.

2. **Define the message loop method**: This method gets called as soon as a message is available.
3. **Create the window**: As soon as that happens, the messages start flowing in.
4. **In the message loop, see whether there is a message available**: If that message happens to be `WM_CLOSE`, close the application. If you want to handle the message, do so. If not, pass it on to the default handler that all apps get.

That is all there is to it.

The source code on the GitHub repository for this book contains a sample. I have not included it here since the sample requires a lot of boilerplate code that takes up several pages. I decided to leave it out of this chapter since Windows Messages are not used except for certain specialized cases. However, if you are interested, just look at the sample code. With the preceding explanation, you can follow along just nicely.

Now you know how Windows Messages work, we can take the next step and look into other means. We begin simple enough: pipes.

Working with pipes for local IPC

Pipes originally came from Unix but have also found their way to other platforms. A pipe is like a direct connection between two systems. It is very lightweight and easy to set up. You can use them to communicate between processes on the same machine and between machines across a network. Theoretically, you can communicate between Linux and Windows using pipes. I said theoretically because since the implementation of the pipes on both platforms is so different, you have to jump through many loops to get that working. In fact, the work you must do to get it working is so intensive that you might as well use other ways, such as sockets, to achieve that same result. That will be much easier to pull off.

There are two types of pipes: **named pipe** and **anonymous pipe**. The named pipe is the simplest of them.

Named pipes

Named pipes are a great solution if you want to communicate from one process to another on the same machine. Communicating over a network is not complex but requires more thought concerning security and access rights.

In .NET, you can use the `NamedPipeServerStream` and `NamedPipeClientStream` classes to get this working.

The code is straightforward. For example, let us look at a server waiting for a connection. We also added a client that connects to that server. As soon as the connection is established, the server sends a message to the client, which will be displayed on the screen.

Here is the server code:

```
using System.IO.Pipes;

"Starting the server".Dump(ConsoleColor.Cyan);
await using var server = new
    NamedPipeServerStream("SystemsProgrammersPipe");
"Waiting for connection".Dump(ConsoleColor.Cyan);
await server.WaitForConnectionAsync();
await using var writer = new StreamWriter(server);
writer.AutoFlush = true;
writer.WriteLine("Hello from the server!");
```

Again, I am using my `Dump()` extension method here to colorize the messages on the screen quickly.

First, I create an instance of `NamedPipeServerStream`. As a parameter, I give it a unique name. If I use a name that is already registered, I get access to that other named pipe. The names are unique on your machine but are gone once `NamedPipeServerStream` is disposed of.

Then, we wait for a connection. When a client connects, we create `StreamWriter`, give it the named pipe server stream, and write the data to the stream.

We use `AutoFlush` on the writer: we don't want data hanging around.

Let's look at the client code:

```
using System.IO.Pipes;
await using var client = new NamedPipeClientStream(".",
    "SystemsProgrammersPipe");
"Connecting to the server".Dump(ConsoleColor.Yellow);
await client.ConnectAsync();
using var reader = new StreamReader(client);
string? message = await reader.ReadLineAsync();
message.Dump(ConsoleColor.Yellow);
```

This code should look familiar. We create an instance of `NamedPipeClientStream` (instead of a server) and give it two parameters. The first is the name of the computer on the network (in our case, our own computer as specified by the dot). The second parameter is the name of the pipe. Obviously, this should be the same as we used for the server stream.

We connect the client to the pipe, create an instance of `StreamReader` with that client, and read the data. Lastly, we display the data coming from the server.

Anonymous pipes

Anonymous pipes work more or less the same way as named pipes do. They provide a lightweight way of connecting processes to each other. However, there are differences between the named pipes and the anonymous pipes. The following table highlights the most important ones:

Feature	Named pipes	Anonymous pipes
Identification	Named. You can find them using the name.	Unnamed. You have to know the runtime handle to connect.
Communication	Both local and networked.	Only local.
Peers	Multiple clients per server. Can be set up to handle bidirectional conversations.	One-on-one only. Also, one way only
Complexity	More complex. Allows for asynchronous communications, also able to do fire-and-forget scenarios.	More simple. Straightforward one-way parent-child communication.
Security	Supports ACL to enable secure communications.	No security features are available.
Speed	Slower due to more control.	Fast. Almost no overhead.

Table 6.2: Comparison of features between named pipes and anonymous pipes.

The code to set up an anonymous pipe is actually quite simple. Let's start with the server code:

```
using System.IO.Pipes;
await using var pipeServer = new
    AnonymousPipeServerStream(PipeDirection.Out, HandleInheritability.
    Inheritable);
$"The pipe handle is: {pipeServer.GetClientHandleAsString()}".
    Dump(ConsoleColor.Cyan);

pipeServer.DisposeLocalCopyOfClientHandle();
await using var sw = new StreamWriter(pipeServer);
sw.AutoFlush = true;
sw.WriteLine("From server");
pipeServer.WaitForPipeDrain();
```

Let me walk you through this.

First, I create an instance of `AnonymousPipeServerStream`. This class handles all the setting up of the communication. We can tell that it can either send or receive code. We cannot use the supplied `PipeDirection.InOut` enum: that will throw an exception. Remember: anonymous pipes are one-way.

We need to make sure the handle can be inherited as well. This is because the client needs to "inherit" this handle. After all, this is the only way we can identify the pipe. There is no name; it is anonymous!

We call `GetClientHandleAsString` so we know what to use on the client side.

When you create `AnonymousPipeServerStream`, it automatically creates a client as well. This can be handy if you want to communicate inside your process. However, if another process needs to talk to this server, you have a problem. Anonymous pipes are single-connection only. The call to `DisposeLocalCopyOfClientHandle` removes the local client, so we have room for another client.

Then, we create a stream, give it the pipe, and write to it.

Finally, we call `WaitForPipeDrain`, a blocking call that only continues if the client has read all the data.

The client is even more simple:

```
"Enter the pipeHandle".Dump(ConsoleColor.Yellow);
var pipeHandle = Console.ReadLine();
using var pipeClient = new AnonymousPipeClientStream(PipeDirection.In, 
pipeHandle);
using var sr = new StreamReader(pipeClient);
while (sr.ReadLine() is { } temp)
    temp?.Dump(ConsoleColor.Yellow);
```

We read the handle from the console first. This is the output from our server, so we have that available. Then, we create the client by creating an instance of `AnonymousPipeClientStream`, telling it to be ready for incoming data, and giving it the handle.

Then, we create `stream` and read from it. That's it!

There is one big caveat. Suppose you write these two console applications and you run them. In that case, you see that as soon as you try to create an instance of that `AnonymousPipeClientStream`, you get an `InvalidHandle` exception. The reason is that Windows separates the processes, ensuring security is as high as possible. If you run two processes, they cannot reach each other's handles. So, it cannot access the pipe, which means you cannot communicate. I am afraid there is nothing we can do about that. If you think about it, it does make sense, though. You can only have one-on-one communications. So, if multiple console apps connect to the server, how do you ensure this one-on-one behavior? The answer is: you cannot.

If you want separate console apps, you should use named pipes instead.

However, if you want to use the example I supplied, you can ensure the client and the server run in the same address space. You do this by launching the client from the server. That looks like this:

```
Process pipeClient = new Process();
pipeClient.StartInfo.FileName = @"pipeClient.exe";
```

```
// Pass the client process a handle to the server.
pipeClient.StartInfo.Arguments =
    pipeServer.GetClientHandleAsString();
pipeClient.StartInfo.UseShellExecute = false;
pipeClient.Start();
```

Do not forget to change the client to get the handle from the `args` parameter given to the `Main` method instead of getting it from the user through the console.

The secret here is the line where we set `UseShellExecute` to `False`. If it is `True`, the client starts in another shell, thus isolating it from the server. By setting this to `False`, we prevent that and can access the handle and, consequently, the pipe.

If they fit your scenario, anonymous pipes are a great addition to your communications toolbelt. They are fast and lightweight, just the sort of thing we love as systems programmers. However, there are other ways to communicate that might even be better, although they are not as simple. Let's talk about sockets…

Using sockets to establish network-based IPC

Sockets are awesome. They are a bit like the Swiss Army knife for communications. The downsides of pipes and Windows messages are gone when you move to sockets. Of course, nothing comes for free, so be prepared to spend a lot of time thinking about error handling and memory management. Still, once you get the idea, sockets are not hard to use.

Sockets are endpoints of a connection over a network between two systems. Of course, the systems can live on the same machine, but they can also be at different ends of the world. Thanks to all the hard work people have done building networks since the 1960s, we can now reach all sorts of machines worldwide.

Networking 101

Computer networks have been around for a long time. However, each supplier had its own way of making machines talk to one another. Over time, standards emerged. As it goes with standards, there were many to choose from. These days, we have more or less standardized on setting up a network, so you no longer have to worry about that.

But before we dive into the specifics, we need to talk about **Open Systems Interconnection (OSI)** first.

OSI is a layered architecture where you can describe how a network works. Each layer builds on top of the previous one (with the apparent exception of the first layer).

There are seven layers, and this is what they describe:

- **Level 1 – Physical**: This is what describes the hardware. For example, what a cable looks like, how the switches are working, the electrical voltages that are applied, and so on.
- **Level 2 – Data Link**: This describes how systems connect over the physical layers. Here, we describe how ethernet or Wi-Fi works. The MAC addresses (unique number per network device) are defined here.
- **Level 3 – Network**: This one is all about routing and addressing. There are several protocols defined on level 3, such as **Internet Control Message Protocol** (**ICMP**), which is used for network diagnostics and error reporting, **Address Resolution Protocol** (**ARP**), used for address resolution, Bluetooth, and, of course, **Internet Protocol** (**IP**), both v4 and v6.
- **Level 4 – Transport**: This layer is responsible for end-to-end communication and reliability. TCP and **User Datagram Protocol** (**UDP**), the topics of this chapter, live in this layer.
- **Level 5 – Session**: this manages the sessions between applications.
- **Level 6 – Presentation**: This layer ensures the data is presented in a format other systems can understand.
- **Level 7 – Application**: here are the applications that use the network.

The hardware and the operating system handle levels 1 through 4. Levels 5 through 7 are ours to take care of.

Almost all systems use TCP as a transport layer, but sometimes people choose UDP. I start by explaining TCP and how to use it, and I move to UDP at the end of this part. IP is more or less a given. We could choose other network-level protocols, but that would make life unnecessarily complicated.

Setting up the session (level 5) is where we write the code to set up the connection on the client or server. The presentation, level 6, is about how we package the data: how we serialize, what encoding to use, and so on. We have covered that already extensively. Level 7 is just our app; I leave that one to you.

So, let's write some level 5 code!

A TCP-based chat app

The "hello-world" application for networking is a chat app. That sort of app allows us to investigate how systems can connect and exchange data without dealing with technicalities about what kind of data is passed between them. The type of data is part of the application, which we learned is level 7 in the OSI model. We do not care about that here. Level 6 is presentation, but for a simple chat application, we can get away with something straightforward: we take a string and encode that in UTF8 bytes (and back again, of course). Since the OS takes care of levels 1 up to 3, we only have to deal with 4 and 5.

Let's make it happen.

The One Where Processes Whisper

I want to use TCP here, which is an excellent protocol that gives us reliability and guarantees the order in which the data arrives. It is also effortless to set up.

The server looks like this:

```
01: using System.Net;
02: using System.Net.Sockets;
03: using System.Text;
04:
05: "Server is starting up.".Dump();
06:
07: var server = new TcpListener(IPAddress.Loopback, 8080);
08: server.Start();
09:
10: "Waiting for a connection.".Dump();
11:
12: var client = await server.AcceptTcpClientAsync();
13: "Client connected".Dump();
14:
15: var stream = client.GetStream();
16: while (true)
17: {
18:     var buffer = new byte[1024];
19:     var bytes = await stream.ReadAsync(buffer, 0, buffer.Length);
20:     var message = Encoding.UTF8.GetString(buffer, 0, bytes);
21:     $"Received message: {message}".Dump();
22:
23:     if (message.ToLower() == "bye")
24:         break;
25:
26:     "Say something back".Dump();
27:     var response = Console.ReadLine();
28:     var responseBytes = Encoding.UTF8.GetBytes(response);
29:     await stream.WriteAsync(responseBytes, 0, responseBytes.
            Length);
30:
31:     if (response.ToLower() == "bye")
32:         break;
33: }
34:
35: client.Close();
36: server.Stop();
37: "Connection closed.".Dump();
```

Since so much is happening, I decided to use line numbers here. That makes it a bit easier to refer to what I am explaining.

In line 7, we create a new instance of the `TcpListener` class. This class handles all the details about communications, but it needs some information from us about that. We give the constructor two parameters that tell it all it needs to know. The first is the address we use. The address is the unique identifier for a network adapter, such as your ethernet or Wi-Fi adapter. This IP address is part of level 3, the network level of the OSI model. It is part of the IP specifications. However, multiple applications can simultaneously use a network adapter in a computer. We can specify a port number to ensure all the applications get the data they need and send it to the correct application on the other end of the line. This more or less arbitrary number decides what application connected to that IP address gets the data. This port number is part of level 4 of the OSI model. I said the number is more or less arbitrary. Technically, you can choose whatever number you desire, but there are conventions about these numbers. Since the port decides what application gets or sends the data, standards help ensure we all use the same ports for the same applications. Web servers, for instance, listen to port 80 unless they use the secure HTTPS protocol. That one uses port 443. There are a lot of "reserved" numbers, but technically, nothing stops you from using port 80 for your chat application. I would not recommend doing so, though: it confuses other people.

I want to ensure our chat server listens on port 8080, a "free to use" number.

I have used the word "listening" a few times here. Listening means that the application waits for another process, either on our machine or on an external one, to connect. Compare it to waiting for the phone to ring: you are listening for your ringtone and ready to pick it up if it goes.

Since your machine can have multiple network adapters, you must specify which one you want to listen to. In this case, I chose a fixed IP address, `IPAddress.Loopback`, which translates to the `127.0.0.1` IPv4 address. This address is the local machine, not attached to any actual adapter. In other words, we only listen to connections from the same physical machine.

Line 8 is straightforward: we start the server. With the call to `AcceptTcpClienAsync` in line 14, we tell the server to accept any incoming connection.

Multiple clients can connect to the same server at the same time. The client here is what represents the connected client. We only expect one client, so we do not have to deal with sessions. Remember: session management is level 5 of the OSI model. We assume one and only one client, and we store that in the variable client. The type of client is `TcpClient`, in case you were wondering.

This call is blocking, and only continues when a client is connected, something we tell the user with the message on line 15.

As soon as we have established a connection, we open a stream to access the client's data or to enable us to send data to that client. This stream, of the `NetworkStream` type, is bidirectional. We store that stream in the variable stream in line 17.

Data comes in binary. Therefore, we use `ReadAsync` to read a buffer of data. I assume that no incoming data exceeds 1,024 bytes. You probably cannot make that assumption in a real-world application, so you must keep reading until you have all the data. Here, we store that data in a byte array of 1,024 bytes long (lines 20 and 21) and convert that to a UTF8 string (lines 22). This is how our data is presented, which is level 6 of the OSI model. As soon as we have that string, we display it. If the string is "bye" we take it that the client wants to disconnect. Otherwise, we allow the user on the server end to enter a response and send that string to the client after converting it to another byte array. We use the same stream here.

If the stream contains no more data or someone uses the word "bye" in the conversation, we close the connection (line 37) and stop listening (line 38).

The client is very similar in code. Here it is:

```
01: using System.Net.Sockets;
02: using System.Text;
03:
04: "Client is starting up.".Dump(ConsoleColor.Yellow);
05:
06: var client = new TcpClient("127.0.0.1", 8080);
07: "Connected to the server. Let's chat!".Dump(ConsoleColor.Yellow);
08: var stream = client.GetStream();
09:
10: while (true)
11: {
12:     "Say something".Dump(ConsoleColor.Yellow);
13:     var message = Console.ReadLine();
14:     var data = Encoding.UTF8.GetBytes(message);
15:     await stream.WriteAsync(data, 0, data.Length);
16:     if (message.ToLower() == "bye")
17:         break;
18:
19:     var buffer = new byte[1024];
20:     var bytesRead = await stream.ReadAsync(buffer, 0, buffer.Length);
21:     var response = Encoding.UTF8.GetString(buffer, 0, bytesRead);
22:     $"Server says: {response}".Dump(ConsoleColor.Yellow);
23:     if (response.ToLower() == "bye")
24:         break;
25: }
26:
27: client.Close();
28: "Connection closed.".Dump(ConsoleColor.Yellow);
```

In line 6, we create a new instance of the `TcpClient` class. Again, we have to give it an IP address and a port. This time, we have to use an actual number. We use `127.0.0.1`, so we are looking for a server on the same machine. The port is again `8080`; otherwise, our server never sees any connection coming in.

This call is again blocking, so it will not continue until a connection has been made. We can access the stream once we have a connection, as in line 8. This stream is, once again, of the `NetworkStream` type, so we have a bidirectional connection.

We do the same thing as we did for the server. We assume a message size of 1,024 bytes or less. We convert strings to and from byte arrays using UTF8 as encoding. We use the word "bye" to signal a desire to stop talking, and we use `client.Close()` to finalize the connection.

As you can see, the code is very similar to the server's. We simplified many things here: we do not consider having multiple clients connecting to one server. We make many assumptions about the message size and have to fall back or retry mechanisms in case things go wrong. When working with connections across machines, things go wrong often, so you must be aware of that and code accordingly. However, since that has nothing to do with the actual networking code, as I have shown you here, I can safely leave that to you to figure out.

UDP

TCP is a great protocol, but it is not the only one. **UDP** is more straightforward and lighter. Of course, that comes with disadvantages as well. I outline the differences between the two protocols in the following table:

Consideration	TCP	UDP
Main objective	Reliability	Speed
Ordering	Order guaranteed	No guarantee about the order of messages
Handshaking	Yes	No
Error Checking	Yes	No
Congestion control	Yes	No
Use case	Web browsing, chatting, file transfer, email	Video streaming, online gaming, VOIP

Table 6.3: TCP and UDP compared

TCP is reliable. Message almost always arrives. When things go wrong, TCP tries to resend the data until it has been delivered. UDP doesn't care about that. It just tries to get the data out there as fast as possible.

TCP ensures that messages arrive in the same order as they have been sent. UDP, however, does not: messages could arrive at the destination in a different order than how they left the origin.

TCP makes sure the other end is ready to communicate. UDP just starts sending data.

TCP checks the data to see whether errors have occurred during transmission and can even fix some. UDP does not care: as long as the data is sent, it is happy with it.

If the network gets congested, TCP can slow down transmission to help alleviate that. UDP dumps data as fast as possible, regardless of network conditions.

TCP is best used when you must have a reliable, error-free way of transmitting data. For instance, with chat, the message must come across as intended, in the correct order. UDP, however, is all about speed. Video streaming comes to mind: if part of the data stream is lost sometimes, it is not a big deal. Slow streams, however, are killing the experience.

UDP is not often used, but it can be a valuable tool in your belt.

Using shared memory to exchange data between processes

So far, we have been sending messages to other processes on the same computer. With named pipes and sockets, we could have used other machines as well. That's the beauty of those protocols: they are network agnostic. However, if you are sure you want to stay on the same machine, using pipes or sockets can be a burden. These methods are not the fastest way to communicate. In those cases, you might be better off using **shared memory**.

Shared memory is effortless to set up. And yes, of course, that comes with downsides. There is almost no way to secure the data or to prevent collisions. However, it is fast; really, really fast. So, let's look at a sample.

First, we look at how to write data to shared memory:

```
using System.IO.MemoryMappedFiles;
"Ready to write data to share memory.\nPress Enter to do
    so.".Dump(ConsoleColor.Cyan);
Console.ReadLine();
using var mmf = MemoryMappedFile.CreateNew("SharedData", 1024);
// Create a view accessor to write data
using MemoryMappedViewAccessor accessor = mmf.CreateViewAccessor();
byte[] data = System.Text.Encoding.UTF8.GetBytes("Hello from Process
    1");
accessor.WriteArray(0, data, 0, data.Length);

"Data written to shared memory. Press any key to
    exit.".Dump(ConsoleColor.Cyan);
Console.ReadKey();
```

Shared memory is like having a file that only exists in memory. It's a block reserved in memory. It has a name you can use to identify it. Again, it is just like a file. Here, we create a new instance of the `MemoryMappedFile` class, giving it a name and a size. (in our case, 1,024 bytes). If you want to use that file, you must get `MemoryMappedViewAccessor`. You can get that by calling `CreateViewAccessor` on the `MemoryMappedFile` instance.

You can then read and write data to and from that accessor.

Reading from that shared file is just as easy. Here is the code:

```
using System.IO.MemoryMappedFiles;
"Wait for the server to finish. \nPress Enter to read the shared
    data.".Dump(ConsoleColor.Yellow);
Console.ReadLine();
using var mmf = MemoryMappedFile.OpenExisting("SharedData");
// Create a view accessor to read data
using MemoryMappedViewAccessor accessor = mmf.CreateViewAccessor();
byte[] data = new byte[1024];
accessor.ReadArray(0, data, 0, data.Length);
$"Received message: {System.Text.Encoding.UTF8.GetString(data)}".
    Dump(ConsoleColor.Yellow);
```

We use almost the same code as the writer. However, instead of creating a new file in memory, we open an existing one. We do not have to specify the size but must know the name.

Once we have that file, we can use the same code to get an accessor. With that, we can read the data and display it. Simple, isn't it?

Again, this is a speedy way to share data between processes on the same machine. However, the downsides are something to be aware of. For instance, any process that knows the name of the shared memory block can access it. There is no security whatsoever. Of course, you can circumvent that by using encryption.

Another downside is that there is no built-in mechanism to notify processes of new or changed data. You have to use things such as semaphores and mutexes to do that. You can set up `FileSystemWatcher` with actual files to get notified, but that is not available for these shared files in memory.

Another potential downside is that it is Windows only. That might limit your options for deployment later on.

But all in all, shared memory is a great way to quickly share large amounts of data across processes on the same Windows machine. Use it to your advantage!

Overview of RPCs and how to use them for IPC

So far, we have looked at ways we can share data. In most cases, developers use this to do just data: send a payload from one system to another. However, the payload can also be something else. They can be commands to instruct a piece of software to do something. Instead of storing, transforming, and using data in systems, we can tell other systems to perform actions. In that case, we talk about RPC.

To control a system from the outside, establish a communication line, ensure your security is in order, and define a protocol.

There are many ways to do this. In the old days, we used to have SOAP, DCOM, WCF, and other techniques to do so.

> **RESTFul services versus RPC**
>
> You could consider RESTFul services to be some kind of RPC. However, they are not the same, and I do not want to go into RESTful services here. There are many similarities, but the basic idea behind RESTful services is that they are all about resources. Calls to web services are usually used to retrieve data from a server. Technically, you could set up RESTful services to accept commands only, in which way they are RPC. It's like calling a calzone a pizza. Technically, that is correct, but there are enough differences in practice to warrant a different approach. Therefore, I have decided not to include RESTful services in this book. If you choose to use RESTful services to communicate with your system, by all means, be my guest.

Basically, it's all very simple. You think of a way to structure and send commands over the line. This works fine as long as both parties understand what is going on. Of course, you don't have to reinvent the wheel: several well-established standards exist to do this. Later in this chapter, I show you how to do this with gRPC. However, as with all standards, they come with a cost. Sometimes, you do not need the additional complexity an established framework gives you. Sometimes, you just want to send a simple command to a system. Suppose your scenario allows for a less secure and unknown protocol. In that case, you can improve your speed and memory by having your own protocol.

JSON RPC is one of the most used ways to do this yourself. Let's have a look.

JSON RPC

JSON RPC is just encapsulating your commands in a JSON structure, sending them off over the wire, intercepting them at the other end, and doing whatever the command tells the system to do.

Let's begin with defining a command we want to send:

```
[Serializable]
internal class ShowDateCommand
{
    public bool IncludeTime { get; set; }
}
```

I want the client to inform the server that it needs to print the current date. I might want to include the current time as well. So, this is the command we created: `ShowDateCommand` with the `IncludeTime` field.

In my sample, I have put the client and the server in the same application, each running on a different task. I did that for the sake of simplicity. Of course, if you want to send commands to a different part of the same application, RPC is overkill. It's not even correct: it's not remote at all. However, for this demo, it works just fine.

For communications, I have chosen a named pipe. It's easy to set up and could be used to send messages across the network. Besides those considerations, I had no real reason to choose this option, so you can do whatever you want.

The server part looks like this:

```
internal class Server(CancellationToken cancellationToken)
{
    public async Task StartServer()
    {
        "Starting the server".Dump(ConsoleColor.Cyan);
        await using var server = new
            NamedPipeServerStream("CommandsPipe");
        "Waiting for connection".Dump(ConsoleColor.Cyan);
        await server.WaitForConnectionAsync(cancellationToken);
        using var reader = new StreamReader(server);
        while (!cancellationToken.IsCancellationRequested)
        {
            var line = await reader.ReadLineAsync();
            if (line == null) break;
            $"Received this command: {line}".Dump(ConsoleColor.Cyan);
            var command = JsonSerializer.
                Deserialize<ShowDateCommand>(line);
            if (command is { IncludeTime: true })
                DateTime.Now.ToString("yyyy-MM-dd
                    HH:mm:ss").Dump(ConsoleColor.Cyan);
            else
                DateTime.Now.ToString("yyyy-MM-dd").Dump(ConsoleColor.
                    Cyan);
        }
    }
}
```

The class, called `Server`, has one method named `StartServer`. It creates an instance of `NamePipeServerStream` with the `CommandsPipe` name. Then, it waits for a client to connect. As soon as that happens, we read the data coming in. As soon as we get a string, we deserialize it to the correct format and perform the task it is told to perform: it prints out the current date and optionally includes the time.

The client looks like this:

```
internal class Client(CancellationToken cancellationToken)
{
    public async Task StartClient()
    {
        var newCommand = new ShowDateCommand
        {
            IncludeTime = true
        };
        var newCommandAsJson = JsonSerializer.Serialize(newCommand);
        "Starting the client".Dump(ConsoleColor.Yellow);
        await using var client = new
            NamedPipeClientStream("CommandsPipe");
        await client.ConnectAsync(cancellationToken);
        await using var writer = new StreamWriter(client);
        $"Sending this command: {newCommandAsJson}".Dump(ConsoleColor.
            Yellow);
        await writer.WriteLineAsync(newCommandAsJson);
        await writer.FlushAsync();
    }
}
```

The client creates an instance of `ShowDateCommand` and sets `IncludeTime` to `true`. Then, it creates `NamedPipeClientStream` with the correct name and connects to the server. Finally, it sends the JSON over the wire. That's all there is to it.

For completeness, I give you the code that initializes both the server and the client in the `Main` method of the program:

```
var cancellationTokenSource = new CancellationTokenSource();
"Starting the server".Dump(ConsoleColor.Green);
var server = new Server(cancellationTokenSource.Token);
Task.Run(() => server.StartServer(), cancellationTokenSource.Token);

var client = new Client(cancellationTokenSource.Token);
Task.Run(() => client.StartClient(),
    cancellationTokenSource.Token);
"Server and client are running, press a key to stop".
    Dump(ConsoleColor.Green);
var input = Console.ReadKey();

"Stopping all".Dump(ConsoleColor.Green);
```

I create instances of `Server` and `Client`, starting them in `Task.Run()` and wait for the user to press a key. In the background, `Server` and `Client` do their thing, telling you all about it with the calls to `Dump()`. Please pay attention to the thread IDs in `Dump` – they can be pretty informative for learning about threading (or refreshing your memory).

This technique is simple and very fast. However, it only works if you know both ends of the equation: the server and the client must follow your proprietary protocol. If that is not the case, you are better off using a standard. One of those standards is gRPC. Let's look at that next.

Overview of gRPC and how to use it for IPC

One of the leading ways to establish a straightforward way of communication between processes these days is gRPC. The acronym **gRPC** stands for either **Google remote procedure call** or the recursive name gRPC remote procedure call. You can pick whichever you like. Google developed it as a public version and improvement of their internal framework, Stubby.

gRPC uses **Protocol Buffers** (**Protobufs**). This is a format that describes the available commands, the messages, and the parameters you can pass. Protobufs are compiled into a binary form, resulting in faster data transfers. The system is built on HTTP/2, so we can use multiplexing (multiple requests over the same TCP connection). HTTP/2 has many more advantages over the older HTTP/1.x, most of which involve efficiency.

Cross-language and platform support was also one of the leading drivers. So, you can be sure gRPC can be used on many devices.

Suppose we want to rebuild our example of a system that can be remotely instructed to display the current date (with or without time). In that case, we first have to define the message structure. However, before we do that, we need to add a couple of NuGet packages to our server application:

Package	Description
`Google.Protobuf`	Handles the proto files
`Grpc.Core`	The core implementation of gRPC
`Grpc.Tools`	Contains, amongst others, the compiler for proto files
`Grpc.AspNetCore`	Needed to host the server in our application

Table 6.4: NuGet packages for our gRPC server

In a C# console application, add a new file called `displayer.proto`. This is just a text file. I like to put them in a separate folder, which I call `Protos`. The compiler takes this file and creates a lot of C# for us.

The file looks like this:

```
syntax = "proto3";
option csharp_namespace = "_02_GRPC_Server";
service TimeDisplayer {
    rpc DisplayTime (DisplayTimeRequest) returns (DisplayTimeReply);
}
message DisplayTimeRequest{
    string name = 1;
    bool wantsTime = 2;
}
message DisplayTimeReply{
    string message = 1;
}
```

Let's dissect this.

First, we tell the system what format this is. We use `proto3`, which is the latest and recommended version.

Then, we tell the system what namespace to put them in when it generates the C# files. As you can imagine, this option is C# only. It is a helper option that helps us keep our code organized.

Then, we define the service. We have one service called `TimeDisplayer`. It has one RPC method called `DisplayTime`. It takes `DisplayTimeRequest` as a parameter and returns something of the `DisplayTimeReply` type.

`DisplayTimeRequest` and `DisplayTimeReply` types are defined below that. They are messages, and they can contain parameters. I added a name to show you how to add a string. For the request, I also added a bool, indicating whether we want to show the time.

The parameters need to be ordered and numbered. This way, if somehow the message gets scrambled, both systems still know what the data looked like initially.

Visual Studio usually knows how to handle this if you add a `.proto` file to your application. However, if this doesn't happen (and I have seen it go wrong occasionally), you must instruct the compiler on how to handle this file. In your `csproj` file, just add the following section:

```
<ItemGroup>
  <ProtoBuf Include="Protos\displayer.proto" GrpcServices="Server" />
</ItemGroup>
```

That should be enough to get the compiler on the way.

Let's build the server!

I have added the code for the server in my console application. Since the compiler takes our .proto file and compiles all the necessary code for us, we can use the following:

```
internal class TimeDisplayerService : TimeDisplayer.TimeDisplayerBase
{
    public override Task<DisplayTimeReply> DisplayTime(
        DisplayTimeRequest request,
        ServerCallContext context)
    {
        var result = request.WantsTime
            ? DateTime.Now.ToString("yyyy-MM-dd HH:mm:ss")
            : DateTime.Now.ToString("yyyy-MM-dd");
        result.Dump();
        return Task.FromResult(new DisplayTimeReply
        {
            Message = $"I printed {result}"
        });
    }
}
```

Our `TimeDisplayerService` class is derived from the `TimeDisplayer.TimeDisplayerBase` base class. This base class is generated out of our .proto file. As you can see, the `TimeDisplayer` name matches what we have in that .proto file.

We have one method here, called `DisplayTime`. Again, this matches what we have in our .proto file. The code is pretty simple; it just takes an instance of `DisplayTimeRequest`, looks at the `WantsTime` parameter, and returns the result.

Usually, gRPC servers run on some sort of webserver, and adding this code to an ASP.NET application is straightforward. But, of course, you can run it anywhere you want, which is something we, as systems programmers, really can use. So, if you're going to run this code in a console application, you can set that up as follows. In the primary method of your program, add the following:

```
"Starting gRPC server...".Dump();
var port = 50051;
var server = new Server
{
    Services = {TimeDisplayer.BindService(new
        TimeDisplayerService())},
    Ports = {new ServerPort("localhost", port, ServerCredentials.
        Insecure)}
};
server.Start();
```

```
Console.WriteLine("Greeter server listening on port " + port);
Console.WriteLine("Press any key to stop the server...");
Console.ReadKey();
await server.ShutdownAsync();
```

We create a new instance of the `Server` class. This comes from the `gRPC.Core` NuGet package we installed. We give it the services we want to use (in our case, `TimeDisplayerService`) and define the network address and port we decide to use. I do not care about credentials here, but you can use SSL, TLS, and other ways of security.

We start the server and wait for the user to press any key. Then, we stop the server again.

Up next: the client.

Again, we need to add some NuGet packages to our console application. These are the ones you need:

Package	Description
`Google.Protobuf`	Handles the proto files
`Grpc.Net.Client`	The client implementation for gRPC
`Grpc.Tools`	Contains, amongst others, the compiler for proto files

Table 6.5: NuGet packages for our gRPC client

First, we need a `.proto` file. To be more precise, we need the same `.proto` file we used on the server. So, it is best to link to that file instead of recreating it. However, if you like typing, be my guest and create a new one. Just make sure these files remain in sync when you make changes.

We do not need a specific client class; we only have to add the following code to our `Main` method in the program:

```
"Starting gRPC client... Press ENTER to connect.".Dump(ConsoleColor.
Yellow);
Console.ReadLine();
var channel = GrpcChannel.ForAddress("http://localhost:50051");
var client = new
TimeDisplayer.TimeDisplayerClient(channel);
var reply =
    await client.DisplayTimeAsync(
        new DisplayTimeRequest
        {
            Name = "World",
            WantsTime = false
        });
Console.WriteLine("From server: " + reply.Message);
```

We start with a wait for the user to press a key. Since I start the server and the client simultaneously in my solution, I might get timing issues if the client is slightly faster than the server in setting up the connection.

Then, we call `GrpcChannel.ForAddress()` with the correct parameters to set up the connection. With that connection, we call the `DisplayTimeAsync` method with a correct `DisplayTimeRequest` setup. The result should come back and show you what the server did.

That is all there is to it! We now have a fully functional server and client application, talking to one another over gRPC.

Differences between JSON RPC and gRPC

As you saw, setting up a gRPC server and client is not too complicated. But still, it adds a bit of complexity to your code. If you do not need the advantages of gRPC, you can use JSON RPC instead. But when do you pick which one?

If your messages get big, gRPC is the far better choice. Remember when I said IO takes a long time? Well, JSON files are usually much bigger than their binary equivalent. gRPC uses that smaller binary format, so data transmission is much faster when using that.

However, JSON is more readable, more debuggable, and easier to interpret for humans. The code is also easier to set up. The `.proto` files are something you have to get used to. Next to that, the compiler needs to transform the `.proto` files into C# classes, and they make your system more complex.

All in all, it depends on your scenario. However, for easy reference, I have outlined the differences between JSON RPC and gRPC in the following table:

Feature	gRPC	RPC with JSON
Serialization format	Protobufs (binary format)	JSON (text format)
Performance	Generally higher due to binary serialization, initial setup and connection might be slower	Lower than binary formats but quicker to set up (depending on the communication setup)
Protocol	HTTP/2	Typically HTTP/1.1
Streaming	Supports bidirectional streaming	Limited support, usually request-response only
Type safety	Strongly-typed contracts (Protobuf)	Loosely typed, prone to runtime errors
Language interoperability	High (supports many languages natively)	High (JSON is universally supported)
Network efficiency	More efficient (smaller payload, HTTP/2 features)	Less efficient (larger payload, HTTP/1.1)

Feature	gRPC	RPC with JSON
Error handling	Rich error handling with explicit error codes	Typically relies on HTTP status codes
Deadline/timeouts	Native support for specifying call deadlines	Usually managed at the application level
Security	Supports various authentication mechanisms	Varies, usually added at the application layer

Table 6.6: Differences between gRPC and JSON RPC

As you can see, although gRPC and RPC with JSON share many features, each has their own use case. Pick whichever works best for your scenario.

Next steps

Everybody needs somebody. That truth has even been the title of a song. The same goes for systems, especially those not meant to be used by humans. They need something to tell them what to do and what data to do it with. They need to communicate with each other. You have now seen the many ways you can use to set up communications.

We have looked at Windows Messages, the old-school communication style (although Windows still uses it for internal communications). We have looked at both named and anonymous pipes. Then, we looked at the most used way for computers to talk to one another: sockets. While at it, we investigated the OSI model a bit to understand where we need to write code and where we can leave that to others.

We also looked at a speedy way to share data on the same machine using shared memory.

Finally, we investigated how we can issue commands by using JSON RPC and gRPC.

Now, we should be ready to take the next step. After all, besides talking to our code, we can use the operating system to help us. Windows offers many services we might need or can use to our advantage, which is the topic of the next chapter.

7

The One with the Operating System Tango

Working with Operating System Services

Computers are complex machines. They can have many different forms, different peripherals, and different functions. Yet, a lot of different machines can run the same software. As long as the hardware fits in a pretty broad set of boundaries (for instance, running a specific CPU architecture), your software does not care what the underlying machine looks like.

The reason this all works is that we have abstraction. You hardly ever deal with the actual hardware. There are always layers of software to go through, each layer adding a level of abstraction. That sounds complicated, but it is a good thing. Without this, we would have to rewrite our software for all possible combinations of hardware. Imagine a user swapping out an old-style hard drive with spinning discs for a more modern, faster SSD. Then, they have to come to you so you can recompile your system to accommodate that. I am sure you do not want to spend your time on that if possible.

The lowest level of software, the one running closest to the hardware, is the **Basic Input/Output System** (**BIOS**). This system interfaces between the actual hardware and the levels above. The BIOS knows how to access a particular area on a storage medium. It knows how to reach a network card and get the bits and bytes to the levels on top of it. It is the gatekeeper to the actual hardware.

In short, the next level of abstraction is the **operating system** (**OS**). These days, the difference between the OS and user programs is not very well defined anymore. Windows, for instance, is an OS. however, it also comes with many user programs, such as a photo viewer and a calculator. However, the OS does come with many utilities we, as systems programmers, can use. These utilities or systems in the OS help us do tasks without worrying about the little details while still being able to run on many different machines. This chapter explains some of the more handy utilities Windows offers us.

This chapter looks at some of the services Windows makes available to us. These are the items we will learn about in this chapter:

- The Windows Registry
- Worker Services
- Windows Management Instrumentation (WMI)
- Registry and WMI – risks and how to avoid them

We also will look at the risks involved and how to minimize them. After all, we are probing deep into Windows, and when things go wrong, they usually go wrong very badly.

Let's begin with the Registry first!

Technical requirement

You can find all the sources and complete samples for all the things we discuss here in the GitHub repository at `https://github.com/PacktPublishing/Systems-Programming-with-C-Sharp-and-.NET/tree/main/SystemsProgrammingWithCSharpAndNet/Chapter07`.

If you, however, want to build the samples from scratch, you need to install some NuGet packages.

For the WMI samples, you need to install the `System.Management` package.

The Windows Registry

Almost all systems have settings. These settings persist; they are still there after a system shutdown, reboot, or whatever reason. The contents of these settings vary; they could be anything your system needs. It could be a connection string to a database, a location where you can store files, the font used to generate reports, and so on. Anything you cannot know in advance while writing the software or that a user or system administrator might want to change should be in a separate location from your system.

In the past, Windows applications and systems used **INI files**. An INI file is an elementary file structure. They consist of sections, each with a key/value pair of data. A section is part of the file that is surrounded by the [and] characters. The key/value data is a line such as `mykey=myvalue`. Each section or data line is on a separate line, and that is it.

We placed the INI file in a known location, usually in the same directory as the main application files.

These days, we do not use INI files that much anymore. The .NET BCL does not have classes for them, although third-party NuGet packages can help you if you decide to go with INI files.

The most obvious alternative for the INI file is the settings file. The settings file is usually in a JSON format, making it easy to work with. You can find them in the same place we used to put INI files: we usually place them alongside the main application.

JSON allows for a much more complex structure with a hierarchy in your settings. JSON is still much readable for humans, just as the INI files were. That might be useful if a system administrator needs to change the settings.

However, a JSON file is not always the best way to store settings. There are downsides to this approach. One of the alternatives to the file-based settings is using the Windows Registry. Allow me to explain what that is and how to use that first, and then I will outline both options' pros and cons.

What is the Windows Registry?

The Registry is a hierarchical database in Windows where systems can read and write all sorts of data. The data itself is a collection of key/value pairs. The keys are strings; the values can be strings, numeric, or binary.

> **Binary data in the Windows Registry**
>
> Yes, you can store binary data in the Registry. However, that doesn't mean it is a good idea. The theoretical limit is 1 MB per value, but I vigorously recommend not doing that. If you only have a couple of bytes, then storing and reading binary data is a great idea, but if you want to store larger amounts of data, you are better off using a different mechanism. Having large amounts of binary data in your Registry might slow down the complete machine, not just your application. Microsoft recommends using a maximum of 1 or 2 KB per entry for your binary data. Above that, you should move your data away to another location.

The Registry is organized in a tree-like structure. Each entry can be a key, a subkey, or an entry. The entry is the lowest level in the Registry: an entry cannot have a sub-entry.

Maybe I can clarify this by showing you a bit of the Registry on my machine.

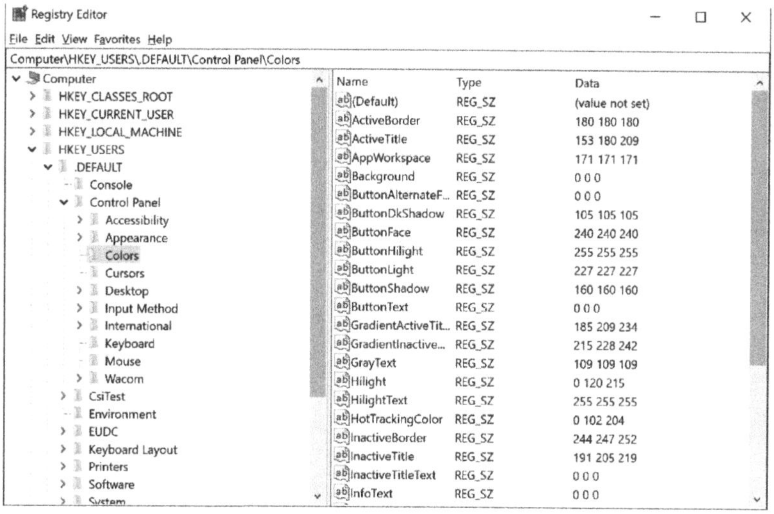

Figure 7.1: The Windows Registry

Figure 7.1 shows a small part of the Windows Registry on my machine. On the left-hand side, you see the tree structure with all the keys; on the right-hand side are the contents of the currently selected key. This image shows the settings for the colors used in the Control Panel. These are the default settings; you can have different settings per user.

That is one of the big advantages of the Registry: you can store settings per user and have the system figure out which to use when. You do not have to deal with that.

There are 5 top-level keys. I explain these in the following table.

Key	Description
HKEY_CLASSES_ROOT	This mainly connects files to applications: for instance, what application should Windows start if you double-click a file in Explorer?
HKEY_CURRENT_CONFIG	This contains information about the hardware profile used by the local computer at startup.
HKEY_CURRENT_USER	All information about the current users and their preferences is stored here. If you change the theme of Windows, this is where it ends up.
HKEY_LOCAL_MACHINE	Contains configuration information particular to this computer, as shared by all users.
HKEY_USERS	Here, you will find all user profiles known on this computer. For each user, their preferences and info are stored.

Table 7.1: Top-level Registry keys

I am not being truthful here. Some top-level keys I just mentioned are handy shortcuts to other keys. For instance, HKEY_CURRENT_USER maps the currently logged-in user in HKEY_USERS, and HKEY_CLASSES_ROOT is a subkey of HKEY_LOCAL_MACHINE\Software. But these root keys are there to help you. For instance, instead of looking up the ID of the current user and then finding that entry in HKEY_USERS, you can open the HKEY_CURRENT_USER key and be assured you get the correct data.

Each top-level key can have sub-keys. Each sub-key can have its own sub-keys. In total, you can go to 512 levels deep. Each top-level and sub-level key can have one or more key/value data pairs.

This data has a data type. The following table shows the available data types.

Win 32 type	C# type	Description
REG_NONE	None	No data type
REG_SZ	String	A null-terminated string

Win 32 type	C# type	Description
REG_EXPAND_SZ	ExpandString	A string containing unexpanded references to environment variables
REG_BINARY	Binary	Binary data in any form
REG_DWORD	Dword	A 32-bit binary number
REG_MULTI_SZ	MultiString	An array of null-terminated strings, terminated by a double null character
REG_QWORD	Qword	A 64-bit binary number
-	Unknown	An unsupported registry data type

Table 7.2: .NET Registry data types

Table 7.2, however, could use a little explanation.

The Win32 API supports many data types. However, the CLR has fewer of them available. The ones we can use are part of an enum called `RegistryValueKind`. These enums defined are the ones I list in the C# type column.

The types that are provided should be enough for you. However, sometimes, you need to use specialized ones. For instance, the Win32 API supports a datatype named REG_RESOURCE_LIST. You use this type to store resource-related data. Unfortunately, the C# enum does not provide an equivalent for that. In those cases, you can use the Unknown type.

ExpandString can be pretty valuable. If you want to store information about the location of a file, you can use a macro such as %PATH%. This macro is the current path in your system. However, the path is stored like that string: %PATH%. If you specify ExpandString as the type, the OS translates that string into the actual value if you read that data.

But honestly, you probably use String, Binary, and DWord the most. The others are there in case you need them, though.

How to access and store data with the Windows Registry

When writing to the Registry, you must first decide where to store that data. For instance, if you want to store something specific for the current user, you would probably use HKEY_CURRENT_USER as your root key. As systems programmers, we are more likely to choose a key such as HKEY_LOCAL_MACHINE or HKEY_CURRENT_CONFIG. These locations are independent of the current user, which is a more likely scenario for us. But, of course, if your use case warrants it, use any key you want.

Since the Registry is a hierarchical database, you must specify a hierarchy. In other words, you must think of a tree-like structure to store your data.

I see several subkeys in my machine's root key: HKEY_LOCAL_MACHINE: HARDWARE, SAM, SECURITY, SOFTWARE, and SYSTEM. In the SOFTWARE subkey, I see a lot of sub-subkeys, many of which are names of software vendors on my machine.

If you want to write to the Registry, you have to think about this: the location does not matter much, but for administrators who are maintaining the machines our software runs on, it has to be logical where you put things.

Let's assume we want to store the first time our software runs on a particular machine. If it has never run before, we store the current date-time. If it has run before, we retrieve that data: we never change the first-run date.

To store that information, we need to take the following steps:

1. Find the HKEY_LOCAL_MACHINE\SOFTWARE key.
2. Create a subkey called SystemProgrammers.
3. Create another subkey called Usage.
4. Store the date-time in binary, in a key called FirstAccess.

Of course, we can only take the last step if that key doesn't exist yet. If it does, the software has run already. In that case, we retrieve the value belonging to that key and show that the user.

This is what that all looks like:

```
var key = Registry.LocalMachine.CreateSubKey(@"Software\
SystemsProgrammers\Usage");

var retrievedKey = key.GetValue("FirstAccess");
if (retrievedKey == null)
{
    // create the value
    key.SetValue(
        name: "FirstAccess",
        value: DateTime.UtcNow.ToBinary(),
        valueKind: RegistryValueKind.QWord);
    "First access recorded now".Dump(ConsoleColor.Cyan);
}
else
{
    if (retrievedKey is long firstAccessAsString)
    {
        var retrievedFirstAccess =
            DateTime.FromBinary(firstAccessAsString);
        $"Retrieved first access:
            {retrievedFirstAccess}".Dump(ConsoleColor.Cyan);
    }
}
```

First, we create the subkey. If it already exists, we get a reference to it. We don't have to specify each subkey individually; we can give this method the whole path. In our case, `Software\SystemsProgrammers\Usage`, which we store in the `LocalMachine` root key.

Then, we try to read the value belonging to the `FirstAccess` key. If that is `null`, we haven't created it yet. So, we do that by calling `key.SetValue`. I specify the type to be `QWord`, but the API is smart enough to figure that out by itself: you can omit that if you want to. I like to be clear in my intentions, so I specify it anyway.

If the key does exist, we retrieve it. We have to do some casting from `long` before we get to `DateTime`, but after that casting, we can show the results.

> **Running this sample**
> Working with the Registry usually means you have to run with elevated privileges. This code only works if you run Visual Studio as Admin. But don't worry: the OS informs you soon enough if you forget that. You cannot write to the Registry on this level as a regular user.

If you want to be more careful with the data you store in the Registry, you can apply some security. After all, since anybody can open the Registry by using the Registry Editor application, you might want to limit access to specific keys. Fortunately, the people who designed the Registry thought of the same thing. So, they enabled security features on it.

If we want our key to only be accessible to the current user, we can add some security info.

So, in our sample code, after creating the key, add the following snippet:

```
var currentUser = Environment.UserName;
var security = new RegistrySecurity();
var rule= new RegistryAccessRule(
         currentUser,
         RegistryRights.FullControl,
         InheritanceFlags.None,
         PropagationFlags.None,
         AccessControlType.Allow);
security.AddAccessRule(rule);
key.SetAccessControl(security);
```

First, we get the name of the current user, which we store in the appropriately named `currentUser` variable. We need this to tell the Registry whom we want to give access to (or deny access from) our key.

We create a new instance of the `RegistrySecurity` class. Then, we create a new `RegistryAccessRule`, giving it the name of the user, and decide we want this rule to apply to everything (complete control), that it is not going to be inherited by child classes, not propagated to child classes, and that we want to allow this user to take complete control (the other option is to deny access).

Then, we add the access rule to the security object, which is applied to the key. There you go – a secured key!

> **A word of advice – limit what you store in the Registry**
>
> Working with the Registry is straightforward. However, I want to stress something: do not fill out the Registry if you do not need to. Also, if you have an installer of your service, make sure that the uninstaller removes all keys you have created. A cluttered Registry is one of the best ways to slow down Windows. There is a reason companies make money selling Registry cleaner apps. Don't be one of those developers who mess up their users' Registry!

Of course, the Registry is not the only place we can store our values. Sometimes, the overhead is just too much and we do need that to achieve our goal. Let's have a look at the difference between using the Registry and using plain JSON settings files.

Comparing the Windows Registry to JSON settings files

You might be surprised how easy it is to work with the Registry. With only a couple of lines of code, you can store and retrieve the information you need. You can easily distinguish between current and other users' data. Or, more likely in our case, you can ensure the data is accessible for all services on the current machine.

However, there is nothing wrong with having a local file with settings. After all, there is a reason Microsoft gives you a `settings.json` file if you create a new project. That's the best way to isolate your settings. The settings you use in your application are right next to your executable. Anyone who needs to change them can go to that folder and make changes if needed.

What do you choose? Which one do you use when?

Well, let's compare them.

Windows Registry

The Windows Registry has a couple of specific features that make it a good choice for certain scenarios. This is what they are:

- **Centralized storage**: The Registry is centralized and controlled by Windows. This location is where people tend to look for settings.
- **User and machine-specific settings**: With the Registry, you can have specific settings for the current user, all users, the local machine, or everybody. You can place your settings in one or more of these locations and have the OS figure out when to use which one.
- **Security features**: Adding rights or revoking rights is built in the Registry. You can specify on a very granular level what users can and cannot do with your keys.

- **Performance**: Reading from the Registry can be faster than reading files, especially if the data you are working with is small.
- **Support for complex types**: The Registry can handle more than just strings and numbers. If your use case demands a more exotic data type, chances are the Registry has got you covered.

Local JSON files

JSON files are used a lot. There are several reasons people like this structure. Here are some of them:

- **Simplicity and portability**: JSON files are straightforward. They are easy to write to and read from. Another bonus is that these files are easy to transfer between systems.
- **Human readable and editable**: You can easily edit the JSON files: they are just text files, and the structure is easily understood.
- **No dependencies on Windows**: The Registry is Windows only. JSON files are everywhere.
- **Version control-friendly**: Since JSON files are text, systems such as Git can handle and version them.
- **Avoiding system corruption**: If you mess up the Registry, you risk bringing Windows to a complete halt. Or, in a slightly less lousy case, wreak havoc on other applications. With JSON files, the worst that could happen is that you render your application useless.

So, if your app is Windows only, and you need security and want to benefit from centralized, multi-user settings, go for the Registry.

If you value simplicity, cross-platform compatibility, and easy version control, local JSON files are a better choice.

Just make a decision based on what you need.

To summarize, most applications need to have access to settings. You could store them in local JSON files or go for the more versatile but slightly more complex Registry.

We have looked at what the Registry does, how to read data from it, and how to write data to it. We compared the Registry to local JSON files, and we can now decide when to use which one.

Worker Services

So far, all of the samples I gave you are console apps; straightforward but aimed at you, the reader, so you can see what happened. However, in real life, systems programmers do not need a console to write output or read input. We deal with software that talks and listens to other software. Systems software usually does not have a user interface. A **console window** is a form of user interface, which we do not need.

I will continue to use the console since that is a straightforward way to show you what happens, and in those applications, we can focus on the core of what I am trying to show you.

However, in the real world, our applications work mainly behind the scenes. One of the ways to do that is to build services.

A **service** is a standalone application that has no user interface. It does the work quietly behind the scenes. It does communicate with the outside world, but it does so through one of the many ways described in previous chapters: through network connections, files, pipes, and so on.

Traditionally, if you wanted a service, you had to create a **Windows Service**. Before you say: "Well, duh, of course," let me explain that a Windows Service is a different type of application and project in Visual Studio. Just as a console application differs from a WPF application, a Windows Service is its own type.

A Windows Service is an application that runs without a user interface. Starting and operating them is not something a user does. Windows is responsible for that. There are dozens of services running on a Windows machine at all times, controlling your system and providing the background services you need.

The following image shows a part of the list of services running on my machine. As you can see by the scrollbar, this is just a tiny part of the total amount of services.

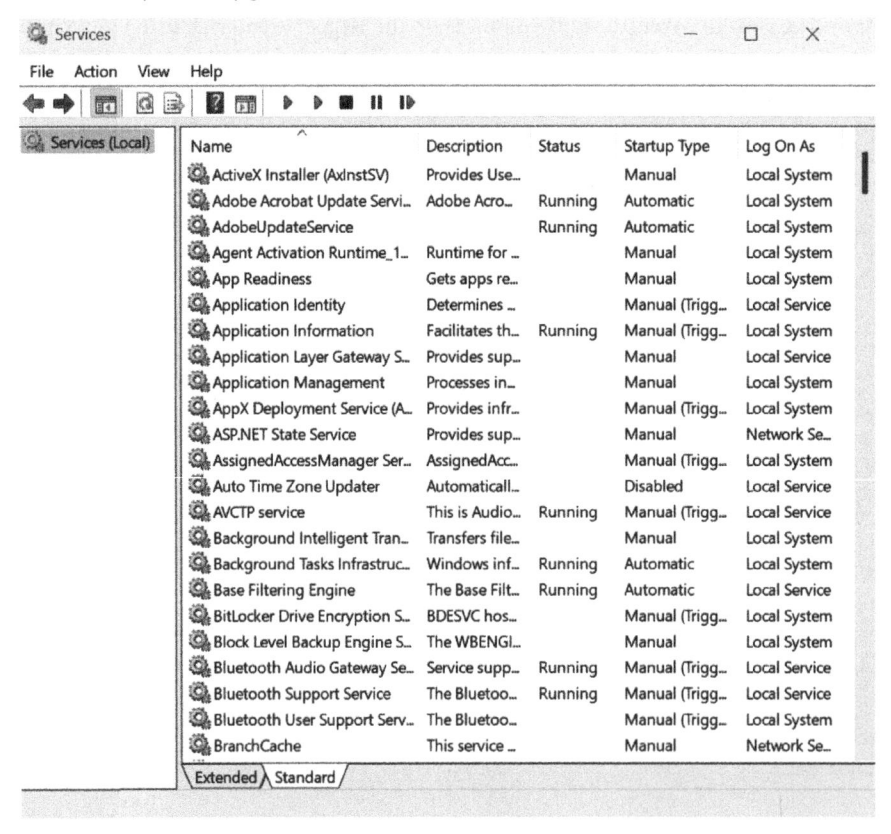

Figure7.2: Running Windows Services

As you can see, the services have a name, a description, a status, a startup type, and a specific kind of user that controls them.

The name and description are self-explanatory. The status can be one of a set of possibilities, but in most cases, they are either running or stopped. There are other statuses, but you hardly ever see those.

The startup type tells us how the service is started. It can be done automatically as soon as Windows starts. It can be done automatically but with a delay, so Windows waits a bit before starting them. This allows you to have other services up and running first. It can also be manual: Windows doesn't start them at all. There are some other options as well. Last, we see the **Log On As** column. This column defines under what security principle the service runs. The security principle defines what rights the service has.

Windows Services are powerful, and they are still around. However, in Visual Studio, you can't create them anymore. That's not entirely true but bear with me for a moment.

The current way to write service-like applications is by using the Worker Service template.

Worker Services are the cross-platform equivalent of Windows Services. If you run a Worker Service on Windows, you can still benefit from the features of Windows Services. That's why I said it wasn't entirely true that you cannot create them anymore. The CLR has incorporated the Windows Services into the Worker Service.

A Worker Service is much easier to build and debug than a Windows Service. Since Windows controls the Windows Service, you had to perform tricks and magic to debug them. However, a Worker Service can run like a console application, albeit with added benefits.

Docker support

If you create a new `Worker Service Project` in Visual Studio, you first get the standard dialog asking you about the name of the project, the location of the project, and the name of the solution. That is hardly surprising; you get that with every type of project. However, if you enter those details and click **Next**, you get a different version of the following dialog. For a console application, Visual Studio wants to know which version of the runtime you want (and whether you want to use top-level statements or not). With a Worker Service, Visual Studio asks you whether you want a Docker container. Your screen probably looks like the following image:

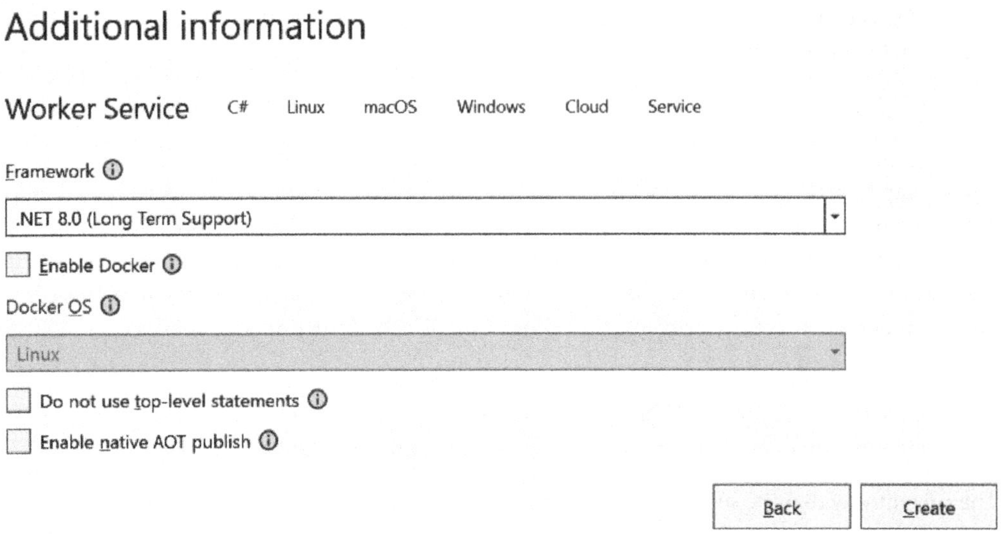

Figure 7.3: Extra information needed to create a Worker Service

If you check the box before **Enable Docker**, you can select the OS you want to use. This is usually a choice between Windows and Linux if you have WSL2 installed. Visual Studio creates a docker file for you, and you can now run your service in a container. Isn't that awesome?

Developing your services and running them on Docker is extremely powerful. Visual Studio allows you to write your source files on your Windows machine, then deploy them to a Docker image and spin up a container with your code running. The debugger even allows you to debug your service from Visual Studio while running in the Docker container.

Unfortunately, I shall not be covering that here in this book. That topic warrants a book on its own. However, to show you your options, we will write a bare-bones worker service and run it on a Docker if you have that installed. If you haven't, that's also fine: the worker runs the same on Windows as on Linux in a Docker container. So, you pick the strategy you think works best for you.

Dissecting the Worker Service

In Visual Studio, you can select Worker Service as a template. If you do that, you get asked the question we already discussed: what version of the framework do you want, and do you want Docker support? If you do, what OS should it run on?

In my example, I have enabled Docker support and chosen Linux as the OS. It does not matter what you decide to do: the C# code is the same no matter what.

The bare minimum of a Worker Service has a bit more code than a regular console application, but the main files are `Program.cs` and `Worker.cs`.

My application looks like this in the Visual Studio solution window:

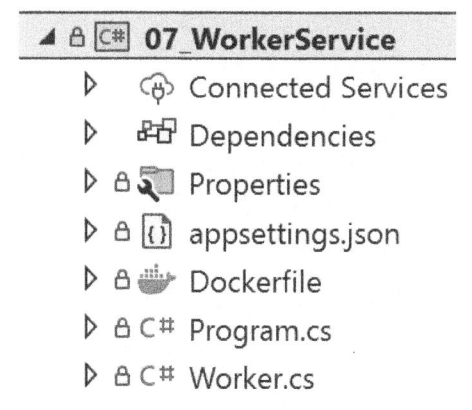

Figure 7.4: The layout of the Worker Service in Visual Studio

The `Program` class is not even that interesting. It contains, next to the namespace declaration, the following code:

```
var builder = Host.CreateApplicationBuilder(args);
builder.Services.AddHostedService<Worker>();
var host = builder.Build();
host.Run();
```

Let me outline the steps I took to get to these results:

First, we create an instance of the `HostApplicationBuilder` class. We do that by calling `CreateApplicationBuilder` on the static `Host` class.

The `builder` instance allows us to register classes. That way, we can use dependency injection. The template adds one service for us: the `Worker` class.

Next, we build `host` (of the `IHost` type), and finally, we run it.

The more exciting code is in the `Worker` class. As the name implies, that's where all the work happens. We do not call it a Worker Service for nothing!

Let's take a look at that `Worker` class:

```
public class Worker : BackgroundService
{
    private readonly ILogger<Worker> _logger;
    public Worker(ILogger<Worker> logger)
    {
        _logger = logger;
    }
```

```
    protected override async Task ExecuteAsync(CancellationToken
      stoppingToken)
    {
        while (!stoppingToken.IsCancellationRequested)
        {
            if (_logger.IsEnabled(LogLevel.Information))
            {
                _logger.LogInformation("Worker running at: {time}",
                  DateTimeOffset.Now);
            }
            await Task.Delay(1000, stoppingToken);
        }
    }
}
```

If you want to rename this class, you can do that, of course, as long as you also change the registered class in the `Program` class. Also, if you want to build multiple classes next to `Worker`, you can also do that. Again, do not forget to add them to `builder` in the `Program` class.

So, what is going on here?

The base class is `BackgroundService`. This class takes care of all the plumbing. It is an abstract class with the `ExecuteAsync(CancellationToken stoppingToken)` abstract method. So, you must write that method yourself (or let the template do that, as we did here.)

The constructor of our class gets a default instance of `logger` that allows us to write things to the console when running. This `logger` is available to us through the magic of dependency injection.

In the `ExecuteAsync` method, we keep looping until `CancellationToken` signals we want to stop. In the loop, we output a message and wait for a second before going to the next iteration.

If you run this, you will see the output. If you have Docker Desktop running, you can also run it on Docker. Just select Docker as what you want to run instead of your application. Visual Studio builds the image, deploys it, starts a container, and hooks the debugger to allow debugging.

In the output window of Visual Studio and Docker Desktop itself, you can see the results: the output of our loop is printed there.

Controlling the lifetime of the service

A Worker Service is meant to run forever. Well, maybe not forever, but at least as long as your machine runs. It is in there in the background, doing its job. It might be doing something worthwhile or waiting for incoming messages over a file, network, or any other way we discussed. It does its job and then returns to waiting for the next assignment.

But what if you want to stop the service when it has fulfilled its purpose? Let's rewrite the code a bit. Add a private variable to our Worker Service call `_counter` of the `int` type.

Then, change the loop in `ExecuteAsync` to look like this:

```
protected override async Task ExecuteAsync(CancellationToken
stoppingToken)
{
    while (!stoppingToken.IsCancellationRequested)
    {
        if (_logger.IsEnabled(LogLevel.Information))
        {
            _logger.LogInformation("Worker running at: {time}",
              DateTimeOffset.Now);
        }
        await Task.Delay(1000, stoppingToken);
        if (_counter++ >= 9)
        {
            break;
        }
    }

    _logger.LogInformation("Worker stopped at: {time}",
      DateTimeOffset.Now);
}
```

After waiting one second, we checked to see whether the loop had been run 10 times. If it has, we break out of the loop. Then, we print a message to tell you it has done so.

Run it and watch. You notice that it works as expected but that Visual Studio does not return to normal: it keeps debugging. However, there is nothing to debug! If you break, you see that Visual Studio still executes the call to `Host.Run()` in `Program`. Apparently, there is no way out!

Well, of course, there is. In this case, all we have to do is tell `Host` that we want it to stop working. We can do that quite easily.

We use dependency injection again. One of the services available to us is an instance of a class that implements the `IHostApplicationLifetime` interface. Let's add that to the constructor of the `Worker` class:

```
private readonly IHostApplicationLifetime _hostApplicationLifetime;
public Worker(
    ILogger<Worker> logger,
    IHostApplicationLifetime hostApplicationLifetime)
```

```
{
    _logger = logger;
    _hostApplicationLifetime = hostApplicationLifetime;
}
```

We get that instance and store it in a local field.

Then, in the `ExecuteAsync` method, just after where we log that we have finished the loop, add the following line:

```
_hostApplicationLifetime.StopApplication();
```

That's all there is to it. The `Host` instance now gets the message telling it to stop working and return to the OS.

Wrapping up Worker Services

Worker Services are excellent if you want a piece of code running in the background without any user interface, only meant to be called by other software. Does that sound familiar? That is precisely what systems programmers strive for. Worker Services are your best bet here. They can do anything you want. They can open ports on a TCP connection, watch folders for files, have named pipes to wait for data and process it, wait for network connections, and much more.

In short, they are a much better place to do all that work than the console applications we have been writing so far. You can still register them as services in Windows, so they start up automatically as soon as Windows starts.

The code is simple enough. Ensure your code is initiated from the `Worker` class, and you are good to go.

We will stick with the console applications in the rest of this book. Not because they are a better way to do systems programming (they are not) but because they are so easy and do not get in the way when I am working on explaining new topics. But now you know: everything you can do in a console application can (and should) be done in a Worker Service. You can deploy your code on Linux machines or Docker platforms if it is cross-platform and does not use Windows-only APIs. It is all up to you!

WMI

System programmers work closer to the OS than other, more user-oriented programmers. We often need to know more about the state of the OS than others do. We might need to keep track of the memory used, the hardware state, and other lower-level items. Luckily, Windows allows us to do just that. We can have a window (no pun intended) into the engine room, so to speak.

WMI is the tool to use. It's like the Swiss Army knife for managing items in Windows. WMI is part of the Windows OS that allows you to access and manipulate all sorts of system information and settings. This is Windows only, of course. In Linux, there is no built-in, out-of-the-box alternative to WMI. If you want to do this on a Linux machine, use external libraries and tools.

What can you do with WMI? You'd better ask, "What can't you do with WMI?" Let me show you some of the more common uses of WMI:

- **Monitoring system health**: You can check on CPU load, available memory, disk usage, and so on.
- **Managing hardware and software**: You can get information about installed software, manage printers, and even play around with BIOS settings.
- **Automating tasks**: You can use WMI to automate tasks, such as monitoring and restarting a service if necessary.
- **Event notifications**: We already saw the possibility of watching a folder or a file, but we can do much more. We can get notifications for almost anything that happens on the system.

There are many more things you can do with WMI. However, let's focus on these first. Before we begin looking at some samples, you need to install a NuGet package: `System.Management` from Microsoft. This package replaces the older `System.Management` assembly that was part of the .NET Framework.

How to use WMI

The primary way of interacting with Windows is by querying it. The `System.Management` NuGet package gives us access to a class named `ManagementObjectSearcher`. This class allows us to create queries and run them against Windows. The searcher usually returns a collection of `ManagementObject` instances, which you can interact with. These `ManagementObject` instances reflect something in your system. This class has an indexer, so you can query that object to get the information you are searching.

`ManagementObjectSearcher` can search over a lot of different types of data providers. That means you might have to limit the search by giving it a scope first.

The query itself is a string that starts with `SELECT`. It is just like a database.

Be careful what you do, though; we are opening the hood of the engine and poking around in places we are usually not meant to be poking around in. Most of the queries run on WMI require elevated privileges. You need to be a local administrator to make some changes or see some of the data. That means that all safeguards are out of the window. You are on your own. With great power comes great responsibility, right?

All of the following samples only run on Windows. Visual Studio is smart enough to see that: if you follow along, you will see many warnings about that. To be specific, you get the `CA1416` warning a lot. This warning says `This call is reachable on all platforms. ManagementObjectSearcher is only supported on: Windows`.

To get rid of that, add a pragma to the top of the file:

```
#pragma warning disable CA1416
```

This instruction tells the compiler not to bother: we know what we are doing. Now, the compiler gets out of your way and lets you be responsible for all damages that might occur if you still try to run this on Linux.

But enough of the scaremongering. Before we get into a heated debate on the pros and cons of being a local admin, we have to measure the heat a bit. Let's measure the temperature of our CPU!

Reading the CPU temperature

Most of the BIOS implementations allow the system to read the current CPU temperature. Other vendors of motherboards might have other ways of reading temperatures in the system, one of which might be the CPU. It all depends on the vendor. However, if your system supports it, you can easily read the current temperature. You could use that information to scale down your work in your system if you notice you are making the CPU work too hard. But how do we get that temperature? The code is relatively simple:

```
public void ReadTemperaturesUsingMsAcpi()
{
    var scope = "root\\WMI";
    var query = "SELECT * FROM MSAcpi_ThermalZoneTemperature";
    var searcher = new ManagementObjectSearcher(scope, query);
    try
    {
        foreach (var o in searcher.Get())
        {
            var obj = (ManagementObject)o;
            var temperature = Convert.
                ToDouble(obj["CurrentTemperature"]) / 10 - 273.15;
            $"CPU Temperature: {temperature}°C".Dump();
        }
    }
    catch (ManagementException)
    {
        "Unfortunately, your BIOS does not support this
            API.".Dump(ConsoleColor.Red);
    }
}
```

First, I identify the scope of the query. In this case, it is `root\\WMI`. Then, I create the query string, where we select everything from the `MCAcpi_ThermalZoneTemperature` class. As I said before, this results in a collection of `ManagementObject` instances. In this case, the collection consists of one item. This item has an indexer, and if we request the `CurrentTemperature` field, we get the current temperature of the CPU in tenths of Kelvin. We multiply that result by ten to get to the actual Kelvin value and then convert that to degrees Celsius. If you want to go to Fahrenheit, be my guest.

As I said, not all vendors supply this option. I use an older laptop from 2018 quite frequently, but it does not give me this information. I see `ManagementException` on that machine when I try to get the results. However, I got the results on my beefy desktop machine as expected.

There is another class you can use to query for the temperature. The query for that is `SELECT * FROM Win32_TemperatureProbe`, and the scope for that query is `root\\CIMV2`.

However, there can be multiple probes in your machine. Some motherboards also support measuring the temperature of other components, such as the GPU. To be honest, `Win32_TemperatureProbe` is even less commonly implemented than `MCAcpi_ThermalZoneTemperature`.

Reading the BIOS

The BIOS is the lowest level of abstraction on your machine. This level is where all the logic gets translated into voltages fed into the hardware. Wouldn't it be nice to see what is going on there? Well, you can, with the power of WMI!

Let's get some basic information out of the BIOS and display that. Here we go:

```
public void ReadBIOSDetails()
{
    // Create a management scope object
    ManagementScope scope = new ManagementScope("\\\\.\\ROOT\\cimv2");
    scope.Connect();
    // Query object for BIOS information
    ObjectQuery query = new ObjectQuery("SELECT * FROM Win32_BIOS");
    using ManagementObjectSearcher searcher = new
      ManagementObjectSearcher(scope, query);
    foreach (var o in searcher.Get())
    {
        var queryObj = (ManagementObject)o;
        "---------------------------------
            ".Dump(ConsoleColor.Yellow);
        "BIOS Information".Dump(ConsoleColor.Yellow);
        "---------------------------------
            ".Dump(ConsoleColor.Yellow);
        $"Manufacturer:
            {queryObj["Manufacturer"]}".Dump(ConsoleColor.Yellow);
        $"Name:
            {queryObj["Name"]}".Dump(ConsoleColor.Yellow);
        $"Version:
            {queryObj["Version"]}".Dump(ConsoleColor.Yellow);
    }
}
```

For this example, I have used a different constructor. Instead of passing in the scope and query as strings, I construct these two items first using the managed `ManagementScope` and `ObjectQuery` wrapper classes. This way of working achieves the same result but might be more readable to future developers working on this code.

The structure is similar to the previous example. We create an instance of a `ManagmentObjectSearchers` class, feed it the scope and query, and then query the results. In our example, we get the manufacturer, name, and version.

You can read many more properties from the BIOS, such as the capabilities. These describe what hardware is supported on that machine. As a systems programmer, you probably can imagine how this could be handy to know.

Controlling the Windows Update service

We discussed Worker Services earlier in this chapter. However, wouldn't it be nice if we could write software that allows us to monitor the state of those services and act upon them if needed? Well, we can with WMI.

In the following sample, we look at the status of a generic service: the Windows Update service. This service is part of the OS and is responsible for dealing with updates: monitoring, downloading, and installing them. Ideally, that service should always be up and running. Let's see what we can do with WMI to achieve that:

```
public void ControlService()
{
    // Define the service. In this case,
    // we're using the Windows Update service
    string serviceName = "wuauserv";
    // Define the query to get the service
    string queryString = $"SELECT * FROM Win32_Service WHERE Name = '{serviceName}'";
    // Create a query to get the specified service
    ManagementObjectSearcher searcher =
        new ManagementObjectSearcher(queryString);
    // Execute the query
    foreach (var o in searcher.Get())
    {
        var service = (ManagementObject)o;
        // Check the service state before trying to stop it
        if (service["State"].ToString().ToLower() == "running")
        {
            // Stop the service
            service.InvokeMethod("StopService", null);
            // Wait a bit for the service to stop
```

```
            System.Threading.Thread.Sleep(2000);
              // Start the service again
              service.InvokeMethod("StartService", null);
              $"{serviceName} service restarted
                  successfully.".Dump(ConsoleColor.Cyan);
        }
      }
  }
```

In this example, I do not specify a scope. Windows then assumes the default scope of root\CIMV2, as we saw before. Generally, it would be best if you used a scope. Specifying a scope limits the areas where WMI executes your query, which improves the speed tremendously. I just wanted to show you this approach here so you know it is an option.

We are looking for a service with the name of wuauserv, the Windows Update service. If we find it, we get the current state. It should be "running." If it is, we stop it, wait for two seconds and restart it.

There you have it: you can now control services inside your code!

Watching USB devices

Sometimes, you might be depending on specific hardware. Let's assume you are reading data from a USB device. Wouldn't it be nice to be informed when the user removes the device? That would prevent embarrassing errors in your code, right? Again, we have WMI coming to our aid!

This is the code to do just that:

```
public void StartListening()
{
    string wmiQuery = "SELECT * FROM __InstanceDeletionEvent WITHIN 2 " +
        "WHERE TargetInstance ISA'Win32_USBHub'";
    ManagementEventWatcher watcher = new
      ManagementEventWatcher(wmiQuery);
    watcher.EventArrived += new EventArrivedEventHandler(USBRemoved);

    // Start listening for events
    watcher.Start();
    "Unplug a USB device to see the event.\nPress ENTER to
        exit.".Dump(ConsoleColor.Cyan);
    Console.ReadLine();
    // Stop listening for events
    watcher.Stop();
}
```

The query tells the system to look at an event called `__InstanceDeletionEvent`. This is the event that Windows raises once something is deleted on the computer. In this case, we look for something in the list of devices registered in `ISA 'Win32_USBHub'`. In other words, we want to be notified if a USB device is deleted from the system. `WITHIN 2` means we want to check every 2 seconds. So, there might be a delay.

This time, we create a new object. The watcher is a new instance of the `ManagementEventWatcher` class. We give it the query, set up a callback in case the event happens, and start watching. When we are done, we stop watching again.

The event handler looks like this:

```
private void USBRemoved(object sender, EventArrivedEventArgs e)
{
    // Get the instance of the removed device
    ManagementBaseObject instance = (ManagementBaseObject)
        e.NewEvent["TargetInstance"];
    // Extract some properties
    string deviceID = (string)instance["DeviceID"];
    string pnpDeviceID = (string)instance["PNPDeviceID"];
    string description = (string)instance["Description"];
    var message =
        $"USB device removed:" +
        $"\n\t\tDeviceID={deviceID}" +
        $"\n\t\tPNPDeviceID={pnpDeviceID}" +
        $"\n\t\tDescription={description}";
    message.Dump(ConsoleColor.Yellow);
}
```

As soon as the event occurs, this code gets called. `eventargs` of the `EventArrivedEventArgs` type contains much information. Amongst others, it has `TargetInstance` in it. `TargetInstance` has all sorts of information we can display.

We could have used another approach: we could have queried the `Win32_DeviceChangedEvent` class. That would have been a bit easier, but that gives us less information than our current solution. This is typical for WMI: there is usually more than one way to get the desired results.

Play around with it; start the code and unplug several devices from your machine. See what happens!

> **Final words about WMI**
>
> WMI is very powerful. You can do all sorts of things that are typically unavailable to a regular .NET application. However, there are downsides: WMI is highly resource intensive. We set the event watcher in the last sample to only run once every two seconds to mitigate that a little bit.
>
> WMI is somewhat obscure. You have to figure out the queries yourself; there is not much information that teaches you all the available options. Of course, the Microsoft documentation has plenty to say about this topic, but it is not as straightforward as you might be used to. There is quite a steep learning curve if you want to dive into this. That leads to another risk: you can quickly get things wrong.
>
> WMI allows you to interact with lower parts of the system, which can cause catastrophic results. Another risk is that it unadvertly displays security-sensitive information. So, be careful what you do with it. As always, test what happens if you use this technique.
>
> However, if you are careful, you can do many cool things!

We have seen some really nice things here. You might be tempted to sprinkle a lot of Registry and WMI code over your systems. However, before you do that, let's take a peek into the downsides: there are potential risks we should talk about!

Registry and WMI – risks and how to avoid them

Nothing comes for free. That also applies to OS services: there is a price to pay. The complexity of the code isn't too high; I am sure you could follow along. No, the price you have to pay lies elsewhere: mistakes can be hard to spot and even harder to fix. The risks are pretty high: an error could lead to unpredictable behavior of the machine. You could bring down a complete server if you do things wrong.

Of course, we are all brilliant developers. We do not make mistakes, right? However, just in case we have a moment of weakness (we all know that 14 hours of developing software in one sitting is not the best idea), I want to tell you about the risks and how to avoid them as much as possible.

But before I do that, we have a whole chapter (*Chapter 11*, to be exact) about debugging. That's where we will dive into the nitty gritty details of that topic. But here, I want to focus on what might go wrong when working with the Registry and WMI.

The Windows Registry

As mentioned before, the Windows Registry is where the OS and most applications running on it store and read their settings. These could range from simple values about the user preferences to details about installed peripherals.

Making a mistake here could result in an application not working as expected. However, it could also result in the machine breaking down completely. So, you'd better be careful when dabbling around in the Registry!

There are several steps you can take to mitigate the risks. Let's go through them.

Backup

If you start experimenting with the Registry, the best tip I can give you is to back up your current settings. You can export and import keys and subkeys in the Registry Editor tool (`regedit.exe` in your Windows directory). That means you can easily roll back your changes when you make a mistake. If you are doing this in your application, you might consider reading your app's settings and storing them before applying changes. Of course, you do not do that when storing simple settings, but this might save you when you need it for more threatening situations.

Proper tools

In the end, the Registry itself is a collection of files on the storage medium of your computer. After all, the data needs to be stored somewhere. It is no secret where these files are stored. For instance, you can find the `HKEY_LOCAL_USER` settings in the `UsrClass.dat` file in the `%UserProfile%\Local Settings\Application Data\Microsoft\Windows` folder. However, I would not recommend messing around with these files yourself. Use the tools. The aforementioned Registry Editor is a great way to read and change settings. If you want to do this in your software, use the tools the BCL and the Win32 API give you. If you are curious about what happens to the Registry in run time, the free Process Monitor tool from SysInternals is invaluable. It can give you a live view of all processes working with the Registry. It might surprise you how often the Registry is used!

Keep it minimal

The Registry is not meant to store large amounts of data. It is for smaller items, such as settings and preferences. Use it wisely: do not store too much data there. A good solution would be to have larger amounts of data stored in a file and store the location of that file in the Registry in a well-known place. This way, you can differentiate between different users (since the Registry keeps track of the user and presents you with the correct `HKEY_LOCAL_USER` instance) but still have a place to store more data.

Logging is your friend

Loggings is always a great tool when debugging your code, but this is especially true when dealing with the Registry. When something goes wrong, logs can be a lifesaver. Next to that, logs can help you understand your software's flow and clarify why specific paths in your code were taken. When developing, you can never have too many log files. However, you might want to turn down the amount and verbosity of your logs when you go into production.

Error handling

Error handling should be a no-brainer. Use try-catch blocks as much as you can. Do not catch the generic `Exception` class, but be specific. After all, the *only catch the exceptions you can handle* rule is still valid.

Software that works with the Registry might encounter exceptions such as `SecurityException`, `IOException`, and `UnauthorizedAccessException`. Be mindful of those. Catch them and return your software in a known state before continuing the flow.

Also, please log these instances!

Test in an isolated environment

When dealing with the more risky areas of the Registry, you might want to do that on a different machine than your daily device. You do not need to switch to a different machine but can use other techniques. You can quickly deploy a **virtual machine** (**VM**) locally or in the cloud. With Azure, making a VM and deploying and running your code is extremely easy. If it all works, that's fine. If it doesn't, all you have to do is delete the VM and try again.

Another good approach is to use Docker. If you switch Docker from Linux containers to Windows containers, you can deploy your Worker Services to Docker and then work on the isolated, local Registry in that container. If it goes wrong, no harm is done. If you also log to a persistent file stored outside the container so that it lives on after the container crashes, you can do a post-mortem conveniently.

Potential risks when dealing with WMI

WMI can be very powerful. You can query your system without having to resort to the Registry. You can also change settings, start services, configure network settings, and much more.

However, WMI is not easy. The documentation is out there, but you must look for it and piece it together yourself. However, there are some tips and tricks I can give you to get up to speed with WMI and use it to your advantage.

Start with the basics

Know your **WMI Query Language** (**WQL**). It is a bit like SQL for the WMI system. Since you often pass in the queries to the WMI in strings, you should be careful not to make typos. They are notoriously hard to spot. Knowing the syntax of WQL can help in those cases.

One often-made mistake is not using the correct namespace when querying the system. Although most queries run against the `ROOT\CMIV2` namespace, not all do. Make sure you use the correct namespace.

Use the right tools

When learning about WMI, you might want to play around with it first. There is an almost unknown tool that comes with Windows called `WBEMTest`. You can start that by entering that term into the **Search** field in Windows.

This tool is a quick entry into the WMI. The user interface looks like it comes straight out of Windows 95, but it is a nice way to investigate WMI. For instance, if I want to know more about my BIOS vendor, I can use the code we looked at before or enter that in `WBEMTest`. That looks like this:

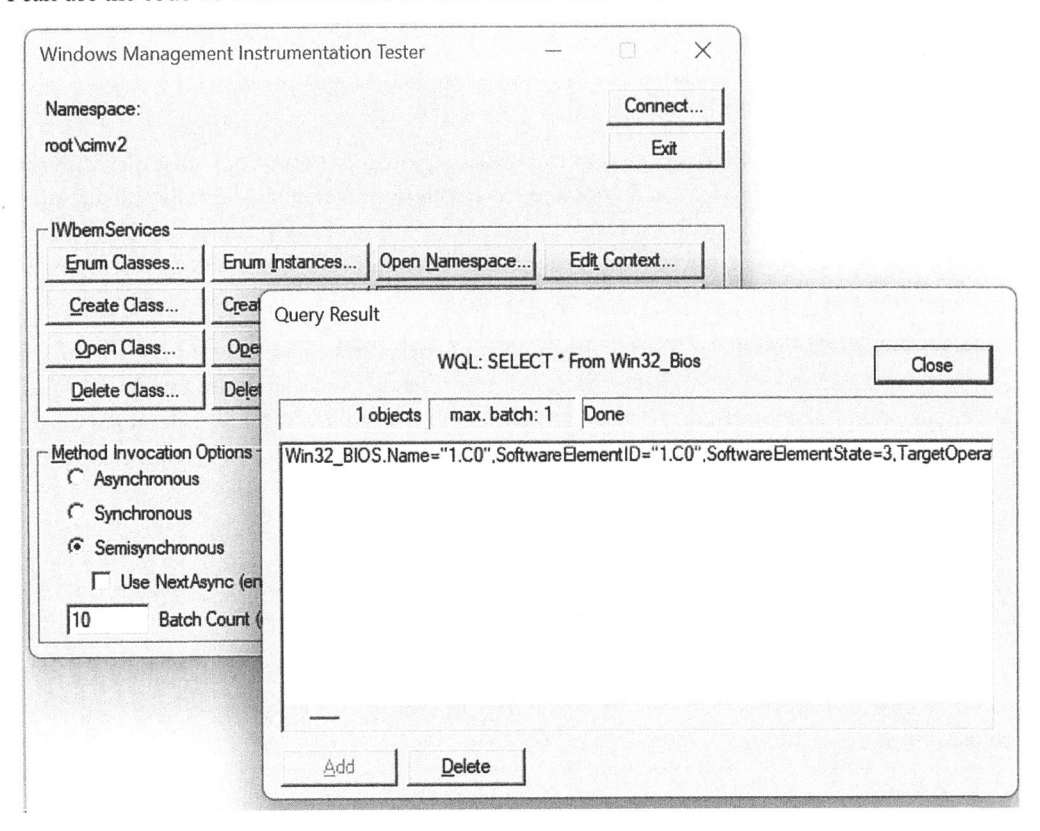

Figure 7.5: WBEMTest querying the BIOS

This image shows `WBEMTest` in action. In the top left corner, I connected the app to the `ROOT\CMIV2` namespace. Then, I clicked on **Query** and entered the `SELECT * FROM Win32_BIOS` query. I got the results you see in the bottom right window.

Powershell is also a great way to interact with WMI before incorporating WMI into your system. You can use the `Get-WMIObject` cmdlets to interrogate the system. For instance, getting the information about the BIOS results in the following:

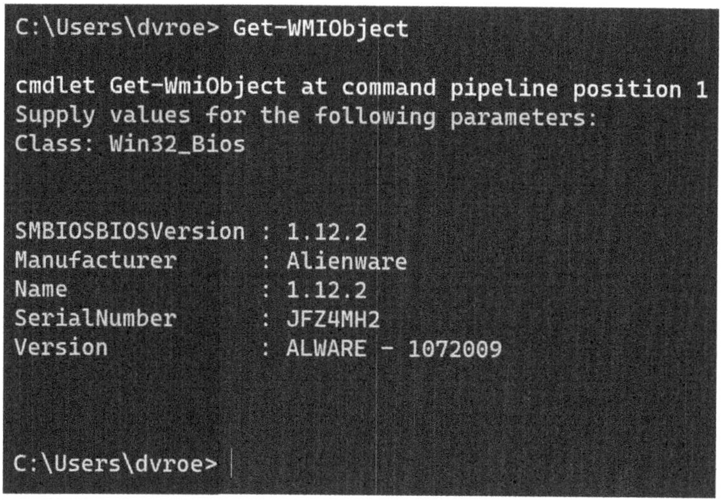

```
C:\Users\dvroe> Get-WMIObject

cmdlet Get-WmiObject at command pipeline position 1
Supply values for the following parameters:
Class: Win32_Bios


SMBIOSBIOSVersion : 1.12.2
Manufacturer      : Alienware
Name              : 1.12.2
SerialNumber      : JFZ4MH2
Version           : ALWARE - 1072009



C:\Users\dvroe>
```

Figure 7.6: Get-WMIObject in PowerShell

As you can see, I can enter `Get-WMIObject`, then pass the name of the object I want to interrogate (`Win32_Bios`), and I get all results nicely formatted.

Improve your code

The tips I gave you for handling the Registry also apply here: catch the right exceptions and log as much as possible.

The most seen exception when working with WMI is `ManagementException`. Of course, we also saw queries not supported on specific platforms. Be aware of those issues and handle them appropriately.

Logging is also a great way to debug your WMI code. Log as much as you can during development to know what is happening when things go south.

Performance and memory considerations

As systems programmers, we care deeply about performance and memory usage. WMI can significantly slow down your app. Especially when polling too often, you will see a degradation of your performance. Avoid frequent polling. You do not need to check the temperature every millisecond, anyway.

Also, do not forget to dispose of all CLR classes dealing with the WMI properly. If handles to those classes remain open too long, you might exhaust the available resources. That is a great way to bring your system to a screeching halt. Let's not do that!

One final note: WMI relies on the WMI service. Yes, that is a Windows Service. If that service is not running, WMI does not work. That will not likely ever happen, but that situation might occur. So, if things do not work as you expect, please also check that service.

Of course, all other tips and tricks I gave you throughout this book also apply. There is nothing magical about WMI, Worker Services, and the Registry. It is just that they might need a bit more attention to avoid getting into weird situations.

Next steps

Windows gives you many tools to use. These tools are deeply integrated into the system. Most of them are never used by applications used by users. But for us, as systems programmers, this is different. We are working closer to the metal, so it is good to know what that metal offers us.

I suggest you play with the Registry Editor and see what hidden gems you can find there. Next to that, learn WQL. Many tools offer a nice interface to the WMI, but in the end, you will have WQL strings in your application. You might as well start to learn about them.

Finally, learn Docker. Docker is a great way to package your applications and a valuable debugging tool. You can use Docker to isolate your potentially dangerous code. If things go wrong, all you need to do is delete the running container and start again. Of course, everything we discussed in this chapter is only available on Windows, so you must use Windows containers on Docker. When you are sure your code works fine, you can use it on real Windows machines.

In this chapter, we looked at all the tools that Windows give us; tools we can use in our code to do things that are hard to do if we had to write everything ourselves. We learned about the centralized settings storage mechanism called the Registry.

We also learned about the ways we can query the OS and even the underlying hardware through the use of WMI. We talked about how to use them and we talked about how to avoid some of the risks involved.

Now, with these skills under our belt, it is time to escape the confinement of the single machine and venture into the land of networking. Systems these days rarely run in isolation on one machine. They communicate. They talk to each other. We should be looking into networking next. So, hook up your dial-up modem and follow along for the road down the network protocols!

8
The One with the Network Navigation

Building High-Performance Networking Applications

Software seldom lives in isolation. The same can be said, to a greater extent for system programs. Since these programs do not directly interact with the user, they rely on other software to give them input, read their output, and be told what to do. That "other software" often lives on the same machine, but just as often, that software runs elsewhere.

We have so far discussed how to transfer data to and from our applications and briefly looked at networking. This chapter focuses on that specific topic: networking. Be prepared to go deeply into the world of interconnected software!

In this chapter, we will go through the following topics:

- The fundamentals and the OSI layers
- Exploring the System.Net namespace (including the most used protocols)
- Working with System.Net.Sockets to have more control
- Asynchronous, non-blocking networking
- How to improve networking performance
- Networking errors and time-out, and how to deal with those

We are about to break out of the box and connect to the outside world. Let's go!

Technical requirements

All of the code samples for this chapter can be found at `https://github.com/PacktPublishing/Systems-Programming-with-C-Sharp-and-.NET/tree/main/SystemsProgrammingWithCSharpAndNet/Chapter08`.

The fundamentals

We have already talked about the OSI model. But just as a quick refresher, the OSI model defines the layers that make up the system, allowing us to communicate with other systems. The layers span from the lowest layer, which describes the voltages a network adapter should be able to handle, up to the highest level, which describes the application that uses networking.

A walk down the OSI layers

I want to walk you through all the layers again, detailing what happens in each. To do this, I want to discuss a user using FTP to send data. **FTP**, which stands for **File Transfer Protocol**, is an older, hardly used technique to send data to remote machines or to get data from those remote machines.

FTP used to be the best way to achieve that, but the lack of security features made people move to other means. We will discuss some of those later, but we can still use FTP for our walk-down of the OSI model. It makes things a bit easier to understand.

An FTP client can be as simple as a console application. Actually, almost all FTP clients are just that. There are GUI-based clients, but they act as wrappers around the FTP commands.

To transfer a file, a user fires up the FTP client, specifies the server to connect to, and optionally passes in the credentials. Then, the user uses commands such as `GET` and `PUT` to transfer the file. Another command is `LS`, which is used to get the contents of a remote directory. We also have `MKDIR` to create a remote directory and other such commands.

So, let us assume that the user is sitting at their machine and wants to log in to the remote computer. To do that, the user types `ftp username:password@127.0.0.1` at the command prompt. This does a few things:

1. It starts up the command-line version of FTP
2. Then it tells it to connect to a computer found at address 127.0.0.1 (which is, as you probably remember, localhost)
3. It supplies a username and a password that the server needs.

After a few seconds, the client lists all files in the requested location. But what happens in the computer when the user presses the *Enter* key?

After starting the application, the FTP client takes over.

The commands and data flow through the OSI levels. Let me show you what happens:

- **Layer 7**: The application runs on OSI level 7, the application level. The FTP protocol in the application then sets up the connection. FTP creates two connections: one for control commands and one for data transfer.
- **Layer 6**: In the presentation layer, the system converts the commands into the appropriate format. In this case, it is simple: the `open` command is translated from whatever string format it was into an 8-bit ASCII format. If encryption is needed, that is also taken care of here. After all, layer 6 is all about how to present the data.
- **Layer 5**: The session layer then takes over. This layer is where the actual connection to the remote machine is made. This layer keeps an eye on the connection to make sure it is reliable and stable. It also closes the connection when it is no longer needed.
- **Layer 4**: After that, the transport layer makes sure the data containing the command is broken into smaller packets and sends them out in the correct order. FTP uses TCP, meaning layer 4 is responsible for rearranging data packets that are out of order when data is received. Error checking is also something that happens here.
- **Layer 3**: The network layer is where the **Internet Protocol** (**IP**) lives. This protocol in layer 3 is responsible for finding the best route to the remote machine. It also handles packet forwarding and rerouting.
- **Layer 2**: Then, we get to the data link layer. This layer adds data to the packets, such as the MAC address of the next machine the data needs to get to. It is responsible for node-to-node communication. If you use Wi-Fi, this layer prepares the data to be sent over the radio waves.
- **Layer 1**: Finally, we reach the physical layer. This last layer is where the data is actually transmitted. This layer translates the data into radio signals if you use Wi-Fi. It deals with all the hardware issues, such as the frequencies used and the strength of the signal.

Luckily, most of this is done at the OS or BIOS level. We do not have to worry about frequencies when setting up a network connection. We usually deal with **layers 7** and **6**, and sometimes **5**. We write the application (**layer 7**). We define the presentation (**layer 6**) if we have our own protocol. And we might sometimes have to worry about the actual connections, so we deal with **layer 5** occasionally.

> **Tip**
> The BCL and the CLR have many classes, tools, and helpers, allowing us to focus on the fun without worrying about the details. But sometimes, as system programmers, we must worry about those details. These details can be the difference between a great, fast, and stable system and a mediocre one. But do not worry: we cover it all here in this chapter!

Before we can do that, let us look at commonly used ways to transmit data over a network.

Exploring the System.Net namespace

Chances are, if you need a way to transmit data, someone else has already figured out the best way to do this.

For instance, you could write all the code to transfer a file to and from a machine or use FTP and rely on existing software.

In fact, there are many ways to transfer data. Many of those ways are so standardized that they are part of the BCL. You can use them without dealing with third-party NuGet packages. Let us discuss some of the offerings in the System.Net namespace and see what we can do with them.

Understanding HTTP/HTTPS

HTTP was the protocol that enabled millions of users to finally use the internet. Before HTTP, the only way to exchange data was through technically complicated protocols, most of which had to be controlled through the command line. When Sir Tim Berners-Lee published his ideas about the World Wide Web and the accompanying **Hypertext Transfer Protocol** (**HTTP**), people with little or no technical background could also use the net. Web browsers made it easy to go around and find information. Of course, when I say easy, I mean easier than before. In the early 1990s, we had no Google or Bing, so finding interesting sites was a struggle compared to today.

HTTP democratized the internet. Before that, it was the realm of scientists and the military, with a few nerds sprinkled in for good measure. Yes, I was one of those nerds: I first used the internet through SMTP, Gopher, FTP, and Usenet in 1987. HTTP and the WWW made it all so much easier.

Programming for it was not that easy. However, with the current frameworks, getting data from an arbitrary site anywhere on the globe only takes a couple of lines of code. Let me show you:

```
using var client = new HttpClient();
try
{
    string url =
        "https://jsonplaceholder.typicode.com/posts";
    HttpResponseMessage response =
        await client.GetAsync(url);
    response.EnsureSuccessStatusCode();
    string responseBody =
        await response.Content.ReadAsStringAsync();
    responseBody.Dump(ConsoleColor.Cyan);
}
catch(HttpRequestException ex)
{
    ex.Message.Dump(ConsoleColor.Red);
}
```

In the first line, we create an instance of the `HttpClient` class. This class is a helpful little helper: it takes away much of the complexity of the older `HttpWebRequest`. Although `HttpWebRequest` does offer some advantages over `HttpClient` (for instance, more control over the headers, the option to set time-outs, and the ability to use synchronous data transfers if needed), `HttpClient` is by far the better choice.

> **Testing with dummy servers**
>
> If you want to play around with HTTP and HTTPS, you need a reliable and easy-to-use website to connect to. The `https://jsonplaceholder.typicode.com/` URL is a great site to use in those cases. It gives you several endpoints to connect to, read from, and send data to. It is simple to use, and it is free. Please have a look at that site to see what it offers.

After declaring the URL, we call the `GetAsync` method with that URL. This asynchronous operation returns an instance of the `HttpResponseMessage` class. That class contains all we need to read the data from the remote server.

The next call is just a shorthand for some straightforward error checking. Calling `EnsureSuccessStatusCode` does very little besides looking at the return code from the server, and it throws an error if it is not in the 200 range. As you probably know, HTTP requests return a numeric status code that tells you what the result of the call is. Everything between 200 and 299 means your call worked. Codes such as 404 mean the site is unreachable, and so on.

This single method makes your code much more readable than `if` statements.

If all is okay, we continue by reading the actual data. The response has several properties, one of which is `Content`. Other properties are the status code, the headers, and so on.

`Content`, of type `HttpContent`, is a wrapper around `Stream` that allows us to read data from the server. In our case, we call `ReadAsStringAsync`, which takes all data the server can give us and returns that to us as a string. Of course, this all happens asynchronously.

Finally, we display that string on the console.

This is the simplest example of using HTTP I can think of. All classes shown here have many more use cases, methods, and helpers that can benefit you. I suggest you look at the documentation of `HttpClient`, `HttpResponseMessage`, `HttpContent`, and the rest to see what else you can do with them. In the meantime, let's look at some other protocols.

FTP

We saw FTP before. I used it to illustrate the flow of actions through the OSI model. But we never thoroughly explored what we can do with it.

FTP is an older technology. It is not in use that much anymore, but it is still beneficial. It is a quick, easy-to-understand technology to transfer files between machines and control remote file systems, regardless of the underlying operating system. It is fast and reliable. Most operating systems support FTP both as a client and as a server.

In Windows, you can enable the FTP server by going to the **Program and Features** section of the settings in the control panel, and there, under **Internet Information Services**, you can see the option to install the FTP server. Alternatively, you can click *Win + R* and then enter the optional features. See *Figure 8.1* to see what it looks like.

Figure 8.1: Installing FTP Server on Windows

However, make sure you know what you are doing. One of the reasons we do not use FTP that much anymore is that it is not secure by default. To transfer files, it would be better to use something such as SFTP, which is a secure version.

But good old FTP is still your friend if you want to communicate in a secure environment (such as in a Kubernetes cluster) and transfer files quickly and easily.

So, how do you read the contents of a remote directory? Simple: use this piece of code!

```
public static void FetchDirectoryContents(string ftpUrl, string
username, string password)
{
```

```
    var request = (FtpWebRequest) WebRequest.Create(ftpUrl);
    request.Method = WebRequestMethods.Ftp.ListDirectoryDetails;
    request.Credentials = new NetworkCredential(username, password);
    try
    {
        using (var response = (FtpWebResponse) request.GetResponse())
        {
            using (var streamReader = new StreamReader(response.
  GetResponseStream()))
            {
                var line = string.Empty;
                while ((line = streamReader.ReadLine()) != null)
                    Console.WriteLine(line);
            }
            $"Directory List Complete, status {response.
                StatusDescription}".Dump(ConsoleColor.Cyan);
        }
    }
    catch (WebException ex)
    {
        var status = ((FtpWebResponse) ex.Response).StatusDescription;
        $"Error: {status}".Dump(ConsoleColor.Red);
    }
}
```

As you can see, the code here is pretty straightforward. We create an instance of `WebRequest` and cast it to a subclass: `FtpWebRequest`. We specify what we want to do by setting the method to `ListDirectoryDetails`. We add some credentials if needed and get a stream containing the data we need. Of course, we handle exceptions as well.

Great! But wait... this is actually not so great.

If you do this in your editor, you will see warnings: `WebRequest` (and thus `FtpWebRequest`) has been marked obsolete. They have been superseded by the much better `HttpClient`. Unfortunately, that one cannot be used with FTP sites: it is only meant for HTTP traffic.

I believe Microsoft made a mistake here. But it is their framework, so they can do what they want. The good news is that plenty of NuGet packages can do what we want them to do. One is *FluentFtp*, which you can find at the `https://github.com/robinrodricks/FluentFTP` URL. Here, I would like to mention that I am not affiliated with this or any other NuGet package I mention in this book; these are just the packages I use. Of course, many different options are available, so just pick whatever works for you.

Email protocols

HTTP is the most used protocol on the public-facing internet, both in the number of servers handling it and in the percentage of data dealt with. But second to that is SMTP. **SMTP**, which stands for **Simple Mail Transfer Protocol**, is used for email. SMTP is just one of the protocols related to emails. Let's look into each one of those:

- **SMTP**: The Simple Mail Transfer Protocol is used to send mail over the Internet. It is connection-oriented, meaning its primary task is to ensure a connection between the client sending the mail and the server processing it. It is reliable (meaning it can be recovered if data is lost in transit).

- **POP3**: POP3 is the third iteration of the **Post Operation Protocol**. This protocol deals with the other side: SMTP ensures the mail gets delivered to the server, and POP3 allows the users to read their mail from the server. POP3 allows for offline access to email, but it can only access one mailbox at a time. If you want to read multiple mailboxes (or accounts, if you will), you need to set up more than one POP3 connection.

- **IMAP**: IMAP stands for **Internet Message Access Protocol**. This protocol is also meant to read mail from the server. But this protocol can read multiple mailboxes in one go. IMAP can access, search, manipulate, and delete your emails without downloading them. It can send these commands to the server in an RPC way (we discussed RPC extensively in *Chapter 7*).

- **MIME**: Despite not having a P at the end of the acronym, **MIME** is also a protocol. It is the acronym for **Multipurpose Internet Mail Extension** protocol. As the name suggests, it is an extension, allowing us to have attachments, multimedia, and non-ASCII characters in our mail messages.

All these protocols enable us to have a functional, complete mail experience.

Sending an email

That being said, most software sends mail messages; it hardly ever reads them. So, let's look at a simple sample of how to send an email in code. The sample code I provide consists of three parts. Let's look at them:

```
using System.Net.Mail;
// Create the mail message
MailMessage mail = new MailMessage();
mail.From = new MailAddress("dennis@vroegop.org");
mail.To.Add("dearreader@thisbook.com");
mail.Subject = "Hi there System Programmer!";
mail.Body =
    "This is a test email from the System Programming
      book.";
```

Obviously, we need a message. Otherwise, why would we connect to an SMTP server?

The message is of type `MailMessage`. It needs a sender, and it can have multiple recipients. Those recipients can be in the To, CC, or BCC fields. To, CC, and BCC are all lists, so you can add multiple recipients. Of course, you need to supply at least the To recipients.

We can supply a Subject field. I would really encourage you to do that, of course. Then we have a Body, which contains the message we want to send.

Once we have the message, we can create an instance of the `SmtpClient` class.

You need to have access to a real SMTP server, of course. Most internet service providers have them, so please look up how to connect to them in their documentation. You usually need a username and password to authenticate yourself. In the old days, there were anonymous servers, but in these days of spam, those are very hard to find.

We have to specify the server's address and port (port 25 is the old port; port 587 is the new, secure one, and the preferred port to use), and you can specify whether you want to use SSL. That code looks like this:

```
// Set up the connection to the SMTP server
// And no, this is NOT a valid SMTP server. Use your own :)
SmtpClient client =
    new SmtpClient("smtp.vroegop.org");
client.Port = 587;
client.EnableSsl = true;
client.Credentials =
    new System.Net.NetworkCredential(
        "dennis@vroegop.org",
        "MySuperSecretPassword");
```

And finally, we can send the message!

```
// Send the email!
client.Send(mail);
```

Once you have set up the client, you can send multiple messages using that same client instance. You do not have to worry about setting up connections. You can just call Send, and it all works.

Sending HTML messages

The previous example works fine, but the message is kind of bland. These days, messages are much more colorful and pleasant to look at. The way to do that is to send an HTML message. You can do that by just putting HTML in the Body field and setting the `IsBodyHtml` property of `MailMessage` to true. But that is not the best way to do that for the following two reasons:

- Not all clients support HTML. The readers must decipher the HTML to find the body text if their client does not support HTML.
- Messages only containing HTML are usually marked as spam.

The best way to do this is to combine your beautifully crafted HTML body and a more down-to-earth plain text body. You can do that by using the `AlternateView` class. The code to create the mail message looks like this:

```
var multipartMail = new MailMessage();
multipartMail.From = new MailAddress("dennis@vroegop.org");
multipartMail.To.Add("dearreader@thisbook.com");
multipartMail.Subject = "Hi there System Programmer!";

var htmlBody = "<html><body><h1>Hi there System Programmer!</h1></body></html>";
var htmlView =
    AlternateView.CreateAlternateViewFromString(
        htmlBody,
        null,
        "text/html");
var plainView =
    AlternateView.CreateAlternateViewFromString(
        "This is a test email from the System Programming book.",
        null,
        "text/plain");
multipartMail.AlternateViews.Add(plainView);
multipartMail.AlternateViews.Add(htmlView);
```

We create an instance of the regular `MailMessage` class. Most of the fields are the same. But we do not specify a body. Instead, we create two instances of the `AlternateView` class by calling the `CreateAlternateViewFromString` static method. That method takes the content we want to send (either HTML or plain text) and the encoding we use (we set it to NULL, so it uses the default setting for your machine). We do have to specify the content type. The first contains `"text/html"` and the second contains `"text/plain"`.

We then add both parts to the `MailMessage` instance, and we can send it.

The rest of the code stays the same.

That covers some of the higher-level classes. It is now time to go deeper into the rabbit hole.

Working with the System.Net.Sockets namespace

The default protocols are fantastic. They take away a lot of manual work. We do not have to program the HTTP protocol ourselves; we can focus on the content instead. The same goes for SMTP, POP3, and all the other protocols out there. You can find a class or a NuGet package if the protocol you want to use is popular enough.

But of course, sometimes you cannot find that package. Sometimes, you want to write your own protocol. In that case, you have to do all the hard work yourself. But, I have to be honest, I immensely enjoy doing that. There is something nice about writing my protocol, deploying it in my apps, and seeing them work together. And even if you do not enjoy this, there are cases where you have no choice.

The good news is that the good people who wrote the BCL have already done much of the underlying work.

In *Chapter 6*, we encountered the `Socket` class when we discussed how systems can communicate. Sockets were mentioned as one of the options. We wrote a simple chat application that uses TCP/IP to communicate. TCP/IP is one of the ways sockets can connect.

In the chat sample I mentioned, we created instances of the `TcpListener` and `TcpClient` classes. These classes are wrappers around the more generic `Socket` class. They are specifically used for TCP/IP connections and handle much of the plumbing needed to get this to work.

You can use sockets yourself, of course. That means you must do much of the work yourself, giving you more control over what happens.

You can use sockets with TCP and UDP connections. We looked at the differences in *Chapter 6*, so we won't compare them again here. However, you should use the `Socket` class if you want to use UDP: obviously, `TCPClient` will not work. By the way, there is also a `UdpClient` class, with which you can achieve the same result. However, I want you to be aware of the inner workings. That is why I am going with `Sockets` here.

Steps to take when using sockets

When working with sockets, you need to take a number of steps:

1. Choose the right socket. You can use stream sockets. Stream sockets are based on the TCP protocol. It is a reliable, connection-oriented protocol. But you can also choose datagram sockets. These are based on the UDP protocol. They are connectionless, fire-and-forget ways of communicating. It is quick, but you have no guarantee the data will reach the intended recipient.
2. Then, you create the socket. You specify the kind of address you want to use (IPV4 or IPV6), the type of socket (stream or datagram), and the protocol (TCP or UDP).
3. It's time to connect. You either listen to incoming connections or connect to a server somewhere. When you connect to a remote server, you must specify the IP address and the port. If you are listening, you need the port at least, and if you have more network connections, you might want to specify the IP address you are listening to.
4. Sending and receiving data. After all, that's what we are here for, right?
5. When you are done, you must be sure to close the connection. You do not want to hold on to a connection for too long: you might get in the way of other applications.

And that is all there is to it. If I put it like this, it seems straightforward, doesn't it? Well, the devil is in the details!

IPv4 and IPv6

We need to talk a bit about the IP address. The **IP** address, which stands for **Internet Protocol** address, is a unique number identifying a network device. It is unique within boundaries, but we will discuss that later. There are two kinds of addresses we can use: IPv4 and IPv6. As you might have guessed, these acronyms are Internet Protocol version 4 and version 6, respectively.

The first publicly used version was IPv4. IPv5 never saw the light of day, leaving us with two versions. It has always been the idea to replace IPv4 with IPv6 completely, but it seems IPv4 will stay around for a bit longer.

An IPv4 address consists of 4 bytes, thus making it 32 bits long. This size means that there are about 4.3 billion unique addresses in theory. In practice, there are fewer since many ranges are reserved. We have already encountered one of them: the address is `127.0.0.1`. This is the address of the device itself.

Although different systems can reserve different port ranges, there is a common understanding of what ranges we should avoid using or what ranges we can use. These ranges are explained like this:

- **Port 0 – 1023**: Well-known ports. These ports are used everywhere and you should not use them yourself.
- **Port 1024 – 49151**: A lot of the ports in this range are registered and well-known, such as port `1433`, which is used by SQL Server. However, these are not as strictly assigned as the range `0 – 1023`.
- **Port 49152 – 65535**: This range is known as the dynamic or private range. They are usually used for ephemeral or short-lived communications. They are, most of the time, dynamically allocated by the operating system.

Just make sure the port you pick is not yet in use on your intended system!

An IPv6 address comprises 8 sets of 2-byte structures, making it 128 bits in length. You can fit substantially more addresses in that address space: there are about 340 undecillion unique addresses.

> **Big numbers**
>
> Working with computers means you sometimes run into big numbers. This is such a case: an undecillion is 10 to the power of 36. That means the number is 340, followed by 36 zeros. That's a lot of addresses.

The IPv6 address is displayed as a sequence of 8 sets of 16-bit hexadecimal values. For instance, a valid address could look like this: `2001:0db8:85a3:0000:0000:8a2e:0370:7334`.

This is also an interesting address: `0000:0000:0000:0000:0000:0000:0000:0001`. This is the IPv6 version of 127.0.0.1. In other words, this is localhost. However, it is pretty long: there are 7 sets of `0000`. With IPv6 we can omit a range of `0000` values with two colons. So we can shorten the address for localhost to ::1.

Both in IPv4 and IPv6, we have reserved ranges. For instance, everything in the range `192.168.0.0` up to `192.168.255.255` is used for internal networks. You cannot, however, assign these addresses to devices facing the public network. The same goes for the addresses `10.0.0.0 to 10.255.255.255` and `172.16.0.0 to 172.31.255.255`.

Looking up time with sockets

It is time to look at how to do all this for real.

There are servers out there that work as time servers. These servers have one purpose: wait for your connection and then respond with the current date and time. The way they do this is pretty interesting: they calculate the time it takes to send a response and adjust the time accordingly, thus making sure the answer is as accurate as possible.

Let's look at some code:

```
public DateTime GetNetworkTime(string ntpServer = "pool.ntp.org")
{
    // NTP message size - 16 bytes (RFC 2030)
    var ntpData = new byte[48];
    // Setting the Leap Indicator, Version Number and Mode values
    ntpData[0] = 0x23; // LI, Version, Mode
    var addresses = Dns.GetHostEntry(ntpServer);
    var ipEndPoint = new IPEndPoint(addresses.AddressList[0], 123);
      // NTP uses port 123
    using (var socket = new Socket(AddressFamily.InterNetwork,
      SocketType.Dgram, ProtocolType.Udp))
    {
        socket.Connect(ipEndPoint);
        socket.Send(ntpData);
        socket.Receive(ntpData);
        socket.Close();
    }
    return ConvertNtpTimeToDateTime(ntpData);
}
```

The method starts with a default value for the name of the server. We use `pool.ntp.org` as our server, but there are many more out there that would do the trick. They all use the NTP protocol (**NTP** means **Network Time Protocol**, in case you were wondering). NTP is one of the oldest protocols. Systems used this protocol to synchronize the clocks of computers over a network as far back as the early 80s!

The address we use, `pool.ntp.org`, is not a single computer but a pool of thousands of NTP servers, ensuring everybody can get their time. However, we can treat it as a single server. Oh, one word of warning: that URL is meant to be used by NTP clients. They use port `123`, as you can see in the code. If you use your browser to go to that address, you automatically use HTTP and thus port

80 (there is no HTTPS server at that address). This means you get to see whatever the maintainers of that pool want to put there. Do not use your browser to go to that URL; use port 123 as it is intended!

A request to the NTP server needs a buffer of 48 bytes to hold the answer. We need to add some data in that buffer when we connect to the server, telling it what we want. In our case, we give it the value 0x23. This byte consists of 3 groups of bits, each group telling the server something about what we want. Look at the following table to see what these bits mean:

Bits	Name	Description
6–7	Leap Indicator	Indicates whether we want to take the leap seconds a month might have into account. 0 means no adjustment, 1 means the last minute of the month has 61 seconds, 2 means the last minute of the month has 59 seconds, and 3 means the clock is unsynchronized.
4-6	Version	The version of the protocol we want to use. The latest version is 4.
0-3	Mode	0: Reserved 1: Symmetric active 2: Symmetric passive 3: Client 4: Server 5: Broadcast 6: NTP control message 7: Reserved

Table 8.1: Settings for NTP servers

We do not want to use leap adjustment. We are interested in using protocol version 4. And we are a client here. That means we have to do some bit-arithmetic. Working down from the most significant bits to the least significant bits, we get 00 for bits 6 and 7, 100 for bits 4, 5, and 6, and finally, 011 for bits 0 through 4. If we combine this, we get 0010 0011, or 23 in decimal.

We place that value in the first byte in the 48-byte long buffer we shall give to the server.

We have the name of the NTP server (pool.ntp.org), but we need the actual IP address of that machine. After all, sockets need an address and not a string of text. The **DNS**, or **Domain Name System**, can look up the current address belonging to a domain name. In my case, if I run the line var addresses = Dns.GetHostEntry(ntpServer);, I get 4 IP addresses back.

We take the first address we got back and construct an instance of an IPEndPoint class with that address and port 123.

Then, we can create an instance of the `Socket` class. We give it the `AddressFamily InterNetwork`, meaning we want to use IPv4 addresses. We also specify that we'll use a datagram, and thus, we use UDP.

> **Mixing streams, datagrams, TCP, and UDP**
>
> You must specify what socket type and protocol type you want to use. However, if you use `SocketType.Stream`, you must also use `ProtocolType.TCP`. And if you want to use `SocketType.DGram`, you must also use `ProtocolType.UDP`. If you try to mix these (you want datagram over TCP, for instance), you get an exception during runtime. So, be careful what you choose.

We call `connect` on the socket, giving it the endpoint we created. After that, we send the server our 48-byte buffer containing information about `leap`, `version`, and `mode`. Next, we try to get an answer by calling `Receive`, using that same buffer.

Of course, when we get the answer, we close the connection.

Once the answer is received and safely stored in our buffer, we can do some calculations to transform the data into something we can use in a `DateTime` structure. That specific piece of code we call contains conversions between different formats, swapping bits, and more. They have nothing to do with getting data from a server, so I leave it out. The sample on GitHub has that code, so please check that out if you want to see what that looks like.

The code that deals with the socket was not that complicated. But there is a problem with this code. It is what we call **blocking code**. It blocks the entire thread for the duration of the call to the NTP server. Let's fix that.

Async, non-blocking networking

It should be evident by now that you must ensure that all non-instantaneous operations in your code are a potential performance issue. Slow operations can block a process from continuing. File I/O is one of the areas where this is appropriate. Networking is even slower than that. So, everything that we can do asynchronously should be implemented that way.

The good news is that most classes dealing with networking have asynchronous versions of their methods. The bad news is that for `Socket`, it is not as straightforward as you might have hoped. But do not worry: we will tackle this soon!

Making asynchronous calls

In the previous sample, we used the static `Dns` class to get information about the address of the NTP server. We called `GetHostEntry()`, which is a synchronous blocking call. We can fix that quite easily: `Dns` has asynchronous versions of those methods. We can rewrite the call to look like this:

```
var addresses = await Dns.GetHostEntryAsync(ntpServer);
```

Of course, the signature of the method needs to change as well. Instead of having this method declaration: `public DateTime GetNetworkTime(string ntpServer = "pool.ntp.org")`.

We change it into this:

`public async Task<DateTime> GetNetworkTimeAsync(string ntpServer = "pool.ntp.org")`

We made it `async`, changed the return type to `Task<DateTime>` instead of `DateTime`, and renamed the method to have the `Async` postfix.

That was simple enough. We can do the same for the code working with `Socket`. This is the full method:

```
public async Task<DateTime> GetNetworkTimeAsync(string ntpServer = "pool.ntp.org")
{
    // NTP message size - 16 bytes (RFC 2030)
    var ntpData = new byte[48];
    // Setting the Leap Indicator, Version Number, and Mode values
    ntpData[0] = 0x23; // LI, Version, Mode
    var addresses = await Dns.GetHostEntryAsync(ntpServer);
    var ipEndPoint = new IPEndPoint(addresses.AddressList[0], 123);
      // NTP uses port 123
    using (var socket = new Socket(
            AddressFamily.InterNetwork,
            SocketType.Dgram,
            ProtocolType.Udp))
    {
        await socket.ConnectAsync(ipEndPoint);
        await socket.SendAsync(
            new ArraySegment<byte>(ntpData),
            SocketFlags.None);
        await socket.ReceiveAsync(
            new ArraySegment<byte>(ntpData),
            SocketFlags.None);
    }
    return ConvertNtpTimeToDateTime(ntpData);
}
```

This version takes advantage of the async/await pattern, so the calls to the server do not block the threads.

> **Tip**
> Networking code should always use asynchronous methods instead of synchronous ones. Networking is slow compared to the raw speed of the CPU and the local machine, so why waste time waiting on that slow trickle of data from the network adapter?

However, there are ways to improve the performance of your system when you use networking. Let's look at those next.

Networking performance

Since networking is comparatively slow, we have to be smart about ways to improve the throughput of the data. We can control local networks, ensuring we have optic fiber and super-fast routers everywhere, but that does not solve the issues. Even the fastest physical network is way slower than data handled in the CPU. Of course, having fast hardware helps. But it only helps on our own network: we cannot control the hardware on other networks. We must be wise in our code to get the most out of our networking. Once again, it all comes down to us, the developers!

Connection pooling

A connection represents an open line between a client and a server. Let's look at the following line of code:

```
var client = new TcpClient("my.server.com", 123);
```

This single line of code is simple enough: this creates a connection to a server called my.server.com on port 123 and returns the open connection. Fine. We've seen that before. But let me show you what happens when you run that line of code:

- **Name resolution**: The framework uses DNS to look up the address of that connection, translating the my.server.com string into the correct IPv4 or IPv6 addresses we can use.
- **Socket creation**: The Socket class is instantiated, allocating the memory for it and ensuring it is available.
- **Connection attempt**: The socket tries to connect to the IP address it found for the address. This is a multi-step process, and it requires a couple of round trips to the server. These are the steps:
    I. **The client sends SYN**: A message with the payload SYN is sent to the server. Basically, the client is asking, "Hey, can we talk?"
    II. **The server sends SYN-ACK**: The server is listening on the port, and if the SYN message comes in, it responds with SYN-ACK, acknowledging that it is ready to talk.
    III. **The client sends ACK**: The client confirms that it received SYN-ACK, that apparently the network works fine, and that they can talk.

When all this has happened, the communication line is open and ready for use. We can start sending and receiving data.

As you can see, a lot of work is involved in that simple line of code. You can imagine that the handshaking between the client and the server takes a lot of time. Network connections are expensive!

There is no getting around this. These steps need to be taken. But there is no reason to do them more than you need to. If you have a connection to a server, you might reuse it as well. We call that connection pooling. We create a pool of connections, and whenever something in our system needs to talk to the server, we return the already-created connection.

Unfortunately, the BCL does not have a class for this. But it is not too hard to write one yourself. You could do it like this.

We create a class called `TcpClientConnectionPool`. The signature looks like this:

```
internal class TcpClientConnectionPool : IAsyncDisposable{}
```

We have three methods in that class:

```
public TcpClient? GetConnection(){}
public void ReturnConnection(TcpClient? client) {}
public async ValueTask DisposeAsync(){}
```

Before we look at what those methods do, we need to create two private fields in the class:

```
private readonly ConcurrentBag<TcpClient?> _availableConnections = new();
private readonly int _maxPoolSize = 10; // Example pool size
```

When you create a pool to hold objects, you need a place to store them. We use `ConcurrentBag<T>` here. `ConcurrentBag` is a thread-safe collection that has the following characteristics:

- **Thread safe**: You can add, access, and remove objects without worrying about locks or other threads running amock. This class handles the details for you.
- **Unordered**: There is no specific order. In our case, this is just fine. However, if you want to use something like FIFO, you should use a class with an order built in.
- **Duplicates are allowed**: You can add the same object to the collection if you want.
- **Performance**: This class is optimized for scenarios where the same thread adds or removes items but performs pretty well in mixed scenarios.

The `GetConnection()` method pulls an object from the pool if one is available. If one is not, it creates one for you. Here it is:

```
public TcpClient? GetConnection()
{
    if (_availableConnections.TryTake(out TcpClient? client))
        return client;
    if (_availableConnections.Count < _maxPoolSize)
    {
        // Create a new connection if the pool is not full
```

```
            client = new TcpClient("my.server.com", 443);
        }
        else
        {
            // Pool is full; wait for an available connection or throw an
            // exception
            // This strategy depends on your specific requirements
            throw new Exception("Connection pool limit reached.");
        }
        return client;
}
```

In this example, I throw an exception when the pool has reached the maximum allowed objects. You want to limit the number of TcpClient instances in your code: they take up quite a lot of memory and underlying handles, so having an unlimited amount of them lying around might not be the best idea.

If there is room in the pool but no items are available, we create a new one and return it to the caller. The idea is that after using, the caller returns the object, and we store it in the collection, ready for another user to pick it up. We use lazy initialization here: we only create TcpClient when needed.

If you want, you can create all 10 instances in the constructor of this class. That makes the initialization of the class slower, and it uses more memory, but it is much faster during the object's lifetime.

When the connection user calls this method, it gets an active and open connection. When the user no longer needs TcpClient, it needs to be returned so it can be stored in the pool and ready for the following user. That method looks like this:

```
public void ReturnConnection(TcpClient? client)
{
    // Check the state of the connection to ensure it's still valid
    if (client is { Connected: true })
    {
        _availableConnections.Add(client);
    }
    else
    {
        // Optionally, handle the case where the connection is no
        // longer valid
        // e.g., reconnect or simply discard this connection
    }
}
```

We can do some checking when we get TcpClient back. For instance, I usually check to see whether it is still connected here. It is a bit like a library: when you return your items, they expect them to be pristine. We do the same here. If there is something wrong, we can fix it or not even add it back to the pool. I'll leave that up to you.

Finally, when the connection pool is disposed of, we do some cleaning up:

```
public async ValueTask DisposeAsync()
{
    foreach (var client in _availableConnections)
    {
        if (client is { Connected: true })
        {
            await client.GetStream().DisposeAsync();
        }
        client?.Close();
        client?.Dispose();
    }
}
```

We go through all the remaining instances of `TcpClient` in our collection, close them if needed, dispose of the underlying stream, and dispose of the instances themselves. This makes sure we leave no connection open. My mother taught me this at a very young age: always clean up after yourself!

To finalize this part, this is how you would use this class:

```
await using var connectionPool = new TcpClientConnectionPool();
TcpClient? myConnection = connectionPool.GetConnection();
try
{
    var myBuffer = "Hello, World!"u8.ToArray();
    // Use the connection
    await myConnection.Client.SendAsync(myBuffer);
}
finally
{
    connectionPool.ReturnConnection(myConnection);
}
```

I first create an instance of `connectionPool`. Obviously, you would not do that in each method call that needs a connection, but for this simple example, it is all right.

Then I try to get a connection by calling `GetConnection()`.

Then I get some bytes by taking the `Hello, World` string, postfixing that with u8 to ensure it is UTF-8 and then converting it to a byte array.

I can use my pooled connection to send that string to the server. Finally, I can put the connection back in the pool.

This sample is limited in functionality and lacks a lot of the code you would need before taking it into production. But I am sure it will help you get on your way.

What we are doing is caching our connections. But caching can help in a lot of other ways as well.

Caching

Caching stores data nearby so you can reuse it instead of going to the server each time. That sounds simple enough: it can be a huge performance booster. Getting an object from a memory location on your machine instead of going to a remote server each time sounds like a no-brainer, right? But there are some potential pitfalls you need to take into account. Here are the most important ones:

- **Stale data**: Data might change. For instance, our NTP sample changes every millisecond. That being said, you might retrieve it from the server once and then add the local time that's elapsed since you got it. It will eventually run out of sync (NTP servers are much more precise than your local machine), but I am sure it will not be that big of an issue soon. But data will get stale. You have to take that into account if you store data locally. How often will data change? How important is it that I have the latest version?

- **Memory overhead**: Storing items locally on your machine takes up local memory. Storing large amounts of (large) objects takes up a lot of data, which might slow down your total application. It might even lead to out-of-memory exceptions. You must decide what you use frequently and what can be left on the server.

- **Complexity in cache invalidation**: If data gets stale, you have to renew it. That requires code to monitor the data and refresh it when needed. That code can get quite complicated. You might have a separate thread that monitors your local cache, or you might decide when something pulls that data from the cache. Either way, you have to write a lot of monitoring code. That might overly complicate your software.

- **Security concerns**: Data on your machine is not always safe. If you store sensitive data on the local machine, it might be susceptible to snooping, especially if you store that cached data on a storage medium. Be sure to handle sensitive data safely.

- **Costs of cache misses**: When your application relies on getting data from the cache and only has it read from the remote server when you have a cache miss (thus, the item is not in the cache yet), you might have introduced a performance bottleneck. The logic of going through the cache, only to go out to the server if the data is not available, takes time. If the data you need is not needed that often, this is probably not the best case for caching.

- **Inconsistent data**: Suppose your app uses data from the cache, but another system or part of your system uses data from the server. In that case, there might be discrepancies between the data. This is not only stale data, but it means that two systems use different data – data they expect to be the same. If that might be an issue, caching might be a bad idea.

Caching can speed up your application, but be aware of the risks involved. Before implementing this, you should consider the potential risks and benefits.

Compression and serialization

If transferring data over the wire is slow, transmitting or requesting less data can help. So, compression and how you serialize data can help. In earlier chapters, we looked into compression and serialization, so I will not go into detail here. But please remember: if there is one place where it helps a lot when you use compression, this is the place. You can speed up network communications if you reduce the payload by compressing it first. And of course, choosing the correct serialization technique also helps.

Since we already looked at how to do compression, I will not show you it again here. You already know how to use the `GZipStream` class in the `System.IO.Compression` namespace (yes, that was a hint).

Keep-alive connections

Creating a `TcpClient` is not that expensive per se. Opening a connection to a server is expensive, however. It can help to keep connections open as long as you can. The `HTTPClient` class is very good at that: it is built so that you can leave the connection open for a long time without getting in your way. If you use sockets, you can do something similar. However, keeping a connection open when you do not need it anymore is not a good idea. If you do not need it, please close the connection. Otherwise, by all means, keep it open. Of course, if you keep a connection open, you also affect the other party. A client that clings to a connection also limits the server. You have to think about this a lot and make the right decisions.

Networking errors and time-outs

When dealing with networks, there is one rule you have to keep in mind. That rule is: *assume that the other party is not answering your call.*

Servers go down. Connections can drop. Networks are unreachable. There are a whole lot of issues that will (not might!) happen.

You must use defensive coding to ensure it doesn't impact your code too much. Of course, if you rely on an external machine to get the data you need, and that machine is not available, you have a problem. But maybe you can get around it. Perhaps you can cache older data. Or, you can retry if something goes wrong.

Let me help you with some strategies you can use to deal with hiccups in the network.

Using the HTTPClient wisely

The `HTTPClient` class has some neat tricks to help you with making the use of it more stable. For instance, connection pooling comes free and out of the box in this handy class. And they built that connection pooling in a pretty clever way.

The general advice is to create one instance of `HTTPClient` and use that throughout your system. The class is smart enough to pool connections to a server. If you use the same `HTTPClient` to get data from another server, the class creates a new pool, so those connections also get pooled.

Of course, be careful what you do: do not generate connections to hundreds of servers if you do not need them. They still take up memory in your system.

Another way to make `HTTPClient` more resilient is to use a default configuration for your connections. I always ensure I set `DefaultRequestHeaders` so I know that I can handle the data coming in.

And I always make sure I have a `TimeOut` on my instance. That way, I know that the `HTTPClient` will not have to wait too long for data from the server.

I suggest you use something such as a `Factory` to create your instances. I use one that looks like this:

```csharp
internal static class HttpClientFactory
{
    private static HttpClient? _instance;
    public static HttpClient? Instance
    {
        get
        {
            if (_instance == null) CreateInstance();
            return _instance;
        }
    }
    private static void CreateInstance()
    {
        var handler = new HttpClientHandler()
        {
            UseCookies = true,
            CookieContainer = new CookieContainer(),
            UseProxy = false
        };
        _instance = new HttpClient(handler);
        _instance.DefaultRequestHeaders.Clear();
        _instance.DefaultRequestHeaders.Accept.Add(new
          MediaTypeWithQualityHeaderValue("application/json"));
        _instance.DefaultRequestHeaders.Add("User-Agent",
          "SystemProgrammersApp");
        _instance.Timeout = TimeSpan.FromSeconds(5);
    }
}
```

This static class creates an instance of `HTTPClient` for me if needed. It tells the handler that it needs to use `Cookies` and that I do not want a proxy on my connection. I also set `DefaultRequestHeaders` and asked it to accept `application/json` data. I also added a nice user agent so the server knows who it is talking to. Finally, I set the `timeout` to 5 seconds.

If I need an `HTTPClient` instance, I can get it like this:

```
var client = HttpClientFactory.Instance;
var response = await client.GetAsync(
        "https://jsonplaceholder.typicode.com/posts");
if (response.IsSuccessStatusCode)
{
    string content = await response.Content.ReadAsStringAsync();
    $"Received: {content}".Dump(ConsoleColor.Yellow);
}
```

The first time I needed that client, it built it. But the second time and after that, it will pull it from the connection pool, making it a lot quicker and more resilient to mistakes.

I also ensure I do not use the `GetStringAsync()` method or `GetStreamAsync()` directly from `HTTPClient`. I first get the `Response` (of the type `HttpResponseMessage`) to check whether the result is valid. As we have seen, this is what the `IsSuccessStatusCode` property tells us.

This way, your communications with an HTTP server will become faster and much more stable.

Implementing retries with Polly

But of course, things will still go wrong. The server might be busy, or the network might be congested. The best way to get around that is to try again, and then again, until either it works or you give up.

You could write that logic yourself, but you would be better off using a standard library. The most used library that implements this is called **Polly**.

So, let's install that NuGet package in our application first. You can do so in the CLI by using this command:

```
Install-Package Polly
```

Once you have done that, we can change our `HttpClientFactory` class a bit.

First, add a new `private static` field to that class:

```
private static AsyncRetryPolicy<HttpResponseMessage> _retryPolicy;
```

This is our `RetryPolicy`, which we will apply to the requests.

At the end of the `CreateInstance` method in the `HttpClientFactory` class, add a call to a new method: `SetupRetryPolicy`. The method looks like this:

```
private static void SetupRetryPolicy()
{
    _retryPolicy = Policy
        .Handle<HttpRequestException>()
        .OrResult<HttpResponseMessage>(r => !r.IsSuccessStatusCode)
        .WaitAndRetryAsync(
            3,
            retryAttempt => TimeSpan.FromSeconds(Math.Pow(2,
              retryAttempt)),
            (outcome, timeSpan, retryCount, context) =>
            {
                $"Request failed with
                  {outcome.Result.StatusCode}.".Dump(ConsoleColor.Red);
                $"Waiting {timeSpan} before next
                  retry.".Dump(ConsoleColor.Red);
                $"Retry attempt
                  {retryCount}.".Dump(ConsoleColor.Red);
            });
}
```

In the static `Policy` class, we call the `Handle()` method. We give it the `HttpRequestException` type parameter. This way, the framework knows the trigger to start retrying. We also tell it to retry if `HttpResponseMessage.IsSuccessStatusCode` is set to false.

If one of those conditions arises, we tell the policy to `WaitAndRetryAsync`. We ask it to give it three retries after the first failure. The following parameter tells the `Policy` to wait for 2, 4, or 8 seconds (2 to the power of the retry number). So, it waits twice as long each time to give the server time to get its stuff in order.

We also give it a delegate that the framework will execute as soon as it starts to retry. In this case, we print out some messages to the console, telling it what failed, how long it will wait before it tries again, and how many times it has tried already.

With that in place, we can rewrite how we ask the `HTTPClient` for data. In the previous example, I showed you how to get the `Instance` from the factory and then use that instance directly. I want to move that code to `HttpClientFactory` as well. But the call to the server must be wrapped up in our new `Policy`. The method looks like this:

```
public static async Task<HttpResponseMessage> GetAsync(string url)
{
    return await _retryPolicy.ExecuteAsync(
        () => _instance.GetAsync(url));
```

Instead of the user of our class calling `GetAsync(url)`, we do it for them using this wrapper method. But we wrap up that call in `_retryPolicy.ExecuteAsync()`.

Change the original code that uses this factory to look like this:

```
var client = HttpClientFactory.Instance;
var response = await HttpClientFactory.GetAsync(
        "https://jsonplaceholder.typicode.com/posts2");
if (response.IsSuccessStatusCode)
{
    string content = await response.Content.ReadAsStringAsync();
    $"Received: {content}".Dump(ConsoleColor.Yellow);
}
```

Instead of calling `client.GetAsync()`, I now call `HttpClientFactory.GetAsync()`. The rest hasn't changed. Well, that's not entirely true. I also altered the URL a bit. I am not asking for `posts2` instead of `posts` in that URL. And that doesn't exist. That should trigger our retry mechanism.

Run it and see what happens. There you go – retries done the right way!

The circuit breaker pattern

A similar pattern is the circuit breaker pattern. This pattern detects when connections are in a fault state and prevents the system from making calls to the server for a predefined period. If the connection raises errors, the circuit breaker opens and stops all communications to that server for a while. After that cooldown period, it opens a bit to allow another quick peek at the server. If it seems to work, it allows full traffic. Otherwise, it will give up and let you know things have gone wrong.

The circuit breaker is also part of the Polly NuGet package.

Validating network availability

Trying to connect to a server that doesn't exist will result in errors. But what happens if your own network has an issue? In that case, it would look like all servers worldwide are down.

That last scenario doesn't seem so likely, so verifying that our network is healthy would be nice before we blame the entire internet.

It turns out that it is not too hard to do so. All you need is one line of code:

```
bool isHealthy =    System.Net.NetworkInformation.NetworkInterface.
GetIsNetworkAvailable();
```

That's all there is to it.

You can also interrogate each network adaptor in your machine like this:

```
foreach (NetworkInterface ni in NetworkInterface.
GetAllNetworkInterfaces())
{
    $"Name: {ni.Name}".Dump(ConsoleColor.DarkYellow);
    $"Type:{ni.NetworkInterfaceType}".Dump(ConsoleColor.DarkYellow);
    $"Status: {ni.OperationalStatus}".Dump(ConsoleColor.DarkYellow);
}
```

We can iterate through all network adapters and see what their status is. That can help us to select the suitable adapter and thus the right IP address if we want to be resilient against errors and failures.

Monitoring and logging

This one goes without saying: *the best way to solve issues is to log and monitor what is happening*. If you have extensive logging, you are much more likely to find problems if they occur. But let's not worry about that too much for now.

If you follow these tips and tricks, you will still face network issues. They are inevitable. But at least network failures will not bring your system down.

Next steps

In this chapter, we took a deep dive into networking. We broke out of the confines of the local machine and looked at all the good stuff that the BCL gives us when it comes to connecting to the outside world.

We looked at default protocols such as HTTP, FTP, and SMTP. We also looked at sockets in case the predefined protocols are not good enough, such as when you want to look up the current time from a time server. We dove into asynchronous networking and talked a lot about performance and making our networking error-proof and more robust.

Let's be honest: almost no computer these days runs on its own. Most machines and thus the software running on them, are somehow connected to the outside world. Especially the things we as system programmers are interested in are not used by users, but instead by other software. Some of that software lives on other machines. This means it is imperative you know about networking. And now you do!

We did not talk about security and logging. Logging is something we touch on in *Chapter 10*. Security is the topic of *Chapter 12*. Yes, these topics are so important they deserve their own chapter.

But before we go there, let's take a little trip to other platforms. Since systems programming works closely with devices, I thought it would be fun to dive into another device and see if we could talk to some fancy hardware. So, let's go there next!

9
The One with the Hardware Handshakes

Hardware interaction and control

As system programmers, we never deal with users. We deal with other software. That other software could be on the same machine, or it could be on another machine. And sometimes, we deal with hardware. That hardware could be part of our machine, hardware attached to our machine, or hardware somewhere else.

In this chapter, we will look into all of these options. We will look at interacting with hardware directly and connecting to remote devices, and we will dive deep into the world of serial communications.

In this chapter, we're going to cover the following main topics:

- Connecting to a serial port on Windows.
- Setting up an Arduino device
- Programming a simple program on an Arduino
- Getting data from a serial port
- Handling events from the outside
- Debugging code depending on external devices
- Make this sort of code as reliable as possible
- All in all, we have much ground to cover. Join me in exploring this new land of exotic hardware!

Technical requirements

In this chapter, we will dive into some external hardware. I will show you how to talk to an **Arduino microcontroller** through a serial connection.

If you do not have access to such a device, do not worry. I will also talk about how to mock these devices so that you can test your code before deploying it on an actual device. You can follow along and try out the code if you encounter these devices later.

As always, you can download the source code for these samples from the GitHub repository at `https://github.com/PacktPublishing/Systems-Programming-with-C-Sharp-and-.NET/tree/main/SystemsProgrammingWithCSharpAndNet/Chapter09`.

Connecting to serial ports

It is time to have some fun. Let's break out of the confinements of the machine we are working on and step into the world of peripherals.

However, before we look at the code, we have to see how software communicates with hardware.

The path to the hardware

Let's say we have an application connecting to some hardware. It doesn't matter what kind of hardware, but let's say we want to send data to a USB port.

Sending data from our application to the device involves several steps where the data is transformed. It is slightly like the OSI layer we discussed in the previous chapter.

It all starts with our application. We devised the C# code to send data to the USB device. We have downloaded the correct NuGet packages, installed the frameworks, written the code, and compiled it into an executable.

When that executable runs, that code is called the correct code in the .NET libraries installed on your machine when you installed the runtime or the SDK. The BCL has a class called `SerialPort` that receives the commands from your code and translates them to the next layer, where the .NET runtime hands over the commands to the operating system. In our case, that is Windows. Windows looks at the data and where it needs to go and decides it cannot handle it. It is hardware, so the operating system calls upon the device driver for the USB port.

The device driver ensures it has everything needed for the specific hardware it is written for. It knows about baud rates, parity, stop bits, and so on. Once that is all figured out, the device driver sends the data to the USB/serial controller. This controller is a bit of hardware that physically connects to the port.

Once the data has come that far, it leaves our system on a set of wires, out of our machine, and on its way to some other hardware.

A lot is going on, but we hardly see it. All we see in our code is the following:

```
using var serialPort = new SerialPort(
    "COM3",
    9600,
    Parity.None,
    8,
    StopBits.One);
serialPort.Open();
try
{
    serialPort.Write([42],0, 1);
}
finally
{
    serialPort.Close();
}
```

We create an instance of the `SerialPort` class. We give it the parameters it expects. First, we need to specify which port we want to talk to. Computers usually have more than one serial port. In the old days, computers did have a minimal number of physical ports. They were either parallel ports, capable of sending multiple bits simultaneously, or serial ports, which could only process one bit simultaneously. The serial ports were also called **Communication Ports**, shortened to **COMs**. In my example, we connect to the third one because I happen to know there is hardware attached to that port that I can talk to.

I also give it the speed – in my case, 9,600 baud.

> **Baud versus bits per second**
>
> There is a common misconception about the best way to describe the speed of communications. We used **baud** for the older COM ports. The term *baud* is named after the French scientist Jean-Maurice-Emile Baudot (1845–1903), who worked on a system to allow multiple transmissions of a single telegraph wire. Baud stands for the number of signal changes per second.
>
> *Bits per second* means just that – how many bits per second can we send? Since baud is analog and can combine signals, there is no direct relationship between baud and bits per second.
>
> However, in most cases, they are pretty close. 9,600 baud can be considered to be around 9,600 bits per second. But don't rely on it!
>
> On a related note, a byte does not have to be 8 bits. A byte transmitted over a wire can be as long as 12 bits, depending on the communication settings.

We also define **parity as none**. We set the data packet to be 8 bits. We also add 1 stop bit.

The settings I have given here (no parity, 8 bits, and 1 stop bit) are the default settings, but you could have omitted them. However, you must ensure the device on the other side of the line uses the same settings. You can imagine what a mess it would be if you send 10 bits per byte, some of which are for error checking, and the other side expects only 8 bits to be sent per byte. It is better to be clear about this sort of thing.

Once we have `SerialPort`, we can open the connection. And when that is done, we send 1 byte over the wire. Somewhere in the chain from our application to the actual wires, the parity, conversion to the correct number of bits, and stop bits are added or converted, but we have nothing to do with that. The BCL, OS, and device drivers take care of it.

Of course, we finalize it all by closing the port again.

Receiving data is just as simple, but we will look at that later on.

Why do we care?

Serial communication, especially over COM ports, is old-school technology. These days, we use a wired network, Wi-Fi, Bluetooth, or USB if we want to connect to other hardware. Or, at least, that is what you might think.

For most software developers, this is true. They will hardly ever encounter a thing such as a serial port. But we system programmers are not like most software developers. We deal with hardware. And often, that hardware is old. Or at least the design of that hardware is old.

For instance, many factories have robots. A lot of them communicate over serial ports. Medical devices are another example. It takes a very long time to certify medical equipment, so the manufacturer is usually very reluctant to change part of the hardware just because a new kind of cable has been announced. They tend to stick to what works. As long as serial communications work well enough, they keep using them.

Industrial CNC machines, barcode scanners, and GPS receivers are all examples of hardware still used widely today that rely on serial ports. We system programmers are the developers most likely to encounter those devices.

So, it's crucial that you know what serial communication is and what it does. But, of course, how can you program for it?

Although you are not likely to see actual D-Port-style serial connectors on computers anymore (unless you specifically add one), serial ports are still a thing. The difference between those older ports and what we use today is that we use virtual COM ports.

The operating system and the device drivers channel communication through the USB port to the outside world, mimicking the older ports. The D-style ports had multiple pins for power, ground, data, TX signals, and much more. These days, the USB devices take care of that. But if you want to connect to one of these older machines, you can get cheap and simple USB-to-serial (or, technically, RS232) converters.

I suspect we will have serial ports for a long time to come. That is why I'm spending so much time discussing them here in this chapter.

A word about parity, data sizes, and stop bits

We set the serial port in the previous sample to use no parity, 8 data bits, and 1 stop bit. But what does that mean?

Usually, you do not need to care about how the actual hardware communicates. If you want to load a file from your storage medium, you are not bothered by the internal workings. You do not care whether the medium is a super-fast SSD or a slow SD card inserted somewhere. You choose where to store your data, and you are good to go. The operating system and device drivers take care of the rest.

For COMs, this isn't an option. You do not have to worry about the voltages across the wires, but you have to know a bit more about how the devices want to communicate. Oh, in case you are wondering, for low-speed USB devices, the voltages are between 0.0V and 0.3V for a zero and between 2.8V and 3.6V for a one. Now you know.

So, what do we need to know if we want to communicate over a serial communication line? Well, there are four parameters we need to decide on. Both the sender and the recipient need to agree on this. The serial protocol does not care: it only knows how to put ones and zeros on that line. We need to tell our software what that data means.

The parameters we need to set are the speed, whether we want to use parity, the size of a data packet, and whether we want to use stop bits.

Speed

Speed is essential. We specify the speed as the number of changes in voltages per second. We do not specify it in bits per second. This distinction is important because a bit is a discrete unit. A bit is a bit. Nothing more, nothing less. But a bit does not exist in the world of electronics; all we can deal with is a flow of electrons, making up voltages (I am really oversimplifying things here, but the basic idea is valid).

If a wire has a high voltage for a second, followed by a low voltage for a second, we have no idea what that means. It is just that – one second of high voltage, followed by one second of low voltage.

But if we establish that we can do four changes per second, we can determine that we got eight changes; the first four were high, and the second four were low. Then, we can agree that we had four 1s, followed by four 0s. Thus, in two seconds, we transmitted the bits 11110000. But if we would have established that we can do eight changes per second, the data would have been 11111111 00000000. And that is an entirely different number.

The baud rate, which we use to specify the speed, tells a system how much data is transmitted in a certain time or how long it takes to send one element (OK, this is a bit) over the wire.

It's all about timing, which can help hardware do some rudimentary error checking. I will explain this when we talk about stop bits.

Parity

Sometimes, data gets messed up. We are dealing with electrical connections here, which can sometimes be unreliable. Sometimes, the voltage drops or a spike occurs, getting in the way of the data we want to send. There are several advanced ways to handle this, but the oldest and easiest way to do some rudimentary checking is by using parity.

Three kinds of parity checks exist – **even, odd, and none**. None is the simplest – we do not want any checks.

The other two, even and odd, mean we add one extra bit to each data packet. That extra bit is either a one or a zero, so the total number of ones in the packages, including the parity bit, is an even or odd number.

Let's say we want to transmit the following sequence of 4 bits – 1011. If the parity is set to even, the system counts the number of ones in that message. It notices there are three, which is an odd number. We need to make it even, so the system adds a one to the package and sends that over the wire, resulting in the bits 10111.

If we had chosen to send 1001 over the wire, the number of ones is already even, so there is no need for an extra one. The system adds a zero and sends 10010 over the wire.

On the receiving end, the system counts the numbers of one in the package and checks to see whether it is indeed an even number. If that is not the case, something has gone wrong. The system can then ignore that package or request a resend.

Of course, if we had set the parity to odd, it would have only added a one if the number of ones in the data package was even.

If two bits flip instead of just one, the system falls apart. There is no way to tell that that happened with this simple setup. There are other ways to do that, but you must implement them yourself.

Parity does add data to a package, slowing communications down slightly.

The data size

How significant is a byte? I guess you are inclined to say 8 bits. But in the early days of computing, this was not a fixed number. There were lots of 10-bit-based computers. Data transmission was slow and expensive back then, so they decided they could get away with sending only 7 bytes if they wanted to send text. After all, most ASCII characters fit in 7 bits. So why send extra data? I know that these days, it is hard to imagine people worrying about an extra bit, but remember that times change. For instance, the first modem I used to connect my computer to the outside world had a transmission speed of 1200/75. That means it could receive with a speed of around 1,200 bits per second, or roughly 120 bytes per second. But I could only upload with 75 baud. That is around 10 bytes per second. Removing one bit can make a big difference in those cases!

`SerialPort` allows you to choose the size of your data package. This size is the number of bits each package contains, not counting the parity bit or any stop bits. You can choose between 7 or 8 bits. Technically, you could specify other sizes. In reality, you never encounter that in practice.

7 bits is enough for ASCII characters. If you use 8 bits, you double the amount of information you can transmit in one single go, but you also make it a bit slower. In the world of serial communication, this can be important.

The default is 8 bits, but if you want to really get the most out of your system, 7 bits might be a good idea.

Stop bits

Then, we have **stop bits**. Stop bits are added to a data package to signal that it is the end of that package. You can decide between 1, 1.5, or 2 stop bits. The system adds these bits to the end of the package, usually ones. Adding data achieves three things – first, it signals the end of the package. It helps detect timing issues or errors and allows the hardware to catch up.

Stop bits are not actual bits; they are not data. They do not reach the software at the end of the chain. Instead, they are a fixed amount of time when the voltage is high. This explains why we can have 1.5 stop bits. There is no *half a bit*, but you can set the voltage high for half the time it takes to transmit one bit. Remember when I said that timing can help detect errors? This is what I was talking about.

If the receiving system thinks it has received the agreed-upon 8 data bits and parity bits, it expects a stop bit (assuming we set the stop bit to 1). If the voltage on the line is low, something has gone wrong. Combined with the parity bit, this can detect simple errors.

The stop bits can be 1, 1.5, or 2 *bits* long (remember that they are not bits but the amount of time it takes to send a bit). Adding extra time between two packets means that a receiving system has time to process the bits it got, calculate the parity, and pass it on to the rest of the system before the next package arrives. Again, in these days of ultra-fast hardware, it seems weird to take that into account, but when serial communication was devised, adding 1, 1.5, or even 2 *bits* of pause could mean the difference between an excellent working system or a barrage of errors.

Working with an Arduino

I do not have a medical MRI machine nearby, so I cannot show you how to connect to one of those using the discussed techniques. However, I do have another device lying around – an Arduino Uno.

Arduinos are really cheap microcontrollers. Although an actual Arduino can set you back $20 to $30; comparable devices with the same capabilities can be found for about $5 to $7. For that price, you get a good running microcontroller that you can connect to your computer, program against, and use to hook up all sorts of hardware.

The hardware is simple – a CPU, a USB connector, a little memory, and an EEPROM that can hold your program. Also, an Arduino has pins that you can use to connect to other hardware.

You can program your Arduino with a free tool called the Arduino IDE. Now, this book is about systems programming with C# and .NET, and not about Arduino. But I need to talk about this briefly in case you decide to get an Arduino and follow along. If you do, great! If you don't, continue reading until we get to the part about faking hardware.

I chose Arduino because it uses a serial port to communicate with your computer. It is cheap, and many people have one lying around somewhere. Then, we can build an elementary device to talk to and have it talk to us. Do not worry if you have no experience with these devices; I will explain everything you need to know to follow along.

We need to write some software for the Arduino. The code is simple and included in the GitHub repo that accompanies this book.

But before we look at the code, let me explain the device we will create.

The device

I want our Windows machine to be more susceptible to the world outside its enclosure. I want it to be aware of sounds. I want a device that warns Windows when a loud noise is detected.

We could use a microphone and plug that into the correct ports, but a microphone is complicated. It can record sounds in high fidelity. I do not want that; I only want to know whether there is a loud sound, not what kind of sound it is. Furthermore, we can only have one microphone in use at a time. So, if we were to use the microphone, we would not be able to use our machines to make Teams calls or anything like that.

It's best to offload that work to a separate device. To do that, we need a couple of things:

- An Arduino or a compatible device
- A breadboard. This is a piece of plastic with wires, allowing us to plug in hardware and connect them without soldering.
- A KY-037 sound detector. This very simple device puts out a voltage as soon as it "hears" a noise. They cost anywhere between $1.50 and $3.00.
- An LED and a 200 ohm resistor (optional). I thought it would be fun to light up an LED when the device hears a sound. You do not need this; the Arduino has a built-in LED we can also use.
- A USB cable to connect it all to our machine.
- Some wires to connect the different parts.

The schematics for this device look like this:

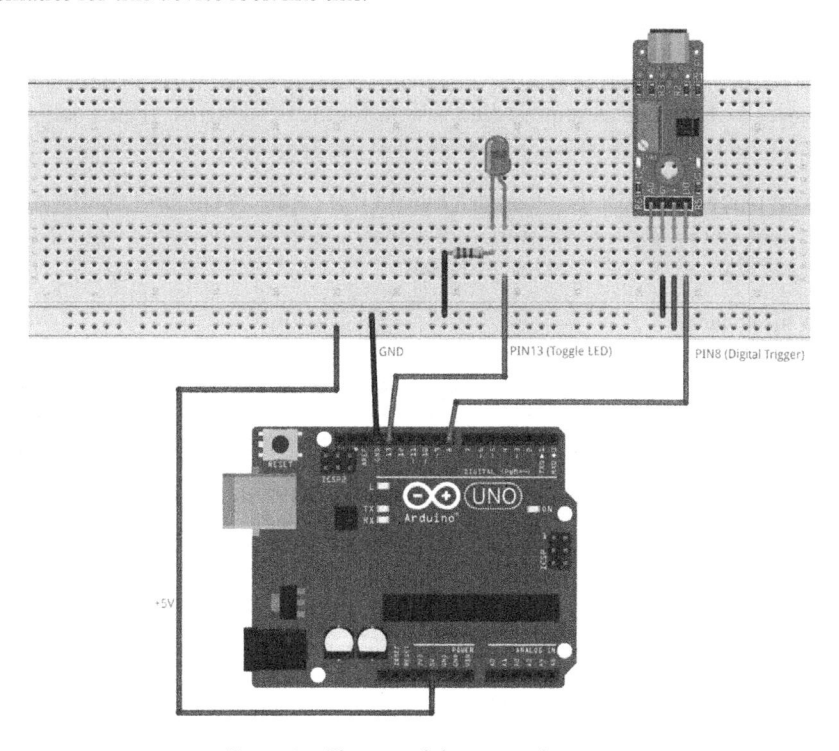

Figure 9.1: The sound detector schematics

If you have never worked with this sort of electronics before, do not worry. It is not as scary as you might think. The thing at the bottom of the preceding figure is the Arduino. As I stated earlier, it has pins we can connect wires to hook it up with other hardware. I have used four wires here. The one from the bottom to the breadboard (the white piece of plastic) is connected to a 5-volt power supply from the Arduino. I have connected it to the lowest row on the breadboard.

The breadboard works like this – all the little holes on the lowest row are electrically connected. That means if I plug in a wire with 5 volts on one of the holes in that row, all the other holes in that same horizontal row will also have 5 volts. The same happens with the second row from the bottom; they are also all horizontally connected. I use this for the ground connections. I hook one of the holes up with the Arduino's **GND** (meaning **ground**) pins. All the wires I plug into the second row are connected to the ground.

The red piece of electronics you see is connected to the breadboard. Except for the lowest two rows of the breadboard, each column is also connected. That means if I plug something into the hole in the first column (above the two bottom rows), all the holes above it are also connected. Columns are isolated from each other.

The breadboard consists of two halves – a bottom and a top half. These two halves are entirely isolated; no wires run from one half to another. So, the top half of the breadboard is a mirror of the bottom half.

I plugged the KY-037 (the red thing in the schematic) into the breadboard. I connected the 5-volt from the first row to the correct column. I did the same for the GND signal. Then, I connected a wire from the leftmost pin of the KY-037 directly to pin 8 of the Arduino.

I did a similar thing for the LED; the plus side of the LED is connected to pin 13 of the Arduino, and the negative side is connected to a 200-ohm resistor that, in turn, is connected to the GND row of the breadboard (and, thus, to the GND of the Arduino).

Are you with me so far?

The idea is simple – if the KY-037 detects a sound, it will (if powered by the 5 volts from the Arduino) put a voltage on the D0 line connected to pin 8 on the Arduino. If that happens, the microprocessor can pick that up and put a voltage on pin 13. That will light up the LED.

If the sound is dropped, the voltage on pin 8 will also go to LOW, and we can program the Arduino to stop the LED. That is, of course, achieved by removing the voltage from pin 13.

The Arduino software

We need to instruct the Arduino on how to behave. That means we have to program it. We can use the free Arduino IDE to write and deploy our software to the device. The device itself is simple; it can only have one program. That program starts as soon as the device is powered on and does not stop until the power is removed. There is no real operating system, no loading, and no multitasking.

The program itself is also straightforward. It consists of two parts. The first part is a method called `setup()`. This method is called as soon as the program starts (or as soon as the Arduino powers up). It is called only once and is a good place to do some initialization.

There is another method called `loop()`. This method is, as the name suggests, a loop. The Arduino goes through the code in `loop()`, and restarts at the beginning of `loop()` as soon as it reaches the end. And that's it. Of course, you can (and should) write your own methods and functions, but this is needed to get the device going.

The programming is done in C (technically, it can be C++, but let's not go there). The IDE can compile the code for you and deploy it to an attached Arduino. When you connect your Arduino through a USB cable to your machine, the IDE recognizes it and knows how to talk to the microcontroller.

The software I want to use looks like this:

```
#define LedPin 13
#define SoundPin 8
int _prevResult = LOW;
void setup() {
  pinMode(LedPin, OUTPUT);
```

```
  pinMode(SoundPin, INPUT);
  Serial.begin(9600);
}
void loop() {
  int soundPinData = digitalRead(SoundPin);
  if(soundPinData != _prevResult){
    _prevResult = soundPinData;
    if(soundPinData == HIGH)
    {
      Serial.write(1);
      digitalWrite(LED_BUILTIN, HIGH);
    }
    else
    {
      Serial.write("0");
      digitalWrite(LED_BUILTIN, LOW);
    }
    delay(100);
  }
}
```

And that's it.

Let's explore it.

First, I define some constants. I create the `LedPin` constant and set it to 13. This pin 13 is the number of the pin we connect the LED to see whether sound is detected. I chose pin 13 because most Arduino devices have a built-in LED on the board, connected to pin 13. So, if you do not want an external LED, you can look at the board and see the same effect.

I also define the pin that the KY-037 uses to send the signal back to us, pin 8, and I call it `SoundPin`. There is no specific reason I chose pin 8; it was conveniently located on the Arduino, so I could easily attach it to the breadboard.

Then, we have the `setup()` method. Again, this is used to initialize the system. We do three things here:

- We set the direction of pin 13 to `OUTPUT`; we do this by calling `pinMode(LedPin, OUTPUT)`. This direction means that the Arduino can use this pin to write to. We need this to turn the LED on or off.

- We set the direction of pin 8 to `INPUT`, by calling `pinMode(SoundPin, INPUT)`. Now, the Arduino knows we want to read from that pin instead of writing to it.

- We open the serial port. We do that by calling `Serial.begin(9600)`. This opens the serial connection through the USB connector to whatever it connects. We tell it we have a speed of 9600 baud. We could have specified the parity, packet size, and the number of stop bits, but the defaults (no parity, 8 bits, and 1 stop bit) are good enough for us. We need to remember these settings, as we will need them at the receiving end as well.

Then, we can look at the `loop()` method.

We begin with reading from the `SoundPin` pin. We do that by calling `digitalRead(SoundPin)`. Remember that the KY-037 adds voltage to the device when it hears a sound. We can read that result; the voltage level is translated into a one or a zero. We compare that with the results of the previous reading; if the value is different than before, we suddenly hear something (or stop hearing something). If that is the case, we determine whether there was a sound and add that information to the serial bus; we use `Serial.write(1)` or `Serial.write(0)` to send that value. You can as quickly send a string over the serial port by calling `Serial.PrintLn("My data")`. However, we do not need that in this case.

Then, depending on the conditions, we turn the LED on or off. Just like we used `digitalRead()` to read the state of a pin, we can now use `digitalWrite()` to set the state.

Finally, we call `delay(100)` to give the sound 100 milliseconds to die out.

And then it starts all over again; we are in a loop after all.

That's it. Upload that program to the Arduino and watch what happens. If you make a noise, you will see the LED light up. You haven't seen the effect of a `serial.print()` yet, but we will fix that next.

Receiving serial data with .NET

We have done a lot already. But that was just the setup to get to where we really want to be as system programmers – dealing with code in our C# programs.

I have written a sample that does just that; it opens the serial port, and it gets data. That in itself is not too hard; I have shown you how to open `SerialPort` and write data to it. Reading data from that same port is just as easy; `SerialPort.ReadLine()`, for instance, is one way of doing it.

However, there are a lot more considerations when dealing with other hardware, and that's what we will discuss here.

First, the sample I provide is not a console application. It is a worker service. I chose this template because I want this code to work quietly in the background and only do something when data comes in on the serial bus. This is the closest we can get to writing a device driver in .NET. Second, USB and serial ports are brittle. It's not that they fail a lot, but it is extremely easy to remove a device and plug it in again. You can never be sure that the device you need is attached to your computer.

Users rarely remove their primary hard drive. Network adapters tend to stay inside. Network cables can be removed but hardly ever are. USB devices, however, are plugged in and removed again all the time. Sometimes, that happens intentionally, and sometimes, your cat decides to play around with that thing with blinky lights and wires hanging out of it (yes, that happened to me when I was writing this chapter).

If we cannot rely on the presence of the device we want to talk with, we need to make sure it is there before we do something. We also need to handle a scenario where the device gets unplugged while working with it.

Luckily, we already know how to do this. In previous chapters, we looked into **Windows Management Instrumentation (WMI)**. That allowed us to investigate the hardware attached to our machine, and we saw that it could raise events if something changed. That sounds like something we can use here.

Watching the COM ports

I created a class called `ComPortWatcher`. As the name suggests, this watches the **COM ports** on my machine. The class implements the `IComPortWatcher` interface, which looks like this:

```
public interface IComPortWatcher : Idisposable
{
    event EventHandler<ComPortChangedEventArgs>? ComportAddedEvent;
    event EventHandler<ComPortChangedEventArgs>? ComportDeletedEvent;

    void Start();
    void Stop();
    string FindMatchingComPort(string partialMatch);
}
```

The interface declares two events. These events get called when a device we are interested in is plugged into a computer or when such a device is removed again. Other classes can subscribe to these events and take action.

We have a method called `Start()` that starts watching the ports. `Stop()` does the opposite – it stops watching the ports.

I also added a method called `FindMatchingComPort(string partialMatch)`. All devices have a set of properties, sometimes including the Caption. That Caption contains some information about the device attached to our machine. In the case of the Arduino, `Caption` contains the `Arduino` string and the actual COM port. This method tries to find that string and extracts the correct COM port, so we can use that to open the serial connection.

Let's look at the implementation. We will start with the easiest, `FindMatchingComPort(string partialMatch)`. This is what that looks like:

```
public string FindMatchingComPort(string partialMatch)
{
    string comPortName;
    var searcher = new ManagementObjectSearcher(
```

```
            @$"Select * From Win32_PnPEntity Where Caption Like
               '%{partialMatch}%'");
        var devices = searcher.Get();
        if ( devices.Count > 0)
        {
            var firstDevice = devices.Cast<ManagementObject>().First();
            comPortName = GetComPortName(firstDevice["Caption"].
               ToString());
        }
        else
        {
            comPortName = string.Empty;
        }
        return comPortName;
}
```

I am skipping a lot of error checking and safeguarding; otherwise, the code becomes too long to read. I am sure that you can spot what I left out and figure out how to do that yourself. Here I have focussed on only the essential parts.

First, I create a new instance of the `ManagementObjectSearcher` class. I give it the `"Select * From Win32_PnPEntity Where Caption Like '%{partialMatch}%'"` search string. This searches through all Plug and Play devices and tries to match the caption of those devices with whatever string we pass in. Again, in my case, I give it the `Arduino` string.

If there are no matches, we simply return an empty string, stating that no Arduino devices are found. However, if one is found (I only check for one; this is one of those areas you can improve a lot on), I take that caption and use some **regular expression (RegEx)** code (in the `GetComPortName()` method) to extract the name of the COM port.

That RegEx code looks like this:

```
private string GetComPortName(string foundCaption)
{
    var regExPattern = @"(COM\d+)";
    var match = Regex.Match(foundCaption, regExPattern);
    return match.Success? Match.Groups[1].Value : string.Empty;}
```

This code is pretty straightforward. We take the `"(COM\d+)"` RegEx pattern, which means we look for the string COM, followed by one or more numbers. Then, we return that part of the string. The caption of the port on my machine looks like `Arduino Uno (COM4)`, so this method returns, in my case, the COM4 string.

The Start() method of this class sets up the watchers. We have two private members in the class:

```
private ManagementEventWatcher? _comPortDeletedWatcher;
private ManagementEventWatcher? _comPortInsertedWatcher;
```

These are the WMI watchers that can trigger events when something interesting happens. What we define as interesting is specified in the Start() method. Here it goes:

```
public void Start()
{
    if (_isRunning)
        return;
    var queryInsert = "SELECT * FROM __InstanceCreationEvent WITHIN 1 " +
                      "WHERE TargetInstance ISA 'Win32_PnPEntity' " +
                      "AND TargetInstance.Caption LIKE "
                      "'%Arduino%'";
    var queryDelete = "SELECT * FROM __InstanceDeletionEvent WITHIN 1 " +
                      "WHERE TargetInstance ISA " 
                      "'Win32_PnPEntity' " +
                      "AND TargetInstance.Caption LIKE "
                      "'%Arduino%'";

    _comPortInsertedWatcher = new 
        ManagementEventWatcher(queryInsert);
    _comPortInsertedWatcher.EventArrived += HandleInsertEvent;
    _comPortInsertedWatcher.Start();

    _comPortDeletedWatcher = new ManagementEventWatcher(queryDelete);
    _comPortDeletedWatcher.EventArrived += HandleDeleteEvent;
    _comPortDeletedWatcher.Start();
    _isRunning = true;
}
```

First, I check to see whether this is not already running. There is no point in doing this twice. Then, I define the query string that defines the searches for both inserting and deleting devices.

When a device is inserted, the __InstanceCreatedEvent class in the operating system gets information about that device. We query for that class, but only if the target is a Plug and Play device (Win32_PnpEntity) and Caption contains *Arduino*. I am not interested in any other device.

I create a similar query string for the deletion event.

Then, I create an instance of that Watcher class, give it the query, and set up the event handlers. Finally, I call Start() on the watchers so that they start doing what they are meant to do.

The `Stop()` method stops the watchers and cleans them up. There is nothing special there, but you can look at the code in the GitHub repository for further details.

The event handlers are slightly more interesting than the `Stop()` method. Have a look:

```
private void HandleInsertEvent(object sender, EventArrivedEventArgs e)
{
    var newInstance = e.NewEvent["TargetInstance"] as
      ManagementBaseObject;
    var comPortName = GetComPortName(newInstance["Caption"].
      ToString());
    Task.Run(() => ComportAddedEvent?.Invoke(this, new
      ComPortChangedEventArgs(comPortName)));
}
```

This method is called when the watcher sees an exciting event in the operating system. We take `EventArgs` (of type `EventArrivedEventArgs`), take the `NewEvent` property, and get the `TargetInstance` member. We cast that to its correct type, `ManagementBaseObject`, and remove the caption. Then, we extract the COM port name and call any attached event handler. Since I know the attached event handler will start the serial communication, I wrap it in a `Task.Run()` method, making it work asynchronously and, thus, stopping it from blocking the current thread. Remember that all things that take time, such as I/O, should be written as asynchronous code.

The event handler for the delete event looks similar.

With this class in place, we can sit back and relax. We can ensure a COM port is available when needed, and we can take action if it gets unplugged.

Wrapping the serial port

There is a slight problem with the serial port class in .NET. It is not written for this day and age. It is a leftover from a much slower world. It is not asynchronous. And that can be a problem. Serial communications are slow enough already, and all calls to it block the thread it runs on. We need to wrap the class into something more modern.

I created an interface that shows us how to do this:

```
public interface IasyncSerial
{
    bool IsOpen { get; }
    void Open(string portName,
        int baudRate = 9600,
        Parity parity = Parity.None,
        int dataBits = 8,
```

```
        StopBits stopBits = StopBits.One);

    void Close();
    Task<byte> ReadByteAsync(CancellationToken stoppingToken);
}
```

The interface has an `IsOpen` property that can help us prevent more than one connection from opening. We have the `Open()` method, and I wrote it so that the parameters are there, but when a user of this class omits them, the serial port gets created with the default settings.

We have a `Close()` method that closes the connection.

I also added a `ReadByteAsync()` method that reads 1 byte from the device. I do not need more; our sound detector device only sends 1 byte at a time.

Let's look at the implementation.

First, I have a private member in the class:

```
private SerialPort? _serialPort;
```

We have already encountered the `SerialPort` class, so the implementation of the `Open()` method should be familiar:

```
public void Open(
    string portName,
    int baudRate = 9600,
    Parity parity = Parity.None,
    int dataBits = 8,
    StopBits stopBits = StopBits.One)
{
    if (IsOpen) throw new InvalidOperationException("Serial port is
      already open");
    _serialPort = new SerialPort(
        portName,
        baudRate,
        parity,
        dataBits,
        stopBits);
    _serialPort.Open();

    IsOpen = true;
}
```

Nothing special happens here – we create an instance of the `SerialPort` class, give it the correct parameters, and then open it. That's it.

`Close()` is even simpler – it only calls `Close()` on the `_serialPort` member. OK, it does that and a bit of cleaning up.

`ReadByteAsycn()` is a lot more interesting. It is the reason we wrote this class. Here it is:

```
public Task<byte> ReadByteAsync(CancellationToken stoppingToken)
{
    return Task.Run(() =>
    {
        if (!IsOpen) throw new InvalidOperationException("Serial port
          is not open");
        var buffer = new byte[1];
        try
        {
            _serialPort?.Read(buffer, 0, 1);
        }
        catch (OperationCanceledException)
        {
            // This happens when the device has been unplugged
            // We pass it a 0xFF to indicate that the device is no
            // longer available
            buffer[0] = 255;
        }
        return buffer[0];
    }, stoppingToken);
}
```

Again, we wrap the synchronous calls in `Task.Run()` so that the whole thing becomes asynchronous. We return that `Task` to the caller.

We call `_serialPort?.Read(buffer,0,1)`. This results in one byte of data, if available. If no data is available, this call is blocked until the data is there. That is why we use `Task.Run()` – we do not want to block our entire system and wait for a single byte to come in.

However, if the device is removed from our system while waiting for that data, we get `OperationCanceledException`. That makes sense; we are waiting for data from a device that no longer exists. We catch that exception and return the `0xFF` byte. Since we know we can only get a 0 or a 1 from the Arduino board (that's how we programmed it), we can safely use this magical number here to indicate an error.

Let's see how we can use these two classes.

Making it all work together

I mentioned that we are building a worker service. This service runs in the background and does not influence other codes or programs. The default template gives you a class called `Worker`, where we can do the actual work. We shall add our code to this `Worker` class.

But before doing that, we need to change the `Program` class slightly. One of the nice things about the worker service template is that it gives you dependency injection for free, out of the box. We can use that to register our `IAsyncSerial` and `IComPortWatcher` interfaces and their accompanying classes. That way, we do not have to create instances ourselves.

The `Program` class needs to be changed to look like this:

```
var builder = Host.CreateApplicationBuilder(args);
builder.Services.AddTransient<IComPortWatcher, ComPortWatcher>();
builder.Services.AddTransient<IAsyncSerial, AsyncSerial>();
builder.Services.AddHostedService<Worker>();
var host = builder.Build();
host.Run();
```

As you can see, we registered our new interfaces and classes, making them available for anyone needing one. And that *anyone* in our case is the `Worker` class. Let's look at the constructor:

```
public Worker(ILogger<Worker> logger,
    IAsyncSerial serial,
    IComPortWatcher comPortWatcher)
{
    _logger = logger;
    _serial = serial;
    _comPortWatcher = comPortWatcher;
    _comPortName = _comPortWatcher.FindMatchingComPort("Arduino");
    _deviceIsAvailable = !string.IsNullOrWhiteSpace(_comPortName);
    _comPortWatcher.ComportAddedEvent += HandleInsertEvent;
    _comPortWatcher.ComportDeletedEvent += HandleDeleteEvent;
    _comPortWatcher.Start();
    if (_deviceIsAvailable) StartSerialConnection();
}
```

We set the incoming instances of our classes and then look for a COM port attached to an Arduino. If there is one, we can set the `_deviceIsAvailable` variable to true.

We add the events that get called when the device is inserted or deleted. Then, if a device is already available, we start the serial connection.

That method, `StartSerialConnection()`, looks like this:

```
private void StartSerialConnection()
{
    if (_serial.IsOpen)
        return;
    _serial.Open(_comPortName);
    _deviceIsAvailable = true;
}
```

Since we have already done the hard work in the `AsyncSerial` class, we can simply call it _serialOpen(_comPortName).

The event handler for `ComportAddedEvent` does more or less the same thing:

```
private void HandleInsertEvent(object? sender, ComPortChangedEventArgs e)
{
    _comPortName = e.ComPortName;
    _logger.LogInformation($"New COM port detected: {_comPortName}");
    if (!string.IsNullOrEmpty(_comPortName))
        StartSerialConnection();
}
```

The event gets the name of the COM port from the `ComPortWatcher` class. So, all we have to do here is save that name and start the communications.

The actual work happens in the `ExecuteAsync` method of the worker. As you probably recall, the runtime calls this part of the class to do the actual work. Usually, this method contains a loop that gets repeated until `CancellationToken` signals that it needs to stop. Our version looks like this:

```
protected override async Task ExecuteAsync(CancellationToken stoppingToken)
{
    while (!stoppingToken.IsCancellationRequested)
    {
        if (_deviceIsAvailable)
        {
            var receivedByte = await _serial?.
              ReadByteAsync(stoppingToken);
            if (receivedByte == 0xFF)
            {
                StopSerialConnection();
                _logger.LogWarning("Device is ejected.");
            }
            else
```

```
            {
                _logger.LogInformation($"Data received:
                    {receivedByte:X}");
            }
        }
        await Task.Delay(10, stoppingToken);
    }
}
```

First, we check whether a device is available. There is no point in reading data if no device is attached, right?

Call the new `ReadByteAsync()` method if there is a device, and check the results. If they return `0xFF`, we have a problem – the device is removed. Otherwise, we just display the data we have.

And that's all there is to it! That was quite a lot. We introduced the Arduino and built our own device from it. We learned what communication over serial ports looks like. We discussed extracting data from our serial ports and how to make it work asynchronously. All in all, I think you deserve a break. We covered a lot of ground here.

Take a look at the complete sample in the GitHub repository to see the little details I left out here. However, with the information I just gave you, you have everything you need to start talking to serial devices!

Faking a serial device

I promised to discuss with you another thing – what to do if you have no device available. Well, there is a reason I used the `IComPortWatcher` and `IAsyncSerial` interfaces. We can mock them in a unit test and write fake code that mimics devices. And that is a pretty good idea, as serial communication is brittle and often fails. If you are developing your software, you want an environment you can rely on. Using these interfaces can help you.

For instance, I can have another implementation of `IComPortWatcher` that contains a `Start()` method that looks like this:

```
public void Start()
{
    _timer = new Timer(2000);
    _timer.Elapsed += (sender, args) =>
    {
        // Trigger the event every second
        if (_deviceIsAvailable)
        {
            ComportDeletedEvent?.Invoke(this, new
                ComPortChangedEventArgs("COM4"));
        }
```

```
            else
            {
                ComportAddedEvent?.Invoke(this, new
                   ComPortChangedEventArgs("COM4"));
            }
            _deviceIsAvailable = !_deviceIsAvailable;
        };
        _timer.Start();
    }
```

If I plug this into my Program class, I can fake ComPortWatcher. The Program class looks like this:

```
#define FAKESERIAL
using _09_SerialMonitor;
using _09_SerialMonitor.Fakes;
var builder = Host.CreateApplicationBuilder(args);
#if FAKESERIAL
    builder.Services.AddTransient<IComPortWatcher,
FakeComPortWatcher>();
    builder.Services.AddTransient<IAsyncSerial, FakeAsyncSerial>();
#else
    builder.Services.AddTransient<IComPortWatcher, ComPortWatcher>();
    builder.Services.AddTransient<IAsyncSerial, AsyncSerial>();
#endif
builder.Services.AddHostedService<Worker>();
var host = builder.Build();
host.Run();
```

As you can see, I can easily switch between the real and fake code by defining the FAKESERIAL. Of course, you can do this better by *defining* this in your build profile and not in the source code. That way, you can choose which version you want to run.

I will leave the implementation of FakeAsyncSerial to you.

So, we have looked at programming your computer to send and receive data to and from the serial port, or COM ports. There are many ways to communicate with the outside world, but COM is still around. System programmers encounter that specific protocol quite often, and now you know how to work with it.

We used an Arduino to mimic an external device. Of course, you might encounter many different kinds of devices. They all have their different use cases and ways of communicating. But they usually use a serial connection if they are attached to your machine through a cable. Now, you have seen how to set up such a connection and a test environment to fake a serial connection. But there is one more thing I want to discuss – how to make this sort of system more foolproof.

Making it foolproof

We already saw that we can use WMI to intercept unwanted removal of devices. USB cables can be removed from a machine easily. One of their selling points is how easy it is to plug devices in and remove them again. From a user's standpoint, that is great. But from a developer's perspective, it is not so great.

And even if the user (or your cat) doesn't fiddle around with the cable, many things can get in the way of a reliable data stream.

Reasons things go haywire

If your software fails, you can easily look up what happened. Well, not really easily – debugging software, especially low-level, multithreaded software, can be challenging. But it is doable.

Dealing with issues from other hardware is much harder to solve. There are so many reasons things can go wrong. Let's go through some of them.

- **Interference**: The cables used for serial communication are simple – several copper wires carry the electrical signal. All cables are sensitive to interference, regardless of their use. Interference is the effect that happens when electrical signals cause a change in the electromagnetic field around them, which in turn can cause changes in other wires. In practice, you might notice errors if you have a long serial cable and leave that coiled up next to your device. The answer is to have shielded or shorter cables or ensure they are isolated from others.

- **Bad cables**: Of course, even if you have a short, straight cable with no other cables nearby, you still might get errors. The cables might be damaged. The connectors might be faulty. The only way to test this is to use a metering device to check the cables and hardware. But even that does not always tell you all you need to know. Sometimes, the strains of copper are partially broken, meaning that sometimes they conduct the signals, and sometimes they don't.

- **Incorrect baud rates**: As explained earlier, the baud rate describes the number of signal changes per second. Both ends of the communication must use the same speed for their data. If you do not have that correctly set up, it might seem like everything works fine. However, you might get weird data streams instead of your expected valuable data.

- **Buffer overflows**: Data streams need to be processed. Sometimes, that processing takes too long, so the driver must buffer the incoming data stream. The idea is simple – the device driver puts all data into a buffer as it comes in and passes that data on when the application asks for it. However, the buffer fills up if the application cannot handle that amount of data in time. Ultimately, the buffer is full; there is no unlimited amount of memory it can use. That will trigger errors on a very low system level, and the buffer overflows.

- **Driver issues**: All hardware communicates through the driver. The driver is the last piece of software your commands or data pass through before they are translated into voltage differences.

The driver is a piece of software written specifically for the hardware you have on your machine. It acts as a translator between the operating system and the hardware. But ultimately, it is software. And software can go wrong. Hence, drivers can also go wrong. If that happens, it is difficult to see why things do not work as expected. Drivers making mistakes are very hard to trace.

- **Port misconfiguration**: As we saw, we need to set up a connection in a certain way. We must inform the system about the parity, the number of bits in a data package, and the number of stop bits we want. If we mix these settings up, we get data that does not make sense. Not all vendors of the devices you want to use are good at specifying the format they expect. Therefore, you might have to play around before it all works as it should.

- **Hardware failures**: Ultimately, everything between your software and the device you talk to consists of many hardware components. And all of them can go wrong for several reasons. The port may be bad, or the barcode scanner might not work correctly. There could be so many things that go wrong when dealing with hardware.

- **Wrong data format**: Serial communication is very basic. You get a stream of bits, and they can be grouped into a set of bytes. But then what? What does that mean? The format in which the data is translated must be clear at both ends; otherwise, you cannot understand each other.

- **Parity bit errors**: Parity is an excellent way of detecting errors. But what if two bits *flip*? Parity does not help you there; if the sender sends 4 values of 1 over the wire, the parity bit might be set to 0 (if *parity = even* is used). But if one of these 1 values changes to 0, and a 0 value changes to 1, you still have a valid parity. However, the data might not make sense at all.

- **Cosmic radiation**: This one is improbable, but it has happened. Cosmic radiation is, as the name suggests, radiation from space. It is around us all the time. It does not cause harm, but sometimes, every now and then, it hits a piece of hardware. And when that happens, 0 might become 1, or vice versa. This is even more unlikely to happen inside your computer; there is a lot of protection around your processor and memory. But this might happen a bit more often with a cheap serial cable.

As you can see, there are a lot of things that can go wrong, and most of them are hard to prevent in your code. OK, I agree that the cosmic radiation issue is not a regular occurrence, at least not regular enough to worry about it (unless you write software that cannot go wrong under any circumstances, such as that used for medical equipment).

There are ways to harden your code so that it doesn't suffer too much from these potential issues. Let's investigate what we can do.

Hardening your code

There is very little you can do about failures on the hardware side. That just happens. But you can ensure your code doesn't come to a screeching halt when the inevitable occurs.

Using Try...Catch

Using `Try...Catch` is one of the best ways to make sure your system stays in a predictable and manageable state. Do not try to catch `Exception`; instead, be more specific about the kinds of exceptions you catch and how you handle them.

For instance, your code should look like this:

```
try
{
    // Attempt to read from the serial port
}
catch (TimeoutException)
{
    // Handle timeout, possibly retry
}
catch (IOException ex)
{
    // Handle I/O errors
    // Log or attempt recovery
}
```

Catch all sorts of exceptions separately and deal with them.

Implementing a robust connection loop

I already mentioned this, but it is worth repeating – connections can get lost. Monitor the state of your connections, as we did earlier with the WMI objects. If something happens that should not have happened, deal with it and let the connection die gracefully.

Ensuring thread safety

If you are accessing your serial connections from multiple threads, use mechanisms such as a lock or semaphores to make your code as thread-safe as possible. You must prevent concurrent readings and writings in a system initially designed for a single-thread communication mechanism.

The use of CancellationToken

For long-running operations such as serial communication, ensure all methods carry `CancellationToken`. Then, when handling the data streams, keep a close eye on that token to see whether the system wants to cancel the operation.

Resource management

You only have a limited number of virtual serial ports and even fewer physical ports in your system. That is why you must be very careful to release the handles on the devices if you do not need them anymore.

The best way to do this is to be sure you clean up after you are done; implement the `IDisposable` pattern. Try to limit the time you use a device, and always ensure you release it.

Logging and monitoring

As always, logging and monitoring are the best ways to keep track of what is going on. Without adequate logging, it is very hard or even impossible to trace what happens when things go wrong. Logging and monitoring are valuable tools to help you understand the specifics of an interaction with external hardware, especially during development. We discuss monitoring in *Chapter 10*, but remember that you need to do this, especially when dealing with external hardware.

All in all, there are things you can do to make your software as robust as possible. But nothing comes for free; there is a performance overhead to all of this. But trust me – it is worth it. These days, software runs extremely fast, especially when compared to the slow speed at which most serial communications take place. You have plenty of time to check errors and ensure smooth communication. But do not make things too slow; as soon as you start getting buffer overflow errors, you are no longer helping a system. As always, test and measure before taking steps.

Next steps

I hope you enjoyed our little field trip to devices outside the realm of our computer. Connecting other hardware to a machine can be much fun. As I said before, dealing with external devices is a very likely scenario for system programmers. The likelihood of encountering older, serial-based communication mechanisms is pretty high in our world.

We have discussed what serial communications are and what devices use them. We examined their protocols, especially the parity, data packet size, and stop bits. We looked at an Arduino device that measured sounds and received data from that over a serial line. We also looked at what you can do if you do not have such a device at hand.

We made the software testable and discussed the disasters that can or will happen when dealing with serial devices. Finally, we looked at some tips you can use to make your software more resilient against these failures.

All in all, we did a lot of exploring. I repeatedly mentioned how important it is to log what is happening and that you should monitor your software, especially when dealing with external hardware; logging and monitoring are sometimes the only ways to figure out what went wrong.

So, the next chapter is all about logging and monitoring. Are you ready for that?

10

The One with the Systems Check-Ups

Logging, Monitoring, and Metrics

Now and then, software fails. Whether we like it or not, that is simply a fact of life. We make mistakes during development. Other people make mistakes. The environment changes. A network becomes unstable. These are all reasons the system might not behave as we intended.

Testing can help. A good and solid set of tests can show you the errors in your work and help make your system more robust. However, sometimes things still go wrong. Let's face it: building software is a creative art form and thus subject to influences beyond our control. So, when things go wrong and our systems do not do what we thought they would be doing, we need a way to look into their workings. That can help us figure out what happened and what we can do to fix things.

This is where logging and monitoring comes into play. Logging helps us write important information and store it in a well-known place. Logging is part of our code base. Monitoring is watching the system from the outside to track what is happening. In this chapter, I will show you exactly how to do everything from a systems developer's perspective.

In this chapter, we will learn about the following topics:

- What logging frameworks are there?
- How do I set up the correct levels of logging?
- What is structured logging?
- How can I monitor my logs outside my system?
- What is monitoring?

- How do I set up monitoring?
- What should I monitor or log?

I hope you are as excited about this as I am!

Technical requirements

In this chapter, we look into monitoring and logging tools. One of the tools I often use is **Seq**. I am not affiliated with them; it is just a tool I like to use. You can download a free-to-use personal version at https://datalust.co/download. You can download the installer or run the tool as a Docker image. To use this, you have to install Docker on your environment. I suggest you go to https://www.docker.com/products/docker-desktop/ to learn more about Docker. If you want to play around, I suggest you choose the Docker version. You can run the image locally by invoking the following command from a terminal:

```
docker run -d
    --restart unless-stopped
    --name seq
    -e ACCEPT_EULA=Y
    -v c:\data:/data
    -p 80:80
    -p 5341:5341
    datalust/seq:latest
```

This Docker command downloads the image from `datalust/seq`. It listens to ports `80` for the **User Interface** (**UI**) and `5341` to intercept logs. All settings are stored in the `C:\data` folder, so you must create that folder beforehand (or change the `-v` property in the Docker command).

I will also show you how to use Prometheus in this chapter. To get that up and running, you could do the same thing. Either download the software from their website at https://prometheus.io/ or run it in a Docker container:

```
docker run -d
    --name prom
    -p 9090:9090
    -v c:\data\prometheus.yml:/etc/prometheus/prometheus.yml
    prom/prometheus
```

You need to have a `prometheus.yml` file that contains information about what you want to monitor. I will show you what that file looks like later in this chapter, where I will also explain what each part does.

We will be using a lot of NuGet packages as well; they are all mentioned in the paragraphs where I discuss each of them and how to use them.

You can download all code samples mentioned in this chapter from our GitHub repo at `https://github.com/PacktPublishing/Systems-Programming-with-C-Sharp-and-.NET/tree/main/SystemsProgrammingWithCSharpAndNet/Chapter10`

Available logging frameworks

Logging has been around forever. In the early days of computing, operators would walk around the machines and note whatever they saw happening to them. If a light blinked when it should not have blinked or vice versa, they wrote it down a journal somewhere. Later, systems would log everything they could onto paper and punch cards. If systems did something unexpected, the operators could go to the paper trail and figure out what had caused the event. After that, people used serial monitors that logged everything onto a separate device.

These days, we hardly use punch cards anymore. However, we still log. There are many frameworks out there that help you get the job done. In this chapter, I will explain three of those frameworks. They all have pros and cons. I will highlight these as much as possible. That way, you can make your own decisions about what to use and when to use it.

Default logger in .NET

Microsoft offers a **default logger**. We have seen it before: if you create an ASP.Net application or, as we have done, a worker process, you will get a logger framework for free. This framework is surprisingly full-featured. This framework offers enough features to satisfy the needs of most developers. So, let's have a look at it!

As I said, many of the templates in Visual Studio already include the standard `Logger` class. Some templates, however, do not have this. So, let's have a look at how to add it. We'll begin with a clean, empty Console application.

The first thing we need to do is add the correct NuGet package. In this case, you need to install `Microsoft.Extensions.Logging` in your project. Once you have done that, you will have access to the logging framework.

In your main project, you can set up the logging like this:

```
using Microsoft.Extensions.Logging;
ILoggerFactory loggerFactory = LoggerFactory.Create(builder =>
{
    builder.SetMinimumLevel(LogLevel.Information);
});
var logger = loggerFactory.CreateLogger<Program>();
logger.LogInformation("This is some information");
```

This code works. If you run it, you will not get any errors. However, you will also not get any output, so that is pretty useless, to be honest.

This is because the framework is quite flexible. It can handle all sorts of outputs to various destinations. However, you have to specify what you want.

Let's fix this. Install another NuGet package; this time, we need the `Microsoft.Extensions.Logging.Console` package. Once you have installed that, we need to change the code in the `LoggerFactory.Create()` method to look like this:

```
var loggerFactory = LoggerFactory.Create(builder =>
{
    builder.AddConsole();
    builder.SetMinimumLevel(LogLevel.Information);
});
```

In the second line, we added the Console as a way to output.

If you run the program this time, you will get the desired information:

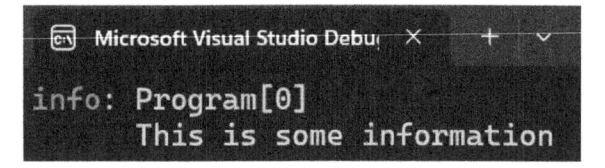

Figure 10.1: Output from the log

OK. We got something on our screen. Let's see what we have done so far since I deliberately skipped over some steps.

`LoggerFactory` is a factory class that can create instances of a class that implements `Ilogger<T>`. We set up `LoggerFactory` by hooking up the desired outputs (in our case, Console; we'll add others later). We also gave it the minimum log level we wanted.

Let's dive into this. I want to discuss log levels and configuration, as well as the different tools we have.

Log levels

Not all messages are equally important. If you are starting out on your project, you will probably want to log a lot. You can output anything you want and you will probably do so. You can write the contents of variables, loop controls, where you are in the flow, and so on. Anything that can help you understand the flow of your program as you run it is a candidate for logging.

However, once you have written and tested your software, you will probably not want all of that information anymore. You might want to log exceptional cases and errors, but that is about it.

To achieve that, you must remove all the logging code that you do not need anymore. Alternatively, you could wrap up the code in `#IF` / `#ENDIF` statements and thus effectively remove the calls when you recompile using a different `#DEFINE`. However, that means changing your code. That could lead to side effects. If you later find a bug and decide that you need that code in again, you will need to rewrite or recompile the system.

`Loglevels` eliminates that problem.

Each log message we write has a level. In the preceding example, we used `Log.LogInformation()`. That means that we want to write something informational. There are other levels we can use as well. What you use them for is entirely up to you. However, in general, there is meaning to each level. These are the levels we can use with `ILogger`:

Log level	Description
Trace	This refers to the most detailed messages. These messages may contain sensitive application data and are therefore not recommended to be enabled in a production environment unless they are necessary for troubleshooting and only for short periods.
Debug	This displays messages that are useful for debugging. It is less verbose than Trace, but more than Information.
Information	This allows the system to show informational messages that highlight the general flow of the application. It is useful for general application insights.
Warning	This is all about messages that highlight an abnormal or unexpected event in the application flow, but which do not otherwise cause the application execution to stop.
Error	These are messages that highlight when the current flow of execution is stopped due to a failure. These should indicate a failure in the current activity, not an application-wide failure.
Critical	This is about messages describing an unrecoverable application, system crash, or catastrophic failure requiring immediate attention.
None	This results in no messages being logged. This level is used to turn off logging.

Table 10.1 Log levels in Microsoft Logger

There are two ways in which you can specify what level your message has to be. You can use one of the dedicated log methods (such as `LogInformation`, `LogTrace`, `LogDebug`, and so on) or the generic `Log()` method. That looks like this:

```
logger.Log(LogLevel.Critical, "This is a critical message");
```

You just call `Log()` and then give it the `LogLevel`. Whatever method you choose, you can decide what level the log is supposed to be on.

However, that only solves a part of the issue. We want to be flexible in what we output to the screen. That's where the `SetMinimumLevel()` method on the `ILoggingBuilder` comes into play.

The method determines what the log is writing to the chosen output channels. If you set it to `Information`, all calls to the log are processed if they are of the Information level or higher. In other words, all calls to `Log.LogTrace()`, `Log.Debug()`, `Log.Log(LogLevel.Trace)`, and `Log.Log(LogLevel.Debug)` are ignored. So you can, in one line, determine what you do and do not want to appear on the logs. You specify the level and all information on that level or above is outputted. The rest is ignored.

During development, you might want to set the level to Trace. After extensive testing, you might want to set it to `Critical` or maybe `Error` during production.

Using a Settings file

Of course, we are not there yet. If you want to change the log level, you still need to change the code and recompile the system. Let's change that so we can use something else.

Add a new file to your program called `appsettings.json`. Make sure you change the `Copy to output directory` property to `Copy if newer`; you need this file next to the binaries.

The file should look like this:

```
{
  "Logging": {
    "LogLevel": {
      "Default": "Information"
    }
  }
}
```

Now, we need to add a couple of NuGet packages. Install `Microsoft.Extensions.Configuration.JSon` and `Microsoft.Extensions.Logging.Configuration`.

When we have done that, we will add the following code that actually reads the configuration:

```
var configurationBuilder = new ConfigurationBuilder()
    .AddJsonFile(
        path: "appsettings.json",
        optional:true,
        reloadOnChange:true);

var configuration = configurationBuilder.Build();
var configurationSection=
    configuration.GetSection("Logging");
```

This code creates a `ConfigurationBuilder` and then adds the JSON file we just added. We set the `optional` parameter to `true`; if people decide to remove the file, our app will still work. We also specify that the `reloadOnChange` parameter is `true`. As you have probably guessed, the configuration is reloaded when the file changes.

The following is relatively straightforward: we call `Build()` to get the `IConfiguration`, then call `GetSection`(Logging) to load that specific part of our JSON file.

We need to do some work on our `LoggerFactory` as well. Change it to look like this:

```
var loggerFactory = LoggerFactory.Create(builder =>
{
    builder.AddConsole();
    builder.AddConfiguration(configurationSection);
});
```

Instead of hardcoding the log level, we will now give it the configuration section from the JSON file.

Lastly, let's change the code that does the actual logging a bit. I will wrap it in a continuous loop:

```
while (true)
{
    logger.LogTrace("This is a trace");
    logger.LogDebug("This is debug");
    logger.LogInformation("This is information");
    logger.LogWarning("This is warning");
    logger.LogError("This is an error");
    logger.LogCritical("This is a critical message");
    await Task.Delay(1000);
}
```

Run your program and see all the different ways of displaying your message. Open another terminal window, navigate to the compiled application folder, and change the log setting in the `appsettings.json` file. As soon as you save the file, you will see a different behavior in the application. Depending on your desire, it will display more or fewer lines of logging.

Now, you can add all the logging you want to your application, use `Trace` during debugging and development, and then move to `Critical` or `Error` if your system is ready for production. You can quickly return to a more detailed debugging level as soon as something happens. All of that is done without recompiling!

Using EventId

Having different debugging levels is nice, but that is not enough to structure the information if you have a lot of messages. To help you create a bit of order in the logging chaos, you can use the `EventId`.

All log methods have an overload that allows you to add an `EventId`. An `EventId` is a class that contains an ID in the `integer` form and a name in the `string` form. What those are is entirely left up to you. The name is not even used in the logs, but it is there for your convenience during development. We can create an `EventId`, or multiple, as follows:

```
var initEventId = new EventId(1, "Initialization");
var shutdownEventId = new EventId(2, "Shutdown");
var fileReadingEventId = new EventId(3, "File Reading");
```

I just made up a bunch of categories: `Initialization`, `Shutdown`, and `File Reading`. This is just an example; I am sure that you can come up with much better names.

When you log something, you can use an `EventId` to indicate that the message you log has to do with a certain part of the system. That looks like this:

```
logger.LogInformation(initializationEventId, "Application started");
logger.LogInformation(shutdownEventId, "Application shutting down");
logger.LogError(fileReadingEventId, "File not found");
```

The output now looks a bit different:

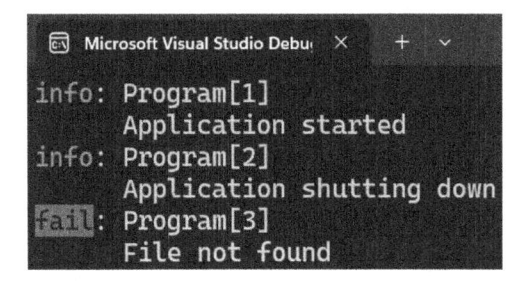

FIgure 10.2: Output of logging with an EventId (or multiple)

Next to the `Log` type and the `Program`, you can see the number between brackets. That is the number of the `EventId` type. In our case, 1 was initialization, 2 was shut down, and 3 was file reading. Again, these strings are never used and, unfortunately, are not shown on the screen. However, having these numbers in there can help you find the areas that you are interested in.

Using Type information

There is one last thing you can use to organize your logs. I didn't explain it earlier, but you must have noticed that when we created the instance of our `logger`, we gave it a `Program` type parameter:

```
var logger = loggerFactory.CreateLogger<Program>();
```

Since we called `CreateLogger` with the `Program` type, we see the `Program` string on the screen in the logs.

You can create several instances of the `ILogger` interface, each with its own type attached to it. That way, you can create different loggers for each application part. If you have a part of your system that handles printing and the main class is called `Printer`, you can create a logger of the `Printer` type like this:

```
var printLogger = loggerFactory.CreateLogger<Printer>();
```

All logs written to the `printLogger` instance will now show `Printer` in their log lines instead of `Program`. Of course, it doesn't really matter what you pass in that parameter. You can use the `Printer` logger in your main program if you want to. It is just decoration that helps you organize the output of the logs. That's it. There is no logic behind it.

> **Using categories wisely**
>
> I suggest you use these categories, but use them sparingly; too many will only clutter your logs. I usually create empty classes just for use in the logger creation. That way, I can get a nice set of logger instances without relying on internal code that nobody outside should see. However, I will leave that entirely up to you.

Now that we have basic logging out of the way, it is time to look at some popular alternatives that offer some other nifty tricks we can use. Let us begin with NLog!

NLog

Microsoft is not the only company that offers a logging framework. There are others out there, each with their own strengths and weaknesses. One of the more popular ones out there is **NLog**.

NLog was created by Jared Kowalski in 2006 as an alternative to the popular log4net solution, which is a port of the immensely popular log4j Java logging solution. Kowalski aimed to build a logging solution that was high in performance but also flexible in the configuration of the settings.

Setting up NLog

To use NLog, you need to install the corresponding NuGet package. The name of the package is simply `NLog`.

Once you have installed that package, we must create a configuration file. To do that, add a new XML file to your project (do not forget to set the properties to `Copy if newer` so that the project can find the file when it runs). By convention, this file is called `NLog.config`, but you can choose any name. The file should look like this:

```
<?xml version="1.0" encoding="utf-8" ?>
<nlog xmlns=http://www.nlog-project.org/schemas/NLog.xsd
      xmlns:xsi=http://www.w3.org/2001/XMLSchema-instance
      >
```

```xml
<targets>
  <target
    name="logfile"
    xsi:type="File"
    fileName="${basedir}/logs/logfile.txt"
    layout="${date:format=HH\:mm\:ss} ${logger} ${uppercase:${level}} ${message}" />
  <target
    name="logconsole"
    xsi:type="Console" />
</targets>
<rules>
  <logger name="*"
          minlevel="Info"
          writeTo="logfile,logconsole" />
</rules>
</nlog>
```

You can control almost all of NLog through this configuration file. You can set up all parameters in code, but that kind of defeats the purpose of NLog. I suggest that you use the configuration file and avoid setting things in the code. That is unless you have a really good reason to do otherwise, of course. After all, it is still your code, not mine.

Now, it is time to start logging. In your program, add the following code:

```csharp
using NLog;
LogManager.Configuration =
    new XmlLoggingConfiguration(
        "NLog.config"
    );
try
{
    Logger logger = LogManager.GetCurrentClassLogger();
    logger.Trace("This is a trace message");
    logger.Debug("This is a debug message");
    logger.Info("Application started");
    logger.Warn("This is a warning message");
    logger.Error("This is an error message");
    logger.Fatal("This is a fatal error message");
}finally{
    LogManager.Shutdown();
}
```

First, we will load the configuration in the LogManager. You usually have one setup for all your logging needs in your entire application, so you might as well do this first.

Then, we will call `GetCurrentClassLogger()`. This call is the equivalent of the call to `CreateLogger<T>` in the Microsoft framework. It ties the current class name to the logger so you can categorize your logs.

If you want other loggers to be associated with different classes, you can do so by calling something like this:

```
var otherLogger = LogManager.GetLogger("OtherLogger");
```

This call creates another logger with the same configuration but will show `"OtherLogger"` in the output this time.

The rest of the code is self-explanatory, except for the line that says `LogManager.Shutdown()`. This line is needed to flush out all logs in the code and ensure that no message is left behind.

Log levels in NLog logging

As with the Microsoft framework, you can specify which level you want to see in the log files. The levels for NLog are comparable, but there are minor differences. The following table shows the available options:

NLog level	Description
Trace	This provides the most detailed information. Use this for the most low-level debug information.
Debug	This provides coarse-grained debugging information. It is less detailed than Trace.
Info	Informational messages that highlight the general flow of the application come with this level.
Warn	Potentially harmful situations of interest to end users or system managers that indicate potential problems are flagged at this level.
Error	Error events of considerable importance that will prevent normal program execution but might still allow the application to continue running are flagged here.
Fatal	This level focuses on very severe error events that will presumably lead the application to abort.
Off	This involves no logging at all.

Table 10.2: Log levels in NLog

As you can see, the levels are almost the same; they are just named differently. That makes it harder to remember when you switch from one framework to another, but we can do nothing about that. We have to memorize the terms, I guess.

NLog targets

You control NLog through the configuration file. That is one of the two main principles that drove the development of NLog (the other being that NLog should be highly performant).

In the sample we have worked on, we wrote the logs in both the Console and a file. In the `settings` file, we have defined different targets where NLog writes the logs. Currently, more than 100 different targets are available, some of which are part of the core package and some of which require a NuGet package.

Let's have a look at another target. We currently use `Console`, but we can replace that with `ColoredConsole`. That is part of the default package, so we do not have to add a NuGet package.

In the configuration, add a new target to the `targets` section. It looks like this:

```
<target
  name="logcolorconsole"
  xsi:type="ColoredConsole"
  header="Logfile for run ${longdate)"
  footer="-----------"
  layout="${date:format=HH\:mm\:ss} ${logger}
${uppercase:${level}} ${message}" />
```

This segment tells NLog that we want to use a new target of the `ColoredConsole` type. We can call it `logcolorconsole`.

We also specified a header that should display the `Logfile for run` text and then the current data. I also added a footer that consists of a simple line. The layout section is the same as the one we used with the file: we display the time (in the `HH:mm:ss` format), the name of the logger (which is `Program` or `OtherLogger`, depending on the line we are on), the level of the log in uppercase, and finally the message itself.

You can vary this as much as you want and add or remove elements at will. You can also set up rules on what to display depending on various factors, such as the level.

We must also add it to the rules. Just for simplicity, I removed the file and console as a target and used the new `logcolorconsole` one:

```
<rules>
  <logger name="*"
          minlevel="Info"
          writeTo="logcolorconsole" />
</rules>
```

If you run the sample after making these changes, you will see a set of colorful lines. Yes, you can change or alter the colors based on the level. The options are almost endless.

As I said, there are over 100 targets available. Let me give you a shortened list of some of the more commonly used targets:

Target name	Description	NuGet package
File Target	Logs data to files on a disk with options for filenames, directories, rotations, and archiving	NLog
Console Target	Sends log messages to the standard output or error streams; useful during development	NLog
ColoredConsole Target	Sends log messages to the Console with color coding based on log level	NLog
Database Target	Logs messages to a database using parameterized SQL commands	NLog
EventLog Target	Writes log entries to the Windows Event Log; ideal for Windows apps	NLog.WindowsEventLog
Mail Target	Sends log entries as email messages; suitable for alerts and monitoring	NLog.MailKit
Network Targets	Includes WebService, TCP, and UDP targets for logging over networks	NLog
Trace Target	Sends log messages to .NET trace listeners, integrating with other diagnostics tools	NLog
Memory Target	Logs messages to an in-memory list of strings, mainly for debugging purposes	NLog
Null Target	A target that does nothing; useful for disabling logging in certain scenarios	NLog

Table 10.3: Targets in NLog

I recommend you look at the documentation at `https://nlog-project.org/config/` to see the different options and the settings per option. It is pretty extensive!

Rules in NLog

In addition to the targets, you can set rules in NLog. The rules define which target is used under which circumstances.

In our example, we used one rule: all logs should go to the Console and `file` targets or the `ColoredConsole` target, which we named `logcolorconsole`.

Let's change that a bit; I want to make it more intelligent. Change the rules section so that it looks like this:

```
<rules>
   <logger name="*"
           minlevel="Trace"
           writeTo="logfile" />
   <logger name="Program"
           minLevel="Warn"
           writeTo="logcolorconsole" />
   <logger name="OtherLogger"
           minLevel="Info"
           writeTo="logconsole" />
</rules>
```

We now have three rules:

- The first is the catch-all. By writing `name="*"`, we tell the system to take all loggers. The minimum level we want is Trace, the lowest level, so we want all messages (yes, you can also define a maximum level). We define the target as a **logfile**. This target is the one that writes to a file.

- The second rule only applies to the logger that has the name `Program`. Thus, all loggers are created by calling `GetCurrentClassLogger()` using our `Main` method. We raise the minimum level to Warn; we are not interested in anything below that. The file catches this. We want to see them in nice colors, so we specify the `writeTo` parameter as `logcolorconsole`.

- All messages sent to the logger named `OtherLogger` are the subject of the third rule. We want all messages of the Info level or above, and we want to see them processed by our colorless, default Console logger.

Run the sample. See how messages on different loggers get sent to the right place.

Asynchronous logging

Remember when I said that anything that takes longer than a few clock cycles should be done asynchronously? Well, NLog allows you to log to databases or network connections. They definitely have long-running operations. Unfortunately, there is no such method as `LogAsync()` in NLog. However, there is another solution to this.

There is a target called `AsyncWrapper`. As the name suggests, this is a wrapper around other targets that make them work asynchronously. All you have to do is add that to the configuration like this:

```
<target
  name="asyncWrapper"
  xsi:type="AsyncWrapper">
  <target
```

```
    name="logfile"
    xsi:type="File"
    fileName="${basedir}/logs/logfile.txt"
    layout="${date:format=HH\:mm\:ss} ${logger} ${uppercase:${level}}
${message}" />
  </target>
```

Although the methods are still synchronous, NLog places all the log messages in a queue on a separate thread and writes them to the target on that thread instead of on the calling thread. You can set several variables to determine how long the delay must be, how long the queue can become, and so on. However, we have eliminated our delay when writing to a file, a database, or a network connection. I strongly suggest that you use that wrapper for anything besides Console!

Two useful but often neglected additional settings

There are two more things I want to show you in the configuration file.

The root element, NLog, can have a property named `autoReload=true`. If you set that, you can have NLog pick up changes in the log file while the application runs. We saw a similar option with the Microsoft logger; it is good to know that NLog also supports this.

With all the available rules, targets, variables, and other things you can set in the configuration file, you might wonder what to do if things go wrong.

The people behind NLog thought of that as well. You can turn on logging for NLog itself. All you have to do is change the root entry to look like this:

```
<nlog xmlns=http://www.nlog-project.org/schemas/NLog.xsd
      xmlns:xsi=http://www.w3.org/2001/XMLSchema-instance
      autoReload="true"
      internalLogFile="${basedir}/logs/internallog.txt"
      internalLogLevel="Trace"
      >
```

I have added the `internalLogFile` and `internalLogLevel` properties. Adding these properties results in NLog logging its internal logs to the given file. Doing this might help you find issues in your logging. It is all becoming a bit metaphysical, but you can log better by logging the workings of the log. Give it a try!

Serilog

There is one more framework I want to share with you. Serilog is a popular logging framework that first saw the light of day in 2013.

The idea behind Serilog is that it allows for structured logging. So far, all the logs we have seen have all just been one-liners with some text. Serilog is built around the idea that structure can bring clarity.

Let me show you what I mean by that. Let's build a sample.

Although Serilog can (and should) be controlled by the settings in a configuration file, I will control this final example exclusively through code. I want to show you how to do that so you have at least seen it once.

However, again, since you want to change logging depending on the state of the system, you are better off having a configuration file that you can change without recompiling.

Of course, we will begin by creating a new Console application and adding some NuGet packages.

Standard logging with Serilog

NLog has targets, and Serilog has **sinks**. You have to install all the sinks you need from different packages. I will only use Console and File in my sample, but there are others: SQL Server, HTTP, AWS, and so on.

You need to install the `Serilog`, `Serilog.Sinks.Console` and `Serilog.Sinks.File` NuGet packages.

Let's write the code:

```
using Serilog;
var logger = new LoggerConfiguration()
    .MinimumLevel.Debug()
    .WriteTo.Console()
    .WriteTo.File(path:
        "logs\\log.txt",
        rollingInterval: RollingInterval.Day)
    .CreateLogger();

try
{
    logger.Verbose("This is verbose");
    logger.Debug("This is debug");
    logger.Information("This is information");
    logger.Warning("This is warning");
    logger.Error("This is error");
    logger.Fatal("This is fatal");
}
finally
{
    await Log.CloseAndFlushAsync();
}
```

This code should look familiar. We create a configuration, this time all in code; we create a logger and log our messages. We end with a `CloseAndFlushAsync()` to ensure nothing is left in some buffer.

There is nothing special about this code. OK, the new thing here is the `RollingInterval`. This property determines when the system should create a new file. You can set that to anything from a minute to a year. If you do not want to create a new file at any point, you can also set it to `Infinite`. That way, the system creates the file once and never again (unless you delete it, of course).

Apart from that, there is nothing remarkable about Serilog. However, let's change that. Change the parameters in the call to `WriteTo.File()` so that it looks like the following:

```
var logger = new LoggerConfiguration()
    .MinimumLevel.Debug()
    .WriteTo.Console(new JsonFormatter())
    .WriteTo.File(
        new JsonFormatter(),
        "logs\\log.txt",
        rollingInterval: RollingInterval.Day)
    .CreateLogger();
```

In this code sample, I added a `JsonFormatter` to the output of both the console and the file. When you add a formatter, you tell Serilog to output the logs a certain way. The `JsonFormatter` formatter forces the output to be in (well, you guessed it) the JSON format.

To truly use the structure log, we must change how we log the messages. Let's add one line to the part where we write the logs:

```
logger.Information(
    "The user with userId {userId} logged in at {loggedInTime}",
    42,
    DateTime.UtcNow.TimeOfDay);
```

As you can see, we log a line of text, but instead of building that string beforehand, we do it in the message. In this case, we give it named parameters, `userId`, and `loggedInTime`, and then pass in the values that we want to display.

If you run it now, that last line, after formatting, results in this:

```
{
    "Timestamp": "2024-04-20T11:47:31.5139218+02:00",
    "Level": "Information",
    "MessageTemplate": "The user with userId {userId} logged in at {loggedInTime}",
    "Properties": {
        "userId": 42,
        "loggedInTime": "09:47:31.5125828"
    }
}
```

As you can see, a lot more information is suddenly available. The structure of the logline is such that if we store it in a system somewhere, we can easily query the lines. Later in this chapter, I will show you how this is done.

So, Serilog is comparable to the other two frameworks until you use one of the many formatters. The ability to store the log information to easily query it makes it a very powerful tool to have in your toolbelt!

Log levels in Serilog logging

As you will probably expect by now, Serilog also has levels. Those levels should look very familiar to you. This table shows the levels that Serilog offers and what they are meant to do.

Serilog level	Description
Verbose	This contains the most detailed information. These messages may contain sensitive application data and are therefore not recommended for production unless hidden.
Debug	This level contains information that is useful in development and debugging.
Information	This level contains informational messages that highlight the general flow of the application. It is useful for general application insights.
Warning	Indications of possible issues or service and functionality degradation are included at this level.
Error	Errors and exceptions that cannot be handled or are unexpected are included here.
Fatal	This level focuses on critical errors causing complete failure of the application and requiring immediate attention.
Silent	This is the level for no logging at all (Serilog does not explicitly define a Silent level, but logging can effectively be turned off).

Table 10.4: Serilog log levels

Again, there are no surprises here. As with the other frameworks, you can use this however you want: no one can stop you from adding lots of debug information to the Error level. It is just not a very good idea.

Comparing the logging frameworks

After having seen all of these frameworks, you might wonder: which one should I pick? The answer is simple: choose whichever one you feel most comfortable with.

All frameworks have pros and cons; none are bad or extremely good. They do have different use cases and areas of attention. The following table highlights some of those:

Feature	.NET Logger	NLog	Serilog
Overview	Reliable and integrates seamlessly with .NET	Rich in features, great for a wide range of applications	Excels in structured logging, making data meaningful and searchable
Integration	Deeply integrated with .NET Core, supports dependency injection and configuration settings	Flexible, can be used in various .NET applications, supports multiple targets	Great with .NET applications, especially for structured data stores such as Seq or Elasticsearch
Pros	Minimal setup. Supports structured logging	Advanced log routing and filtering; logs to multiple targets simultaneously	Exceptional at structured logging; supports enrichers for additional context
Cons	Less feature-rich without third-party providers	Configuration can get complex	Might be overkill for simple needs; best features require compatible logging targets
Best for	Projects that need straightforward logging with minimal setup	Applications requiring detailed control over logging, or when logging into multiple places	Projects where structured logging and data querying are priorities

Table 10.5: Comparison between the logging frameworks

You just have to look at your own needs and determine your scenario and way of working best. Pick that tool. My advice is to give the others a go. You might find a new favorite logging framework!

So, we have now looked at logging. We have seen the most commonly used frameworks and how to use them. We have looked at default Microsoft logging; we have had an in-depth look at NLog and its robust collection of targets and rules. Finally, we have looked at Serilog's structured logging approach.

You should be able to use logging from now on. However, logging is part of your application. What if you do not get all the information you need from logging? That is where monitoring comes into play. Let's have a look at that next!

> **A word of caution**
>
> Logging is very useful. In fact, I would suggest that you cannot do serious development on systems without a UI if you do not have extensive logging. However, you must be careful: it is too easy to leak sensitive information about your system. Consider things such as connection strings, credentials, and other sensitive information. Also, you might sometimes accidentally disclose information about the inner workings of your system or even about the organization that this system runs. Be careful. Do not assume that people will not try to move the log level to Trace to see what is happening. Log as much as possible, but be mindful of the dangers!

Logging is one of the best things you can do to solve development and production issues. However, there is more that we can do. We need insights into these logs, but we must also monitor things such as memory usage, CPU usage, and much more. Let's talk about monitoring next!

Monitoring your applications

We need to keep an eye on things as our software runs. During development, we can turn on extensive logging to the console or to a file, which helps us track errors and issues. However, once our code runs on the final machine, it needs to run, and it might be a bit harder to look at all those log files.

Monitoring with Seq

Monitoring the system's state is essential to keep things healthy. One of the great tools we have available to do this is Seq. Seq and Serilog are a match made in heaven!

One of the reasons why Serilog is getting so much attention these days is because of its ability to write logs in a structured manner. We looked at this in the previous section but did not dive into what we could do. It is time to change that.

Since the logs coming from Serilog are formatted in a particular way, we can also store them in a specific way. One of the tools that allow us to do so is Seq. Seq is a tool by the company Datalust. You can get a free personal license from them to play around with your logs. You can choose to install Seq on your machine, or you can choose to download a Docker image that contains everything you need. I prefer the latter, but it doesn't matter which option you choose. The Datalust website clearly explains how to get the bits. You can find the documentation at `https://docs.datalust.co/docs/an-overview-of-seq`. In the *Technical requirements* section of this chapter, I have shown you the Docker command that you will need to execute to get a local version of Seq running.

Once you have done that, you can actually start to use Seq. We need to change our code a little bit. In addition to the packages that we installed earlier to enable logging to `Console` and `File`, we will also need a new package: `Serilog.Sinks.Seq`.

Once you have installed that, we must change the setup of the log a bit. That looks like this:

```
var logger = new LoggerConfiguration()
    .MinimumLevel.Verbose()
    .WriteTo.Console(new JsonFormatter())
    .WriteTo.File(
        new JsonFormatter(),
        "logs\\log.json",
        rollingInterval: RollingInterval.Day)
    .WriteTo.Seq("http://localhost:5341")
    .CreateLogger();
```

As you can see, we added a new `Sink` to our configuration, and this time, we are writing to Seq. I use the default port `5341`, since this is the port that Seq listens to.

If I run the application and go to the Seq dashboard on my machine, I will also get to see the logs there. That looks like this:

Figure 10.3: Serilog captured by Seq

You can clearly see all log messages. They are nicely colored. I have also opened the last message, in which we added some structural information. Seq captures this information and shows you exactly what is going on.

You can also query over the logs by entering a SQL-like statement in the top edit box. That looks like this:

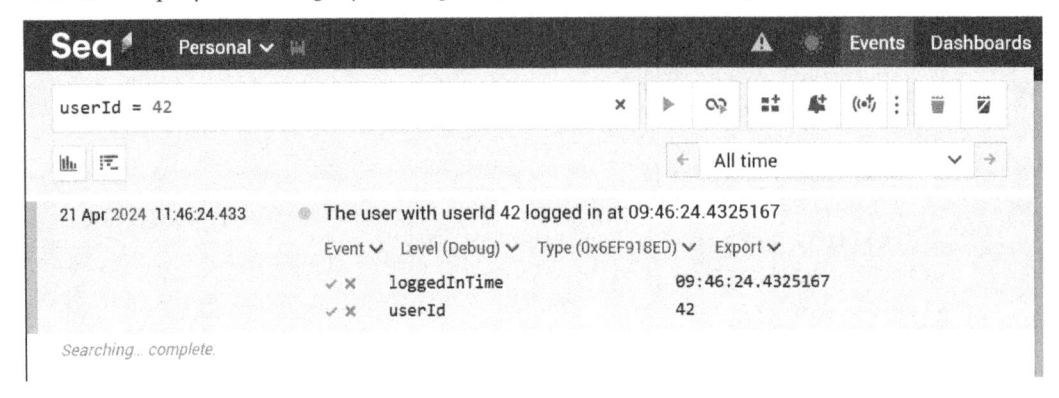

Figure 10.4: Seq dashboard with a filter for user Id.

I added the `userId = 42` query in the edit box. This results in Seq only showing all messages about the user whose `userId` is `42`.

The query language is extensive and you can write complex queries. This means that you can always find what you need even if you log many messages.

Seq is extremely powerful and yet easy to set up. I highly recommend checking it out!

Performance counters

Windows gives us lots of tools to monitor our systems, such as `EventViewer`. We can use those tools in our own systems as well. For instance, there are a lot of performance counters available that you can access both inside and outside of your code.

Let's look at how to get that in our code first.

I started a new Console application, added the `System.Diagnostic` NuGet package, and then wrote the following code:

```
using System.Diagnostics;
using ExtensionLibrary;
#pragma warning disable CA1416
var counter = 0;
var cpuCounter = new PerformanceCounter("Processor", "% Processor Time", "_Total");
while (true)
{
```

```
        if (counter++ == 10)
            // Start a method on a background thread
            Task.Run(() =>
            {
                Parallel.For(0, Environment.ProcessorCount, j =>
                {
                    for (var i = 0; i < 100000000; i++)
                    {
                        var result = Math.Exp(Math.Sqrt(Math.PI));
                    }
                });
                counter = 0;
            });
        var cpuUsage = cpuCounter.NextValue();
        var message = $"CPU Usage: {cpuUsage}%";
        var color = cpuUsage > 10 ? ConsoleColor.Red : ConsoleColor.Green;
        message.Dump(color);
        await Task.Delay(200);
}
```

Near the top of the file, I have created an instance of the `PerformanceCounter` class. This class gives us access to all the performance counters that we have mentioned, so we can also use them in our code. We need to specify the category and the item in that category we want to monitor. In my case, I went for `Processor` and `% Processor Time`, which are indicators of the load on the CPUs

Then, I start a never-ending loop in which I increase a counter. As soon as that counter reaches `10`, I do some silly calculations on all the CPUs available on my machine. These calculations do not do anything useful besides keeping the CPUs busy. All this happens on a background thread, so the main loop keeps displaying how busy the system is.

For readability, I will also change the color of the output if the CPU percentage is over 10%. You might have to change this threshold if you have a slower or faster machine than I do.

If you run this, you will be able to see how busy the system is. You should see a nice green output, but the system will get busier every few seconds, as shown by the red output.

You can measure many items, tracking what the computer is doing. Suppose that you want to find out what you can monitor. In that case, you only need to open the Performance Monitor application on your Windows machine (search for `perfmon.exe`). You can add counters to the main screen; the dialog that shows them is a good source of information. Make sure that you check the **Show**

description box at the bottom of the screen to see what all the counters do. To give you an idea, this is what that screen looks like when you search for the counter that we just used:

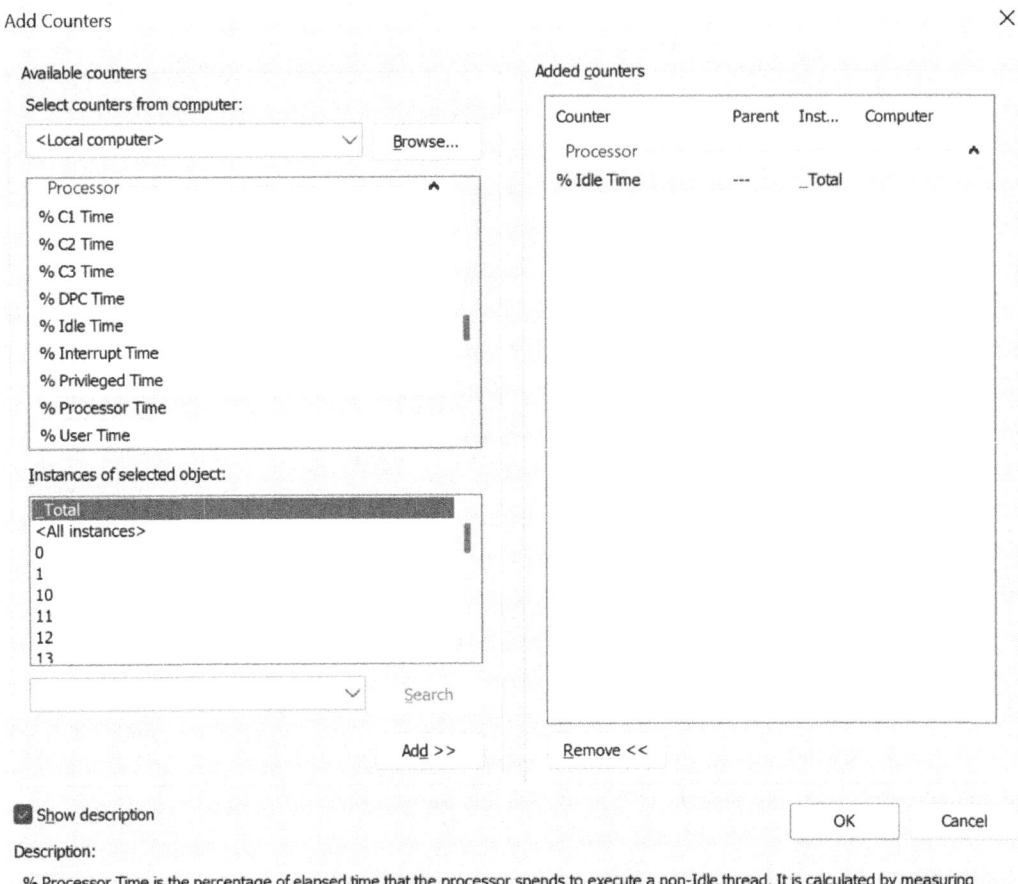

Figure 10.5: Perfmon.exe example with % Processor Time

I suggest that you browse through that list and see what you can find that might be useful. There are even categories specifically for the .NET CLR, so you can see how often the garbage collector runs or how frequently an exception has been raised per second!

Prometheus

Keeping an eye on your system's vital metrics can help you pinpoint issues. If your system suddenly starts using a lot more memory, or if at certain times the CPU usage spikes, you might have a problem that needs fixing. Thus, it is important to track those metrics. As we just learned, we can use the

`PerformanceCounter` class to get the necessary information and do something with it, such as writing it to Seq with Serilog.

However, that is not the only way. There is nothing wrong with the combination of Serilog and Seq. However, their primary goal is to log events. You can use a tool such as Prometheus to track trends, such as CPU usage or memory pressure.

Prometheus is similar to Serilog and Seq: they allow you to write something in your code to an external system that you can look at in your web browser. However, Prometheus is primarily used for ad monitoring and time series databases. It is designed to record real-time metrics in a scalable fashion. It excels at monitoring the state of your applications and infrastructure.

Let's have a look at how all of that works.

The application that you want to monitor needs a NuGet package. So, let's install that. It is called `prometheus-net`. However, that is only part of the equation. As I said, you can use your browser to see the events that you are interested in, so we will also need to install the server.

You can download Prometheus from `https://prometheus.io` and run it on your machine. However, if you are just trying to figure out how it works and see whether this is the tool for you, I recommend downloading the Docker image and running it.

Prometheus needs a configuration file. This is a simple YAML file telling it how to behave. We need to link to that configuration file when we start the Docker image, so let's write that file first.

Open your favorite code editor and create a file called `prometheus.yml` somewhere. I have placed mine in a folder called `c:\data`. The preceding Docker command will ensure that it gets read and used inside the running container. This is what the file looks like:

```yaml
global:
  scrape_interval: 5s
  evaluation_interval: 5s
scrape_configs:
  - job_name: 'c# worker'
    static_configs:
      - targets: ['host.docker.internal:1234']
```

Let's see what is going on here.

The first line defines the `scrape_interval`. This is the interval that determines how often Prometheus looks at the metrics. Since metrics are usually interesting over a longer time, you do not need the system to measure them continuously. In our example, I have set it to do a scrape every five seconds.

The following line defines the `evaluation_interval`. Prometheus can have rules and alerts that fire when a particular metric goes over or under a specific metric. This interval determines how often it checks to see whether the alert needs to be fired. Again, I have set it to five seconds.

These two settings are global; they apply to all the metrics for all the applications that we monitor. We can later change these for each specific metric or application if we want to.

The following section, called `scrape_configs`, defines the specific metrics that we want to collect. In my case, I have given it a name: `C# worker`. Then, we will tell it which server supplies the metrics. Again, in my case, it is `host.docker.internal:1234`. This means that the server runs on that URL with that specific port.

"Wait a minute," you might say, "I am not running a server; I am running a Console application!" Do not worry; Prometheus takes care of this.

The server application of Prometheus calls into the systems it needs to monitor over an HTTP connection. Thus, the clients it monitors need a web server that supplies that information. We do not have to take care of that; Prometheus does that for us.

> **IP addresses in Docker**
>
> You might wonder why I use the `host.docker.internal` hostname as the server address. After all, both Docker and our Console application run on the same system. They both are available on `localhost`, right? That is incorrect; Docker containers all run in their own network (I am simplifying things here, but the idea still works). That means that if the Prometheus server would listen to anything on `localhost:1234`, it would only listen to the virtual network in the image. We need to supply the actual IP address of the machine that runs our application. However, if you do not want to hardcode that, use the `host.docker.internal` DNS name. The DNS system in Docker knows this name. It resolves the actual IP address of the host machine so that the containers in Docker can find the correct machine.

Let's have a look at our code. I have started a new Console application and added the NuGet package. The code itself looks like this. I start by setting up our metrics:

```
Gauge memoryGauge =
    Metrics.CreateGauge(
        "app_memory_usage_bytes",
        "Memory Usage of the application in bytes.");
var server =
    new MetricServer(
        hostname:"127.0.0.1",
        port: 1234);
server.Start();
```

First, I create a `Gauge`. This is like a thermometer that you use to measure metrics. In this case, I will make one that measures `app_memory_usage_bytes`, one of the many metrics that we can use.

Then, we will create an instance of a `MetricServer`. You must specify the host from which the app runs and the port from which it broadcasts the metrics. Remember when I said that Prometheus listens to servers to collect its metrics? Well, this is where we set up that server.

> **IP addresses and Docker, again**
>
> I have used the `127.0.0.1` hostname here. If I used `localhost`, I would get errors for some reason. If I used the machine's actual hostname, I would get errors. Either the app does not start up, or the Prometheus server can't find my app. However, if I specify the IP address here (my actual IP address also works), the system works just fine. So, if you have issues with getting things to work, just try to use `127.0.0.1` here.

Then, I will start the server.

Now, you are ready to send the metrics to the server. I have created a simple method that does this:

```
static void UpdateMemoryGauge(Gauge memoryGauge)
{
    var memoryUsage = GC.GetTotalMemory(forceFullCollection: false);
    memoryGauge.Set(memoryUsage);
}
```

That is basically all that you have to do.

However, let's see what happens when we actually do something. In the main body of my code, I have a simple loop that adds a block of memory every five seconds and then clears them all after 20 seconds, after which the whole thing starts all over again.

The code looks like this:

```
var counter = 0;
List<byte[]> buffer = [];
Random rnd = new Random();
while (true)
{
    if (counter++ % 5 == 0)
        AllocateMemoryBlock(rnd, buffer);
    if (counter == 20)
    {
        ClearMemory(buffer);
        counter = 0;
    }
    UpdateMemoryGauge(memoryGauge);
    await Task.Delay(1000);
}
```

I have defined some variables, such as `counter`, `buffer`, and `rnd`. In the loop, I will either add memory to the system, clear the memory, or do nothing. At the end, I will make sure to call the `UpdateMemoryGauge()` method. Then, the app sleeps for one second.

The `AllocateMemoryBlock()` looks like this:

```
static void AllocateMemoryBlock(Random random, List<byte[]> bytesList)
{
    var memoryToAllocate =
        random.Next(50000000, 200000000);
    var dummyBlock =
        new byte[memoryToAllocate];
    bytesList.Add(dummyBlock);
    "Memory block added".Dump(ConsoleColor.Blue);
}
```

Again, this is silly code; I hope you never write this in actual production code. However, it works here; we want to measure the memory usage of our app, so we might as well allocate lots of it. I have used a randomizer to make the system a bit less predictable because I like the look of the charts a bit better that way.

The `ClearMemory()` is even simpler:

```
static void ClearMemory(List<byte[]> list)
{
    list.Clear();
    GC.Collect();
    "Memory block cleared".Dump(ConsoleColor.Green);
}
```

We then clear the list and clean up the memory by calling `GC.Collect()`, and we will log that to the screen.

That is it! If you run this for a while and open your browser to the default Prometheus URL of `http://localhost:9090`, you can search for the `app_memory_usage_bytes` metric. If you run the app for a while, you will get a nice chart like this:

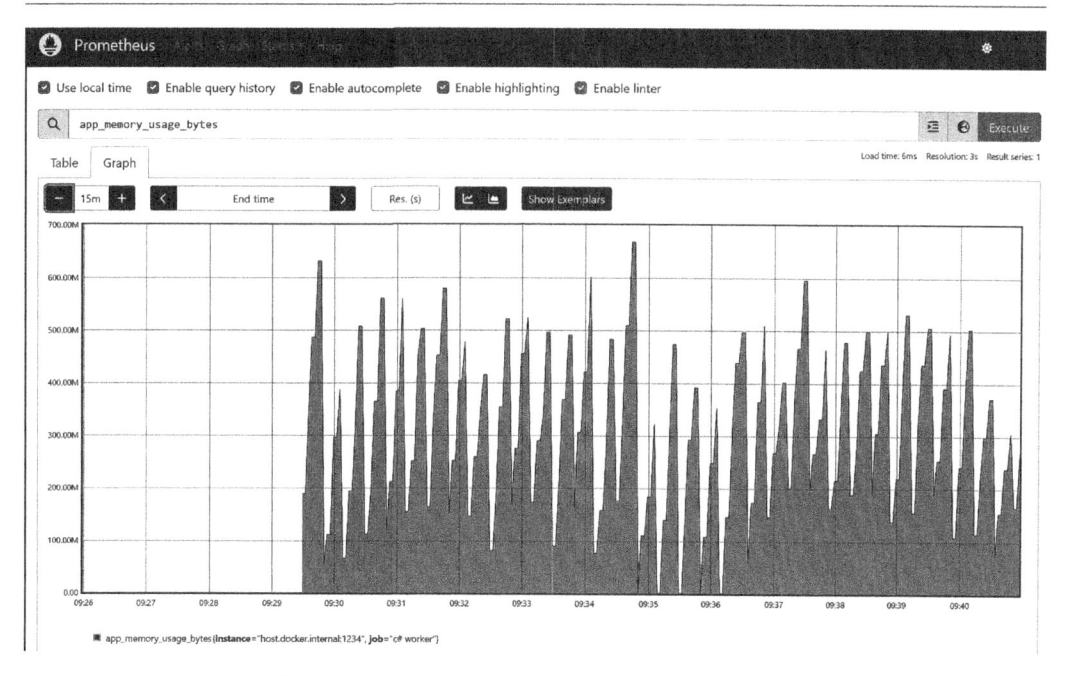

Figure 10.6: Prometheus sampling our memory usage

The chart shows our app in action, depicting how much memory it uses. You can probably also see why I used a randomizer; the chart looks slightly more interesting. However, that is just my personal preference.

You can search for metrics in the top part of the screen, or you can search for jobs. If you specify the `{job = "c# worker"}` search string, you will get over 30 metrics for your app. You can click on each of them to add them to the chart. There is a ton of information there!

Other platforms for monitoring

We have looked at Seq to collect our logs. We looked at performance counters and we looked at Prometheus. These are all great tools and I believe they are the ones that fit us as system programmers the best. However, there are many more systems out there that might work better for you and your specific use case. I will not describe them all in detail; that would justify a book in itself. However, here is an overview of some of the most used ones. If you are interested in them, I suggest that you do research and find out how they can help you!

Tool	Description	Use case
Application Insights	Part of Azure Monitor, it provides APM features and telemetry data	Cloud-based monitoring
New Relic	Offers full-stack observability, including application monitoring	Performance insights
Dynatrace	Utilizes AI for automatic monitoring and problem resolution	Full-stack monitoring
Datadog	Provides monitoring, troubleshooting, and security for cloud applications	Cloud-native environments
ELK Stack	Elasticsearch, Logstash for data processing, Kibana for visualization	Log Management
Nagios	Offers monitoring and alerting services for servers, switches, applications, and services	Infrastructure monitoring
AppDynamics	Application performance management and IT operations analytics	Business performance monitoring

Table 10.6: Monitoring tools

As you can see, there are many options available, so there is definitely something that you can use that fits your specific needs!

Now that you know how to monitor using Seq, performance counters, and Prometheus, we should look at what we are logging and monitoring.

What you should be monitoring or logging

We have seen a lot of ways in which we can log and monitor our systems. However, the question remains: what should you be logging and monitoring? The answer is simple: whatever you need to keep your systems healthy.

OK, that answer is probably the easy way out. Let's be a bit more specific.

Basic health monitoring

You should monitor the overall health of your system. Your application does not live in a vacuum, so you should be mindful of the state of the complete system and how you interact with it. These are some of the items you might want to keep an eye on:

- **CPU usage**: Track CPU usage to determine whether your application is causing a high CPU load
- **Memory usage**: Monitor memory consumption to detect memory leaks or excessive memory usage, which is critical in a managed environment such as .NET, where garbage collection occurs

- **Disk I/O**: Monitor read/write operations and disk usage to ensure that disk I/O is not a bottleneck
- **Network I/O**: Keep an eye on inbound and outbound network traffic, especially if your system communicates with other services

Of course, there are many other metrics you might be interested in, but these are usually the ones that people care about the most.

Application-specific metrics

Of course, your system itself is also something that you should look into. These are the metrics I would suggest you add to your monitoring tool:

- **Thread counts and thread pool health**: It is helpful to know whether your threads are getting starved or whether the pool is overworked
- **Garbage collection metrics**: Track the frequency and duration of garbage collection events to manage memory more effectively and optimize application performance
- **Queue lengths**: If your application uses message queues or similar structures, monitoring their lengths can help you understand throughput and backlogs

These metrics are more geared toward your application than the whole system, so I really recommend that you use these.

Errors and exceptions

Exceptions happen. That is just a fact of life. So, you might want to track those as well. Monitoring tools can capture these exceptions, but I would not solely rely on them. Always log what is happening in your exception-handling code blocks. You should be thinking about these items:

- **Unhandled exceptions**: Log all unhandled exceptions with complete stack traces for debugging
- **Handled exceptions**: Sometimes, knowing about handled exceptions can provide insights into potential issues that are not critical yet but may become problematic

Monitoring errors and exceptions is, in my opinion, a given. You really want to know about these events!

Application logs

Several things are happening around your application that might be worthwhile to keep track of. These are some of them:

- **Start/stop events**: Log when services or components start and stop to understand application life cycle events

- **Significant state changes**: Any change in the state that might affect the application's behavior should be logged
- **Security-related events**: These events include authentication attempts, access violations, and other security checks

Dependency health

Applications rarely work in isolation. There are usually other systems that they depend on. You should track those dependencies as well:

- **Database connectivity**: Regular checks to ensure that your application can connect to databases or other storage systems
- **External services**: Monitor the availability and response times of any APIs or external services that your application relies on

Custom business logic monitoring

Of course, the application does some specific things that only apply to your environment. These might also be targets to monitor. Think about things such as these:

- **Performance of critical operations** such as algorithms or processes central to your application's functionality
- **Data processing rates**, especially in systems that handle large volumes of data or streaming data

These are just some of the things you might add to your toolbelt.

> **Use the right level!**
> Remember: assigning the right level to each event is essential when logging. Not everything should be Information; you must distinguish between an error and debug information. Again, please make sure that you are not leaking sensitive information through your logs.

Next steps

I hope that you took note of all of these items and kept a log of what we have been talking about! Logging and monitoring are extremely important, especially when you do not have a UI. We covered the logging frameworks available to you as a systems programmer in this chapter: the good and default Microsoft log, as well as NLog and structured logging in Serilog.

We also looked at monitoring the health of your system and your application. We looked at Seq to collect our logs, discussed how to use performance counters, and dove into monitoring with Prometheus.

We also talked about what you should be logging and monitoring and why you should do that.

All in all, from now on, you will no longer be in the dark when unexpected things happen. Since they *will* happen, you'd better make sure that you are prepared. A good logging and monitoring strategy can save your life. Well, maybe not your life, but it can help your system. That is what makes it all worth it. After all, a good log can set you on the right track when you want to start debugging your system. Incidentally, that is the topic of the next chapter!

11

The One with the Debugging Dances

Debugging and Profiling System Applications

Debugging is the art of finding errors in your code and ensuring you have all the knowledge to fix them. That sounds simple enough, doesn't it? Well, think again. Debugging can get complicated quickly, and you need good strategies to recover. Luckily, I am here to help you! In this chapter, we're going to cover the following main topics:

- What is debugging? What is **profiling**?
- How do we use **breakpoints**?
- What other debugging tools do we have in Visual Studio?
- How do we deal with multithreaded and asynchronous systems?
- How do we profile and benchmark our code to ensure it runs as fast as possible?

Debugging can get quite time-intensive. So, let's not waste any time and get started.

Technical requirements

As always, you can find the source code for all samples in this chapter in the GitHub repository at `https://github.com/PacktPublishing/Systems-Programming-with-C-Sharp-and-.NET/tree/main/SystemsProgrammingWithCSharpAndNet/Chapter11`.

I only use Visual Studio in this chapter; I am not referring to any of the third-party tools that might do the same job. However, I will provide you with a list of alternative tools at the end of this chapter.

Introducing debugging

True story: I once worked for a manager who claimed he wanted to lay off the testers in my team. He said, "If your team performs better, they will not produce bugs, and therefore we can save on the testers." Obviously, he was wrong. I left that company shortly after this happened.

Developing software is a creative job. People think software development is an exact science that is close to mathematics and physics, but it is not. Sure, the roots look mathematical, but what we, as software developers, do is something else. We take an idea, think of something that does not yet exist, and then turn those ideas into something that can help others. We create something out of thin air by our imagination and ingenuity.

However, the creative mind is sloppy. We cut corners when we are in the flow. We make mistakes trying to realize our vision. Testers and QA professionals are our safety net; they are there to catch the things we forget about. But having a safety net does not mean you can do whatever you want and wing it. Once you have the first outline of your code ready, it is time to switch from being the creative developer to the pensive, analytical developer – the one who looks at their code and notices areas of improvement; and still then you will miss things. So, you test yourself. That is when you find issues. Or, you see the system does not run as smoothly as you expected. Maybe you find the results are not what they are supposed to be. That is when the debugging dance starts: you run the system, you try to pinpoint the area where things go wrong, you fix things, and repeat the whole cycle.

> **Tip**
> Debugging can be a fun journey, or it can be an extremely frustrating experience. I am here to help you move your debugging experiences into a more fun one. If debugging means fixing bugs, then developing means creating bugs. There is nothing wrong with that, as long as you realize this is the case and you can resolve the issues before shipping. Let me help you with that!

Debugging and profiling – an overview

I remember when they taught me how to write Cobol code on the university mainframe. It was a challenge, to be honest. The mainframe was a costly machine with many terminals attached. If you do not know what that means, imagine you have one computer with multiple keyboards and monitors connected to it, where each user can use their session to do their work, isolated from the others.

This worked fine when you had to do some simple stuff, such as working on a document or a spreadsheet; the mainframe could handle multiple sessions well. However, compiling code is something else: that takes a lot of CPU power. They fixed that by having the students submit their code to the compiler, which would then run sequentially at night. You could see what you did wrong when you returned the next day. Imagine forgetting a semicolon somewhere, meaning you have to wait another 24 hours before you can see the results of your fix. That way of working taught me to think about my code very thoroughly.

These days, when I enter C# code, I see the compiler working for me constantly. Visual Studio immediately tells me when I make a mistake.

Debugging

Debugging was out of the question. All we could do was stuff the code with logging messages, run the program, and see the output. Then, we could try to deduce the errors in our code from the log files.

Nowadays, it's so much easier: you can step through your code, see the statements as they are executed, and inspect variables, memory, threads, and so on.

Of course, the requirements of the software have also become much more complex, so writing software in itself hasn't gotten any easier.

But modern debugging tools help – a lot.

Debugging is the process of identifying, isolating, and fixing problems or "bugs" in software. These bugs can be anywhere from simple syntax errors to more elusive logic errors that produce the wrong output or flow.

The compiler helps us fix the most obvious mistakes: a typo in a statement is caught immediately. However, code that compiles does not result in a flawless program. Debugging can help remedy that.

Profiling

Profiling is the twin of debugging. *While debugging aims to find logical errors, profiling is meant to help you find performance errors.* Performance errors can indicate that the system runs too slow, uses too much memory, or other things that stop the software from running as efficiently as possible.

Profiling helps you improve the efficiency of your software. It shows you where the bottlenecks are. Profiling can help you pinpoint where your memory usage goes up and where your logic fails when encountering performance issues.

Profiling can be as simple as logging some timing information or as complex as gathering 24 hours of activities of all your threads and performing a statistical analysis of that data. It all depends on your needs.

Debugging and profiling go hand in hand. With a profile session, you gather the evidence that something is not going as you want it to. You then use debugging techniques to find and fix the errors in your code.

Of course, this process is more like a cycle. You debug, then you profile, then debug to find the issues, fix them, then debug the fixes, then profile the fixes, and so on. It's a never-ending dance. However, it can be quite satisfying: in the end, you have much better code and a better-performing system, and that must make it all worth it!

So, let's investigate the tools we have to do all this magic!

Debugging 101

Visual Studio is a great tool. It has many features that help you during development and the debugging process. So, it is natural to start by looking at Visual Studio first. I will not spend much time on debugging basics in Visual Studio. Still, I think revisiting the most apparent tools we have is immensely clarifying.

Debug builds versus Release builds

Let's talk about that dropdown at the top in Visual Studio, where you can choose between **Debug** and **Release**. I am sure you have a feeling about what this is all about. You pick **Debug** when you are still writing the code, and want to debug your software. You choose **Release** when you are ready to release your product.

However, there is a bit more you should know about those options. Let me start by saying that you can still debug your code if it is built in Release mode. It's just a bit harder.

Let me compare the results of a Debug setting and a Release setting. The following table shows the main differences:

	Debug	**Release**
Purpose	Primarily for development.	Primarily for production.
Optimization	Minimal or no optimization.	Highly optimized for performance and efficiency. The compiler removes unused code and applies various optimizations.
Symbols	Includes debugging symbols (.pdb files), which provide detailed information about the code (e.g., variable names, line numbers, and so on).	No or limited symbols. You can still get a .pdb file, but it will have much less information.
Assertions	Debug assertions are enabled.	Debug assertions are disabled.
Performance	Generally slower because there is no optimization.	Generally faster and more efficient.
Size	Larger files due to extra debugging information.	Smaller because of optimizations and removal of debugging information.

Table 11.1: Comparing Debug and Release builds

I suggest you use Debug builds when debugging. That is what it is for.

Breakpoints

The best tool Visual Studio offers is the mighty **breakpoint**. It is a straightforward construct, but it can help us a lot when trying to understand what is happening inside our application.

In the simplest form, a breakpoint is a code point that stops the program when the application reaches the code statement to which the breakpoint is attached. You can add breakpoints to all sorts of things as long as they are statements. You cannot add a breakpoint to a code comment.

You cannot set a breakpoint on a method declaration, but you can set it on the first { that marks the beginning of the method.

Also, declarations of variables are not a valid target for a breakpoint unless you do an assignment simultaneously.

For instance, look at the following two lines:

```
int x; // Cannot add a breakpoint
int j = 0; // Can add a breakpoint
```

We cannot add a breakpoint to the line where we declare i. We can add a breakpoint to the second line. Technically, that line consists of two parts: the declaration and the assignment; the breakpoint is set on the assignment part.

Namespace declarations and using statements are also invalid targets. Interfaces cannot have breakpoints, just as attribute declarations are excluded.

However, besides these obvious cases, you can place them wherever you want.

What happens when a breakpoint is hit?

We have some software, placed a breakpoint, and ran the software. At one point, the execution point reaches our breakpoint. The question is: what happens then?

First, the execution stops. The program is frozen in time. In Visual Studio, some additional tools come to life:

- **Locals**: This window opens or updates, showing all variables reachable in the current scope
- **Autos**: This window displays variables used in the current line and the surrounding context
- **Watch**: This window shows any variables you might have added to the Watch
- **Call Stack**: This window displays a series of method calls that led up to the current breakpoint
- **Immediate**: This window allows you to type commands, evaluate expressions, or change variable values on the fly

With the program paused, you can inspect or modify variable values if necessary.

This helps you understand what happens in your program. However, it can lead to weird situations if you are not careful.

Let's have a look at what I mean. Imagine you have this code somewhere:

```
int sum = 0;
for (int i = 1; i <= 10; i++)
{
    sum += i;
}
$"The sum of the numbers from 0 to 9 is {sum}".Dump(ConsoleColor.Cyan);
```

This code iterates over the i variable, increasing it and adding its value to the sum variable. If you run this, you get the result of 55. Now, place a breakpoint inside the loop. Run the code again, but after the ninth iteration, you decide you want to see what happens in that loop one more time. So, you change the value of i from 9 back to 0. The sum variable will not make any sense anymore: the outcome is a vastly different value.

This sample is simple, but these side effects can happen quite quickly. Changing variables might have unintended consequences. So, be aware of that.

Threads and breakpoints

Later in this chapter, we will discuss debugging multithreaded applications, but I want to discuss one item here. I said that when the code hits a breakpoint, the debugger stops execution.

Look at this code:

```
ThreadPool.QueueUserWorkItem(_ =>
{
    int inThreadCounter = 0;
    while (true)
    {
        $"In the thread with counter {inThreadCounter++}".Dump(ConsoleColor.Yellow);
        Thread.Sleep(100);
    }
});
int outThreadCounter = 0;
while (true)
{
    $"In the main thread with counter {outThreadCounter++}".Dump(ConsoleColor.Cyan);
    await Task.Delay(200);
}
```

The code is straightforward enough. First, we get a `thread` from `ThreadPool`. An infinite loop logs a message in `thread`, increases a `counter`, and waits for 100 milliseconds.

In the main part of the code, we do something similar but at a different time. Running this program shows that we get two messages from the inner thread for each message from the outer thread. Now, place a breakpoint on the last `Task.Delay()` statement. Run the code, let the debugger hit the breakpoint, wait for a few seconds, and continue the run.

Suppose you do that a couple of times. In that case, you will notice that although the sequence of the messages to the console is slightly different, we still get twice as many messages from the inner thread. In other words, if we pause the outer thread, the inner thread is also paused.

That is good, of course. You do not want other threads to continue, wreaking havoc on the program flow. But let's change things a bit: replace the code where we create the thread with the following:

```
var inThreadCounter = 0;
var timer = new Timer(100);
timer.Elapsed +=
    (_, _) =>
    {
        $"In the timer call with counter {inThreadCounter++}".
Dump(ConsoleColor.Yellow);
    };
timer.Start();
```

Instead of having a `thread`, we now have a `timer`. This code achieves the same effect as our previous code: the `timer` works on a separate `thread` when the time has passed. If that happens, we will log the message and increase the counter.

However, if we repeat the little trick we did with the breakpoint on the code in the last loop, you will notice a completely different behavior. The number of messages from the timer is no longer double the number we get from the main loop; it is much more than that.

A breakpoint does not stop timers. Neither does it stop classes such as `Stopwatch`. Time-based events still happen, so you have a different outcome than expected. Be mindful of that when you use timers!

Features of breakpoints

Breakpoints are more than just markers to show the debugger where to stop the execution. They have some properties that can be helpful if you use them correctly. Most of these settings are accessed by clicking the breakpoint in the **Breakpoints** window and selecting **Settings**. That window looks like this:

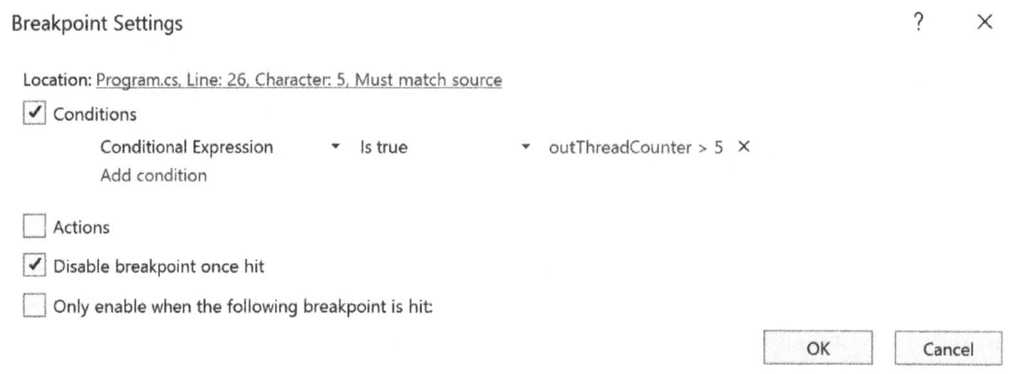

Figure 11.1: The Breakpoint Settings window in Visual Studio

You can also get this window by clicking on one of the settings you get when you right-click the breakpoint bullet in the code editor.

Active and inactive breakpoints

Breakpoints by default are active, meaning that if the debugger comes to the statement containing the breakpoint, the execution stops. But you can also disable the breakpoint: this means the breakpoint is still there, but it does not do anything. This option can be handy if you are debugging some code but want to skip a specific breakpoint at this time but do not want to delete it.

Conditional breakpoints

A conditional breakpoint only breaks when a particular condition has been met. The condition can be a single condition or a set of conditions, all of which must be true. The condition can include variables from the code as well. Let's imagine I want a breakpoint in the previous code sample. I want the breakpoint to be on the line with the `Task.Delay()` code. However, I only want that breakpoint to be active if the `outThreadCounter` variable is larger than 5 and only if that breakpoint has been hit 6 times. In our code, that should be the same (every time we go through that loop, `outThreadCounter` is increased), but if this doesn't happen, you can verify it using this technique.

You can specify this by placing a breakpoint, right-clicking on it, and then choosing **Conditions**.

Action breakpoints or tracepoints

Action breakpoints can be real breakpoints or breakpoints that do not break. But besides breaking (or not), you can also specify that the debugger should write something in the **Output** window. In other words, this is a very lightweight and temporary log system. You can output a static text or the contents of a variable. Underneath the option where you specify the output, you can place a checkmark in the box saying **Continue code execution**. If you check that box, the debugger does not stop at this breakpoint and only displays the required information in the Output window. When you do not stop executing the code and only display some information, we call these breakpoints **tracepoints**.

One-time breakpoint

A **one-time breakpoint** only works once. It stops code execution when the breakpoint is hit and then disables itself. If you want to use it again, you must manually enable it. You create this breakpoint by selecting **Disable breakpoint once hit**.

Dependent breakpoint

The **dependent breakpoint** is only enabled after another breakpoint has been hit. This is particularly useful if you have a method that is called from different places in your code. Still, you only want to debug a particular path. In that case, you create a breakpoint in the flow you are interested in (you might even make it non-breakable so that it only acts as a trigger) and then connect the breakpoint in the method you are interested in into that first breakpoint.

The effect is that the breakpoint is disabled until that first breakpoint is hit.

To see this in action, take our last example. Increase the time for the **Timer** option to 1 second (1000 milliseconds). Then, add a breakpoint to the line where we write the message to the console. Tick the **Action** box in the properties of this breakpoint, but do not add anything to the **Message** dialog. However, make sure you tick the **Continue code execution** box. The settings should look like this:

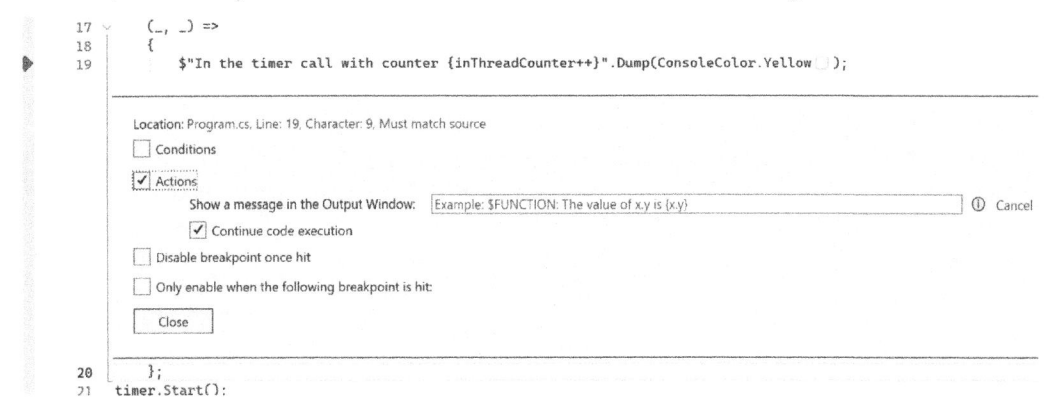

Figure 11.2: Trigger breakpoint

Then, add another breakpoint to the line where we write the console the value of outThreadCounter. This time, change the settings to enable the **Only enable when the following breakpoint is hit** option and select the other breakpoint in the corresponding drop-down menu. That should look like this:

```
24    while (true)
25    {
26        $"In the main thread with counter {outThreadCounter++}".Dump();
```

> Location: Program.cs, Line: 26, Character: 5, Must match source
> ☐ Conditions
> ☐ Actions
> ☐ Disable breakpoint once hit
> ☑ Only enable when the following breakpoint is hit: Program.cs, line 19 character 9
> [Close]

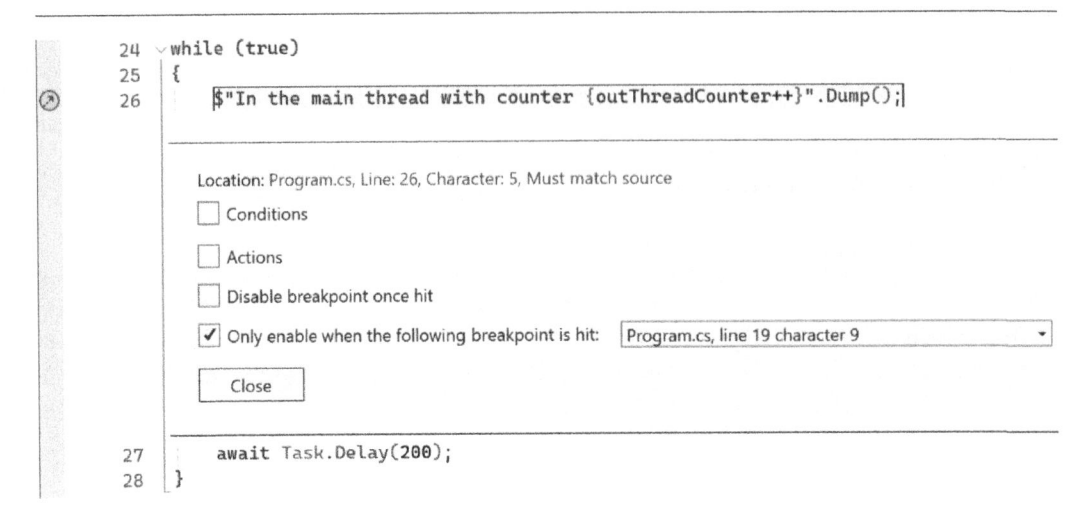

```
27        await Task.Delay(200);
28    }
```

Figure 11.3: Dependent breakpoint

If you run the program, the debugger ignores the last breakpoint during the first second. Then, the execution stops since our first breakpoint has been hit.

Of course, you can combine these settings at will.

> **Adding other breakpoints quickly**
>
> You probably know that you can add breakpoints to your code by clicking in what is known as **the gutter** to the left of the source code. If you do that, a red bullet appears in that gutter to indicate you have added a breakpoint at that position. But did you know you can also right-click in that gutter? If you do that, you get a pop-up menu to quickly add the breakpoints that were previously mentioned. In the long run, this might save you some mouse clicks!

Some other features

Breakpoints have some other nice features that might be helpful. You usually access these in the **Breakpoints** window in Visual Studio by right-clicking the chosen breakpoint. Here are some of them:

- **Breakpoints can have labels**: This way, you can give more meaningful names to the breakpoints.
- **You can group breakpoints**: If you create a breakpoint group, you can add breakpoints to them. This way, you can quickly turn a large group of breakpoints on or off instead of going through them individually.
- **You can search for breakpoints**: In the breakpoints window, you can search for class names, line numbers, output, labels, and so on. This feature might be helpful if you have a large group of breakpoints.
- **You can sort breakpoints by name, condition, hit count, label, and more**: If you still can't find what you need, you might want to reconsider your breakpoint strategy!

Most developers I encounter never come near all these options: all they do is toggle a breakpoint on a line of code to stop execution. But I hope you begin to appreciate the power these tools can bring you.

Debug windows

Visual Studio has a lot of windows that can help you get a grip on what is happening when you debug. Most of these windows are useless when editing code but come to life once the debugger starts. Let's see what we have!

Breakpoints

We already discussed breakpoints, but I want to point out the **Breakpoints** window. This window is where you see all the breakpoints in your application. It also shows additional information about those breakpoints. You can add columns to the window if you need more information. This is an example of what might look like:

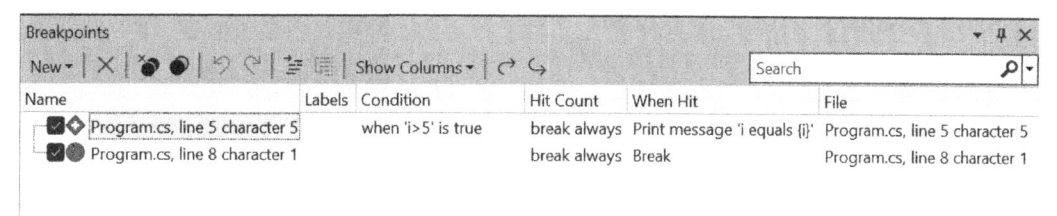

Figure 11.4: The Breakpoints window

You can customize this window to fit your needs.

Locals, autos, and watches

When debugging, you probably want to see the values of the variables in your code. To see the value, you can hover the mouse over a variable in the code editor window. However, there are windows in Visual Studio dedicated to giving you access to that data. Let's explore these.

The **Locals** window shows all the variables in the current scope. That can be pretty useful: you see all variables in the current block without being distracted by other variables.

The **Autos** window is even better: it tries to guess which variables interest you when you break in the code and show them and their values.

Let's have a look at this. We have the following class:

```
internal class MyClass
{
    public int Counter { get; set; }
}
```

We use it in the following code (I added line numbers so I can refer to the lines later on):

```
1: MyClass myClass = new MyClass();
2: int myNumber = 0;
3: while (true)
4: {
5:     myClass.Counter++;
6:     Console.WriteLine($"Counter {myClass.Counter++}");
7: }
```

Now, add a breakpoint on *line 3*. Run the code and see whether your output matches mine. I will step through all lines from *3* up until *7* and show you what the **Autos** window tells me.

The first breakpoint is on *line 3*, so the debugger stops there. It breaks on *line 3*, with the following result in the **Autos** window:

Name	Value	Type
myNumber	0	Int

Table 11.2

Now, step to the following line. Then we get, if we stop on *line 4*, we get the following results:

Name	Value	Type

Table 11.3

As you can see, we get no results. We stopped on {, and no variables can influence the path of the code now. So, there is nothing to show. Let's continue and step to the following line, *line 5*.

Name	Value	Type
myClass	{myClass}	MyClass
Counter	0	Int
myClass.Counter	0	int

Table 11.4

If you step to that line, you will see two items. The top one, myClass, can be expanded so you can see properties that might interest you. In our case, this is myClass.Counter. We also see the myClass.Counter variable separately since the compiler is smart enough to see this is significant in our code.

Let's move to the next line, *line 6*.

Name	Value	Type
MyClass.Counter.get returned	0	int
myClass	{myClass}	MyClass
Counter	1	Int
myClass.Counter	1	int

Table 11.5

That is interesting: the **Locals** window shows us that we called a method (`MyClass.Counter.get`) and got a result. There is also an icon to show you that this is indeed the return value. The "get" returned zero, but then we applied the ++ operator to change the value locally.

The next line, *line 7*, produces this:

Name	Value	Type
MyClass.Counter.get returned	1	int
System.Runtime.CompilerServices.DefaultInterpolatedStringHandler.ToStringAndClear returned	Counter 1	string

Table 11.6

We printed the line of text to the console and did that with the $ interpolation command in front of the string. Now, you can see that doing that caused the `System.Runtime.CompilerServices.DefaultInterpolatedStringHandler.ToStringAndClear()` method to be called, returning the resulting `Counter 1` string. Oh, and we lost `myClass` (well, it's not lost; it's just not shown any more since we will not use it in this scope anymore). As you can see, the **Locals** window is good at showing values of local variables and helping you figure out implicit method calls, such as the string interpolation and property getters!

The **Locals** window is pretty clever at figuring out what you need to see. Of course, if you disagree, there is always the **Watch** window.

The **Watch** window does the same as the previous two debug windows, but it only shows you what you ask it to show. Once the debugger stops the flow of your program, you can right-click on a variable and select **Add to Watch**. The variable will then pop up in the **Watch** window, where you can do the same things as you can do with **Locals** and **Autos**: inspect the variables and change the values if needed.

However, this time, the variables stay there until you remove them. Suppose they go out of scope or are unreachable. In that case, you get an error in the **Watch** window telling you the variable does not exist in the current context. That doesn't harm your experience, though: it will stay there as long as you need it, and if the variable comes back into context (in this or in a subsequent debugging session), it will be back again.

Diagnostic Tools

The **Diagnostic Tools** window almost deserves its very own book. It does many things for us! Let's dive into it.

As with most other debugging tools in Visual Studio, you cannot use the **Diagnostic Tools** until you are at a breakpoint in your code while debugging. We will use a very silly program to show you some of **Diagnostic Tools**' possibilities. It's a **console application**, and the code looks like this:

```
var memoryBlock = new Dictionary<int, byte[]>();
var passCounter = 0;
while (true)
{
    passCounter++;
    var newBlock = new byte[1024 * 1024];
    memoryBlock.Add(passCounter, newBlock);
}
```

I also place a conditional breakpoint on the line with `passCounter++` (so, the first statement is in the while-loop). That condition looks like this:

```
passCounter % 100 == 0
```

In other words, the breakpoint stops every 100 passes.

If we run this, the application will break on the first pass. That makes sense: 0 % of 100 equals 0. You can then open the **Diagnostic Tools** window (if it doesn't show up automatically, you can open it by going to the **Debug** menu, then choosing **Windows**, followed by selecting **Show Diagnostic Tools**). I suggest you make the window bigger than usual so you can see all the goodies it gives us. Mine looks like this:

![Diagnostic Tools window screenshot]

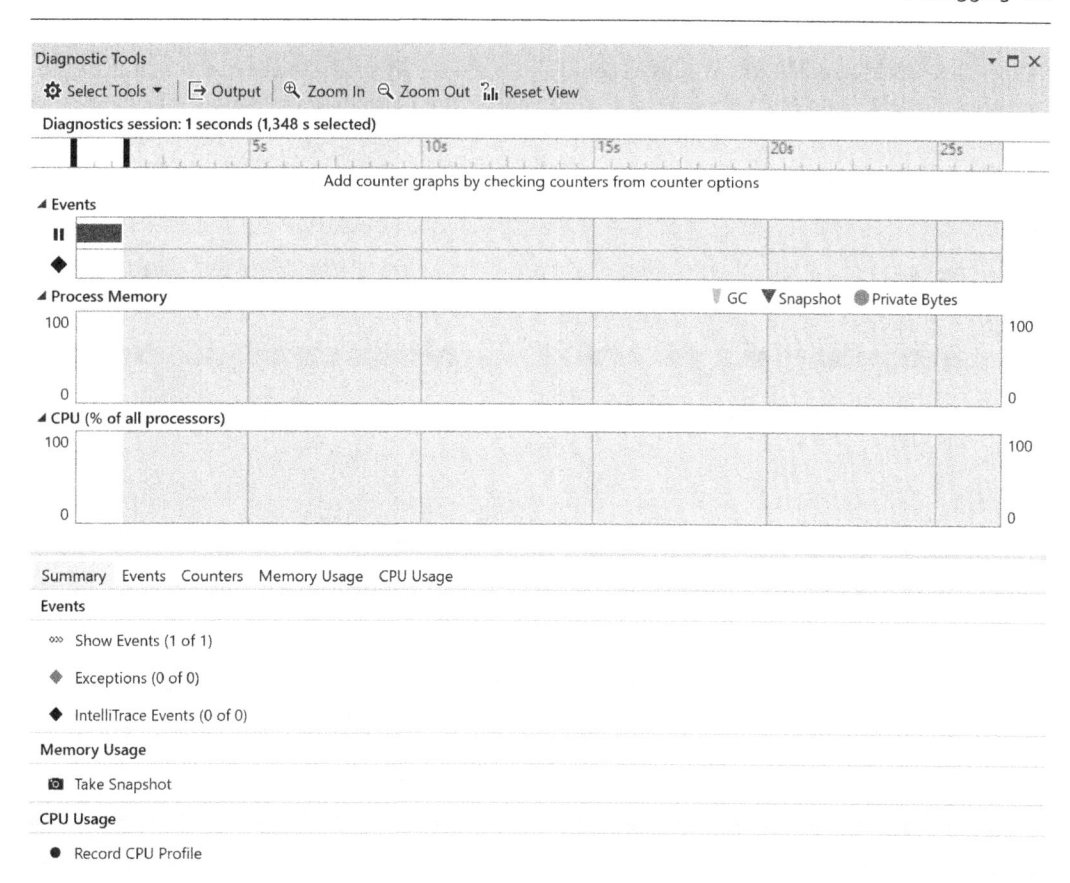

Figure 11.5: The Diagnostic Tools window

At the top of the window, there are some charts. Since nothing has happened yet in our program, these are not very interesting. But that will change! Below the charts, there are some tabs. Initially, you see the **Summary** tab, which summarizes the contents of the other tabs.

In the **Summary** tab, click **Take Snapshot** under the **Memory Usage** title. You can also do that in the **Memory Usage** tab itself. Doing this saves the current memory usage and allows it to be compared to a later point in time. Since our application hasn't done much, this could give us a baseline. So, click on **Take Snapshot**. Then, continue running the program.

If you click **Take Snapshot**, the window should show you the **Memory Usage** tab, which shows the snapshot. Since we continued the program, we are not on the 100th iteration, so we can take another snapshot. Do that. That results in my system in this view:

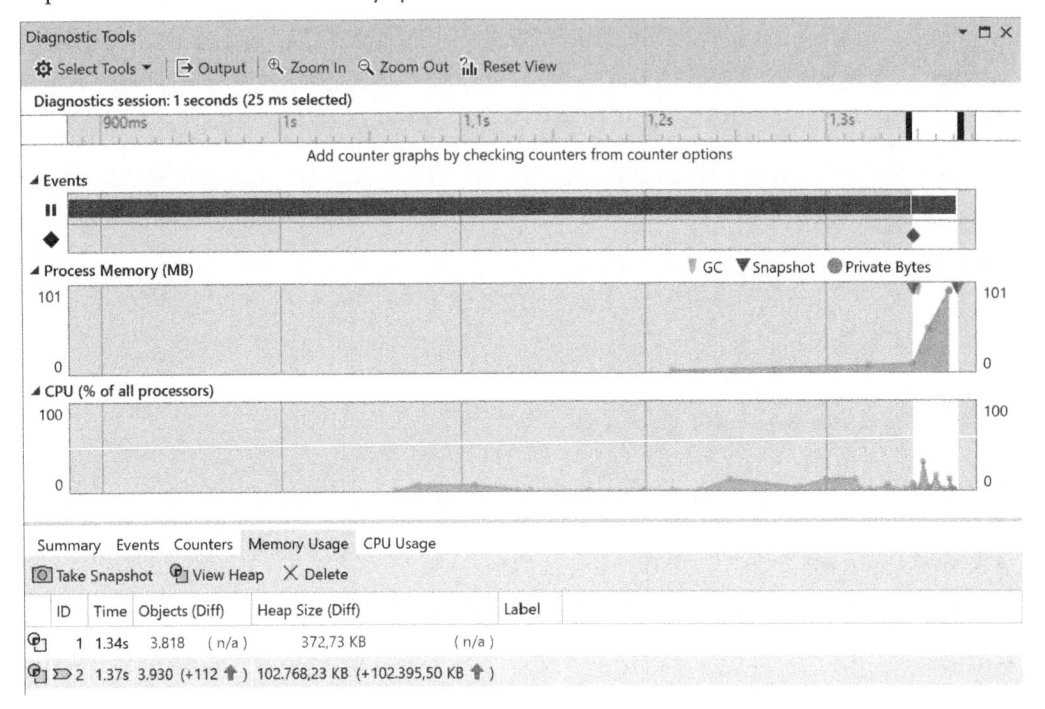

Figure 11.6: Second pass in the Diagnostic Tools window

This is getting more interesting. We can see in the **Process Memory (MB)** chart that we have started to allocate a lot more memory. But the real exciting stuff happens in the **Memory Usage** tab below. You can see a lot here: in the second snapshot, we can see that we have allocated more objects and memory.

You can click on most values, such as **Object Count**, **Object Count Diff**, **Heap Size**, and **Heap Size Diff**. If you do that, you will get more information. Let's click on the **Objects (Diff)**, thus the number +112. On my system, I get this screen (I clicked on the `Count Diff.` column to sort on that.)

Debugging multithreaded and asynchronous code

Managed Memory

Object Type	Count Diff.	Size Diff. (Bytes)	Inclusive Size Diff. (Bytes)	Count	Size (Bytes)	Inclusive Size (Bytes)
Byte[]	+99	+104,858,944	+104,858,944	105	104,882,008	104,882,008
Object	+14	+336	+336	22	528	528
TimerQueue	+8	+704	+704	8	704	704
Action	+6	+384	+504	7	448	568
TimeSpan	+3	+72	+72	3	72	72
AsyncMethodBuilderCore+ContinuationWrapper	+3	+120	+120	3	120	120
Int32[]	+3	+4,016	+4,016	16	7,664	7,664
Func<Object, PropertyValue>	+2	+128	+128	12	768	768
ValueTask+ValueTaskSourceAsTask<Int32>	+1	+80	+552	1	80	552
StringTypeInfo	+1	+64	+104	1	64	104
ConcurrentDictionary+VolatileNode<Guid, List<Microsoft.Extensions	+1	+320	+320	1	320	320
AutoResetEvent	+1	+24	+56	4	96	224
Dictionary+Entry<Int32, Byte[]>[]	+1	+4,752	+103,816,152	1	4,752	103,816,152
Microsoft.Extensions.HotReload.HotReloadAgent	+1	+56	+1,520	1	56	1,520
Total	**+112**	**+104,852,992**		**3,930**	**105,234,66**	

Figure 11.7: Memory snapshot

We have 99 more `Byte[]` objects in memory, resulting in an increase of 104,858,955 bytes of memory.

You can do all sorts of things here. You can click on the line you want to learn more about and then drill down into the source code of that object. That way, you can probably discover why your memory usage is increasing.

A lot is going on in **Diagnostic Tools**. I suggest you play around with it and see what it can tell you about your system!

Debugging multithreaded and asynchronous code

Let's join the league of super debuggers. We are about to embark on a journey into the depths of multithreaded systems and where they go wrong.

Multithreaded code is notoriously hard to debug. Imagine you have two threads that interact with each other, and then things go wrong. However, if you step through the methods in Visual Studio, things work just fine, and that makes sense: some bugs appear only when certain timing conditions happen.

Parallel Watch

What about this: you have multiple threads, and something goes wrong. You want to inspect what happens in that thread. But if you set a breakpoint, how do you know you are in the correct thread?

Fear not: Visual Studio can help with this. Let's start with the following code:

```
var rnd = new Random();
for (int i = 0; i < 10; i++)
```

```
{
    int threadNumber = i;
    ThreadPool.QueueUserWorkItem(_ =>
    {
        var counter = 0;
        while (true)
        {
            $"Thread {threadNumber} with counter {counter++}".
Dump(ConsoleColor.Yellow);
            Task.Delay(rnd.Next(1000)).Wait();
        }
    });
}
```

This code creates 10 threads. Each thread has an infinite loop, displaying some text and counting up. However, each thread does this at a different speed: they all wait for a random time between each iteration.

Place a conditional breakpoint somewhere in that loop, with the condition saying it should break with this condition: `counter % 10 == 0`. Now, run the program.

You see the `counter` value in the **Autos** or **Locals** windows. That can be helpful; that variable is local to the thread you are currently in. Visual Studio did pause all other threads for us, but we have no idea what the state of the data is in those threads. How can we find out?

The answer to that question is this: open the **Parallel Watch** window. Again, you can find this in the **Debug | Windows** menu. On my system, after breaking in my breakpoint, it looks like this:

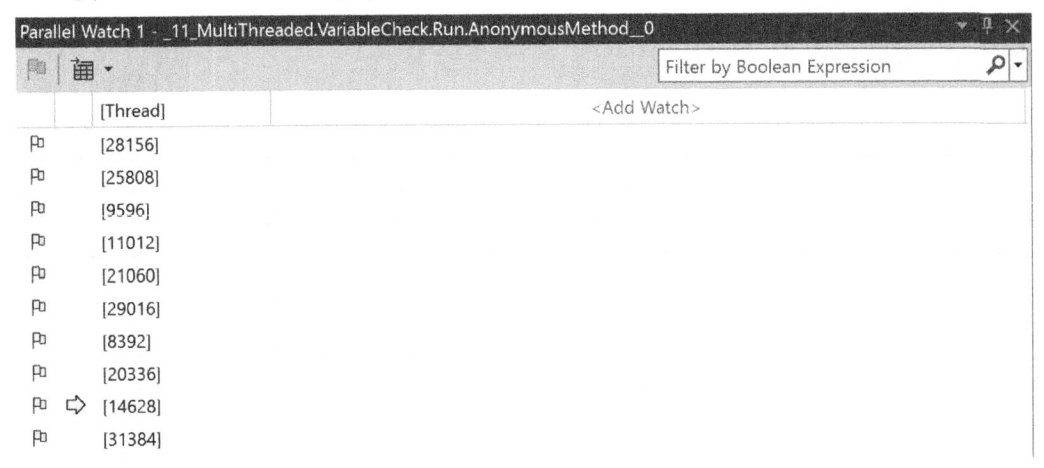

[Thread]	<Add Watch>
[28156]	
[25808]	
[9596]	
[11012]	
[21060]	
[29016]	
[8392]	
[20336]	
⇨ [14628]	
[31384]	

Figure 11.8: The Parallel Watch window

In this particular case, I have apparently stopped execution in thread 14628. That doesn't tell me much.

Add a Parallel Watch

But as you can see, on the top of the window, it says <**Add Watch**>. If I click there, I can enter the variable's name I am interested in. So, I add the `counter` variable there. As soon as I do that, the **Watch** window shows me the value of that variable, but it does that for each thread:

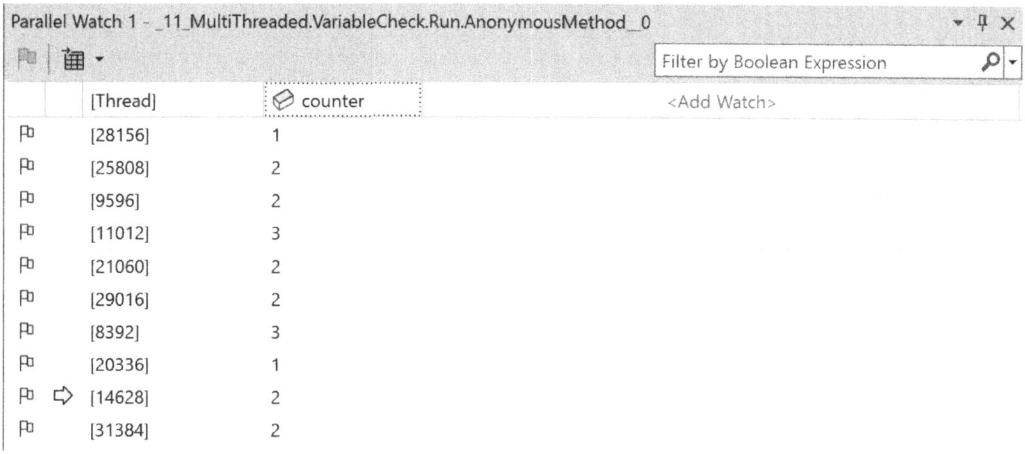

[Thread]	counter	<Add Watch>
[28156]	1	
[25808]	2	
[9596]	2	
[11012]	3	
[21060]	2	
[29016]	2	
[8392]	3	
[20336]	1	
⇨ [14628]	2	
[31384]	2	

Figure 11.9: Parallel Watch with counter added

As you can see in the screenshot, all threads have their version of the `counter`, each with a different value. This is helpful!

Jumping to frames

Although this window is primarily a **Watch** window, meaning it shows the variables you are interested in and their values, there are other things you can do here as well.

Since we stopped somewhere in the loop, you can hover over the variables in your code to see the values. However, as we discovered, those values only apply to that thread. You can add all the variables you are interested in into the **Parallel Watch** window, but what if you just want to see a variable once? Well, the **Parallel Watch** window can help you. Select one of the other threads in that window and right-click on that line, and you will see a context menu. One of the options is **Switch To Frame**. If you do that, the debugger makes the chosen thread the current one, allowing you to investigate the values of all variables in scope for that particular thread.

This way, you can jump between all active threads and inspect all values of all variables in scope per thread.

Freezing and thawing threads

The ability to inspect variables in different threads is a potent tool. You can probably imagine that certain variables affect other threads. Finding issues usually requires a lot of logging and inspections of those logs to determine the results of unwanted behavior. Being able to break the code and see what is happening saves you from a lot of that work.

But sometimes, all those threads running simultaneously can get in the way. In those cases, you might want to focus on one or some threads in isolation. The **Freeze** and **Thaw** options can help in this situation.

Freezing a thread is nothing more than pausing it during debugging. You temporarily halt the execution of one or more threads so you can focus on what is important to you. When you have all the information you need, you can thaw the frozen threads and let them resume their regular work. You can use the **Thread** window, but you can also do that in the **Parallel Watch** window. All you have to do is right-click on the thread you want to freeze and select **Freeze** from the context menu. If you resume the program, the thread you have chosen to freeze will not do anything anymore.

To see that behavior in action, change the number of threads in our code to 2 instead of 2. Rerun the program and see which thread is active when the breakpoint hits. Obviously, one of the threads will cause the breakpoints condition (the `counter` variable in that thread must be a multiple of 10) to be satisfied. If you then resume the program, the other thread will likely be the following thread to stop: it is probably also close to satisfying the condition (I say "probably," since the random behavior of the `Wait()` statement might, in theory, make it possible to act otherwise).

Restart the program and wait for the first time the breakpoint becomes active. This time, right-click on the other thread and select **Freeze**. Resume the program.

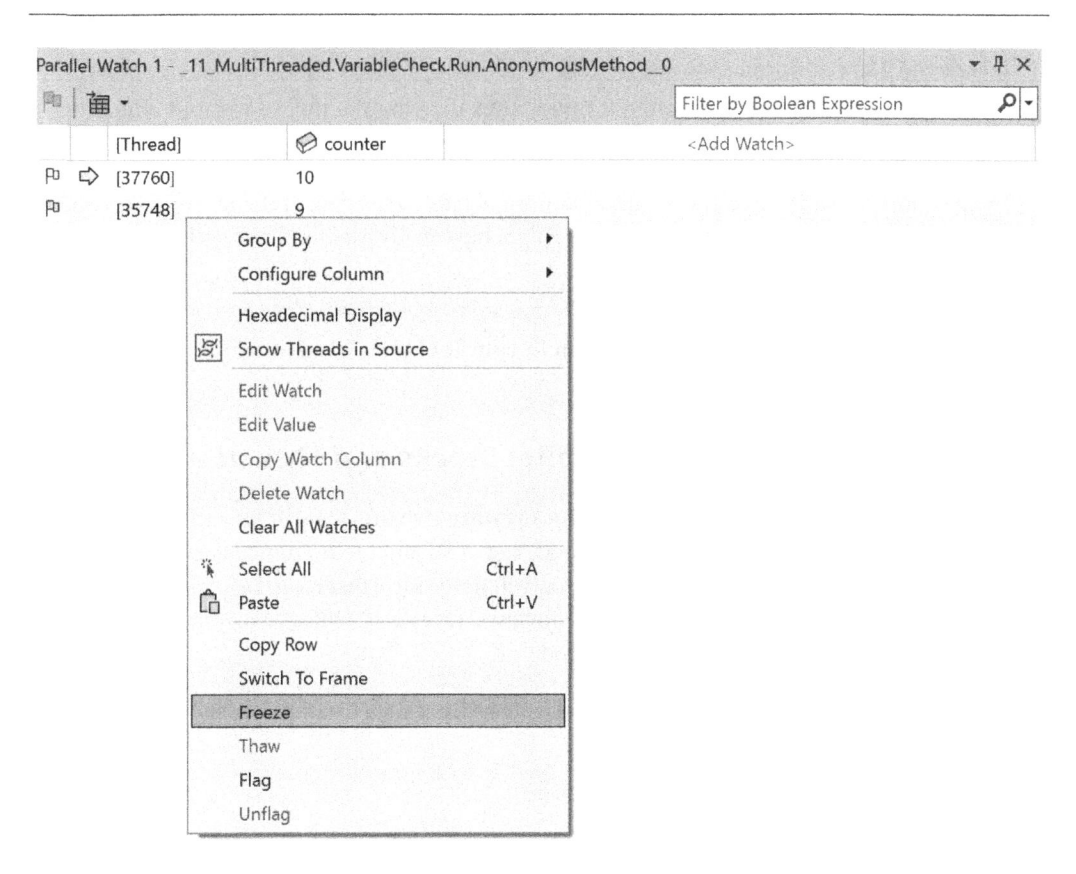

Figure 11.10: Freezing threads in Parallel Watch

A pause symbol should be in front of the chosen thread. Resume the program. When the program breaks again, it will be on the same thread as the first time it did this. If you resume, the third time will also be on that thread. That makes sense: the other thread is not doing anything and thus never satisfies the breakpoint conditions.

Now, you can work on that one working thread to make sure you get what is going on. When you are ready to have the thread join the rest of the program, wait until the breakpoint happens again. Then, you can right-click the frozen thread and "thaw" it. Resume the program and see whether everything is back to normal: the debugger will break as soon as the condition is met in any of the threads.

> **Freeze and Thaw: a word of warning**
>
> As you probably saw, the program continues after thawing the thread without adjusting anything. Typically, the `counter` variable values in both threads should be close to each other. However, after freezing one thread, it falls behind, and it doesn't catch up on that lag anymore. Freezing and thawing threads can have an unpredictable side effect: if the rest of your code somehow relies on that thread running, you might have inadvertently changed the logic flow. So, be aware of that!

Freezing and thawing can be a lovely addition to your tool belt. So, use them if needed, but use them wisely!

Debugging deadlocks with Parallel Stacks and Thread windows

Deadlocks are pretty nasty. Simply put, a **deadlock** is when two threads wait for each other and thus cannot continue. It's like driving your car on a narrow road and seeing someone coming from the other side. One of you will have to back off, or you will never leave that road. Deadlocks are like that, but your application freezes since neither of the involved threads is willing to drive back. I think it is obvious that you would not want that in your code.

However, as simple as the issue sounds, it can be challenging to debug and fix. But Visual Studio is here to help!

Let's begin with a simple program. This is the code:

```
"Starting the threads".Dump(ConsoleColor.Cyan);
var lockA = new object();
var lockB = new object();
ThreadPool.QueueUserWorkItem(_ =>
{
    lock (lockA)
    {
        "Thread 1 acquired lock A".Dump(ConsoleColor.Yellow);
        Thread.Sleep(1000);
        lock (lockB)
        {
            "Thread 1 acquired lock B".Dump(ConsoleColor.Yellow);
        }
    }
});
ThreadPool.QueueUserWorkItem(_ =>
{
    lock (lockB)
    {
        "Thread 2 acquired lock B".Dump(ConsoleColor.Blue);
```

```
            Thread.Sleep(1000);
            lock (lockA)
            {
                "Thread 2 acquired lock A".Dump(ConsoleColor.Blue);
            }
        }
    });
    "Waiting for all threads to finish".Dump(ConsoleColor.Cyan);
    Console.ReadLine();
```

What do we do here? Simply put, we create two threads. They each use a `lock` statement. This means no other thread can enter that scope until the thread that owns the `lock` statement is done. That is not an issue in this code: both threads use a different `lock`. However, we also tried to use the other `lock` object in the thread. Because we have a `Thread.Sleep(1000)` in each thread, both threads have enough time to acquire the `lock` before accessing the other `lock`. But that never happens. No thread can release the `lock` since it waits for the other thread – and vice versa.

Run it. You will see that both threads print out their initial statements about acquiring their `lock`s. And then: nothing. The program is completely frozen. It doesn't do anything anymore. We have a deadlock on our hands.

In this case, what is going on is obvious. Still, I am sure you can imagine these situations can be tricky to find in typical programs. The good news is that Visual Studio usually knows what is happening and can tell us.

Stop the program execution by going to the **Debug** menu, and then clicking on **Break All**. When Visual Studio has the focus, you can also press *Ctrl + Alt + Break*.

Breaking like this stops all threads as if the debugger has hit a breakpoint. Visual Studio stops at one of the three threads (the main thread or one of the bad-behaving ones), and you get a warning like this one:

Figure 11.11: Deadlock detected by Visual Studio

So, at least know what caused the freezing: we have a deadlock. It is time to find out what is going on.

Parallel Stacks

In *Figure 11.12*, you see the **Show Parallel Stacks** option in that dialog box. You can also get the **Parallel Stacks** window through the **Debug | Windows** menu option. Doing that gives you a nice visual representation of all currently known threads. On my machine, that looks like this:

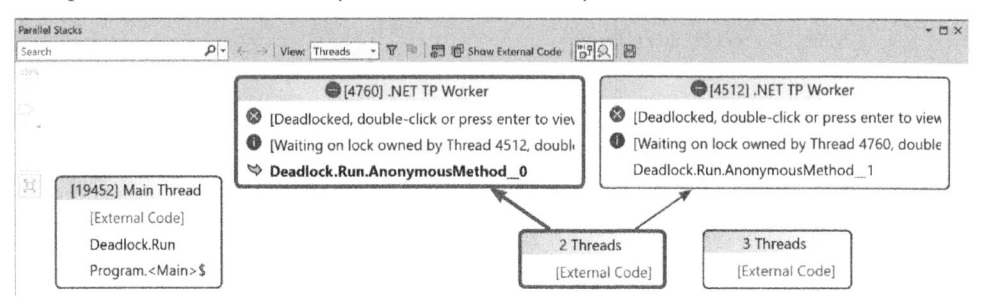

Figure 11.12: Parallel Stacks in action

Since we have very few threads running, spotting the issue is straightforward. The offending threads are marked with a red circle with a white line: the symbol globally known as a stop sign. This symbol indicates the threads that are currently deadlocked. To make it even more apparent, the information box below says [**Deadlocked, double-click or press enter to view**]. You can double-click on the **Waiting on lock** line to jump to the source code for this thread.

This window helps you identify thread issues very quickly. You can see which threads are running, if there are any issues, and where those threads originated from.

But if that is not enough, you can go deeper by looking at the **Threads** window.

Threads window

As you might have guessed from the name, the **Threads** window shows you all the threads you might be interested in. Let's continue with our deadlock example. You have looked at **Parallel Stacks**, but you cannot find what is happening.

So, you open the **Threads** window. On my machine, it looks like this:

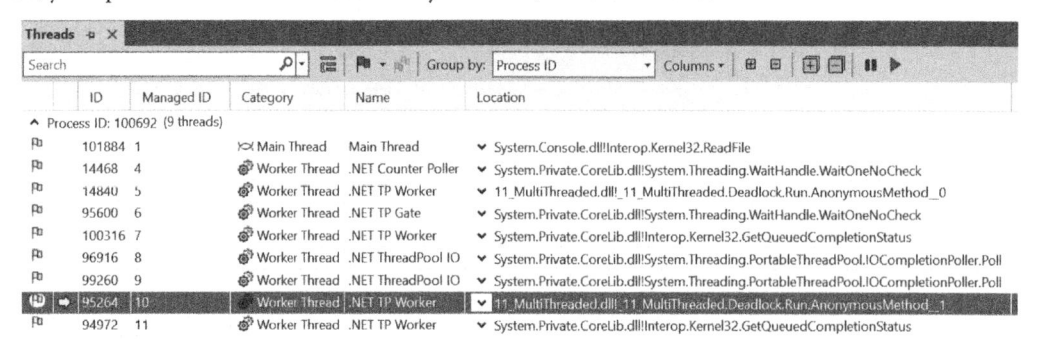

Figure 11.13: The Threads window

These are all the threads currently known in my application. They are all up and running, and the current thread has an ID of `95264` (or managed thread ID `10`). It is a thread from the thread pool since the name is `.NET TP Worker`. You can also see the location: it is in my application.

If you click on the down arrow next to the name, you get more details:

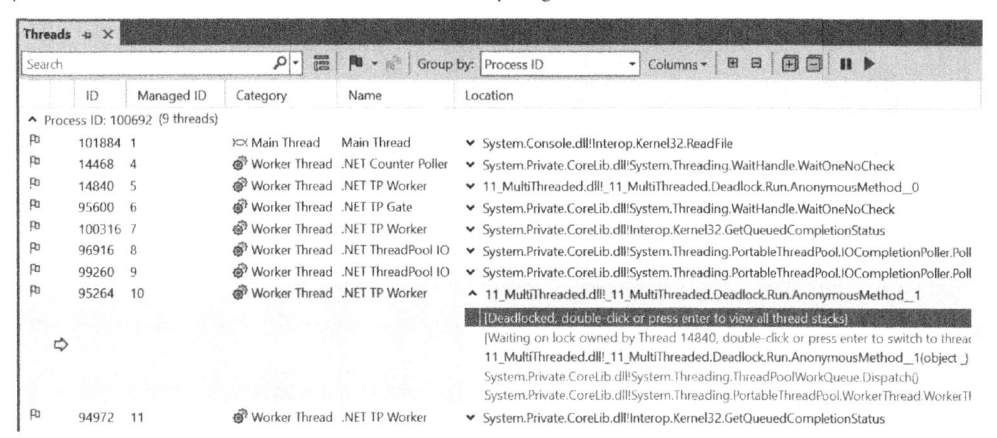

Figure 11.14: The Thread window with more details

As you can see in the screenshot, this gives me more information, including the text that this thread is deadlocked and is waiting on a lock owned by thread `14840`. The **Thread** window also shows information about that particular thread, so you can open that one if you want to. Double-clicking on the location brings you to the source code, where you can investigate what you were doing before the whole thing came crashing.

Debugging threading issues is not easy. But without these tools, they can be found more easily than ever before. Of course, the best course of action is not to make mistakes in the first place, but as I explained to my manager all those years ago, we do not live in that kind of world.

Profiling application performance

By now, we have established that system programmers care about speed. Applications need to be as efficient and as fast as possible. But what if you think your application can go faster but do not know where or what to improve? That is where profiling and benchmarking can help.

Profiling is measuring and analyzing the performance of your application in terms of factors such as CPU usage, memory pressure, network performance, and so on. It's like putting your app under a microscope. Things we look at during profiling are, amongst others, the following:

- **CPU usage**: Identify which parts of your application are using the most processing power
- **Memory usage**: Track how much memory is used and finding memory leaks or excessive allocations

- **Function call frequency**: See which methods are called the most and how long they take
- **Performance hotspots**: Pinpoint areas of code that are slower than they should be

Benchmarking is related, but it is different. Benchmarking is measuring the performance of your code under different circumstances or comparing different approaches. This process involves running predefined tests and capturing metrics. Some of the metrics are the following:

- **Execution time**: Measuring how long it takes for a piece of code to run
- **Throughput**: Assessing how many operations or transactions can be processed in a given period
- **Latency**: Determining the delay between the initiation and the execution of a task

Profiling and benchmarking go hand in hand and are often used together to improve your application.

The prime application

To investigate how we might do this, let's start with a program we want to improve performance. It is a simple program that calculates all the primes in the range 0 – 100,000 and sums them up. It's nothing fancy or helpful, but it requires the CPU to do much work. We also want to see whether we can make things better. So, let's start by looking at the code. First, we create a class called `PrimeCalculator`. That's easy enough. The main method of this class is the `Run` method. It looks like this:

```
public void Run()
{
    var limit = 100000;
    var stopwatch = Stopwatch.StartNew();
    var sum = SumOfPrimes(limit);
    stopwatch.Stop();
    $"Sum of primes up to {limit}: {sum}".Dump();
    $"Time taken: {stopwatch.ElapsedMilliseconds} ms".Dump();
}
```

There is nothing special going on here. We create a `Stopwatch` to time the duration, then call the `SumOfPrimes()` method that does all the actual work. Finally, we display the results and the duration.

Let's look at `SumOfPrimes()` next:

```
private long SumOfPrimes(int limit)
{
    long sum = 0;
    for (var i = 2; i <= limit; i++)
        if (IsPrime(i))
```

```
            sum += i;

    return sum;
}
```

This code is also pretty basic. We loop for all values between 2 and the given limit (2 since 1 is technically not a prime number) and check whether that number is a prime. If it is, we add it to the sum. Let's move to `IsPrime()`:

```
private bool IsPrime(int number)
{
    if (number < 2) return false;
    for (var i = 2; i <= Math.Sqrt(number); i++)
        if (number % i == 0)
            return false;
    return true;
}
```

This method is a lousy implementation to see whether a number is a prime, but it is simple enough to follow. We do this by checking whether the number we give it is divisible by any number that is less than the square root of that number. If it is divisible, it is not a prime.

For example, if I run this on the machine I am writing this text on, I get the sum of 454, 396, 537 and a total duration of 21 milliseconds. I have no idea if that sum is correct; I have no intention of calculating it by hand on my calculator app on my phone. It doesn't matter: we are here to see whether we can spot bottlenecks.

21 milliseconds sounds like a short amount of time, but in reality, it is pretty long. After all, computers are fast these days, so I am sure I can improve on it. We can use the profiling tools from Visual Studio to see where the bottlenecks are.

Profiling in Visual Studio

In Visual Studio, under the main **Debug** menu, you find the **Performance Profile** option. The default shortcut key for that is *Alt + F2*, which might be helpful if you repeatedly run this (and you will!)

If you select that option, you see the following screen:

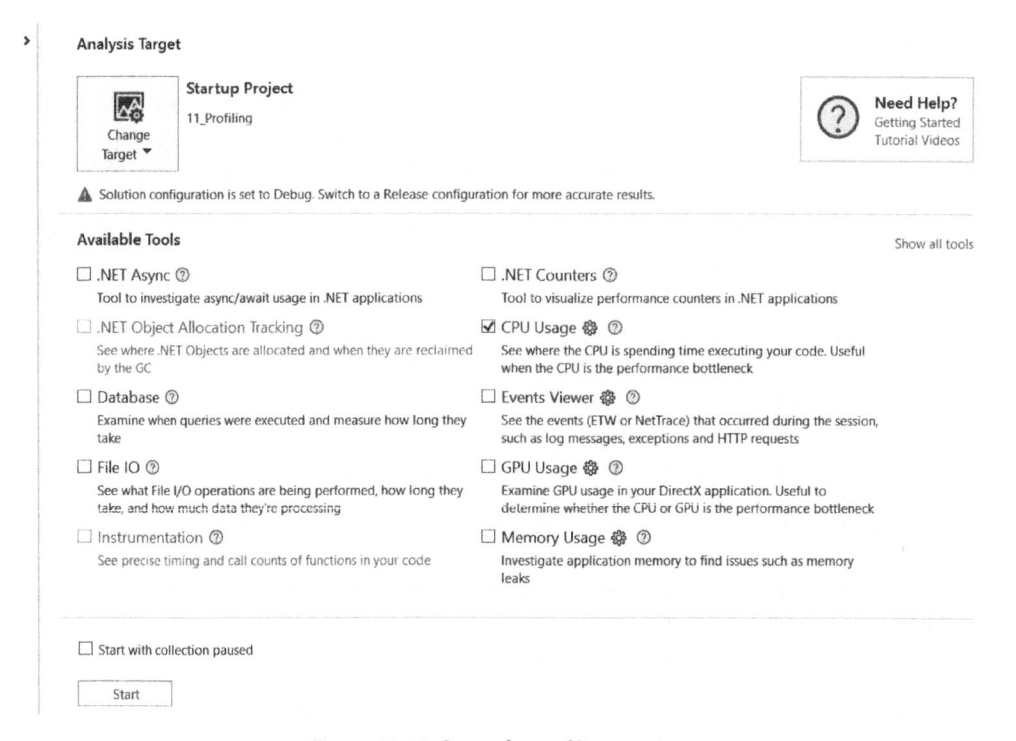

Figure 11.15: Start of a profiling session

Profiling can be done on many different levels. However, the most crucial choice is what you want to profile. By default, this tool chooses the current application. As you can see, in my case, that is the `11_Profiling` project. You can select other projects or running processes, browse for an application, and so on. Click that large **Change Target** button to change if necessary. There is also a warning underneath that button: we might want to switch from a Debug profile to a Release profile. Release is more closely related to what you run in production, so the figures you get are more like the ones you expect to see when you have deployed your application. However, Release mode optimizes your code, making it harder to find programming mistakes. So, I tend to leave it to Debug during development.

Then, you have to decide what you want to see. There are many options here: you might want to see async/awaits, or maybe you are interested in database communications. In my case, I want to know about **CPU Usage**. I also leave **.NET Counters** and **Memory Usage** checked; they might be helpful.

If you click the **Start** button, your program will build and run. In the background, Visual Studio starts collecting the information.

In our case, the program runs and ends, signaling Visual Studio to stop collecting. If your application keeps running, you must stop the program manually or click the **stop collecting** button in Visual Studio.

Once you have done that, Visual Studio shows you an overview of what it has collected.

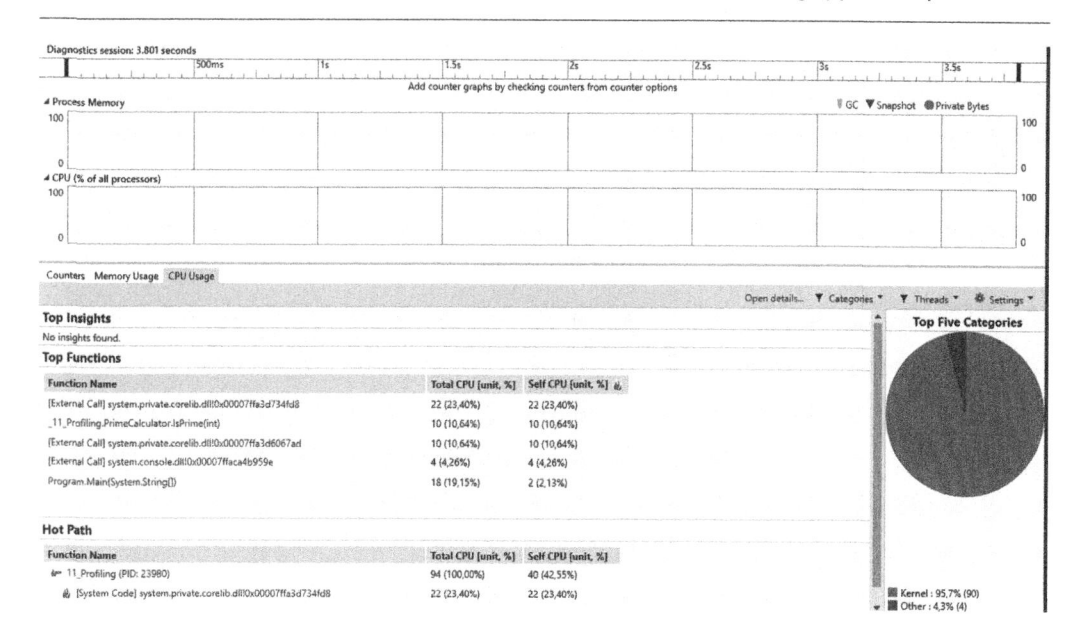

Figure 11.16: First results from a profiling session

The results are not that impressive since we have a straightforward program. However, you can see in the **Top Functions** part that the `_11_Profiling.PrimeCalculator.IsPrime(int)` method takes a lot of time: 10 microseconds, or 10.64% of the total time.

That is good to know, but we want to see whether we can get more information. Click on that line, and you will get another view. You can select what you want to see at the top of that view. By default, you see all data grouped by **Functions**, but I want to see the call path. If you do that, you get this result:

Figure 11.17: The hot path leading to the slowest function

You can click **Show Hot Path** and **Expand Hot Path** to see how the process came to the slowest function.

Finally, you can double-click on a line to see the source code. So, if you double-click on the `IsPrime()` method, you get this:

```
                       31
                       32              return sum;
                       33          }
                       34
                       35          private bool IsPrime(int number)
         1 (1.06%)     36          {
                       37              if (number < 2) return false;
         5 (5.32%)     38              for(var i=2;i<Math.Sqrt(number);i++)
                       39                  if (number % i == 0)
                       40                      return false;
                       41
                       42              return true;
                       43          }
```

Figure 11.18: The slowest lines of code highlighted

Now, it becomes clear that the loop is the slowest part of the `IsPrime()` function. That makes sense: to make this loop work, the CPU has to calculate `Math.Sqrt(number)` every time. That takes time. How to improve that is obvious: pre-calculate that square root and use that variable in the `for` statement. That should speed things up!

As you can see, with the proper tooling, you can identify the bottlenecks in your application. Once you find them, you can restructure your code or replace parts with something faster. But how do you know which algorithm to use to speed things up? The answer to that is this: benchmark them!

Benchmarking different solutions

I know that the `number % i ==0` line is not the fastest way to see whether a number is divisible by another number. However, I am not really sure how much quicker other ways are. To find out, I can use some benchmarking to figure it out.

There are several ways you can start with benchmarking, but in a case such as this, where I have several options for a specific algorithm, I like to use the `Benchmarkdotnet` NuGet package. This free package makes benchmarking simple.

To do this, start a new console application. Add the `Benchmarkdotnet` package to the project. Then, create a new class. I call this class `ModuloTesters` since I want to test the performance of the `Module` operator and any alternatives I can find.

I added a method called `TestModulo`. That method looks like this:

```
[Benchmark]
public void TestModulo()
{
    var numberOfMatches = 0;
    for (var i = 3; i < numberOfLoopCount; i++)
        if (testNumber % i == 0)
            numberOfMatches++;
}
```

As you can see, it is pretty simple. I just go through several iterations (`numberOfLoopCount` is defined as a constant in my class, and I have set it to 100,000) and calculate the modulo (`testNumber` is again a constant; it doesn't really matter what it is, but I have set it to 400). The only thing that makes this method stand out from a typical method is the `[Benchmark]` attribute. This tells the benchmark tool that this method needs to be measured.

In the main program file, we need to kickstart the benchmarking. That is extremely easy: just add this line of code:

```
var summary = BenchmarkRunner.Run<ModuloTesters>();
```

Set the build mode to `Release`, and run without debugging. The `Benchmark` tool will run the methods marked with `Benchmark` a couple of times (well, more than just a couple) and present you with the results.

But before we look at those results, we need to add something. Benchmarking is meant to compare solutions to a problem. Right now, we have one solution: the modulo operator. So, there is nothing to compare against. Let's fix that. Add a new method to the `ModuloTesters` class that looks like this:

```
Benchmark]
public void TestMultiplicationAndDivision()
{
    var numberOfMatches = 0;
    for (var i = 3; i < numberOfLoopCount; i++)
        if (testNumber - i * (testNumber / i) == 0)
            numberOfMatches++;
}
```

This is another way of calculating a module. But is it faster? There is only one way to find out: run the benchmark! If you do that, you see the results. On my machine, it looks like this:

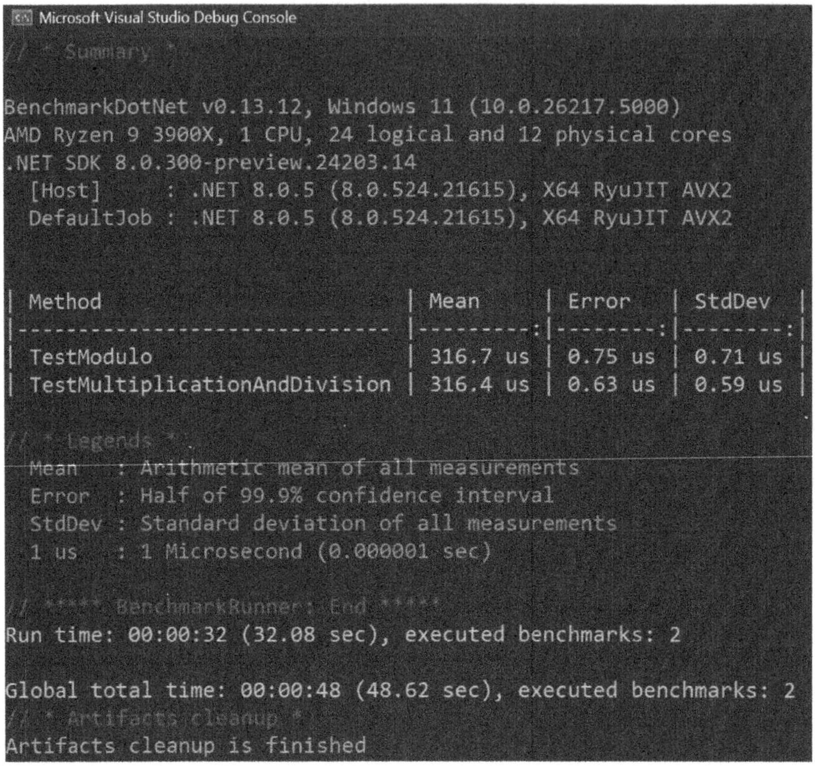
Microsoft Visual Studio Debug Console
// * Summary *
BenchmarkDotNet v0.13.12, Windows 11 (10.0.26217.5000)
AMD Ryzen 9 3900X, 1 CPU, 24 logical and 12 physical cores
.NET SDK 8.0.300-preview.24203.14
[Host] : .NET 8.0.5 (8.0.524.21615), X64 RyuJIT AVX2
DefaultJob : .NET 8.0.5 (8.0.524.21615), X64 RyuJIT AVX2
Method	Mean	Error	StdDev
TestModulo	316.7 us	0.75 us	0.71 us
TestMultiplicationAndDivision	316.4 us	0.63 us	0.59 us
// * Legends *
Mean : Arithmetic mean of all measurements
Error : Half of 99.9% confidence interval
StdDev : Standard deviation of all measurements
1 us : 1 Microsecond (0.000001 sec)
// ***** BenchmarkRunner: End *****
Run time: 00:00:32 (32.08 sec), executed benchmarks: 2
Global total time: 00:00:48 (48.62 sec), executed benchmarks: 2
// * Artifacts cleanup *
Artifacts cleanup is finished

Figure 11.19: Benchmark results

So, the new algorithm is quicker: it takes 316.4 microseconds instead of 316.7 microseconds. Ok, I admit it is not that much faster. Maybe we can do better. You know what? We can. Let's add a third benchmark:

```
[Benchmark]
public void TestMultiplicationAndDivisionInParallel()
{
    var numberOfMatches = 0;
    var localNumberOfLoopCount = numberOfLoopCount;
    var localTestNumber = testNumber;
    var lockObj = new object();
    Parallel.For(3, localNumberOfLoopCount, i =>
    {
        var div = localTestNumber / i;
        if (localTestNumber == i * div)
            lock (lockObj)
```

```
            {
                    numberOfMatches++;
            }
        });
}
```

Since all the calculations can be done independently, we can probably do them in parallel. So, that is what I am doing here: I use the `Parallel.For()` statement to divide the work into jobs that run simultaneously. I need a lock to update `numberOfMatches`, which might slow down the loop. But that is a guess: let's test this. Run the benchmark. This is what I get:

```
// * Summary *

BenchmarkDotNet v0.13.12, Windows 11 (10.0.26217.5000)
AMD Ryzen 9 3900X, 1 CPU, 24 logical and 12 physical cores
.NET SDK 8.0.300-preview.24203.14
  [Host]     : .NET 8.0.5 (8.0.524.21615), X64 RyuJIT AVX2
  DefaultJob : .NET 8.0.5 (8.0.524.21615), X64 RyuJIT AVX2


| Method                                 | Mean      | Error     | StdDev    |
|--------------------------------------- |----------:|----------:|----------:|
| TestModulo                             | 316.65 us | 0.732 us  | 0.649 us  |
| TestMultiplicationAndDivision          | 317.27 us | 0.890 us  | 0.833 us  |
| TestMultiplicationAndDivisionInParallel|  80.88 us | 0.402 us  | 0.356 us  |
```

Figure 11.20: New benchmark results

Now, that is interesting. The addition of `Parallel.For()` made a massive difference in the time spent on that method.

If you think that could benefit your code, you can apply the findings to the actual application you are working on. Of course, I would profile it first, make the changes, and then profile again to see whether you have not added new bottlenecks. But all in all, I think we have made our prime calculator a lot faster!

Other tools

Visual Studio is an excellent tool for debugging and profiling your system. However, it is not the only one. There are many other solutions out there that can help you debug and profile your code. Some of them are paid, others are free. Some are easy to use, some are pretty hard to get to know. I will not discuss the other tools, but I want to give you a small list so you can investigate them for yourself.

Please look at what Visual Studio gives you first. Chances are, what you need is already there!

Debugging tools

There are many debugging tools out there. This is just a sample of what you can try out.

Tool Name	Description	Company
Visual Studio Debugger	Integrated into Visual Studio, supports .NET, C++, and other languages with breakpoints, watch variables, and more.	Microsoft
WinDbg	A multipurpose debugger for Windows, useful for debugging user-mode and kernel-mode code and analyzing crash dumps.	Microsoft
Visual Studio Code Debugger	Built into Visual Studio Code, supports various languages and platforms through extensions, with breakpoints and variable inspection.	Microsoft
Managed Debugger (MDbg)	A simple command-line debugger for .NET applications, offering basic debugging capabilities for managed code.	Microsoft
Debug Diagnostic Tool (DebugDiag)	Assists in troubleshooting application crashes, hangs, memory leaks, and performance issues in user-mode processes.	Microsoft
ProcDump	Command-line utility to monitor applications for CPU spikes and generate crash dumps for analysis.	Microsoft
Microsoft Performance Tools (PerfView)	Performance analysis tool for collecting and analyzing ETW data, valuable for .NET application performance and memory issues.	Microsoft
Son of Strike (SOS) Debugging Extension	An extension for WinDbg that provides insights into .NET runtime internals, aiding in-depth debugging of .NET applications.	Microsoft
Windows Performance Recorder (WPR)	Tools for recording and analyzing performance data on Windows systems, capturing detailed system and application behavior.	Microsoft
Remote Debugging Tools	Tools for debugging applications running on different machines or environments, supporting both managed and native code.	Microsoft
GNU Debugger (GDB)	A powerful debugger for various programming languages, especially C and C++, to see what is happening inside a program.	GNU Project

Tool Name	Description	Company
LLVM Debugger (LLDB)	A modern, high-performance debugger part of the LLVM project, supporting languages such as C, C++, and Objective-C.	LLVM Project
Valgrind	A programming tool for memory debugging, memory leak detection, and profiling, including tools such as Memcheck.	Valgrind Developers
Strace	A diagnostic, debugging, and instructional utility for Linux that traces system calls and signals.	Open Source

Table 11.7: Debugging tools

I do not endorse any of these products; I have merely listed them here for your convenience.

Profiling tools

Profiling tools are also easy to find. A lot of companies next to Microsoft offer solutions for this. They each have their own strengths and weaknesses. So, please look at the following table as a guideline to help you find what is best for you.

Tool Name	Description	Company
Visual Studio Profiler	Integrated into Visual Studio, provides detailed performance and memory usage data for .NET and C++ applications.	Microsoft
WPR	Captures detailed performance data on Windows systems for in-depth analysis.	Microsoft
Windows Performance Analyzer (WPA)	Analyzes performance data collected by WPR, helping to identify performance issues.	Microsoft
PerfView	Collects and analyzes ETW data, useful for investigating performance and memory issues in .NET applications.	Microsoft
.NET Memory Profiler	A powerful tool for finding memory leaks and optimizing memory usage in .NET applications.	SciTech Software
ANTS Performance Profiler	Provides .NET code profiling to find performance bottlenecks, including memory usage and execution time analysis.	Redgate

Tool Name	Description	Company
JetBrains dotTrace	A .NET profiler for performance, memory, and coverage analysis, integrated with Visual Studio.	JetBrains
VTune Profiler	Performance analysis tool for C, C++, and Fortran applications, offering deep insights into CPU and GPU performance.	Intel
Valgrind	Includes a suite of tools such as Cachegrind for cache profiling and Massif for heap profiling, primarily for C and C++ programs.	Valgrind Developers
Google Performance Tools (gperftools)	A suite of utilities for performance profiling and heap analysis, providing insights into CPU and memory usage.	Google
YourKit Profiler	A profiler for Java and .NET applications, offering comprehensive CPU and memory profiling features.	YourKit
Perf	A performance analyzing tool in Linux that provides detailed information on CPU performance, helping identify bottlenecks.	Linux Community
GlowCode	A performance and memory profiler for Windows, focusing on C++ and .NET applications.	Electric Software Inc.
AQtime	An advanced performance and memory profiling tool for various programming languages, integrated with Visual Studio.	SmartBear
Perfino	A Java profiler for production environments, focusing on performance monitoring and problem resolution.	EJ Technologies

Table 11.8: Profiling tools

These tables do not contain all the tools available. New tools are added regularly, while others go away. I suggest you try some of them and stick to what works best for you. Maybe you prefer a CLI solution. Perhaps you want to work with a graphical tool. Whatever your preference is, there is always a tool that fits your needs.

Next steps

Writing code inevitably means making mistakes. That is part of the fun of the job, I believe. Coming up with new ideas, making something out of nothing, and then making it work and improve is a great process. However, you can only do that when you have the right tools and know how to use them.

In this chapter, we have looked at the debugging tools that Visual Studio provides. We looked at what debugging and profiling actually are, discovered the possibilities with breakpoints, and looked at the other helpful debug windows.

We also investigated how to deal with multithreaded applications and the debug challenges they give us. We looked at the windows that could help us and investigated deadlocks.

To top it off, we talked about profiling and benchmarking to uncover performance bottlenecks and how to solve them.

So, we now know how to tackle most of the issues in our code. However, we have one more important thing to discuss: how do we secure our code? What does that even mean? That is a big topic. It is so big that I have a complete chapter about it, and that is what is next. Please, follow along!

12
The One with the Security Safeguards

Security essentials for systems programming

Security is more critical these days than ever. Software never stands alone; it always works with hardware and other software packages. Attackers do whatever they can to find the weakest link in the chain. As developers, we must ensure our software is not the weakest link.

Security is not a "thing" but a mindset and a process. It is a never-ending quest to find the best solution, keeping in mind maintainability and useability. As system programmers, we have to trade off security against performance and memory usage.

This makes building secure software a challenge. But let's be honest – isn't that sort of challenge the reason we chose this profession?

In this chapter, we will cover the following topics:

- Why do we need to care about security as system programmers?
- How to work with strings securely
- How to handle keys in your systems
- What are the requirements around credentials and privileges?
- How do you transfer data safely across a network?

Security is an important but complicated topic. I will not cover everything there is to say about security. Still, as a system programmer, I will touch upon the most important things you should know. But let's not talk too loudly – we must keep our secrets to ourselves! So, make sure nobody is listening in, and then follow me.

Technical requirements

You will find all the code in this chapter at this URL: `https://github.com/PacktPublishing/Systems-Programming-with-C-Sharp-and-.NET/tree/main/SystemsProgrammingWithCSharpAndNet/Chapter12`.

If you want to follow along when I discuss Azure Key Vault, you need a subscription to Azure. You can create one here: `https://azure.microsoft.com/en-us/free`.

Security for system programmers

When I started programming, security was not an issue. Imagine this – my computer had one connection, the one to the power outlet on the wall. And, of course, the computer was attached to a television to display whatever it needed to show. Yes, a TV. I did not have a monitor; I could not afford one back then. I started the machine up, and it would load the OS and the basic programming environment from ROM. And that was it. This setup was extremely secure – there were no attachments to anything that could interfere with my machine and data. I kept the computer in my bedroom, so physical security was also taken care of (no one goes into a teenager's bedroom voluntarily; the mess was unbelievable).

Fast-forward to today. My desktop computer is always on and always connected to the internet. Some systems I have written run on a virtual machine with a cloud provider; others are serverless and waiting for connections.

My firewalls and application gateways inform me that other systems constantly try to connect to all those environments and machines. I have the feeling that all of those machines are under constant threat.

Security is something everybody in the software industry needs to be aware of all the time. Only adding security measures at the end of the development cycle is the best way to ensure attackers have access to your system. You are bound to forget something. Security must be considered at every step, from the initial design to maintaining a running system.

As I said in the second paragraph of this chapter, security is a mindset. You need to ask yourself continuously, "Can someone take advantage of the things I am doing?"

What could happen if we have a vulnerability?

I can almost hear you say, "Hey, I write low-level code, not some fancy customer-facing website. Why should I be bothered with all this?" That is a reasonable response, but there are ways you, as a system programmer, should be very aware of the risks. If you aren't, the results could be catastrophic. Let me outline some of the things that could happen:

- **Privilege escalation**: A lot of the code we write runs with elevated privileges. Hackers who exploit a vulnerability can escalate their privilege from regular users to administrators, giving them extensive control over a system.

- **Data theft**: Hackers who gain access to your system can use that to steal sensitive information, such as the following:
  - User data, such as personal information and credit card information
  - Confidential business data, including trade secrets, intellectual property, and internal communications
  - System logs and configurations that might contain information about other systems, so they can be targeted as well
- **Code injection**: Hackers might exploit vulnerabilities such as buffer overflows or inadequate input validation to inject malicious code into a process. This action might enable them to do the following:
  - **Execute arbitrary commands**: They can run any code, potentially installing malware, ransomware, or other malicious software
  - **Alter system behavior**: Change how a system behaves, causing instability or hiding their activities
- **Denial of service or distributed denial of service**: Attackers can disrupt the normal operation of a system by doing the following:
  - **Overloading a process**: Sending excessive requests or data, causing a system to crash or become unresponsive.
  - **Resource exhaustion**. Consuming system resources such as CPU, memory, or disk space, leading to performance degradation or system crashes
- **Backdoors and persistent access**: Once they have control over a background process, hackers can do the following:
  - **Install backdoors**: Create hidden entry points to re-access a system even if the initial vulnerability is patched
  - **Establish persistence**: Modify a process to restart or maintain their presence on the system, even after a reboot or restart
- **Spying and surveillance**: Hackers can use compromised systems to monitor and collect data over an extended period:
  - **Keystroke logging**: Capture what users type, potentially stealing passwords and other sensitive information
  - **Screen capture**: Periodically take screenshots to monitor users' activity
  - **Network traffic monitoring**: Capture data being sent to and received from other systems

- **Spreading malware**: A compromised system can be used as a launchpad for further attacks:
  - **Lateral movement**: Use a compromised system to move to other systems within a network
  - **Propagation**: Spread malware to other devices or processes, creating a larger attack surface
- **Manipulating data**: Hackers can alter data processed by a background process:
  - **Data corruption**: Introduce errors or malicious modifications to data
  - **Tampering with logs**: Modifying or deleting log entries to cover their tracks makes detecting a breach harder.

As you can see, there are a lot of things that can go wrong if we leave our systems vulnerable. To hammer the point home, imagine a background process that monitors a serial port and handles data from an external device. That process runs 24/7, and since it deals with the lower-level Win32, we run it as an administrator. But we made a mistake somewhere, and a hacker accessed our process. The following is a potential scenario that might happen:

1. **Exploiting the vulnerability**: The hacker finds and exploits a buffer overflow vulnerability in the process.
2. **Privilege escalation**: They escalate their privilege to gain administrative rights.
3. **Data theft**: They extract the entire database of user credentials and personal information.
4. **Installing a backdoor**: They install a backdoor to maintain access and monitor user activities.
5. **Data manipulation**: They alter account balances and change bank information for accounts payable.
6. **Disruption**: Finally, they launch a DDOS attack, bringing your whole company down.

If you think this is exaggerated, I suggest you go online and find articles about security hacks. If you look hard enough, you will find many examples. Most companies are reluctant to share their experiences, but the data is there.

How to protect yourself

If I have scared you a little bit, good. It can be scary. But do not worry too much – following some good security practices can avert many of these risks. In fact, the rest of this chapter is all about what you, as a developer, should do to protect your systems. However, besides the coding aspect of security, there are several other things you should be doing:

- **Holding regular security audits**: Continuously review and audit your code and systems for vulnerabilities. I really would suggest hiring an external party for this. They have a lot more experience, and they are not likely to have the same blind spots as the people who developed the systems.

- **Input validation**: Ensure all inputs are properly validated and sanitized. Just do not trust anything coming in from an external source.
- **Least privilege principle**: Run processes with the minimum necessary privileges to limit potential damages.
- **User modern security practices**: Employ encryption, secure coding practices, and up-to-date third-party libraries.
- **Monitoring and logging activities**: Keep detailed logs and monitor for suspicious activities to quickly detect and respond to breaches.

So, now you know why security is important. Now, let's investigate how to do that in our code.

Working with strings

Your application likely has **strings**. Most of them are irrelevant to the outside world; if you write "Hello World" to a console, an attacker probably couldn't care less about that. But other strings are a lot more interesting to these people. Consider connection strings to a database, for instance. They can be an excellent resource for a hacker. Then, there are other data, such as user information, passwords, and credit card information.

We can distinguish between two types of strings:

- Strings that are part of your code and thus are compiled in the binaries
- Strings that are handled in your code and originate from an outside process or go to an outside process

Let's see whether we can protect this sensitive data.

Protecting settings

First, we deal with the strings in your application that are part of your code base. Think of things such as passwords and connection strings. In an ideal world, you store this information in an external file. The reason for this is that by not having them in your source code, you can change them without recompiling your code.

Imagine that a breach has been detected somewhere in your organization. The security department tells everybody to update their passwords. In your case, that would mean opening Visual Studio, loading the solution, changing the password to the database server, recompiling, and finally, redeploying the system. Or, on second thought, you could just change the password in the config file. I know what I would prefer to do!

Still, having a password in a config file is a pretty bad idea. If you have the password as part of your code, an attacker must decompile your assembly to find it. If we store the password in a text file, all the attacker has to do is open that file and read the password. To counter that, we encrypt the password.

We have discussed encryption several times before, so I am sure you can figure out how to do this. But all the techniques we have looked at so far require a password to be part of the source code, and we just determined that that is a bad idea. Storing a password in a config file to enable decrypting the rest of the file sounds even worse. There must be a better way. There is.

Let's investigate this.

I have a sample application that has some sensitive information. I have this information in a file called `appsettings.json`. You know – a typical .NET-based configuration file. It looks like this:

```
{
  "MyPublicSettings": {
    "Setting1": "Value1",
    "Setting2": "Value2",
    "Setting3": "Value3"
  },
  "MySecretSettings": {
    "MySecretSetting1": "SecretValue1",
    "MySecretSetting2": "SecretValue2"
  }
}
```

We have two sections – insensitive data and data we do not want others to read. We need to protect the latter. Now, the way we handle this is a bit inconvenient. We must write a separate program to encrypt the data before writing the code that uses this file.

Start a new **console application** and add the following NuGet packages:

`Microsoft.Extensions.Configuration`

`Microsoft.Extensions.Configuration.FileExtensions`

`Microsoft.Extensions.Configuration.Json`

`Microsoft.Extensions.DependencyInjection`

`Microsoft.AspNetCore.DataProtection`

These packages are needed to read and use configuration files, and `Microsoft.AspNetCore.DataProtection` is there to protect our data.

To begin, we have to set up the dependency injection infrastructure. The data protection tools use this; they require packages to be injected when required. So, the first lines of our code look like this:

```
var serviceCollection = new ServiceCollection();
serviceCollection.AddDataProtection();
var serviceProvider = serviceCollection.BuildServiceProvider();
var dataProtector = serviceProvider.GetDataProtector("MySecureData");
```

We first create a `ServiceCollection` instance. Then, we call `AddDataProtection()` to that collection so that all required packages are loaded and ready to use. After getting `serviceProvider`, we get an instance of an `IDataProtector` interface by calling `GetDataProtector()`. This method expects a parameter – a string describing the purpose. This string can be anything you want; it acts as a label so that you can group items. Think of it as labeling your encrypted data so that you can later track what belongs to what.

Then, we read the config file into the configuration infrastructure:

```
var configuration = new ConfigurationBuilder()
    .SetBasePath(Directory.GetCurrentDirectory())
    .AddJsonFile("appsettings.json")
    .Build();
```

Do not forget to mark your `appsettings.json` file as `Copy when newer` in Solution Explorer; otherwise, your code will not load it.

OK, now for the funny part – we reread the configuration file, but this time as text. We do this because we will replace the sensitive strings with encrypted versions. This is the code to read it:

```
var json = File.ReadAllText("appsettings.json");
```

The `json` string now holds our complete settings file. It's time to start encrypting!

First, we read the section we want to protect, iterate through all the items in that section, encrypt the values, and then change the strings in the `json` variable. Finally, we write the new string to the configuration file. This is what that looks like:

```
var secretSection = configuration.GetSection("MySecretSettings");
foreach (var key in secretSection.GetChildren())
{
    var originalValue = key.Value;
    var encryptedValue = dataProtector.Protect(originalValue);
    var oldValue = $"\"{key.Key}\": \"{originalValue}\"";
    var newValue = $"\"{key.Key}\": \"{encryptedValue}\"";
    json = json.Replace(oldValue, newValue);
}
File.WriteAllText("appsettings.json", json);
```

The call to `dataProtector.Protect()` does all the hard work for us. It takes a string and encrypts it. We replace the old value with the new one and write it in the file.

If you open the `appsettings.json` file (the one in the folder with the debug build, not the original one!), you will see that the secret strings are not human-readable anymore. So, anyone opening that file will not have access to our secrets!

Reading encrypted data

In an application where you intend to use secret strings, you can simply read the data from the configuration file and decrypt them. That goes like this:

```
configuration.Reload();
var encryptedSection = configuration.GetSection("MySecretSettings");
var someSecretValue = encryptedSection["MySecretSetting1"];
var decryptedValue = dataProtector.Unprotect(someSecretValue);
$"Encrypted value was: {someSecretValue}\nDecrypted this becomes: {decryptedValue}".Dump();
```

First, I reload the configuration to ensure the object has the encrypted strings. Then, I get the section and read the first setting and its value. Finally, I use `dataProtector` to decrypt the string. The result is a lovely, unencrypted, readable string.

Of course, you should not do encryption and decryption in production systems using the same program. You need to split them up. When you do, remember to use the same string for the purpose. If you do not do that, you will get an exception telling you that the decryption did not work. Try this:

```
var secondProtector = serviceProvider.GetDataProtector("AnotherSection");
var decryptedValue = secondProtector.Unprotect(someSecretValue);
```

I call `GetDataProtector()` with a new purpose string, and I use that to unprotect the string. That will not work. If I use `"MySecureString"` instead of `"AnotherSection"`, it works again, even though I have a new `DataProtector`.

Where are the keys?

You may wonder why I never specified a password to encrypt and decrypt. The answer is that the framework generates one for me. It is more or less hidden in the `"%LocalAppData%\ASP.NET\DataProtection-Keys"` folder. This special folder is where the runtime stores and reads the keys. Open that folder, pick one of the XML files, and open it to see what it contains.

You can specify another folder where the system stores the keys. Change the start of the program, where we call `AddDataProtection()` to add the data protection classes to `serviceCollection`, to look like this:

```
serviceCollection
    .AddDataProtection()
    .PersistKeysToFileSystem(new DirectoryInfo(myKeyFolder));
```

This line of code tells the system to use the folder specified in `myKeyFolder` to store the keys.

In a production system, you can distribute the key file and store it in a known location. Of course, any attacker with access to your `appsettings.json` file probably has no problem finding the key file. There must be better ways to deal with this. And there are, but I will deal with that in the next part. First, I want to talk about the strings that are in memory. Those can be hardcoded strings in your code or decrypted strings from your settings file. Are those a potential security risk? Let's find out!

Handling strings in memory

You might think encrypted strings in a configuration file are safe. After all, nobody can read them. Only your program can access them, provided it can access the key file. The program can read and decrypt the settings in memory, making everything safe and secure. Unfortunately, that is not the case. Finding that kind of information in a running program is not hard.

Disclosing strings in your application

Let's assume we have the following code:

```
var myOpenString = "This is my Open String";
Console.ReadLine();
```

I agree. This isn't the most exciting piece of code you have ever seen, but it does what it needs to do. It loads a string in memory and then waits for the user to press a key to abort the program.

Suppose I compile this in release mode and start the handy **WinDbg** tool (you can install that by going to the Microsoft Store and searching for it). In that case, I can do all sorts of inspections on a running program. With some digging around, I finally found this result:

```
Name:          System.String
MethodTable:   00007ffaf832ec08
EEClass:       00007ffaf830a500
Tracked Type:  false
Size:          66(0x42) bytes
File:          C:\Program Files\dotnet\shared\Microsoft.NETCore.
App\8.0.5\System.Private.CoreLib.dll
String:        This is my Open String
```

```
Fields:
              MT    Field   Offset                  Type VT
Attr           Value Name
00007ffaf82b1188  400033b       8          System.Int32  1
instance             22 _stringLength
00007ffaf82bb538  400033c       c          System.Char   1
instance             54 _firstChar
00007ffaf832ec08  400033a      c8          System.String 0   static
000001ee80000008 Empty
```

WinDbg gives me all sorts of information about the `System.String` object found at a specific memory location. Part of that information is the contents of that string – `"This is my Open String"`.

My sample program is straightforward, so finding the information wasn't hard. But the fact that I can actually do this by just attaching it to a running program shows you what a hacker can do. If your program takes encrypted data from an `appsettings.json` file and keeps that string in memory, you might as well not encrypt your data at all.

There must be a better way. And guess what – there is!

Using SecureStrings

We've discovered that strings in memory are not secure. The people behind the BCL thought of this as well and gave us an alternative – `SecureString`.

That sounds like a beautiful idea, but `SecureString` is less convenient than a "real" string. Not by far. However, it does have one advantage – the data in it is encrypted.

Creating `SecureString` is easy enough:

```
using var secureString = new SecureString();
```

But that doesn't really help us. We want some data in it. That's not hard, but you must copy the data one character at a time:

```
var sourceString = "This is a big secret";
foreach (var c in sourceString)
{
    secureString.AppendChar(c);
}
secureString.MakeReadOnly();
```

Now, `secureString` contains some data. The nice thing is that the data is encrypted and not readable anymore. The call to `MakeReadOnly()` is important. By making it read-only, you ensure that the string is not changeable anymore, which helps in performance.

`SecureString` is mainly used to store passwords. A lot of classes in the BCL that need passwords accept `SecureString` as their parameter. For instance, these are some of the classes that can work with `SecureString` instances:

- `ProcessStartInfo`: When starting a new process, you can provide a password as `SecureString` using the `ProcessStartInfo` struct, or by calling an overload of `Process.Start()` that accepts `SecureString`.
- `NetworkCredential`: When you need to identify a resource with a network resource, you can use `NetworkCredential` to pass along the required parameters, such as the username, password, and domain. The password can be an instance of the `SecureString` class.
- `CspParameters` and `X509Certificate`: These are important if you are dealing with certificates, and they also allow `SecureString` instances.

So, now we have a secure string. Great. But we still have an issue. Can you spot it? I will give you a minute while you look at the code that we last discussed.

The problem, of course, is where we seed the secure string. We create a string in memory with the `"This is a big secret"` contents and transfer it to the secure string. But the original string is still in memory.

We would have had the same issue if we had read an encrypted string from a configuration file, decrypted it, and copied it to the secure string. The original, decrypted string is still in memory and can be read externally.

The only way to circumvent it is to erase that provisional string as soon as you finish it. The unencrypted strings should be in memory for as long as possible. Technically, it is still vulnerable, but the attacker has to break the running application exactly when the strings are in memory. The attack window is still there, but it is very, very small.

Erasing a string is not the same as assigning a new value – strings are immutable. When you try to change the string, you get a new instance, and the old data is still readable. The only way to completely eradicate it from memory is to erase the chars that form the string. You can erase a string from memory with something similar to this code:

```
void OverwriteAndClearString(ref string str)
{
    if (str == null) return;
    unsafe
    {
        fixed (char* ptr = str)
        {
            for (int i = 0; i < str.Length; i++)
            {
                ptr[i] = '\0'; // Overwrite with null characters
```

```
            }
        }
    }
    str = null; // Dereference the string
}
```

You have to set the **Allow unsafe** flag to compile this, but once you have done this, you have another tool on your toolbelt. This code goes through the characters in the string and replaces them with '0'. Since 0 denotes the end of the string, it is harder to see the original length of the string.

I am not saying you need to call this method for every string. But suppose you are dealing with strings that you absolutely do not want to leak. In that case, this might solve the intermediate problem of copying data to a secure string.

But where do we get the decryption keys from? We can distribute them as shown previously, but there are other ways. Let's discuss those! However, before doing that, let's think about what we have learned. This was a complicated topic; dealing with strings in memory is not something many C# developers think about. But therein lies the problem – since people do not think about it, they are unaware of any risks.

Conversely, you now know about the risks and are ready to deal with them if you encounter the need for this level of security.

Using key management

Keys are the best-kept secrets of your application. Keys are used to encrypt and decrypt a lot of sensitive data. This means the keys themselves are even more sensitive; they hold the power to unlock all your secrets. Storing a key in a text file next to an executable might not be the best way to treat this valuable piece of data.

How and where you store the keys depends on where you run your program. If your application lives in the cloud, you should use a cloud-based key management system. If you run your systems on a machine you can touch, you need another solution.

Using the Azure Key Vault

The **Azure Key Vault** is a centralized, cloud-based secret and key management solution. It is straightforward to set up and easy to use. Its main purpose is to guard secrets and keys for Azure-based applications. However, it can also be used by applications running on-premise.

I will not teach you how to create a key vault here; plenty of resources can help you. For instance, this is a good resource from Microsoft itself: `https://learn.microsoft.com/en-us/azure/key-vault/general/quick-create-portal`.

Once you have a key vault deployed and have added a secret, retrieving that secret is simple. But before we look at the code to get that secret, we must ensure access to the resource. That means we make notes of the following items:

Item name	Value	Description
Key vault name	`mykeyvault`	The name of the key vault you specified when you created it
Secret name	`MySecretValue`	The name of the secret

Table 12.1: Values to find the Azure Key Vault secret

Obviously, you should change these values to match your setup.

In the C# application, we need to add a couple of NuGet packages:

- `Azure.Identity` to enable authentication
- `Azure.Security.KeyvaultSecrets`

Once you have installed those packages, the code to get the secrets out of the key vault is very straightforward. For instance, you can use this helper method:

```
public async Task<string> GetSecretAsync(string keyVaultUrl, string secretName)
{
    var client =
        new SecretClient(
            new Uri(keyVaultUrl),
            new DefaultAzureCredential());
    var secret =
        await client.GetSecretAsync(secretName);
    return secret.Value.Value;
}
```

This code snippet shows how to use the `SecretClient` class from the previously installed package to access the secrets in the key vault. To authenticate this request, I use the `DefaultAzureCredential` class. Using this class means I authenticate against the Azure URL with the current user's credentials.

In a production system, you would not do that. Instead, you should probably create a registration for your system and use that to authenticate. Authentication in Azure is a topic that deserves its own book, but the following URL should get you on your way: https://learn.microsoft.com/en-us/dotnet/azure/sdk/authentication/?tabs=command-line.

Using environment variables

Even when using Azure (and not using the default credentials), you need to store some sort of access key, secret ID, or user ID and password before you can use the resources. The same applies when you store data encrypted in your `appsettings.json` file – you need a key to decrypt. As we saw in a previous sample, you can ask the .NET runtime to create a key for you and store it in a known place. That is one way of solving this issue, but there is also a much simpler way. We can use environment variables.

> **Warning**
> Environment variables are convenient, but they are not secure – not by a long shot. Everybody can look up their values if they have physical access to the machine. Never store sensitive information in environment variables unless you can be confident the virtual or physical machine is secure.

An environment variable is simply a key-value pair that lives in Windows. It is usually used to contain settings from outside of the process. This is why they can be useful for holding data we need to identify resources; they can change on the fly without changing or restarting our application.

Environment variable scopes

Where precisely these variables live and how long they persist depends on the kind of environment variable. The variables can have a scope that affects where they persist (and how long they do so). These are the options we have:

- **Process scope**: These variables are only available to the process that defined them, or any child processes that the main process spawns. They can be useful for temporary values that can be discarded if the process goes out of memory.

- **User scope**: They are specific to the currently logged-in user. They are available to all processes that run under that user's credentials. These variables persist across logins.

- **Machine scope (or system scope)**: These variables are available to all users and processes on a machine. They require administrative privileges to set and modify but not to read.

- **Session scope**: These variables are scoped to a user session. This scope is more or less the same as the user scope, but the variables are discarded as the session ends. That happens, for instance, if the user logs off.

- **Volatile environment variables**: This is a special category mainly used by a system. They are intended to be temporary. Users typically do not handle or even access these. An example is the settings set during boot time that can be removed once the login process ends.

As you can see, there are a lot of different scopes, some of which most users have never even heard of before. Make sure you pick the correct one!

Setting environment variables

Of course, we can use our C# code to set variables. However, we usually do not do that; in our case, we want to set some secret data outside our application and then use it in our code. This means we have to set the data from the outside. Setting the values is typically done during the installation of our software. However, during development, you have to do it manually.

Setting these variables is very easily done from a PowerShell session, and the exact syntax depends on the scope you want to achieve.

Process scope

I only add this here for completeness. After all, if we set a variable so that we can read it in our application, using the **process scope** does not make sense. The variable is set in the scope of the PowerShell session and thus is not readable in our application. But anyway, here is how you do it. In PowerShell, enter this command:

```
$env:MY_SECRET_ID = 12345678
```

This command creates a new variable named "MY_SECRET_ID" in memory and assigns it the 12345678 value.

If you read the data, you'll be surprised to see that it is almost as simple as setting it:

```
Write-Host $env:MY_SECRET_ID
```

This command should return the 12345678 string.

After setting and reading the data, you might want to erase it. Again, this is very easy to do:

```
$env:MY_SECRED_ID = $null
```

Note that that last command happens automatically if you close the PowerShell session.

User scope

User scope is the first useable scope for our purposes. Setting this variable goes like this in PowerShell:

```
setx MY_SECRET_ID 87654321
```

This command creates a new variable and sets the data. The variable is stored in the Windows Registry under the HKEY_CURRENT_USER\Environment key. Windows keeps this value across reboots. Since the data is stored in HKEY_CURRENT_USER, you can only read the data in processes belonging to that user. That means you can read it during debugging in **Visual Studio** (**VS**), but only if you run VS under the same credentials.

Machine scope

The broadest scope is the **machine scope**. Setting data is just as simple as using the user scope, with one tiny addition:

```
setx MY_GLOBAL_SECRET_ID 87654321 /m
```

The use of /m at the end makes this variable a machine-scoped one. This means it is stored in a different location as well; you can now find this variable in the Windows Registry under the HKEY_LOCAL_MACHINE\SYSTEM\CurrentControlSet\Control\Session Manager\Environment key. This variable is persisted across reboots and is accessible to all users and processes on that machine.

Reading the variables in your code

There is little use in storing data somewhere if it is impossible to read. So, let's investigate how we can use that data in our C# application.

To read the data, you only need one line of code, which is this:

```
string mySecretdId = 
    Environment.GetEnvironmentVariable("MY_SECRET_ID");
```

However, remember that MY_SECRET_ID was set using the user scope. So, if you run your PowerShell command as an administrator, you must also run VS as an administrator. Otherwise, the code returns an empty string.

Do you want to see how to read the machine-scoped variable? I thought you might. This is how:

```
var mySecretdId = 
  Environment.GetEnvironmentVariable("MY_GLOBAL_SECRET_ID");
```

Yes, that is the same code, with the only change being the variable name we are looking for. Not all code in this book is hard to understand!

There are many more ways to handle keys, but you have now seen two of the most used ones. You now know how to use Azure Key Vault and have learned a lot about environmental variables. Let's move on!

Using the right privilege level

Most systems do not need to run as admin. Requiring your application to have admin rights is a potential security risk. It would be best to ensure your application runs on the lowest security level possible to avoid potential leaks.

However, sometimes you have no choice. There are certain cases where admin-level privilege is needed. The bad news is that this happens often in the world where we, system programmers, live. Our systems need an admin level more than a regular program does.

Admin-level scenarios

Let's investigate some areas where elevated privileges are needed if we want our system to do what it needs to do:

- **Filesystem operations**:

    Accessing or modifying system files, such as updating or reading configuration files stored in protected directories. For instance, the `C:\Windows\System32` directory is a good example of a protected directory. You need elevated rights if you want to read something from that folder.

- **Registry operations**:

    Reading and writing operations in the registry do not require administrative rights, unless you want to do something with secured areas. One of those areas is the `HKEY_LOCAL_MACHINE` key. That area cannot be reached without the proper security level.

- **Service management**:

    Starting, stopping, or configuring Windows services is another nice example of requiring admin-level privileges. Also, installing and uninstalling these services need that level of trust. Since we work a lot with background processes, we can imagine scenarios where we need to control those processes from other processes. That means elevating the level again.

- **Network configuration**:

    Modifying network settings is also a reason you might need elevated privileges. These tasks include changing an IP address, configuring network adapters, and adjusting firewall rules.

- **System monitoring and diagnostics**:

    Some of the performance counters or diagnostics tools require elevated privileges. Also, reading system logs in an event or other logs requires admin access.

This is not an exhaustive list; there are other areas as well. If you run into one of those, you will find out soon enough – your system won't work and crash with a nice exception.

Impersonating as an admin

If your system does something from the preceding list, you might be tempted to install your system with admin credentials. That way, you are sure it always works. But as we have discussed before, that is not necessarily a good idea. It would be much better to go to the administrator level only when needed. When done, revert to the regular, less privileged user account.

How can we do that? First, we must create an account with admin-level rights on the machine where our software will run. I would not use the generic administrator account found on machines; you are better off using a dedicated account.

On my machine, I created an account named `MySecureAdmin`. I gave it the extremely safe password `P@ssw0rd!`. No, that's not a password I would use in real life, but for this demonstration, it will suffice. This account is a local admin. And finally, my machine has the name `DennisMachine`. This is all the information you would need if you wanted to log in as an administrator.

The technique to temporarily act as another user in your application is called impersonating. Let me show you how that is done.

I have created a console application and added a new class called `ImpersonationHelper`. The class imports two methods from the Win32 API – `LogonUser` and `CloseHandle`. This is their signature:

```
[DllImport("advapi32.dll", SetLastError = true, CharSet = CharSet.Auto)]
public static extern bool LogonUser(
    string lpszUsername,
    string lpszDomain,
    string lpszPassword,
    int dwLogonType,
    int dwLogonProvider,
    out SafeAccessTokenHandle phToken);
[DllImport("kernel32.dll", CharSet = CharSet.Auto)]
public static extern bool CloseHandle(IntPtr handle);
```

The `LogonUser` API resides in the "`advapi32.dll`" DLL, while the `CloseHandle` API can be found in "`kernel32.dll`".

Next, I declare two constants that we will need later on:

```
private const int LOGON32_LOGON_BATCH = 4;
private const int LOGON32_PROVIDER_DEFAULT = 0;
```

That is all we need to start impersonating. This is the code that does that:

```
public static void RunAsAdmin(
    string userName, string domain,
    string password, Action action)
{
    var returnValue = LogonUser(
        userName, domain,
        password, LOGON32_LOGON_BATCH,
        LOGON32_PROVIDER_DEFAULT,
        out var safeAccessTokenHandle);
    if (!returnValue)
    {
        var ret = Marshal.GetLastWin32Error();
        throw new Win32Exception(ret);
```

```
    }
    try
    {
        WindowsIdentity.RunImpersonated(safeAccessTokenHandle, () => {
            action(); });
    }
    finally
    {
        safeAccessTokenHandle.Dispose();
    }
}
```

Let me explain what is going on here.

The method gets all the required information to log into Windows – the username, password, and domain. We also give it the code we want to run under these credentials in the form of an `Action`.

We call `LogonUser()` and give it the username, domain, and password. Then, we specify the login type; we give it LOGON32_LOGON_BATCH. This type is used for batch servers. Batch servers execute code on behalf of a user without their intervention. In contrast, a standard login would use LOGON32_LOGON_INTERACTIVE. The BATCH option results in higher performance, which is very convenient for us. After this, we give it the login provider and instruct it to use the default provider by passing LOGON32_PROVIDER_DEFAULT.

If all goes well, we will get a pointer in `SafeAccessTokenHandle`. If it does not work, we get an error.

With that handle, we can call `WindowsIdentity.RunImpersonated()`, which in turn calls our action.

Do not forget to call `Dispose()` on the handle!

Using this code is straightforward:

```
var userName = Environment.UserName;
$"Current user: {userName}".Dump();
var adminUserName = "MySecureAdmin";
var domain = "dennismachine";
var password = "P@ssw0rd!";
ImpersonationHelper.RunAsAdmin(
    adminUserName, domain, password, () =>
{
    var otherUserName = Environment.UserName;
    $"Username {otherUserName}".Dump();
});
```

This code uses our new class to temporarily log in as another user. But before that, it shows the current username. I do the same in the `Action`, but the results will differ. We are now logged in as the new user, which should also be shown on the screen.

There is no need to log out – the call to `LogonUser()` doesn't alter the logged-in state of that user; it is just required to get the handle. The moment we dispose of the handle, the impersonation also terminates. This means we are now back operating under the standard credentials. Run this sample and see what happens.

Impersonation is another nice tool in your toolbelt, but use it sparingly. Only increase the trust level in your applications if you absolutely need it. Oh, and I am sure I do not need to remind you that storing usernames and passwords in plain code in your application is terrible, especially if they belong to admin-level users. Right?

Many developers, by default, assume their code needs admin-level privileges. After reading this section, you now know better. We discussed the situations where admin-level is required, but please remember that less is more, especially regarding privilege levels! And if you need admin-level privileges in your code, you know how to take care of that temporarily before returning to a normal level.

How to transmit network data securely

As we have seen, keeping data sensitive on your machine is hard. But things get even more complicated once we leave the safe haven of the machine we control and venture into the wasteland of networks.

I probably do not have to remind you that you should never use a public website that uses an HTTP connection instead of an HTTPS connection. The "S," after all, stands for "Secure." That is what we want – we want our data to be encrypted, and we want to be confident that the server we talk to is secure and belongs to the party we think it belongs to.

The same applies to our code – if we talk to an outside system, we want to ensure that our data is not being tampered with or intercepted. That also applies to other systems when they connect to us – we want to give those users the same sense of security. How do we achieve that? The answer is simple – we do the same as those HTTPS servers. The next question is, how do we implement that? And that is slightly more complicated. But don't worry – I will walk you through it step by step.

How HTTPS works

Let me ask you a question. How do you know you can trust the website you visit? Just because it says HTTPS in the address bar? But what does that mean? How can that be a guarantee? To answer that, we need to look at what HTTPS actually means.

HTTPS stands for **Hyper Text Transport Protocol Secure**. This is a variation of regular HTTP traffic – it has added security. Let's examine the flow:

1. In your browser, you enter a URL: `https://www.microsoft.com`.
2. The browser resolves the domain name to an IP address.
3. The client initiates a TCP connection with the server using a three-way handshake (SYN, SYN-ACK, and ACK).
4. The client sends a `"ClientHello"` message to the server. This message includes the following:

    - Supported TLS versions
    - Supported cipher suites
    - Supported compression methods
    - A randomly generated value (client random)
    - Session IDs and extensions (optional)

5. The server then responds with a `"ServerHello"` message, which includes the following:

    - The chosen TLS version
    - The chosen cipher suite
    - The chosen compression method
    - A randomly generated value (server random)
    - The session ID (if supported and desired)

6. The server sends its digital certificate, including its public key and a digital signature, from a trusted certificate authority.
7. Then, the server may (if required) send a `"ServerKeyExchange"` message.
8. After that, the server requests a client certificate for mutual authentication.
9. Finally, the server sends a `"ServerHelloDone"` message, indicating that this is the end of the handshake.
10. The client then optionally sends its own certificate (if requested).
11. The client sends a `"ClientKeyExchange"` message. The contents depend on the algorithm chosen. For instance, if RSA is chosen, the client encrypts a pre-master secret with the server's public key and sends that to the server.
12. The client sends a `"CertificateVerify"` message to prove it owns the client certificate. This involves signing a hash of the handshake messages using the client's private key.

13. Both parties then generate the session keys (symmetric keys) for encryption and authentication, using the pre-master secret and the random values exchanged earlier.
14. The client then sends a `"ChangeCipherSpec"` message to inform the server that, from now on, all messages will be encrypted using the negotiated keys and algorithms.
15. The server also sends a `"ChangeCipherSpec"` message.
16. The client sends a `"Finished"` message, which is a hash of all the handshake messages encrypted with the session key.
17. The server responds with its `"Finished"` key, with the same sort of information.

From now on, the client and the server can use the keys and algorithms to encrypt and decrypt the data flow.

If you think this sounds complicated, you are right. The good news is that we do not have to worry about this. All of the classes in the BCL dealing with HTTP handle this for us. All you have to do is connect to a secure server, specify that you want to use SSL, and you are good to go.

Certificates and certificate authorities

The preceding steps outline how the client and server exchange keys securely. However, a key question remains – how do they know they can trust each other?

The answer to that question lies in the use of certificates. A certificate is a digital document containing information about the certificate's owner. It includes the following information:

- **Subject**: The entity that the certificate represents (for instance, the website's domain name)
- **Issuer**: Who issued the certificate
- **Public key**: The public key of the entity
- **Validity period**: The date range in which the certificate is valid
- **Serial number**: A unique identifier for the certificate
- **Signature**: The digital signature of the issuer, verifying that the certificate is genuine and has not been tampered with

If you get a certificate from a website, you can use that to verify that the site you are connecting to is indeed the one it claims to be. If the information on the certificate doesn't match what is expected, you had better not use that site.

But how can you be sure that the certificate is valid? This question leads us to the last part of the SSL infrastructure – certificate authorities.

A certificate has to be obtained from a third party. These companies sell certificates, but only after they have verified that the one requested a certificate is who they say they are. We call these companies **certificate authorities** (**CAs**). These authorities are regularly audited to make sure they can be trusted. This starts a whole chain – a CA has its own certificate. However, that certificate is a root certificate; it is implicitly trusted. No organization guarantees the CA's certificate is valid. But if we trust that root certificate, we can assume that all certificates signed with that root certificate are also safe. Then, we can use the secondary certificate to sign another certificate. We can build a whole tree of trusted certificates, all of which can be traced back to the CA that issued the original certificate.

Windows keeps track of all the trusted root certificates and stores them on the local machine. That way, the software can compare the hashes with the data it receives from the HTTPS server and make sure the certificate is secure.

To see these root certificates, run the mmc.exe command on your machine. Then, press *CTRL + M* to add the **Certificates** snap-in. Open the tree on the left to see all the trusted root certificate authorities. This is what it looks like on my machine:

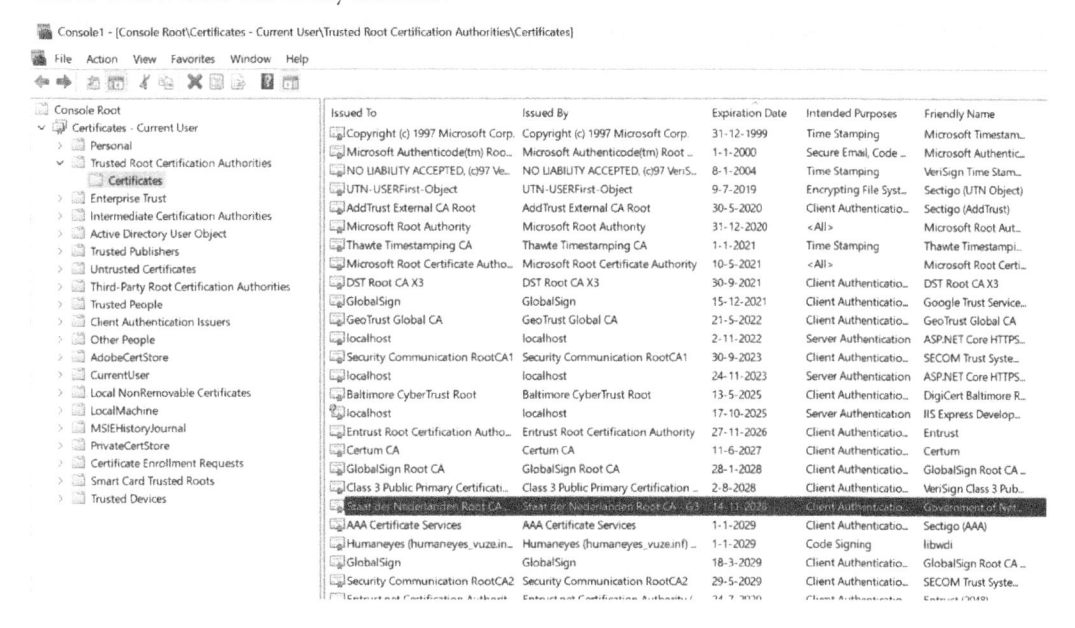

Figure 12.1: Root certificates in Windows

Your list will undoubtedly differ from mine, but these are all trusted root certificates. Windows regularly updates this list to make sure it is still valid.

You must get a certificate from one of these CA organizations to set up a HTTPS server. They all have a slightly different process, so I suggest you investigate some of them to see if they are suitable for you. It doesn't matter which CA you use; all certificates suit your purposes. Some are faster than others, and others are cheaper than others. Just pick what you feel is the best option for you.

> **Be aware of free certificates!**
>
> I will be very clear about this – there are no free certificates to be had at the time of writing. A few CAs issued free certificates, but that doesn't happen anymore. The demands for verification have significantly increased; the CA needs to be more thorough than ever to combat cybercrime. And that costs money. If you see a CA that offers a free certificate, do not fall for it. Remember that if something sounds too good to be true, it probably is. Some CA organizations provide a free certificate, but they have other demands. You have to build your software on their pipelines, or you have to host with them. Ultimately, you still pay for it.

So, now we know what a certificate is and how to get one. But let's be honest – if you want to play around with certificates or are still in development, you might not be ready to purchase a certificate. If that is your situation, then I have good news. There is a free alternative – you can make your own certificate!

Creating a development certificate

Yes, you can create your own certificate. But this is just for experimental or development purposes. You cannot use it in a production system; the verification will fail, since your certificate is not vouched for by a CA.

The tools to create a certificate are part of the SDK installed with VS. Let's make a certificate!

In a developer command prompt or PowerShell terminal, enter the following command:

```
MakeCert -r -pe -ss PrivateCertStore -n "CN=localhost" -sv testcer.pvk testcer.cer
```

`MakeCert`, part of the SDK, is the tool to create a certificate. There are many options, but we do not need most of them. I have given you the minimum we need for our purpose. Let's investigate what we did by looking at the parameters:

Parameter	Description
`-r`	This means the certificate is self-signed and not signed by a CA.
`-pe`	This marks the private key as exportable. The private and public keys are all part of the certificate, so you need this option if you want a copy of the private key.
`-ss PrivateCertStore`	The specifies the certificate store where the generated certificate will be placed. In our case, we use `PrivateCertStore`, one of those entries in the Management console we looked at earlier.
`-n "CN=localhost"`	This is the **distinguished name** (**DN**) of the certificate. We set it to `localhost` (**CN** means **common name**) so that the clients know which domain this certificate belongs to.

Parameter	Description
`-sv testcer.pvk`	We marked the private key as exportable; this option does the export. The private key is stored in the `testcer.pvk` file.
`testcer.cer`	The filename of the certificate

Table 12.2: Parameters for MakeCert

If you run the `MakeCert` command, you will be asked to enter passwords. Make sure you remember them and store them somewhere secure!

This command results in two files – `testcer.cer` (the certificate) and `testcer.pvk` (the private key). Make sure you treat these files as confidential; they contain your private keys.

The certificate can now be used, but not for everything we want to use it for. Later, we will use the certificate to encrypt data streams, but that will require a different format. These tools need a `pfx` format. Luckily, converting a `.cer` file to a `.pfx` file is easy enough. Just enter this command:

```
pvk2pfx -pvk .\testcer.pvk -spc .\testcer.cer -pfx testcer.pfx -po
"password"
```

The `pvk2pfx` tool takes the exported private key and the certificate and converts them into a `.pfx` file. The parameters speak for themselves.

The certificate we created is now stored in the certificate store under the `PrivateCertStore` section. But we also need to store the newly generated `.pfx` file in the certificate store for later use. To do this, enter the following command:

```
certutil -importpfx testcer.pfx
```

In this case, the `certutil` command invoked another handy tool to take the new `testcer.pfx` file and store it in the right place.

And that is all there is to it. We now have our own certificate, so let's secure some network traffic!

Securing TCP streams

If you have a web server, such as IIS, you can import the `.pfx` file there. That way, you can use HTTPS on your local network. Again, this is not SSL; other clients will not accept that self-signed certificate. It is for development only.

However, I am not currently interested in setting up a HTTPS server. I am more concerned about the other network communication types we discussed previously. For instance, how can we secure simple, straightforward TCP communications? If we want to use sockets, how do we secure that? The answer is to use SSL, as we have seen with HTTPS. Let's build some secure code!

I have created two console applications. One is a server waiting for incoming TCP connections; the other is the client connecting to that server.

Let's have a look at the server code first. I have created a new class called `SecureServer`. This class gets a constructor that takes the required information to set up the server. It looks like this:

```
public SecureServer(int port,
    string certificatePath,
    string certificatePassword)
{
    _port = port;
    _serverCertificate = new X509Certificate2(
        certificatePath,
        certificatePassword);
}
```

We pass the file path to the certificate we just created and the password in the port that the TCP socket listens to (I told you to write that down, didn't I?). We store the port number in a local variable and use the other two variables to create an instance of the `X509Certificate2` class.

Next is the method that starts the server. We investigated that before (in *Chapter 8*, *The One with the Network Navigation*), so there shouldn't be any surprises here. Here it is:

```
public async Task StartAsync()
{
    "Server is starting...".Dump();
    var listener = new TcpListener(IPAddress.Any, _port);
    listener.Start();
    $"Server is listening on port {_port}...".Dump();
    while (true)
    {
        var clientSocket = await listener.AcceptSocketAsync();
        _ = HandleClientConnection(clientSocket);
    }
}
```

We create an instance of `TcpListener`, tell it to use any IP address on the machine, and give it the correct port. Then, we call `Start()` to accept incoming connections. In a never-ending loop, we wait for a client to connect. If that happens, we accept the connection with a call to `AcceptSocketAsync()` and pass the handling of the connection to a method called `HandleClientConnection()`. Let's look at that one next.

The first half of the method looks like this:

```
private async Task HandleClientConnection(Socket clientSocket)
{
    try
    {
        await using var sslStream =
            new SslStream(
                new NetworkStream(clientSocket),
                false);
        await sslStream.AuthenticateAsServerAsync(
            _serverCertificate,
            false,
            SslProtocols.Tls12,
            true);
        $"Client connected: {clientSocket.RemoteEndPoint}".Dump();
```

Instead of using a normal stream, we use a specialized one called `SslStream`. This takes `NetworkStream` and a parameter, indicating whether the stream should be kept open when we finish it (we don't want that, so we give it a `False`).

Then, we call `AuthenticateAsServerAsync()` on that `SslStream`, giving it the certificate, tell it that we do not require a client certificate, also tell it that we want to use TLS version 1.2, and finally, inform the method that we want to check the certificate revocation (hence the `True`). This one line of code makes sure the server does all the steps needed for it to set up a secure connection.

The rest of the method is straightforward – we read data coming in and display it. This is the rest of that method:

```
        var buffer = new byte[1024];
        var bytesRead =
            await sslStream.ReadAsync(
                buffer,
                0,
                buffer.Length);
        var receivedString =
            Encoding.UTF8.GetString(
                buffer,
                0,
                bytesRead);
        $"Received from client: {receivedString}".Dump();
    }
    catch (Exception ex)
    {
```

```
            ex.Message.Dump();
    }
}
```

And that is all! Well, almost – we need to use this method as well. But that is even simpler. In the `Main()` method, use this code:

```
var certificatePath = @"d:\Certificate\testcer.pfx";
var certificatePassword = "password";
var server = new SecureServer(
    8081,
    certificatePath,
    certificatePassword);
await server.StartAsync();
```

With all this, we have a working and secure socket server!

Next up, the client! For the client, I did a similar thing. I added a new class called `SecureClient` with the following constructor:

```
public SecureClient(
    string server,
    int port)
{
    _server = server;
    _port = port;
}
```

This constructor takes two parameters – the name of the server and the port it wants to connect to.

Next, we define a method called `ConnectAsync()` that allows the client to connect:

```
public async Task ConnectAsync()
{
    using var clientSocket = new TcpClient(_server, _port);
    await using var networkStream = clientSocket.GetStream();
    await using var sslStream =
        new SslStream(
            networkStream,
            false,
            ValidateServerCertificate);
    try
    {
        await sslStream.AuthenticateAsClientAsync(_server);
        "SSL authentication successful".Dump();
```

```csharp
            var message = $"Hello, server! {DateTime.Now.TimeOfDay}";
            var messageBytes = Encoding.UTF8.GetBytes(message);

            await sslStream.WriteAsync(messageBytes, 0, messageBytes.Length);
        }
        catch (Exception ex)
        {
            ex.Message.Dump(ConsoleColor.Red);
        }
    }
```

This method starts with familiar code – we create an instance of `TcpClient` and give it the server and port. After that, we open `NetworkStream` from that `TcpClient`. But then things get more interesting – we create a new instance of the `SslStream` class, giving it `NetworkStream`, the same `False` that indicates that we do not want to keep the stream open when we are done with it, and a callback method called `ValidateServerCertificate`. After that, we call `AuthenticateAsClientAsync()` to make sure the client and the server exchange messages, as described previously.

The rest of this method is nothing special – we just write the bytes to the stream.

Let's look at the `ValidateServerCertificate()` callback method next:

```csharp
private static bool ValidateServerCertificate(
    object sender,
    X509Certificate certificate, X509Chain chain,
    SslPolicyErrors sslPolicyErrors)
{
    if (sslPolicyErrors == SslPolicyErrors.None)
    {
        "Server certificate is valid".Dump();
        return true;
    }
    "Server certificate is invalid".Dump(ConsoleColor.Red);
    return false;
}
```

This method is called when we create `SslStream` and is part of validating the server's certificate. The method itself is straightforward – we just check to see whether there are any errors in the `SslPolicyErrors` enum. If there are, we return `false`. This is picked up by the `SslStream` class, which will raise an exception.

> **A developers' trick – simplify your development**
>
> If you are developing a solution like this but do not have a valid certificate, there is a quick hack you can use. Change the validation method to always return `True`. That way, your client will accept all sorts of certificates, regardless of their validity. Just do not use this technique in production code!

Using this class is easy. This is the code:

```
var secureClient = new SecureClient("localhost", 8081);
await secureClient.ConnectAsync();
```

Just a word of warning – this is only for development purposes. The code itself is fine for any scenario, but the certificate we created is not. We signed it ourselves, so no real client should accept it. Next, we specified that the server's name is `"localhost"`. This apparently only works on your machine, not across a network. You could change that when you create the certificate, of course.

And there you have it – a working TCP client using a secure channel. You have made it much harder, if not impossible, for a hacker to eavesdrop and listen in on your communications!

Next steps

I have to be honest with you. We only touched briefly on the subject of security. There are hundreds, if not thousands, of books on this topic. But the information I gave you should help you get in the right mindset. Remember that a system is only as secure as the weakest link. And security is something that you should consider from the beginning, not added as an afterthought.

One final warning – do not try to reinvent the wheel and come up with your own algorithms. Your solutions are never as good as what teams of hundreds of crypto and security experts can come up with. Trust them to do their job so that you can focus on yours.

That being said, we did cover a lot of ground. We discussed the following:

- The need for security in modern applications
- How data is represented in memory and how to protect against that
- How to handle keys in Azure Key Vault but also in simple things such as environment variables
- How to deal with the proper privilege level
- How to secure your network communications

However, there is one thing that we mentioned briefly but did not cover in detail – how to pass credentials securely from our development machine to a production environment. How do we ensure the environment variables are set when deploying our solutions? This and other questions are part of the deployment strategies we can use, which happens to be the topic of the next chapter!

13

The One with the Deployment Dramas

Deployment and Distribution

Allow me to make a confession: I love writing code. The whole process that starts with a vague idea, followed by writing the first lines of code, then finding issues and debugging the code, gives me a thrill. There is something magical about creating something out of thin air and seeing it come to life before my eyes.

But there comes a moment when the software is "good enough" and it needs to move into production. After all, we write software with a purpose: it needs to be used. And that usually means moving it away from your development machine to a production environment.

There are many challenges in this process. But don't worry: we will tackle all of them! We will discuss the following topics:

- What does deployment mean?
- How do you use the Publish wizard from Visual Studio?
- What is CI/CD, and how do I use it in Azure DevOps or GitHub?
- How do I build an installer?
- How do I deploy with Docker?

So, if you are ready to let the world see the fruits of your labor but are unsure how to get that out there, this is the chapter for you.

Technical requirements

You will find all the code in this chapter in our repository at https://github.com/PacktPublishing/Systems-Programming-with-C-Sharp-and-.NET/tree/main/SystemsProgrammingWithCSharpAndNet/Chapter13.

If you want to follow along with the CI/CD samples in Azure, you'll need an Azure subscription. You can sign up for a free trial for Azure at https://azure.microsoft.com/en-us/free/.

To have a go with GitHub Actions, you'll need to sign up for a GitHub account. You can get a free one here: https://github.com/signup.

If you want to follow along when we talk about the setup projects, you must install **Visual Studio Extension Microsoft Visual Studio Installer Projects 2022**. You can find this by going to the **Extensions** menu item and choosing **Manage extensions**. From there, in the **Online** tab, search for that extension.

With this tool, you can follow along and build your own installers.

If you want to work with the Docker sample, install Docker Desktop. You can find it here: https://www.docker.com/products/docker-desktop.

All the software mentioned here is free or has a free trial.

From development to production

There will come a moment when you're developing your application when you decide it is time for other people to try out the fruits of your labor. This means moving your application from your development machine to another environment. This could be another developer's machine or a production system.

Depending on the complexity of your system, moving the bits away could involve anything from a simple file copy to building a complex installer application. You also have to think about ways to remove your application from their system and about ways to update or upgrade your application. All these tasks are gathered under the term *deployment*.

Deployment should be as seamless as possible. The users should be able to take your application and prepare it for use effortlessly. This means all the hard work lies with us.

Creating a deployment scenario involves thinking about the following aspects:

- Copying your binaries
- Copying the binaries your system depends on
- Copying additional files
- Setting user rights
- Copying settings and altering them
- Creating and copying secrets
- Altering system settings such as paths
- Registering your application in the host environment

Uninstalling your applications means reversing this process: in an ideal world, an uninstall leaves no trace of your application and the associated files on the host machine.

Upgrading and updating is a mix of these scenarios: deploying new code, changing settings, and removing things you no longer need in the latest version.

If all you have is a simple, standalone console application, deployment is a breeze: just copy the files needed. Suppose you're deploying a complex system, such as a background worker; this needs configuration settings to connect to external systems. In that case, you have a lot more work to do. But there is good news: for each of those and other scenarios, there are strategies to follow. And that is what the rest of this chapter is all about. So, do a final build of your app, do a quick local test, and let's deploy our work!

Publishing and file copy

The easiest way to deploy an application is to use Visual Studio's Publish mechanism. Let's assume I have a simple console application. I don't have any configuration settings that I need to change when running on a production environment. So, I can just copy what I have.

Let's assume we have a simple console application. You've tested it, and you're ready to deliver. There are two options: use **Visual Studio** or use the **CLI**.

Publish using Visual Studio

In Visual Studio, in the **Solution Explorer** area, right-click on your project and select **Publish**. You'll see the following dialog:

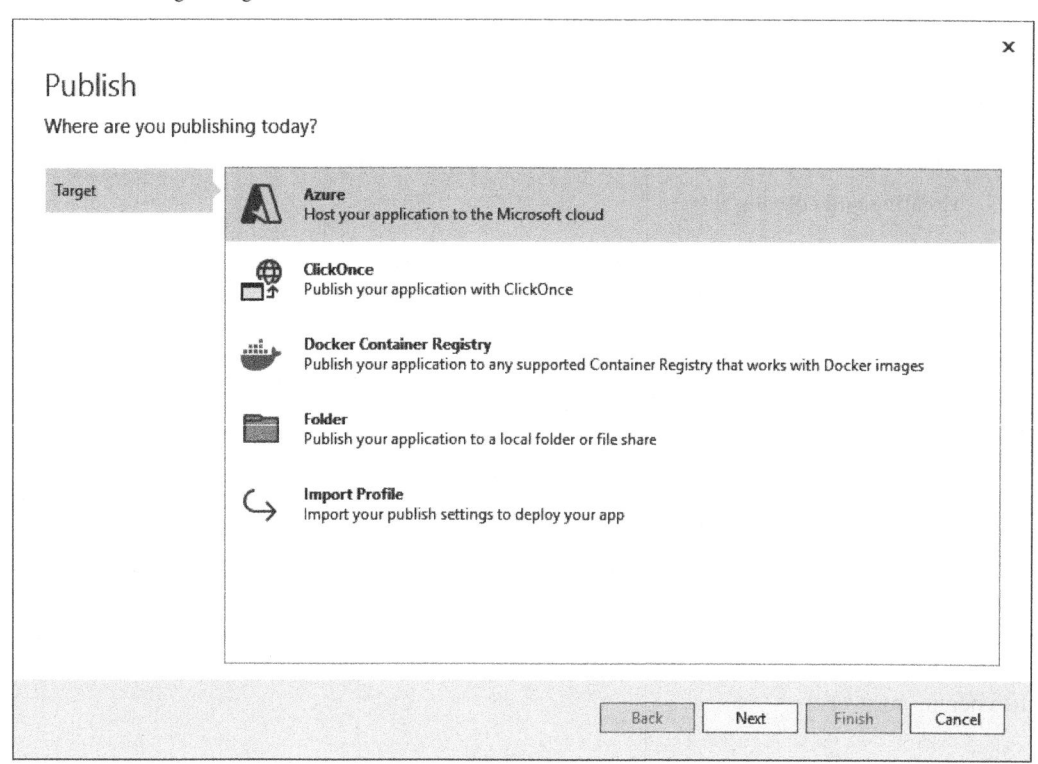

Figure 13.1: Publishing via Visual Studio

There are a couple of options to choose from:

- **Azure**: This means deploying your system to Azure so that it runs there.
- **ClickOnce**: ClickOnce is a technique for building a simple installer. Updates and uninstallation are part of the mechanism. However, ClickOnce is meant for Windows applications that the users start. Therefore, this is not a solution for us system programmers. For that reason, I will not cover ClickOnce here.
- **Docker Container Registry**: This is a great way to package and deploy systems. We will discuss this later.
- **Folder**: This is the simplest way to publish as it just copies all files needed to a folder.
- **Import Profile**: If you've already defined deployment methods, you can use those settings here by importing them.

In this case, we'll choose **Folder**. Upon doing so, you'll get a new dialog asking if you want to use **ClickOnce** for the folder deployment or whether you wish to deploy to the filesystem. Choose **Folder** to pick the latter. At this point, you can enter the path to which you want to publish. For now, leave it as the default setting. Click **Finish**.

Although you clicked **Finish**, it didn't finish publishing. All Visual Studio did was create a publish profile. In this case, it is called `FolderProfile.pubxml`, and you can find it in the **Solution Explorer** area in your project under **Properties** > **PublishProfiles**.

Visual Studio will open the profile and show you what it looks like. From here, we can click the big **Publish** button; however, we might want to tweak the profile before doing that. Click **More Actions** and choose **Edit**. This results in the following dialog:

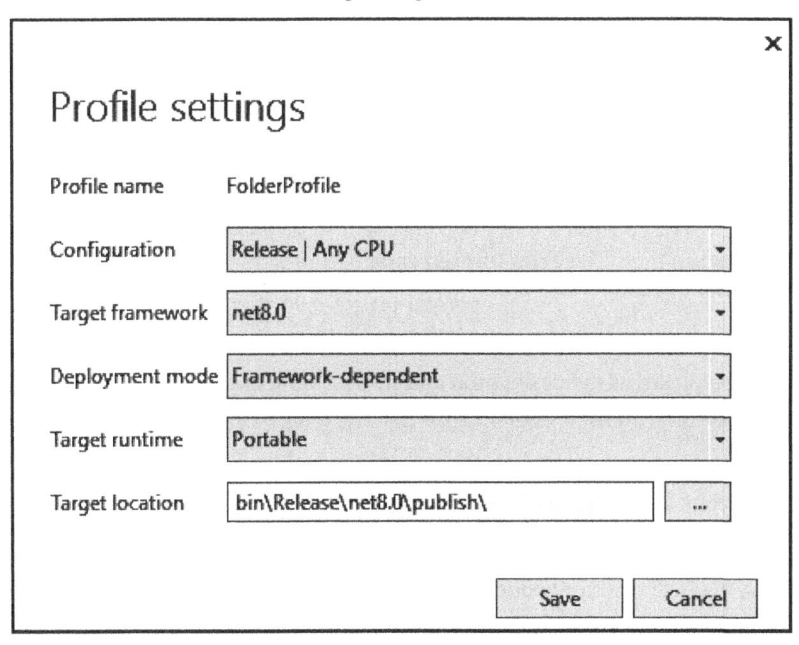

Figure 13.2: The Profile settings dialog

You can tweak the profile a lot here. Let's walk through the options:

- **Configuration**: You can choose any configuration you might have defined in your project. By default, these are the **Debug** and **Release** configurations. I suggest that you use **Release** for deployments.

- **Target framework**: Here, you can choose any compatible and installed framework you want for your application. Just leave this set to what you used when you were building your system.

- **Deployment mode**: Here, you can choose between **Framework-dependent** and **Self-contained**. If you pick **Framework-dependent**, the application will assume the .NET runtime is installed on the target machine. However, if you select **Self-contained**, all needed assemblies will be part of the publication. Your package will be much bigger since it contains everything you need from the .NET runtime. However, it does not rely on others to install the .NET runtime.
- **Target runtime**: This is where you decide on the architecture of the target. If you know what architecture that machine is, you can choose it from the drop-down menu. This results in more optimized code but restricts where you can use it. For instance, if you decide to use Win-X64, you cannot deploy your code to a Linux machine. If you do not want to make that decision, leave it set to **Portable**.
- **Target location**: This is the location where the files will be copied.

Suppose you decided to go with the **Self-contained** option. In that case, you get three additional choices: **Produce Single file**, **Enable ReadyToRun compilation**, and **Trim unused code**.

The first option is self-explanatory: you get one big file instead of dozens of small files. **ReadyToRun** is a form of **ahead-of-time** (**AOT**) compilation. This means the code is pre-compiled and thus starts faster. It is not a real AOT compilation: the resulting files contain both the compiled code and the IL. Still, it saves startup time. The **Trim unused code** option removes all code from the runtime you don't need. Selecting this option makes the final package a lot smaller.

Make your changes and then click **Save**. After that, click **Publish**. When Visual Studio is finished, go to the folder you picked as the destination and inspect what has happened (*hint*: you can click on the **Target location** value in the **Publish Profile** dialog to open an **Explorer** window and go to the location directly).

All that's left is to copy the resulting files to the target machine. Then, you can run it on that machine to see if everything is working fine and you are ready.

Congratulations: you just deployed your application!

Publishing using the CLI

The Visual Studio wizard is very good at helping you build the profile. Still, if you already know what you're doing or want to make publishing part of a pipeline, you can use the CLI to do the same.

The base command is simple – in the directory where you have your `.csproj` file, just run the following command:

```
dotnet publish
```

This command takes all the default settings in the dialog box and uses them to publish your application. Of course, you can change what `publish` does: all you have to do is supply the correct parameters. The following table shows the most common ones and their possible values. Most parameters have two variants – a full parameter name (often preceded by two dashes) and a shorthand (often preceded by one dash):

Parameter	Description	Possible Values
`-o`/`--output`	The output directory to place the published artifacts in	The directory where you want to place the published application
`--sc`/`--self-contained`	Includes the runtime with your application	-

`-f`/`--framework`	The target framework you want to deploy to	`net6.0`
		 `net7.0`
		 `net8.0`

`-r`/`--runtime`	The target runtime to publish for	`win-x64`
		 `linux-x64`
		 `linux-arm`

`-c`/`--configuration`	The build configuration	`Release` `Debug`

Table 13.1: dotnet publish options

If you decide to build a self-contained deployment, you can add three more parameters:

Parameter	Description
`-p:PublishSingleFile=true`	Creates a single file
`-p:PublishReadyToRun=true`	Compiles to Ready To Run AOT binaries
`-p:PublishTrimmed=true`	Removes all unnecessary code from the binaries

Table 13.2: Self-Contained extra options

You could specify that you do not want these options by setting them to `False`, but I suggest that you omit that parameter.

So, to publish your console application to a specific folder, create a self-contained deployment in a single file that's ready to run, and trim all unnecessary code for a `win-x64` architecture running on `net.80`. To do so, issue the following code (all on a single line):

```
dotnet publish
  -o d:\temp\publish
  --self-contained
  -f net8.0
  -r win-x64
  -c Release
  -p:PublishSingleFile=true
  -p:PublishReadyToRun=true
  -p:PublishTrimmed=true
```

Now, if you go to the `d:\temp\publish` folder, you can take the file there, copy that to your production machines, and run it. At this point, you can sit back, knowing your hard work is finally being used.

Using Azure DevOps and GitHub

If your code is meant to be used in the cloud, such as on Azure or AWS, you can use Azure DevOps and GitHub. Which one you pick depends on where you currently have your source code. Both DevOps and GitHub allow for **continuous integration and continuous deployment** (**CI/CD**) scenarios.

> **CI/CD**
> The idea with CI/CD is that when you change your source code, the system notices this and builds your software. Then, it can run tests optionally (in my view, it is not optional, but mandatory). After, it automatically deploys the new binaries to the production environment. This way of working means that you can do a lot of minor, incremental updates to your system and get early feedback on what you did. If this fits your use case, it is a great tool!

Let's look at Azure DevOps first.

Deploying to Azure

I assume you have an Azure DevOps project set up, have defined the working process, and have a repo available to host your code.

You can connect Visual Studio to that project if you have done so. In my case, I have created a simple Function App. A Function App is a service that runs in Azure. In this case, I have decided to use a simple HTTP-based trigger. In other words, the function responds to a REST API call and returns a string with a pleasant greeting. This chapter is not about writing Azure Functions but about deploying code, so I won't dive into the details of how the code works. For now, it's a REST API that you call with a parameter called `name`; it returns a friendly greeting containing that name. That's it.

But to make things more interesting, I have called my program `MyFileConverterFunctionApp`. Trust me: it doesn't do anything interesting.

If you have the code up and running locally, it is time to prepare your system for deployment. There are two steps we need to take.

- Create a publish profile
- Publish the system to Azure

Let's get started.

Building the publish profile for Azure DevOps

Before I show you how to deploy your application to Azure, let's review the prerequisites if you want to follow along. First, you need a project to deploy. But besides this obvious prerequisite, these are the things you'll need:

- An Azure account.
- A resource group (mine is called `SystemsProgrammingRg`).
- A Key Vault to store secrets.
- A storage account. We'll need this for deployment later.

Once you have these, you're ready to start the deployment process.

388　The One with the Deployment Dramas

In Visual Studio, right-click on your project's name and select **Publish**. You'll be taken to the following screen:

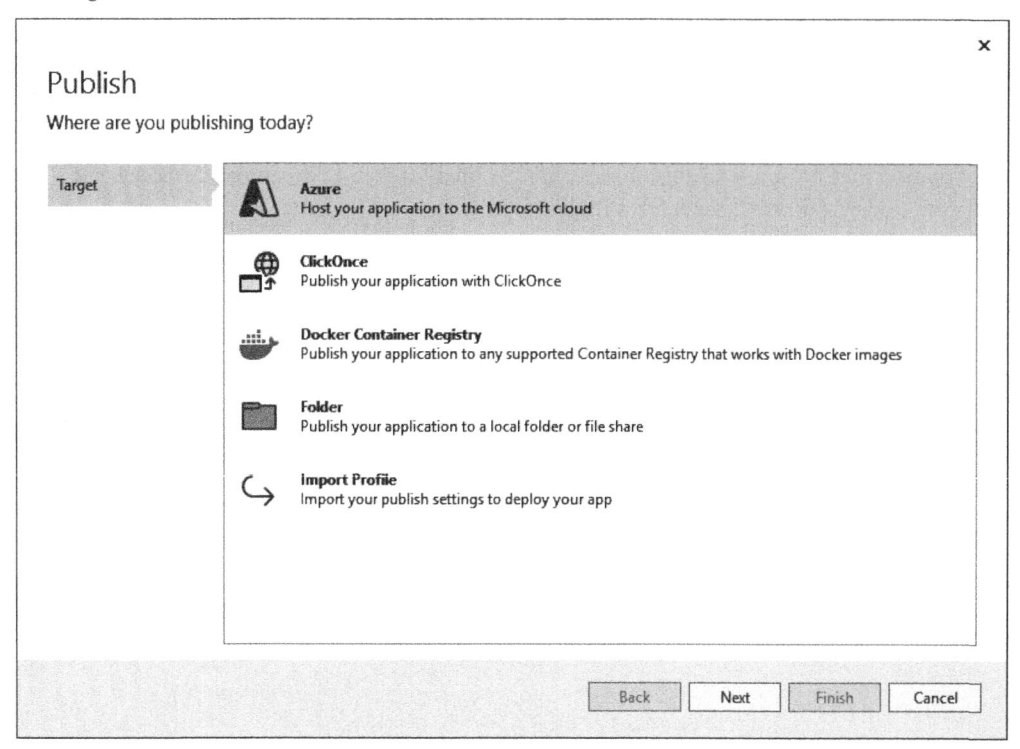

Figure 13.3: Default publishing dialog

Yes, this is the same dialog we saw previously. However, this time, select **Azure** as your target.

The following dialog will ask you what kind of service you want to deploy. I chose **Azure Function App (Windows)**. You could go for a Linux deployment. Don't worry about the container options for now; we will discuss Docker and containers later in this chapter.

Then, we need to tell Visual Studio about the final location of our application. Likely, you won't have a Function App you can use (that wasn't part of the prerequisites, after all), so you can create one now. You'll be presented with a dialog asking you about your environment and preferences. Mine looks like this:

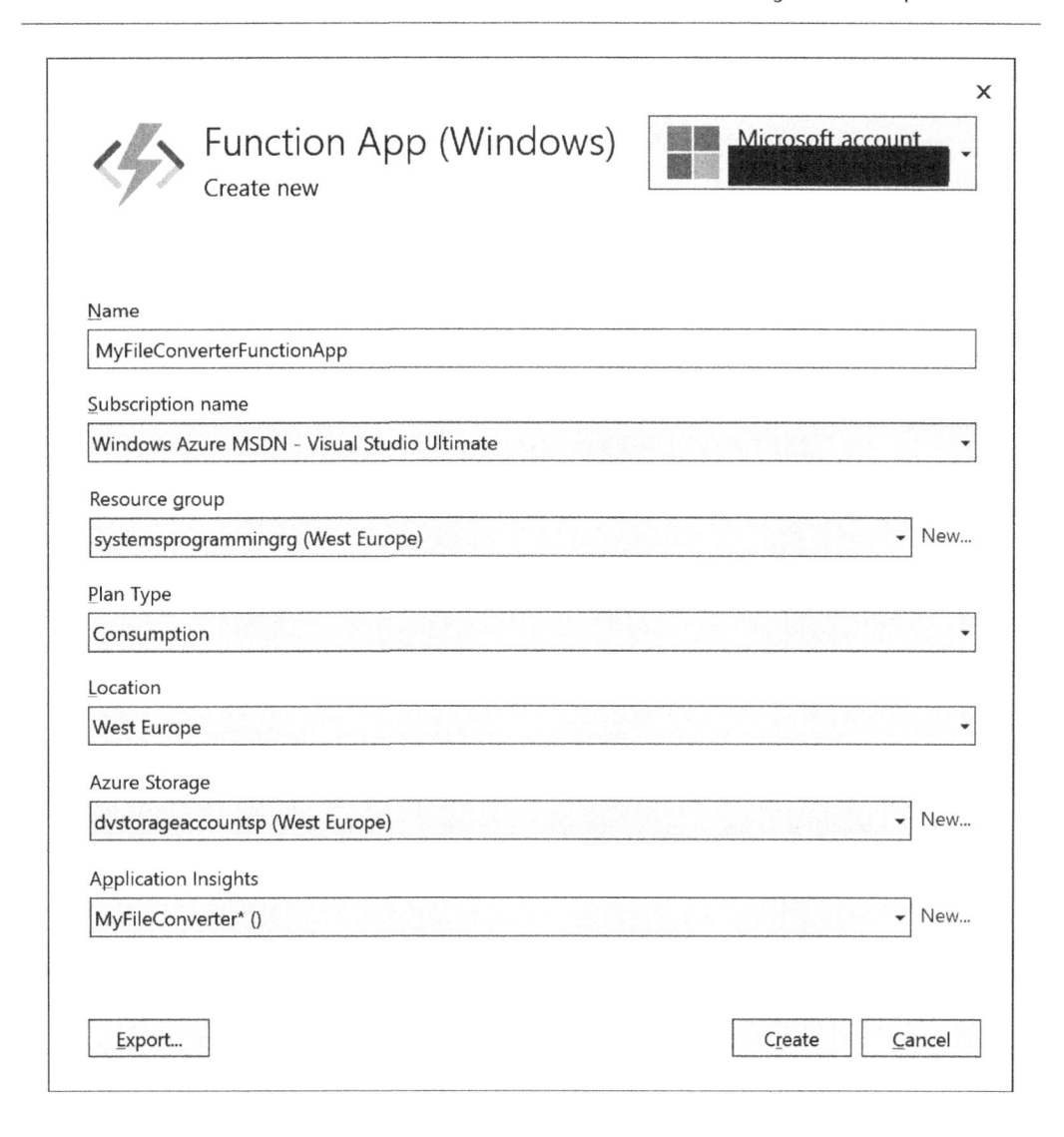

Figure 13.4: Creating a new Function App in Visual Studio

I've blacked out my Azure account details since I want you to use yours. You need to choose the options that are best for you. This dialog is also where you must specify the storage account I told you to create (in my case, it is `dvstorageaccountsp`). I also decided to add **Application Insights**. Using **Application Insights** helps me monitor and troubleshoot my application if needed.

When you click **Create**, the system will build your environment. This takes a while, but we can move to the next screen when it is done. This next screen gives you an overview of all app services in the given resource group and all the deployment slots. Since we haven't deployed yet, this list is empty. Click **Next**:

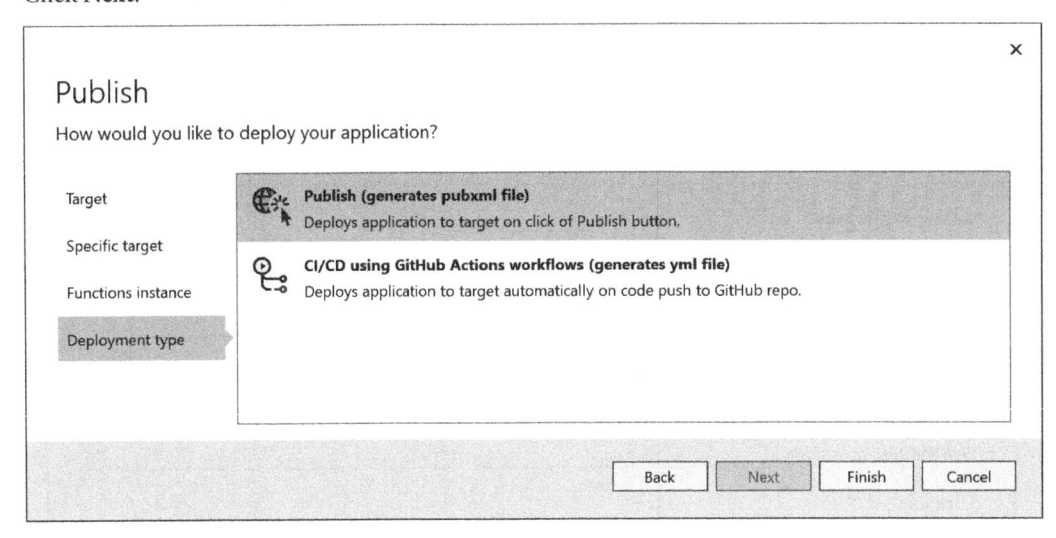

Figure 13.5: Choosing what to generate as a publishing mechanism

We can choose whether to use a publish profile or GitHub Actions here. We will look at GitHub Actions shortly, so let's go with **Publish** for now. Visual Studio will generate the Publish profile for us.

When that is done, we'll get an overview, including a nice, big, inviting **Publish** button:

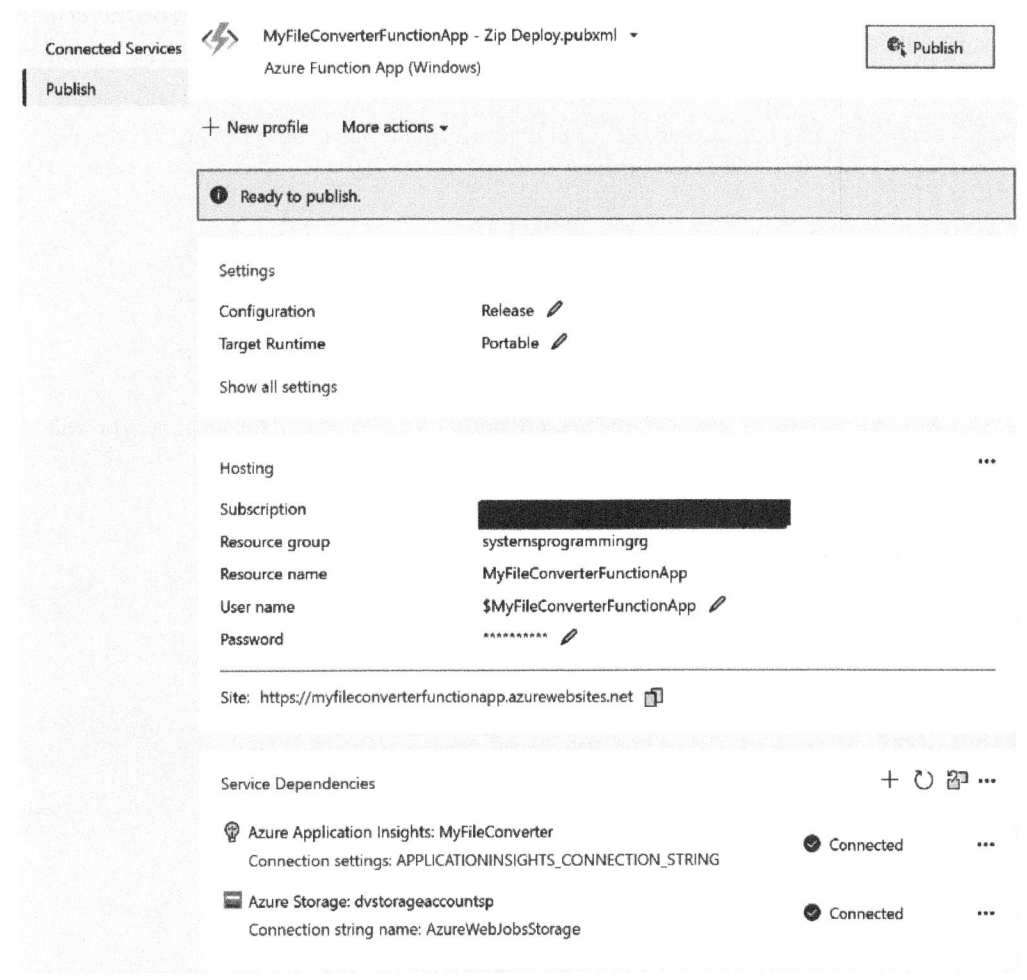

Figure 13.6: Overview of the Publish profile

Let's click that **Publish** button!

Again, this takes a little while, but when your code has been published, you'll get a hyperlink that allows you to go to the resource. You can click that, but it won't be exciting. It's just a web page saying your Function App is up and running.

To see what happened, go to the Azure portal, find your resource group, and locate the Function App we created. There, you can test the function right inside the Azure web portal. Or better yet, open Visual Studio Code (if you have that installed), create a new file called `test.http`, and add the following code:

```
GET https://myfileconverterfunctionapp.azurewebsites.net/api/Function1
Content-Type: application/json

{
    "name": "dennis"
}

###
```

Replace my URL with yours, and click the **Send Request** link at the top of the first line. This will call the server. You'll get some results that should look similar to the following:

```
HTTP/1.1 200 OK
Connection: close
Content-Type: text/plain; charset=utf-8
Date: Mon, 17 Jun 2024 07:07:01 GMT
Content-Encoding: gzip
Transfer-Encoding: chunked
Vary: Accept-Encoding
This HTTP triggered function executed successfully.
```

Your data will be different, but the important part is that we get the `HTTP/1.1 200 OK` result. This shows that our app works!

Enabling continuous integration in Azure DevOps

Pushing to Azure directly from your development environment is convenient. Once you've set up the publishing profile, right-click on your program and click **Publish** to move your changes to Azure.

There is a better way of doing this, though: you can enable CI/CD so that any change you make is automatically deployed.

> ### Branching and CI/CD
>
> In all my samples, I use a single branch: `main`. I push changes from `main` on my machine directly to the online source repositories and let the systems build from that. In a real-world scenario, that is a terrible idea. You should pick up a branching strategy that allows for a good separation between the daily work and the deployments. You need things such as pull requests and merging strategies to preserve the quality of the work. Please don't do what I've done here and have only a single branch.

So, how do we achieve this magic? How do we get our changes "auto-magically" in our production environment? The answer is to use pipelines.

In your Azure DevOps environment, go to the project. You'll see a **Pipelines** tab in the left sidebar. Click that. You'll greeted with a page saying you haven't got any pipelines yet. Let's change that. Click the **Create Pipeline** button. You'll be taken to the following screen:

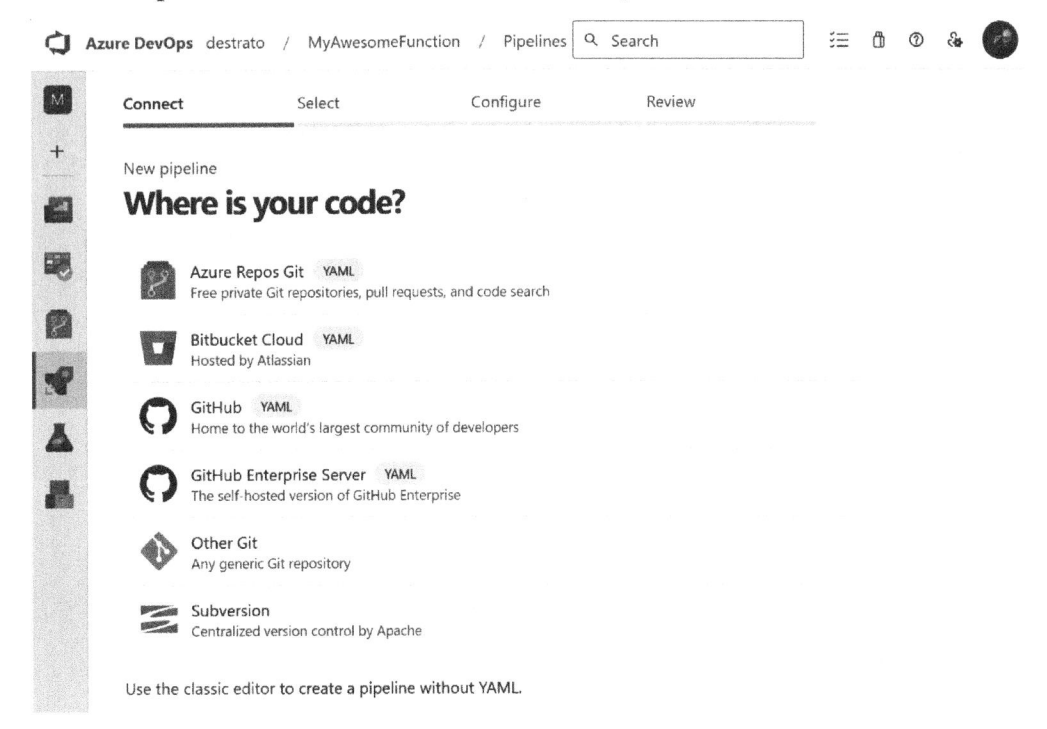

Figure 13.7: Creating an Azure DevOps pipeline

In this case, select **Azure Repos Git**. When you click that, you'll get a dialog asking for your project. Select the repository containing the code you want to deploy automatically.

Once you have done that, you're done. Yes – it was that easy.

You can now run the pipeline manually to see if everything works. Building your solution will take a couple of minutes, but when it's done, you'll see something like this:

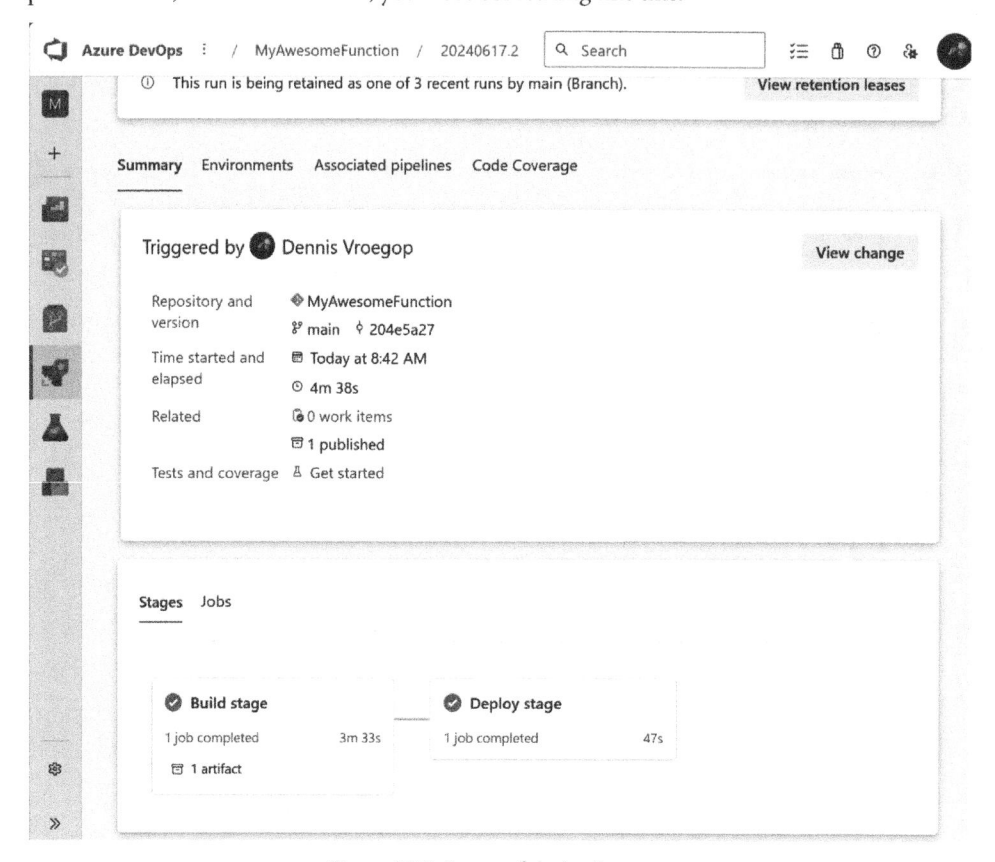

Figure 13.8: Successful pipeline run

To test if your code has been published, rerun the test from Visual Studio Code (or whatever tool you use to test REST calls).

Now, it is time for the cool stuff.

In Visual Studio, make a change to the code. You could do something simple, such as change the text the function returns.

Save your changes and push them to your repository. Once you've done that, go to Azure DevOps and find the pipeline – you'll see that it's already running! Just wait a few minutes until it is done and rerun your tests. You should see that your results have been propagated to the production environment.

That's what I call easy deployment!

In case you were wondering, the pipeline gets all the necessary information from your Publish profile. Remember when I said it was easier to do this if you publish manually first? Now you know why! You should look at the generated YAML files to see how things work. If you're ready to take your deployment skills to the next level, I suggest that you search for this online. Dozens of books have been written on this topic, so I'm sure you can find what you're looking for.

Enabling CI from GitHub

Azure DevOps is a great way to collaborate with people in the same organization. However, if you want to work with people across organizations, GitHub might be a better choice. GitHub is more geared toward open collaboration, such as open source projects. But that doesn't mean you can't have the same continuous integration as you have with Azure DevOps: you can achieve the same thing with GitHub Actions.

Instead of having our source code in Azure DevOps, we host it in GitHub. Originally, GitHub was nothing more than a bunch of repositories, but they have expanded a lot since then. One of the more astonishing things they have added is GitHub actions.

Actions are the equivalent of the pipelines we just looked at. The syntax is different, and they support many more environments than the default pipelines in Azure, but the idea remains the same.

GitHub offers wizards to help you write your Actions, but there is a straightforward way to get our first Action up and running.

Create a new Azure Function project in Visual Studio, but this time store it in your GitHub account. Once you've done that, test it locally and publish it to Azure. I always do this to make sure it works.

Once the publishing is done, create a test for your code using Visual Studio Code or your preferred test tool.

Now, let's set up CI/CD from GitHub!

In the Azure portal, navigate to your function. Then, in the left sidebar, select **Deployment Center**. Then, under **Source**, select **GitHub**. After doing that, you can enter your details. You must log in to GitHub and select the correct organization, repository, and source branch you want to publish.

You'll also need to specify how you wish to authenticate. The GitHub action needs to log in to Azure to deploy your code, so the wizard will create an account for you. Use a user-assigned identity to make this happen. The identity will be created automatically. Once this has happened, click **Save**.

And that is it – you've just set up your first GitHub Action! If you don't believe me, go to your GitHub account, select your project, and go to **Actions**. You should see the action there, and it should show that it has already run as well!

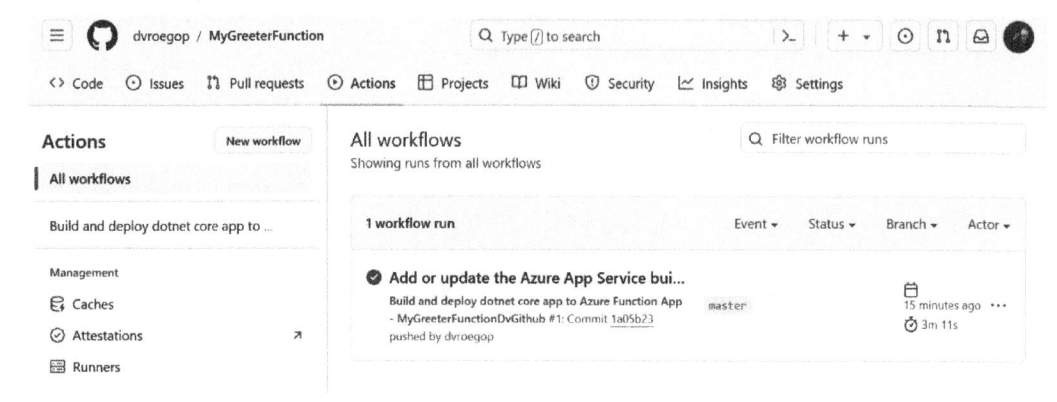

Figure 13.9: First Action

To check that it works as intended, you can change your code, commit the changes to the repository, and see the Action come to life. You can click on the run to see the details. When you're done, it will have updated the code in your Azure environment. Test it and see the changes!

Of course, a lot of our code doesn't run on Azure. As system programmers, we often have to deploy to local hardware. In that case, these techniques won't work. We have to figure out a better way. And there is: using installers!

Building installers with Visual Studio

Installers are nothing new – they were the only way to get an application on your system for a long time. Installers were primarily used to install Windows-based applications on the users' machines. They aren't used that often anymore since this has become obsolete for most use cases. But installers are a great and simple way to get the job done if you wish to install a background worker process and need to do some custom work.

> **Installers and Wix**
>
> The standard Microsoft Installer project works just fine. Still, many developers have moved away in favor of using Wix. Wix is a third-party solution for building installers. It is incredibly versatile, and thus, it is pretty hard to start using. Many books, articles, and how-tos are available to help you get up and running. But in our case, we don't need that complexity. The standard installer is enough for most system programmers. But if you want more control, I urge you to dive into Wix and see what it can do for you.

Suppose you installed the **Microsoft Visual Studio Installer Projects 2022** extension in Visual Studio. In that case, you can add an installer project to your solution.

Let's do that!

Building a simple installer

In the **New Project** dialog, select the **Setup Wizard** template. This will start a typical "next, next, finish" type wizard. There are five steps to follow.

The first one looks like this:

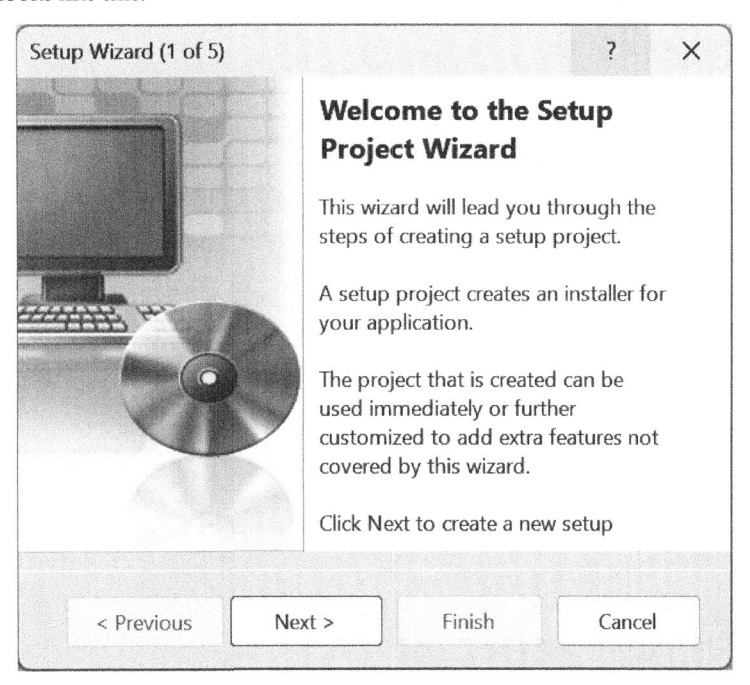

Figure 13.10: Setup Wizard (1 of 5)

The rest of the screens are self-explanatory. The first real question asks you whether you want to build a setup program for a Windows application, a setup program for a web application, or whether you want to create a redistributable package. We want the first option: a setup for a Windows application since that is what a background worker system still is.

Then, the wizard will want to know what you want to install. From the dropdown, select the **Publish Items from...** option. Those are all the executables and dependencies, so we want those.

After, you'll be asked if there are any other files you want to include. There aren't, so just click **Next**. The last step is a summary of the previous steps. Review this page and click **Finish**.

And that's it!

Before we can test it, we need to set some properties. Select your project in the **Solution Explorer** area and look at the **Properties** window. Here, you can fill in all the details you think matter to you. Mine looks like this:

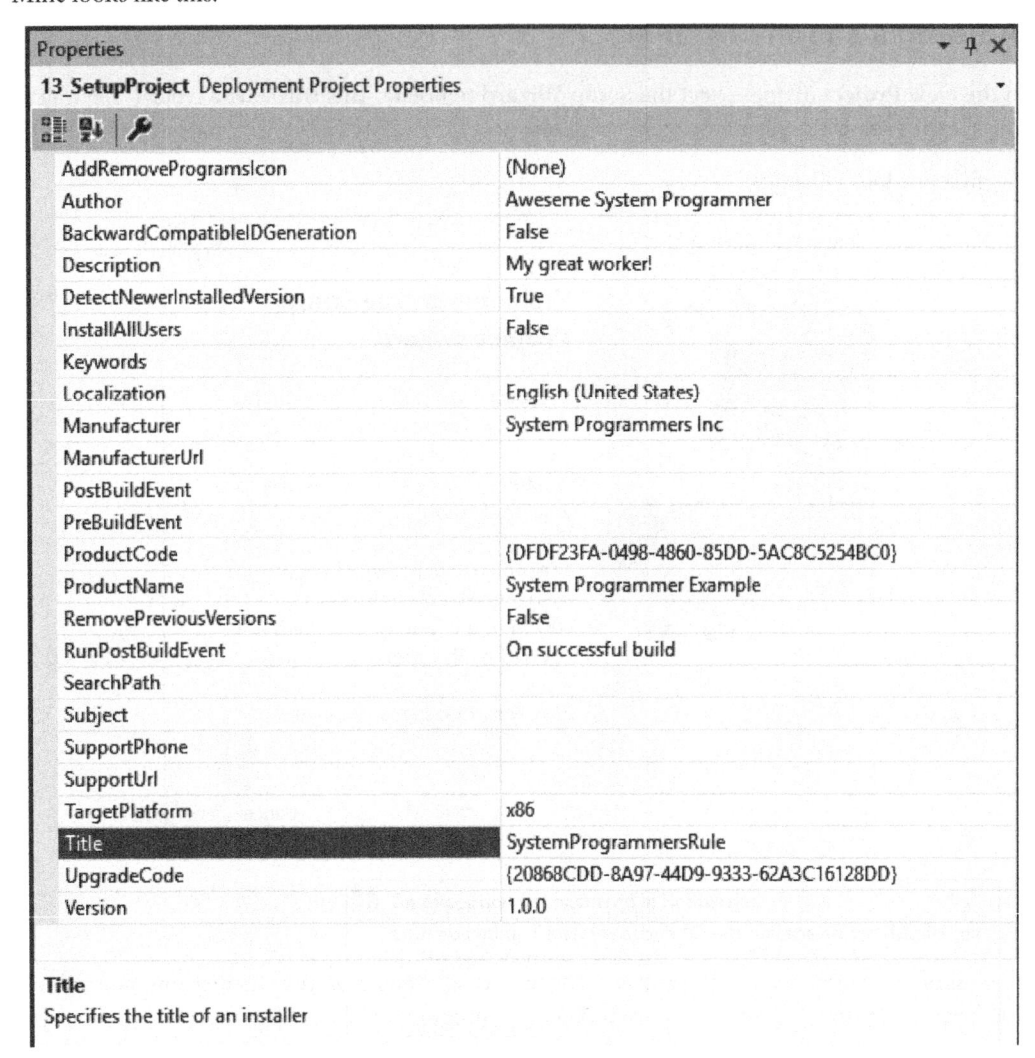

Properties	
13_SetupProject Deployment Project Properties	
AddRemoveProgramsIcon	(None)
Author	Awesome System Programmer
BackwardCompatibleIDGeneration	False
Description	My great worker!
DetectNewerInstalledVersion	True
InstallAllUsers	False
Keywords	
Localization	English (United States)
Manufacturer	System Programmers Inc
ManufacturerUrl	
PostBuildEvent	
PreBuildEvent	
ProductCode	{DFDF23FA-0498-4860-85DD-5AC8C5254BC0}
ProductName	System Programmer Example
RemovePreviousVersions	False
RunPostBuildEvent	On successful build
SearchPath	
Subject	
SupportPhone	
SupportUrl	
TargetPlatform	x86
Title	SystemProgrammersRule
UpgradeCode	{20868CDD-8A97-44D9-9333-62A3C16128DD}
Version	1.0.0

Title
Specifies the title of an installer

Figure 13.11: Setting up project properties

You should at least change the **Manufacturer** property: this will also be the name of the folder the installer creates when installing. By default, the installer assumes you're installing an x86 application, which means your systems will be installed in a subfolder of the `C:\Program Files (x86)` folder. If that's not what you want, change the `TargetPlatform` property from **x86** to **x64** to make `C:\Program Files` the default folder. Of course, you should only do that when your application is indeed 64-bit (the **x64** option) instead of the older 32-bit (**x86**) format.

> **Why is 64-bit X64, but 32-bit X86?**
>
> Sometimes, people get confused by these names. People seem to get that X64 means 64-bit, but why on earth is 32-bit called X86? The answer is rather simple: X64 indeed is just 64-bit, but the X86 refers to the original Intel 8086 processor from long ago, when machines ran 16-bit or at most 32-bit software. It's just a weird thing that you now know and can brag about to your friends!

It's time to test it all out!

Right-click on your **Setup** project, select **Build**, and see if everything builds. If it does, you can right-click on the project again, but select **Install** this time. If all goes well, your system will be installed! You can navigate to the folder you chose during installation and see your files there.

To clean up, you only have to click **uninstall** in Visual Studio.

Writing a Custom Action

This is nice, but it's not enough. Especially for us system programmers, several other things need to be done during or after installation. For instance, a worker process must be registered as a Windows service to start automatically. Or let's say we have a secret that must be encrypted before we can store it in a settings file. How would we do that? The answer is we write a Custom Action.

A Custom Action is some code in an external assembly that gets deployed with the Installer and called at the right time.

It's not hard to write them: it's all done in C#. And we know that language!

First, let's discuss what we want to do.

In the previous chapter, we discussed secrets. We discovered we can use the .NET system to generate keys to encrypt and decrypt data. That key would only work on that machine since it is tied to the installed version of Windows for that particular user. That means we must encrypt any secret in the `appsettings` file on the target machine.

So, suppose we deploy an unencrypted secret in a settings file. In that case, we must make sure that we encrypt the target machine during installation.

In my sample, I am just replacing a placeholder with a new `GUID` to show how it's done. But the principle stands.

Add a new Class Library to the solution. However, there is one caveat: select the **.NET Framework** version of the Class Library. The MSI installer uses the "old" .NET framework, so any add-ons must be built with that technology.

Add a reference to **System.Configuration.Install** to the class library project, as I did here:

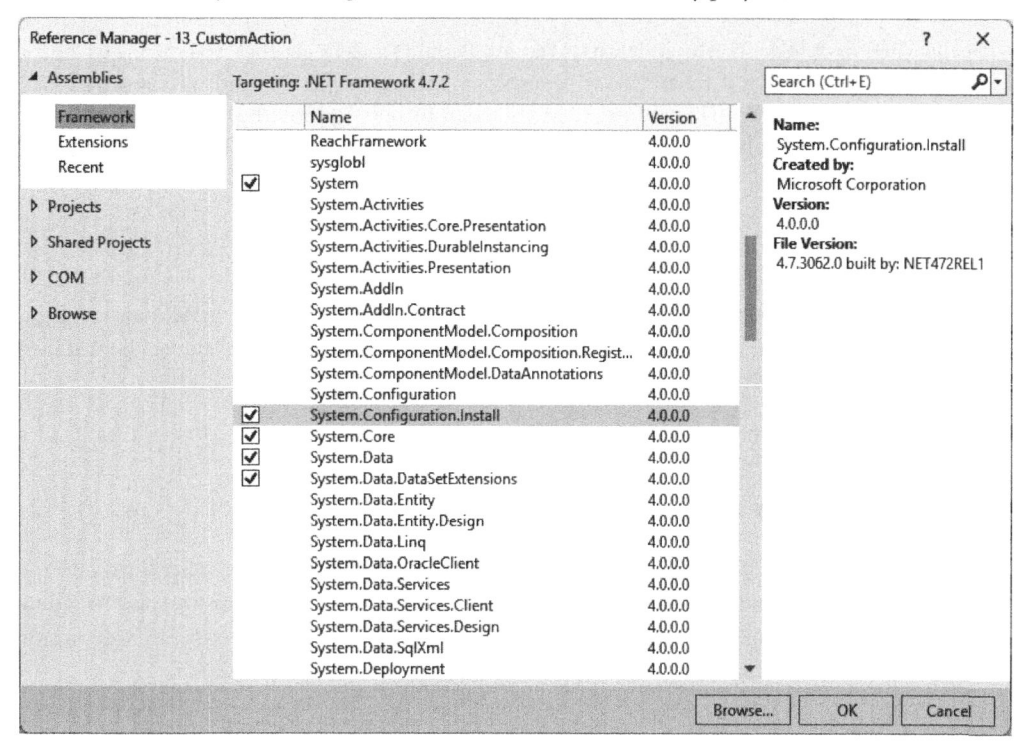

Figure 13.12: Adding the System.Configuration.Install reference

Add a new item to the class library that's of the `Installer` type. You can do that by right-clicking on the project and selecting **Add new item**. In the dialog, you can search for `Installer`. Call it `SecretsInstaller`. This can be seen in the following screenshot:

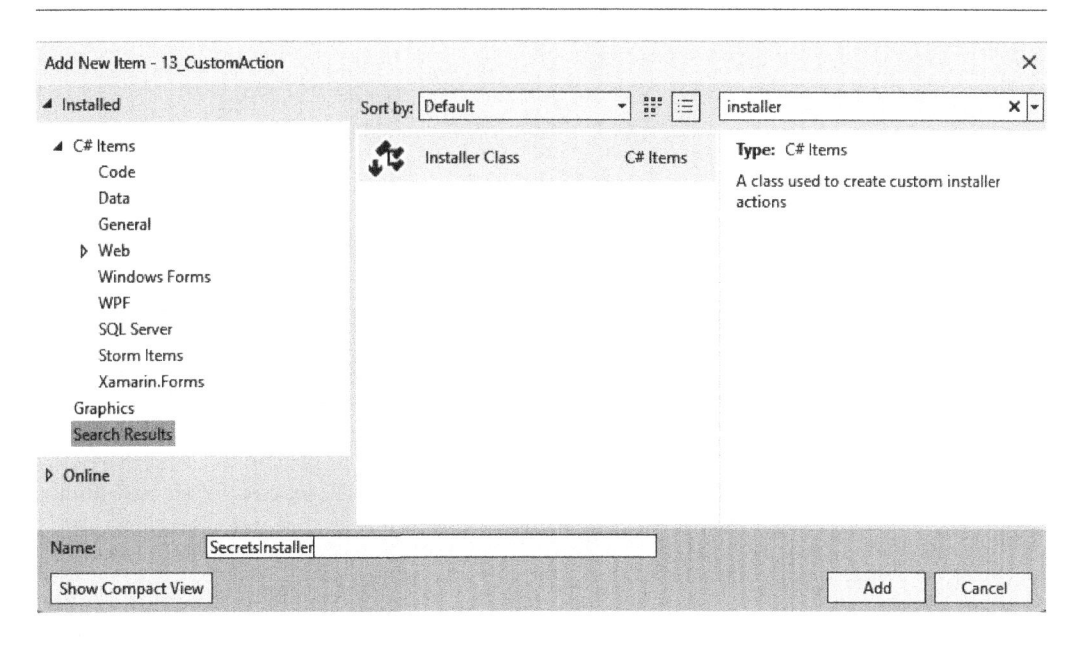

Figure 13.13: Adding an installer class

Change the code so that it looks like this:

```
[RunInstaller(true)]
public partial class SecretsInstaller : Installer
{
    public override void Install(IDictionary stateSaver)
    {
        base.Install(stateSaver);
        var secret = Guid.NewGuid().ToString();
        var targetDir =
            Context.Parameters["targetdir"];
        var appSettingsPath =
            Path.Combine(targetDir, "appsettings.json");
        if (File.Exists(appSettingsPath))
        {
            var appSettingsContent =
                File.ReadAllText(appSettingsPath);
            appSettingsContent =
                appSettingsContent.Replace(
                    "SECRET_PLACEHOLDER",
                    secret);
```

```
                File.WriteAllText(
                    appSettingsPath,
                    appSettingsContent);
        }
    }
}
```

This code gets called by `Installer`. Here, I found the `appsettings.json` file, loaded it in memory, found the `SECRET_PLACEHOLDER` string, and replaced it with a `Guid` value. Finally, I wrote it back to the file.

The interesting part is the line where I get the path to the file. I return to that one later, so keep that in mind.

We need to register this class with `Installer`. Add a new `Installer` class to our class library, `ProjectInstaller`, and change the constructor. This code is even simpler than the last one:

```
[RunInstaller(true)]
public partial class ProjectInstaller : Installer
{
    public ProjectInstaller()
    {
        InitializeComponent();
        var secretsInstaller = new SecretsInstaller();
        Installers.Add(secretsInstaller);
    }
}
```

In the constructor, we create an instance of the `SecretsInstaller` class and add it to our `Installer`. This is a list of classes the install system looks at and then calls `Install` on.

That is all the code we need to write. Let's use it!

Incorporating the custom action in the setup

Go back to **Setup program**. Right-click on the project, select **Add...**, then **Project output**. Select the primary output of the **Custom Action** project. This ensures our DLL is part of the files that are being installed on the target machine.

Right-click on **Setup program** again but select **View**, then **Custom Actions...**.

You should see a screen with four categories. This determines when the custom action should be called. These options are as follows:

- **Install**: This is when all files are installed
- **Commit**: This is when the setup has finalized everything
- **Rollback**: When the setup fails, this is called
- **Uninstall**: When the user decides to install, these actions are performed

In our case, we need to use **Install**. Right-click on that and select **Add Custom Action**. Once again, you'll be presented with a dialog showing the target machine's file structure. These are all the locations where our files can end up. Since we added our project output of the custom action to the regular installation, we can find it in the **Application Folder** area. Select the primary output from your Custom Action and click **OK**:

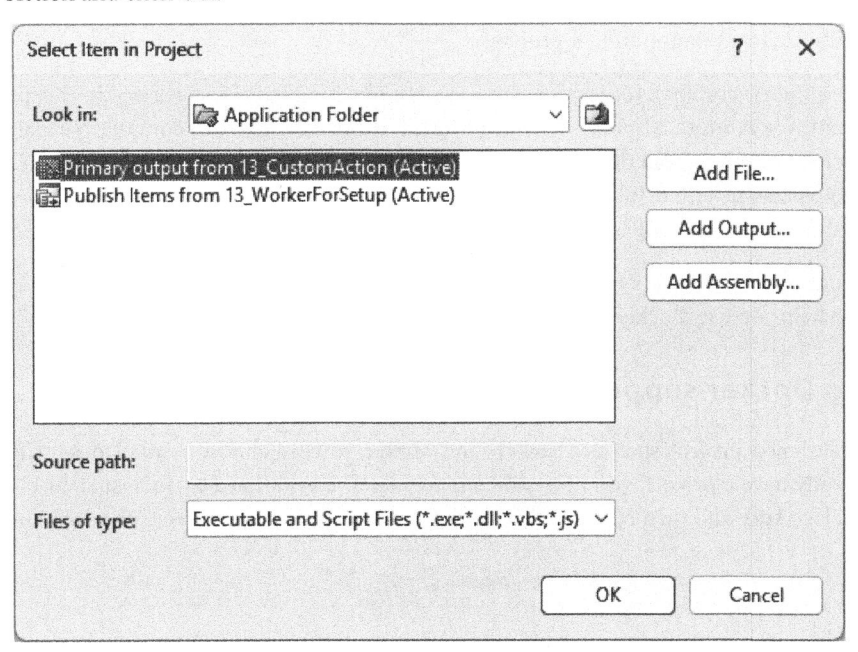

Figure 13.14: Adding the Custom Action assembly

Don't leave the Custom Action view yet. Click on the new item in the **Install** section, and look at the **Properties** area. Here, you can add all sorts of items, but the most important is **CustomActionData**.

This is data from outside that gets passed as parameters to our custom action. Remember when I said I would get back to how I would get the path to the target directory? This is where I do that. Add the following line to that property:

```
/targetdir="[TARGETDIR]\ "
```

Yes. A "backslash, space, closing quote" is at the end of that line. Don't leave those out. Trust me: I spent hours determining why my actions didn't work. The reason: I forgot that extra slash and space. It just doesn't work without it.

And that's all there is to it!

You can now build and then run **Install**.

Look up the folder where the installation took place and marvel at the changes in the JSON file!

Using Docker

The most used excuse developers use when someone complains the system doesn't work as expected is "But it works on my machine!" Of course, the only suitable response is, "We do not ship your machine; we ship software."

Docker aims to be a solution to that problem.

Docker is a highly complex topic. If you're unaware of what it can do, please skip this part of this chapter until you're more familiar with it. In short, Docker can act like a complete virtual machine. This principle means you can develop on that virtual machine, test on that virtual machine, and then deploy that virtual machine. In other words, if it works on that machine, it will work everywhere. The reason it will work everywhere is that with Docker, we ship your machine. Well, the virtual one, at least.

Visual Studio has completely embraced Docker. The IDE comes packed with handy add-ons and wizards to help you use Docker.

Adding Docker support to your background worker

If you create a new project, such as a background worker, you can choose to add Docker support. But if you already have a project, you must add support later. It's not hard to do: just right-click on the project, select **Add**, and then click **Docker support**. You can choose between **Windows** and **Linux**:

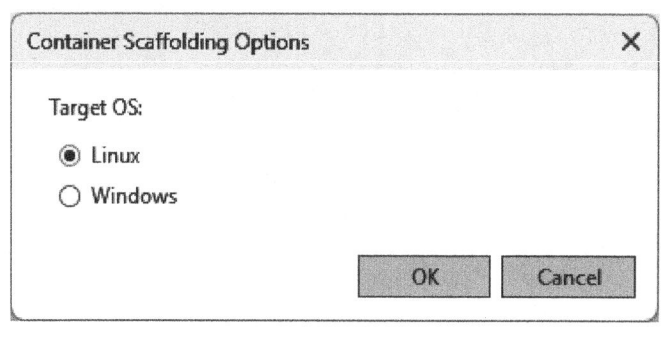

Figure 13.15: Adding Docker to an existing project

> **Docker – using Windows or Linux?**
>
> If you've been working with Visual Studio for some time, you will likely choose Windows over Linux. After all, you probably know that platform very well. Why should you move to Linux? However, containerization comes from the Linux world: it is baked into the core of the operating system. Linux is a far better platform for containers than Windows. If you don't need Windows features, I suggest that you take Linux as the base container. Your apps will benefit from that if you decide to use Docker.

When you do this, a lot of things happen:

- A new file called `Dockerfile` is added to the project
- The `launchSettings.json` file is changed to add Docker
- In the background, all the necessary support images are installed
- The default start action is set to **Container** (Dockerfile)

If you start debugging, Visual Studio will build the Docker image with your binaries and start a container. You can add breakpoints to your code, and Visual Studio will also ensure the debugger is deployed in the container. Hence, it knows how to tunnel the debug information back and forth. The whole process is streamlined: you hardly notice you're running on a Docker image instead of your host machine.

Deploying your Docker images

Once you've finished working on your code base and are ready to deploy it, you must figure out where to deploy it. There are three options:

- Use Docker Hub. This is the standard repository where you can store your images.
- Use Azure/AWS/Google Cloud to store your images. These are much more secure since you control these environments. For instance, you can create a container registry in Azure and then upload your images. Everybody in your organization can then pull that image and run it locally.
- Use your own repository. Suppose you don't want to depend on a cloud provider but want complete control over where your images are. In that case, you can build your own repository.

The third option is the most used one for our scenarios. Of course, you can use Docker Hub or Azure. Nothing is getting in your way. It's just that for the things we build, the third option is probably the best.

Building an actual repository is hard. But the good news is that someone else has already done it. And they have put it in a Docker image. So, all we have to do is download that image and start it up.

But before we do that, we need to think about security. There are many ways to secure the repository, but the easiest (and least secure) way is to assign a username/password. You need some code to generate those, but don't worry: there's a Docker image for that.

First, create a folder named `C:\Auth`. Then, run the following command:

```
docker run --rm --entrypoint htpasswd httpd:2 -Bbn yourusername
yourpassword > C:\auth\htpasswd
```

This command downloads the `http:2` image and runs it, gives it a username of `yourusername` and a password of `yourpassword` (I suggest that you use other values for those parameters), and stores the result in the `htpasswd` file in the `c:\auth` folder.

Now, we can start the repository. Run the following command, all on one line:

```
docker run -d -p 5000:5000
   --name registry
   -v c:\auth:/auth
   -e "REGISTRY_AUTH=htpasswd"
   -e "REGISTRY_AUTH_HTPASSWD_REALM=Registry Realm"
   -e "REGISTRY_AUTH_HTPASSWD_PATH=/auth/
htpasswd"                registry:2
```

This command pulls the `registry:2` image from Docker Hub and starts it. It connects the internal folder, `/auth`, to our `c:\auth` directory and gives it some parameters.

And that's all there is to it.

To use the repo, you must log in:

```
docker login localhost:5000
```

Now, you can tag and push your images there. In my case, my C# worker process image from Visual Studio is called `image13workerfordocker`.

You can tag it by running the following command:

```
docker tag image13workerfordocker:dev localhost:5000/
image13workerfordocker:dev
```

Again, this is all one line. Now, I can push it to my local repository, like this:

```
docker push localhost:5000/image13workerfordocker:dev
```

If I want to reuse my image, I can pull it:

```
docker pull localhost:5000/imagework13fordocker:dev
```

I can use this repository just like I can with the ones at Docker Hub, Azure, AWS, or Google.

Production-ready Docker repository

What I've shown you here is just to show you the uttermost beginnings. The repository isn't secure or stable and doesn't even survive a reboot.

There are several things you need to do if you want to use this in a real production environment:

- Harden the security by using TLS
- Install a volume so that you can store the images instead of using a container (hint: map a volume to `/var/lib/registry`)
- Use actual authentication instead of the single username/password I have just shown you
- Deploy the repository in a fail-safe environment such as Kubernetes

But even with this setup, you can have your own repository. This will ensure that if the code works on your machine, it works everywhere!

Next steps

In this chapter, we discussed many ways you can get your software from your machine to other machines. Some were easy, others were hard. To be honest, this chapter was more about helping you start thinking about deployment. Each topic could fill hundreds of pages. For instance, I mentioned Wix. Well, dozens of books have been written on Wix alone. We discussed CI/CD in Azure in a couple of pages. It turns out people make a complete career out of that topic. We also looked at Docker: people spend weeks, if not months, getting up to speed on that topic.

There are many ways you can get your code out there, and this chapter only scratched the surface.

I wanted to show you the most common ones that fit scenarios we will most likely run into. It is up to you to determine which is the best for your use case and then dive deeper into it.

But before I let you go, I need to say something about the dialog regarding Docker. The dialog asked if you wanted to use Linux or Windows. I suggest that you choose Linux as often as you can. If you think, "But I know very little about Linux," don't worry. The next chapter will tell you all you need to know about that operating system. So, let's have a look, shall we?

14
The One with the Linux Leaps

Systems Programming in C# on Linux

I remember the time when only the really cool kids worked on Linux. Windows was for serious people. That was where the work was done. Sure, many servers ran Unix or Linux, but those working on those platforms were considered somewhat weird. They usually had beards, wore sandals, and spoke a language none of the rest of the people had ever heard.

OK, maybe I am exaggerating. Perhaps this shows how I felt about Linux or how intimidated I was by that operating system and its users. Linux has always been considered a more mature but complex operating system. It is more secure, faster, and better to maintain. It is also more complicated to use. Most of the work is done in the command line, although graphical user interfaces exist.

These days, things are different. Linux is everywhere. And for good reasons, too – Linux is an excellent operating system to run your system in the current online, connected world.

With the introduction of **.NET Core** and **.NET 5**, developers who traditionally only used Windows can also compile their code to run on Linux. And that opens up a whole new world.

Of course, there are downsides. Linux is more complex than Windows, especially if you have worked on Windows for a long time. Even though .NET can run on Linux, not all the classes and tools you might be used to are available.

This chapter is meant to help you get on your way should you want to run your .NET applications on Linux. Don't worry – I do not want you to start wearing sandals or become a typical 1970s-type developer. That is entirely optional. So, let's get your inner penguin out and start hacking on Linux!

In this chapter, we will ask the following questions:

- What is Linux?
- How do I do basic things in Linux?
- How do I develop for Linux?
- How do I deploy to Linux?
- How can I write background services for Linux?

This chapter contains some history, some theory, and a lot of practical information and samples. Are you ready to follow along?

Technical requirements

You will find all the code in this chapter in our repository at this URL: https://github.com/PacktPublishing/Systems-Programming-with-C-Sharp-and-.NET/tree/main/SystemsProgrammingWithCSharpAndNet/Chapter14.

If you want to follow along, you need a Linux machine. But during development, you actually do not need that. All you need is WSL. **WSL** stands for **Windows Subsystem for Linux**. The official name is WSL2, as we are at version 2 these days, but let's stick with WSL here.

WSL is a lightweight virtual machine that runs a Linux distribution (I will explain what that is later on) on your Windows machine. You can quickly move to that machine and use it like a "real" Linux machine. You can even deploy directly from Visual Studio and debug your apps on WSL.

To install WSL, follow these steps:

1. In Powershell, use the `wsl --install` command (you have to be an administrator to do this). Be aware that this might take a couple of gigabytes of hard disk space on your machine.

And that's it. No *step 2*. You can now go to the **Start** menu and search for Ubuntu. That looks like this:

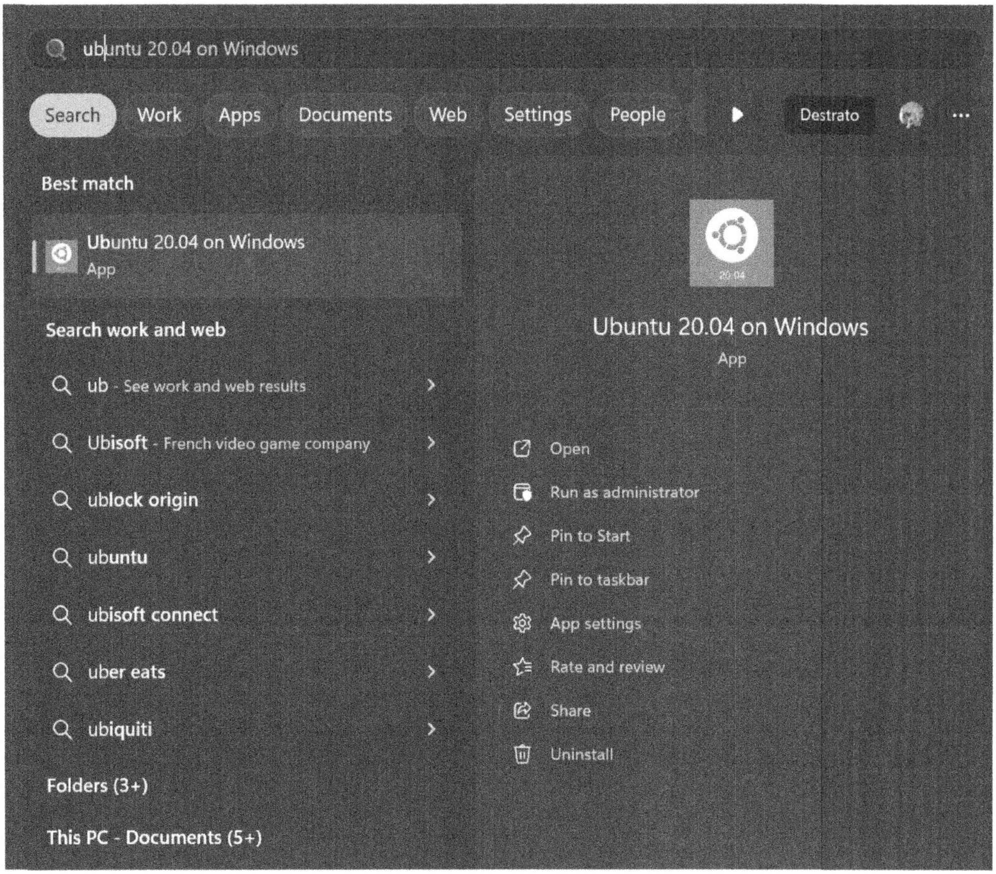

Figure 14.1: Running Ubuntu from the Windows Start menu

Alternatively, you can install other versions of Linux, but I will use **Ubuntu 20.04** in this book. What you pick doesn't matter; just do what you feel most comfortable with.

Alternatively, you can create a virtual machine using HyperV, deploy a Docker container with Linux, get a second machine to install Linux on, or run Linux from a bootable USB stick. The choice is yours.

An overview of Linux

Before discussing how to program for Linux, we should discuss what it is. The short answer is that it is an operating system. While that is absolutely true, it does not sufficiently explain all that Linux can do. I can say that a bike is a transporting device, but that also applies to the Saturn 5 rocket that took astronauts to the moon. We need a bit more information.

A short history of Linux

The history of Linux is quite fascinating. Understanding the timeline and circumstances under which it was developed can help you appreciate some of the design decisions and choices. So, here is a short timeline of the history of Linux:

1. **Early beginnings**

    - In 1983, Richard Stallman announced the GNU Project. The idea was to create a free Unix-like operating system. Unix was the leading operating system in those days. The GNU Project developed many components, but one key piece, the kernel, was missing.

    - In 1987, Andrew S. Tanenbaum created Minix. Minix was a Unix-like system. It was intended for educational purposes and was very popular among students. One of them was a young man named Linus Torvalds.

2. **The birth of Linux**

    - In 1991, Linus Torvalds, a student at the University of Helsinki in Finland, started developing his kernel. It was just a hobby; he wanted to have something to do. On August 25, 1991, he announced his project in a newsgroup posting, seeking input from others. This is what later became the Linux kernel.

    - On 5th October, 1991, Torvalds released version 0.02 of Linux. It could run Bash (a terminal) and GCC (a C-compiler).

3. **Development and growth**

    - In 1992, Linux was released under the GNU **General Public License** (**GPL**), allowing anyone to use, modify, and distribute the software.

    - In the mid 1990s, Linux snowballed in popularity. Distributions, such as Slackware and Debian, were both released in 1993.

    - In 1994, Linux version 1.0 was released. It was a significant milestone; this was the first stable release.

4. **Commercial and community expansion**

    - In 1996, Tux the Penguin was chosen as the official Linux mascot.

    - The late 1990s saw companies such as Red Hat and SUSE begin to offer commercial Linux distributions. Since these also included support, this was the moment enterprises jumped on board.

    - In 1999, IBM announced support for Linux.

5. **The 21st century and mainstream adoption**

    - In 2001, version 2.4 of the Kernel was released, including USB, PC cards, and other hardware support.
    - 2002–2003 saw major companies such as HP and Dell offering Linux on their servers.
    - In 2004, Canonical released its Linux distribution, which was way more user-friendly. This enabled the general public to use it as well.
    - In 2005, Linus Torvalds released a side project called Git. Yes, that Git. The tool you probably use every day. Git was an essential tool for Linux development.

6. **The modern era**

    - In 2011, Linux was the dominant operating system in the server market. It powers the majority of web servers, including those of major companies such as Google, Amazon, and Facebook.
    - In 2013, Google released Android, a mobile, Linux-based smartphone operating system.
    - In the 2020s, Linux continues to dominate the server space, cloud infrastructure, supercomputing, and IOT devices.

One of the key factors that led to the success of Linux was its open source nature. Everybody can look at the sources, download them, adopt them, and do whatever they want. And it is and always will be for free.

Will all this in mind, it is no wonder that we, as system programmers, also need to learn about Linux.

What is Linux?

The name Linux itself can be confusing at times. Let me shed some light on that and help you clarify things.

The Linux kernel

The **Linux kernel** is the heart of what we call Linux. It is the core of the operating system. The kernel manages the systems' hardware and resources, such as memory and CPUs. Some of the key responsibilities of the Kernel are as follows:

- **Process management**: It decides which process runs and for how long
- **Memory management**: It keeps track of every byte in the systems' memory and manages the allocation and deallocation of memory space
- **Device management**: It manages communications with all devices attached to the system
- **System calls**: It also provides an interface between the aforementioned systems and the applications that want to use them

The kernel is comparable with the **Windows NT kernel**.

Other components

Linux usually comes with a set of other components as well. Some of the most commonly found components are as follows:

- **System libraries**: These are essential collections of functions that programs can use to perform tasks, such as file handling and mathematical computations. A good example is the GNU C library, the foundation for most C or C++ programs.
- **System utilities**: These are basic programs necessary for system management. An example is the `init` program. This program manages system startup. Other examples are Bash, a shell program, and various command-line tools.
- **Daemons**: These are background services that perform various tasks, such as handling print jobs, managing network connections, or scheduling tasks.

> **Bash? What is that?**
>
> Names of software or parts in Linux differ from the names you'll find in Windows. Windows is more serious in its naming, while Linux is more playful. **Bash**, for instance, stands for **Bourne Again Shell**, named after its creator, Stephen Bourne. He wanted to create a better shell than the most used shell back then – the Thompson shell. So he merged "born again" with his own surname and came up with this new name. You'll find these kinds of names a lot when working with Linux!

There are a lot more components, and sometimes, the choice of where to place components might seem arbitrary. But in general, this distinction works.

Added software

When you install Linux, you often get a lot more software. These are the user-facing programs and the software that the users interact with. There are command-line-based programs and GUI-based programs. Which ones are distributed depends on what package you have downloaded or purchased.

Distributions

A Linux **distribution**, or "**distro**" for short, is a complete operating system package that includes the Linux Kernel, system libraries, utilities, daemons, and added software. Each distro has its own set of characteristics and is aimed at different kinds of users. In this chapter, I will use Ubuntu. You can easily install this distro – search for `Ubuntu` in the Windows Store and click **Get**.

Hundreds of distros are available, mostly for free, but some you have to pay for. The following table is a list of the most used distros, grouped by usage category:

Category	Distribution	Description
General desktop use	Ubuntu	Known for its user-friendliness, large community, and robust support
	Linux Mint	Based on Ubuntu, popular due to its ease of use and traditional desktop environment
	Fedora	Known for its cutting-edge features and close relationship with Red Hat
Lightweight	Lubuntu	A lighter, faster, and energy-saving variant of Ubuntu that uses LXQt
	Xubuntu	An official Ubuntu variant that uses the XFCE desktop environment
	Puppy Linux	Extremely lightweight, designed to run on older hardware
Privacy and security	Tails	Aimed at preserving privacy and anonymity, based on Debian
	Qubes OS	Focuses on security through isolation, using virtual machines
	Kali Linux	Designed for penetration testing and security auditing
Server and enterprise	CentOS/ AlmaLinux/Rocky Linux	Community-supported rebuilds of Red Hat Enterprise Linux (RHEL)
	Ubuntu Server	The server edition of Ubuntu, known for its ease of use and broad support
	Debian	Known for its stability and robustness, often used on servers
Development	Arch Linux	Favored by developers for its simplicity and control
	Fedora	Offers cutting-edge software and technologies
	openSUSE	Known for its developer-friendly tools and YaST configuration tool
Media production	Ubuntu Studio	Specifically tailored for audio, video, and graphic design
	AV Linux	Custom-built for multimedia content creators
	Fedora Design Suite	Comes with a range of open source creative applications
Education	Edubuntu	An Ubuntu flavor designed for use in classrooms and educational environments

Category	Distribution	Description
	Kano OS	Designed for use with the Kano computer kit, aimed at teaching kids how to code
	Debian Edu/Skolelinux	A custom Debian Pure Blend, designed for educational use
Gaming	SteamOS	Developed by the Valve Corporation for gaming consoles
	Ubuntu GamePack	Comes pre-installed with many games and emulators
	Lakka	A lightweight Linux distribution that transforms a small computer into a full-blown game console
Special Purpose	Raspberry Pi OS (formerly Raspbian)	Optimized for the Raspberry Pi hardware
	Clear Linux	Developed by Intel, optimized for performance and security on Intel hardware
	Tiny Core Linux	An extremely small, highly modular, and flexible Linux distribution

Table 14.1: Some of the available Linux distros

As you can see, there is a distro tailored just for you. However, remember that the kernel is probably the same or at least very similar for all of them. The biggest difference between the distros is the added software and the configuration you get out of the box.

A quick primer to use Linux

In the early days of my career, I knew I was very good with computers. They held no surprises for me. I knew how to control them; I was the master of the machine. That lasted until I sat behind my first Linux machine. That was when I realized I only knew a lot about Windows and how to use that platform. I was at a loss. I could not even get the contents of a directory on the screen.

To my defense, this was in the early 1990s. Linux was just released, and we did not have the wealth of information online that we have today. The World Wide Web had just been invented, search engines did not exist, and information was hard to find. Today, things are more straightforward – there are tons of sources out there that can help you get up to speed with something new.

I'm going to help you learn some of the basics so that you can play around with Linux without pulling your hair out. I am not going to discuss any of the available GUI systems. There are plenty of them, and some of them are very good. But using them is as easy as using Windows. Honestly, real work happens when you are on a command line. So, that is what I focus on from now on.

I also assume you have figured out how to install WSL on your machine and can open a Terminal. I also have a tip – install the Windows Terminal from the Windows Store. The Windows Terminal is an excellent tool for opening different shells, including Linux ones. This is what it looks like:

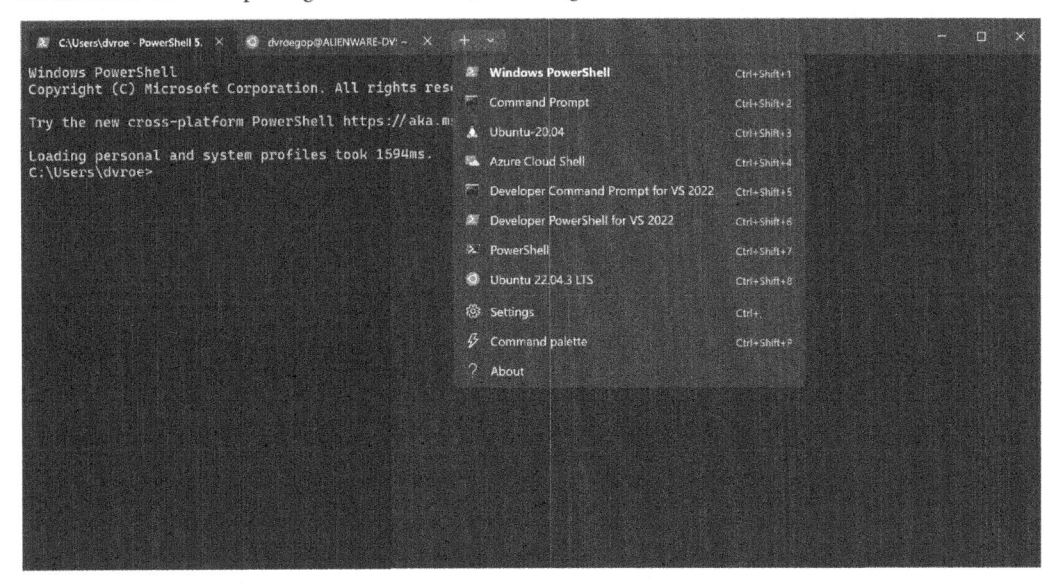

Figure 14.2: A Terminal application opening a new Linux shell

You can open multiple windows, each with its shell. You can open a PowerShell window next to a Ubuntu window and even the old-style Command Prompt. You have everything you need ready at your fingertips.

> **Casing – beware!**
>
> Before we dive into the commands, there is one thing you should know – *Linux is case-sensitive; Windows is not*. Trust me – this has tripped up many people in the past and will probably confuse people in the future. So, keep this in mind. A directory can have two files with the same name that only differ in casing. It is possible to have the `MyAwesomeApp` and `myAwesomeApp` files in the same place. If you come from a Windows background, you will often make this mistake; you cannot find a file that you know is there, which I see a lot. Check your casing.

If you have chosen a Terminal, open the shell for Linux. Now, you are ready to try out some commands!

Basic commands

I want to give you a list of the most used Linux commands with their equivalents on Windows. But before diving into those lists, I want to share the best command – `man`. This keyword opens the manual pages for any command you want to learn more about. For instance, the equivalent of `dir` on Windows is `ls`. Type `man ls` and press *Enter* to learn more about it. Doing this results in pages and pages of information about the command, parameters, and examples. This works for almost all commands.

Basic navigation and file management

Navigating the filesystem is probably essential when using an OS. For Linux, you should know these commands:

Task	Windows command	Linux command	Description
List directory contents	`dir`	`ls`	Lists files and directories in the current path
Change directory	`cd`	`cd`	Changes the current directory
Print working directory	`cd`	`pwd`	Displays the current directory
Copy files	`copy`	`cp`	Copies files
Move/rename files	`move`	`mv`	Moves or renames files
Delete files	`del` or `erase`	`rm`	Removes files
Delete directories	`rmdir` or `rd`	`rmdir` or `rm -r`	Removes directories
Create directories	`mkdir`	`mkdir`	Creates directories

Table 14.2: Navigation and file management commands

The commands work more or less as you would expect. So, try them!

File viewing and editing

If you want to learn more about the contents of a file or edit the contents, these commands are there to do just that:

Task	Windows command	Linux command	Description
View file contents	`type`	`cat`	Displays file contents
Edit files	`notepad`	`nano`, `vi`, or `vim`	Edits files
View file contents (paged)	`more`	`less`	Views file contents page by page

Table 14.3: File viewing and editing

A word of warning – if you start using VI or VIM for the first time, ensure that you have a web page open with the commands to use in those tools. Working with those tools can be pretty complicated when you have no experience with them!

System information and processes

If you want to learn more about the system you are on or are keen to learn about the running processes, give these commands a try:

Task	Windows command	Linux command	Description
Display system info	`systeminfo`	`uname -a`	Displays system information
Display process info	`tasklist`	`ps`	Lists running processes
Kill processes	`taskkill`	`kill`	Terminates processes
Show disk usage	`dir or chkdsk`	`df`	Displays disk space usage
Show file size	`dir`	`du`	Displays file and directory sizes

Table 14.4: System information and process commands

These commands are invaluable when you start to write your own software on Linux. Running these commands gives you a lot of information that you might need later on!

Network commands

As system programmers, we often work with networks or have our software communicate over networks. In those cases, it is good to know how to learn more about the network on our systems. These are commands that can help you:

Task	Windows command	Linux command	Description
Ping	`ping`	`ping`	Checks network connectivity
IP configuration	`ipconfig`	`ifconfig` or `ip`	Displays or configures IP network settings
Trace route	`tracert`	`traceroute`	Traces the path to a network host

Table 14.5: Networking commands

Most of these commands are similar to their Windows counterparts, so you should have no problem remembering and using them.

Package management

Many distros come packed with software, but it is very likely your distro might miss something that you may find invaluable. But don't worry – Linux has tools to install them. This is a short list of some of them:

Task	Windows command	Linux command	Description
Install software	Varies (e.g., `msiexec`)	`apt-get install`, `yum install`, or `dnf install`	Installs software packages
Update software	Windows Update	`apt-get update` or `apt-get upgrade`	Updates software packages
Remove software	Varies (e.g., Control Panel)	`apt-get remove`, `yum remove`, or `dnf remove`	Removes software packages

Table 14.6: Package management commands

You will run into these commands a lot more later on in this chapter.

Elevated privileges

Linux is built around security. One of the effects is that you are more or less forced to run all the commands as a regular user. You are not an administrator, even though you logged in as one. You cannot do everything you want.

You can easily change that. You can give yourself root privileges using the `su` command, meaning **super-user**. **Root** here means you are at the top level of all user rights; you can do anything you want. However, don't do that. I have rarely had a reason to become the root of my systems. In the Linux community, becoming root is frowned upon.

If you need to elevate your rights to do something, use the `sudo` command. This command stands for **super-user do**. Let's assume that you start your command with `sudo`. If so, you give the command the root rights it might need once, and then the system immediately returns to the normal privilege. Only the command on that line can use these elevated privileges.

The first time you use `sudo` in a session, you must supply the administrative password you entered when installing your distro. Your system remembers those credentials for the duration of the session, so you do not have to do that every time.

Let me show you how that works. I use the `whoami` command, which provides information about the currently logged-in user. If I use that command, it returns my name. However, when I do that again, I add `sudo` before it, and it returns `root`. Immediately after that, it reverts to returning my name. This screenshot shows that in action:

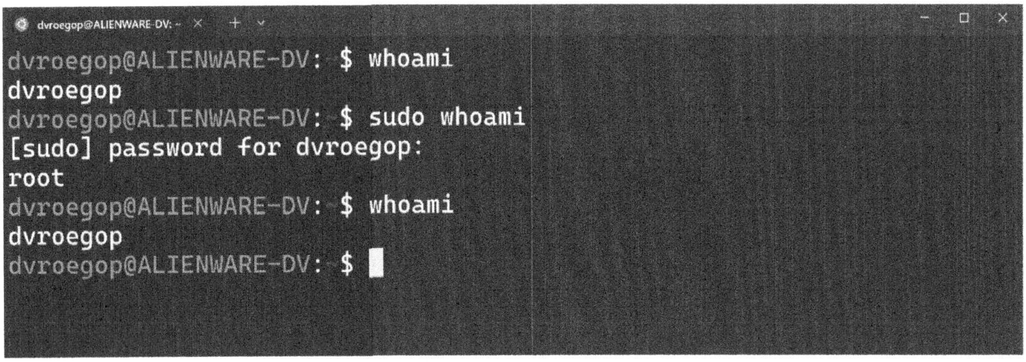

Figure 14.3: Sudo in action

As you can see, it also asks me for my password. If I issue the same or another command and use `sudo`, it will use the cached credentials. But remember that this is only valid in this session. If I open another Terminal window and repeat the same exercise, the system will ask me for my password again.

Using `sudo` is another example of how Linux makes things as secure as possible.

It's useful to know many more commands, but this at least gives you a starting point. Remember that `man` is your friend here!

Now that you can confidently find your way in your Linux distro, it's time to see how we can work with the OS as developers.

Developing for Linux

One of the first pieces of software written for Linux was GCC, created in 1991. **GCC** is the **Gnu C Compiler**, and it was used to build a lot of the software that became part of the first distro later on. You can still use GCC if you want to, but today, there are many other development tools available to use. For instance, Python is part of most distros. So, if you want to use Python, you can type the `python3` command into the terminal, and you are ready to go. But we do not do Python; we do .NET. And that means we have another road to take.

Installing .NET on Linux

I mentioned previously that Linux usually has a lot of development tools pre-installed. However, .NET is not one of those pre-installed environments. The good news is that it is not hard to install.

Before I tell you how to get .NET on the system, I want to discuss my choice of development machines.

I love Visual Studio. I think it is by far the best IDE available. There are others, and I know many people who prefer other tools over Visual Studio, but I am not one of them.

One of the IDEs that many people use is **Visual Studio Code**. And I agree with them that **VS Code** (to use its shorter name) is a great tool. However, I prefer the richness of the complete edition of Visual Studio when I work on a real-world system.

If you prefer VS Code, you can use that, of course. You can install VS Code on many different platforms, including Linux. There are many tutorials online that tell you how to do this.

I have bad and good news if you want to stay with Visual Studio.

The bad news is that you cannot install Visual Studio on a Linux machine. The good news is that you do not have to. You can install it on your Windows machine and then deploy and debug directly on the Linux system. And that is what we will do in the rest of this chapter.

However, to run .NET applications on your Linux system, you must have the Runtime. The Runtime contains all that is needed to run your .NET applications. This is great if you want to prepare your production system for your applications. But if you want to debug and test your applications on a Linux machine, you also need the **.NET SDK**. The SDK contains the Runtime, so you do not need to install both.

Installing the .NET Runtime

Let's discuss installing the Runtime first. Again, you only need the Runtime on machines that will run your software. If you want to compile your code, you need the SDK.

Open a Terminal on your Linux distro (or a Ubuntu Terminal on your Windows machine).

Enter the following commands:

```
sudo apt-get update
sudo apt-get install -y wget apt-transport-https
```

The first command updates all packages on your system. The second one installs the HTTPS transport software if it is not already there. It is probably already on your system, but this ensures that is the case. We need `https` to download the software.

Microsoft ensures all their software is signed, so you can trust it. However, to verify that signature, you need to have their public key. This is how we get that key on our system:

```
wget https://packages.microsoft.com/config/ubuntu/$(lsb_release -rs)/packages-microsoft-prod.deb -O packages-microsoft-prod.deb
sudo dpkg -i packages-microsoft-prod.deb
```

These commands get the keys and install them on our system. Now, we can use them to verify the downloads from Microsoft.

This was all only preparation. Now, it is finally time to install the Runtime. This is how we do that:

```
sudo apt-get update
sudo apt-get install -y dotnet-runtime-8.0
```

First, we make sure everything is updated. Then, we get the Runtime package.

And that's it. If this command finishes, we can test it by running the command:

```
dotnet --list-runtimes
```

You should see the .NET 8 Runtime in the (concise) list of runtimes.

Installing the SDK

If you want to build and debug your Linux distro, you need more software. You must install the SDK. Fortunately, that process is almost the same as installing the Runtime. If you have installed the Runtime, you can enter the following command:

```
sudo apt-get update
sudo apt-get install -y dotnet-sdk-8.0
```

This set of commands first updates all packages and then installs the SDK.

If you haven't installed the Runtime, you first have to repeat all the steps I showed you during the Runtime installation, except for the last one (the installation of the Runtime itself). You still need to update, get, and install the keys.

Test the installation of the SDK by calling the following:

```
dotnet --list-sdks
```

You should now see a list of the SDKS – well, I say list, but you will probably only see one item.

You can further test the installation by doing a quick test, like this:

```
dotnet new console
```

This command creates a new console application. When that is done, do this:

```
dotnet build .
```

This builds .csproj in the current folder. The result ends up in the /bin/Debug/net8.0 folder. The program's name is the same as the folder in which you placed your project. If you didn't create a directory, it is the name of your user. In my case, the program is called dvroegop, so I can run it like this:

```
./dvroegop
```

I can see a friendly `Hello, World` message, so apparently it all works!

Running a .NET background worker on Linux

We have had enough theory for the moment, I think. Let's get practical. Fire up Visual Studio and start a new background worker project. In the wizard, accept all defaults until the project is ready. In the code, we leave everything as it is, including the default template printing a message every second. Run it to see that it all works.

If all goes well, you will have a new background worker running on Windows. Great! But we have seen tons of those already. Let's move our program to Linux. To do that, we have to do a couple of things.

Run your app in the WSL

We can publish directly from Visual Studio to your WSL installation. To do that, do the following.

Open your project, and go to the run menu. In the dropdown, you should see the option to deploy to WSL. This looks like this:

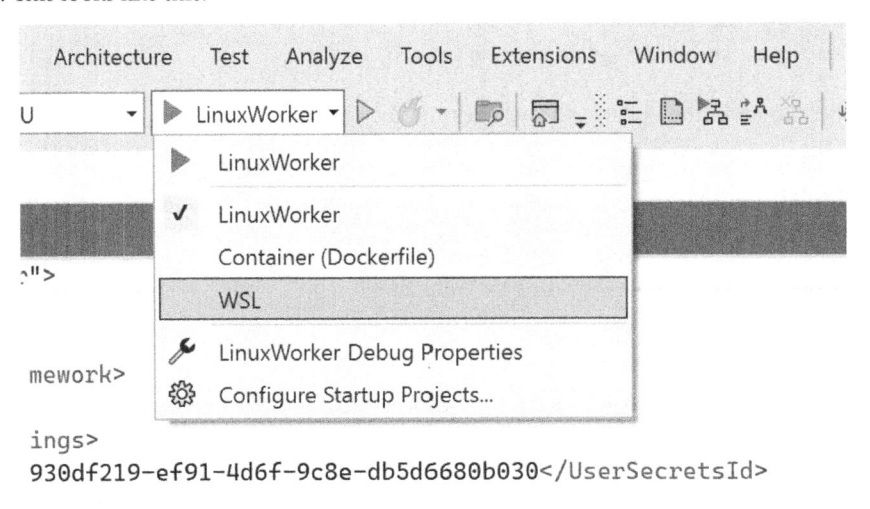

Figure 14.4: Use WSL as your debugging environment in Visual Studio

Select the **WSL** option in the dropdown.

If you have more than one distro installed in WSL, you might get a warning in Visual Studio that the default WSL does not have the correct SDK installed. If that is the case, just click the **Install** button to fix it.

The `launchSettings.json` file in the `Properties` folder of your project should also have the WSL option. This determines which distro Visual Studio will launch. If none is specified, it takes the default. In my case, I have both Ubuntu 20 and Ubuntu 22 installed, so I have to make a choice. I can instruct Visual Studio to take version 22 by changing my `launchSettings.json` to look like this:

```
"WSL": {
  "commandName": "WSL2",
  "environmentVariables": {
    "DOTNET_ENVIRONMENT": "Development"
  },
  "distributionName": "Ubuntu-22.04"
```

The distribution name is an empty string by default, resulting in Visual Studio using the default environment to run your system. Since I have specified my desired distro name, it uses that distro instead.

You can change the default distro by opening a command prompt or using the PowerShell Terminal. Then, get the list of installed distros using this command.

```
wsl --list
```

You will see the list of installed distros on your machine. On my machine, this looks like this:

```
Windows Subsystem for Linux Distributions:
Ubuntu-22.04 (Default)
docker-desktop-data
docker-desktop
Ubuntu-20.04
```

Then, you can pick one to be the default by issuing this command:

```
wsl --set-default Ubuntu-22.04
```

Of course, you can specify whatever distro you want. I happen to like `Ubuntu-22.04`.

What happens is quite interesting. Visual Studio does a lot of work to ensure we do not have to worry about deployment. Here is a simplified overview of what happens when you click **Run** after you select WSL as your environment:

1. Visual Studio builds your project as a cross-platform system.
2. Visual Studio then uses WSL to start up an instance of the subsystem.
3. Using WSL, Visual Studio then copies all the output files to the subsystem.
4. Visual Studio copies VSDBG, which is the remote debugger, to WSL.
5. It sets up VSDBG, giving it the proper permissions and enabling network communication.
6. Visual Studio then starts VSDBG in the WSL and attaches your application.
7. Finally, Visual Studio attaches itself to the running VSDBG instance.

The result is that you can use the IDE just like you are used to. You can set breakpoints, break the application, inspect variables, read system information, and so on. You will see little difference between running your app locally and running it on the WSL.

Deploy your app to a Linux environment

Running your application directly from Visual Studio is pretty cool. Still, ultimately, you want to deploy your app to the system. That's not that hard to do.

In Visual Studio, right-click on your project and choose to publish.

Build a new publish profile like you are used to, with a tiny difference – set the target runtime to **linux-x64**. Setting this framework will ensure that your app runs on Linux!

If you want, you can also deploy your app to your WSL distro. You can use a handy shortcut in Windows Explorer – navigate to the \\wsl.localhost\Ubuntu-22.04\home\[username]\ folder. Make sure to replace [username] with your username from the WSL. You can create a new folder to act as the publish profile recipient.

You can enter that folder in the profile's target location – that way, Visual Studio automatically sends all the artifacts to the right place. My profile settings look like this.

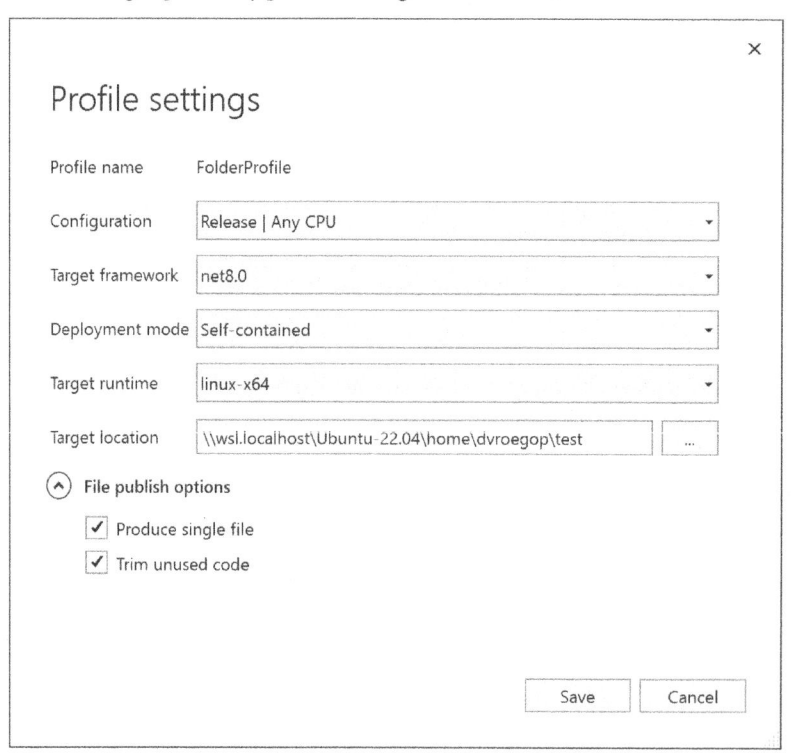

Figure 14.5: A publish profile for a Linux/WSL target

If you do this and then press the **Publish** button, your code ends up where it needs to be. Now, you can run the program from the WSL distro. Of course, if you have another Linux system running, you can use the same mechanism. If you can't make a share, you can always publish it locally and then use a tool such as SCP to copy the files.

I think we have discussed this matter enough. Next, let's discuss developing for Linux!

Make your code cross-platform

The beauty of .NET is that it is cross-platform. The IL runs almost everywhere. If you build an application, it will work on your Windows and Linux machines.

> Running an exe on Linux?
>
> No, you cannot run your Windows exe on Linux. An EXE file is a typical Windows construct. The file layout is specific to that platform, and Linux systems have another way to handle executables. However, the compiler also produces a DLL file if you build your system. That file can be run with the dotnet command. So, if your system is called MyAwesomeApp.exe, you will also find a MyAwesomeApp.dll in the Build directory. On all supported platforms, you can run your application using the dotnet MyAwesomeApp.dll command, which works on Windows and Linux.

But that doesn't mean you can copy your binaries, run them, and expect everything to work fine. There are some caveats you should be aware of. But don't worry – we'll cover them one by one here.

> Permissions in Linux
>
> Here is the first caveat – scripts and applications cannot run by default. They do not have the correct permissions. Each file has a set of permissions, telling the OS what it can do with it. These permissions differ per category. There are permissions for the user, a group, and others. The permissions themselves can be read, write, or execute. You use the chmod (**change mode**) command to set or remove these permissions. Try man chmod to get all the inside information, but remember that to make your application runnable, you have to use the chmod +x [yourapplicationname] command. The +x part tells Linux you can execute it.

Once you get the hang of it, you will find it is easy to switch between Windows and Linux. But to be completely honest, I have been known to try the chmod command on my Windows machine. Don't tell anyone I confessed to this!

How code can help you

The people who made .NET have gone out of their way to make it as easy as possible for those who need to support multiple platforms. Whereas in the "old days," you had to have a lot of compiler directives or even different versions of your code, you can now do a lot in code and have the system figure out how to handle things. Let's look at some of them.

Finding out where you run

Now and then, you want to know what platform a system runs on. There is a class called `OperatingSystem` that helps with that. It is a very simple class, but it can be tremendously powerful. Look at the following snippet:

```
if(OperatingSystem.IsWindows())
    _logger.LogInformation("Worker running on Windows");
else if(OperatingSystem.IsLinux())
    _logger.LogInformation("Worker running on Linux");
```

The `OperatingSystem` class has many more methods like this, but I am sure you get the idea. You can also use this class to determine the software's specific version of a platform if you need to know that. So, all the information you need is available.

Paths and directories

If you played around in WSL using the commands I gave you earlier in this chapter, you might have noticed that paths look quite different from what you may be used to.

For instance, the path to my home directory when I browse in Windows looks like this:

```
C:\Users\dvroe
```

My main drive is the C drive, with a `Users` folder with a subfolder, `dvroe`.

In my Linux distro, my home folder can be found at this location:

```
/home/dvroegop
```

Apparently, it can be found by going to the root, then the `home` subfolder, and finally, to the `dvroegop` folder.

There is no mention of a drive. In addition, all the slashes are the other way around.

Drives are available, but they are in a different place. Linux has a root path called `/mnt`. You can find a folder for all the drives on your machine in that folder. So, in Windows, the drive is the root of all paths; in Linux, it is a subfolder of `/mnt`.

In your code, you should never need to worry about what kind of slashes to use or how to structure your path to contain the right drive. The Path class contains all the tools you need. Look at this code:

```
var directorySeparatorChar = Path.DirectorySeparatorChar;
var pathSeparator = Path.PathSeparator;
var currentPath = Directory.GetCurrentDirectory();
var newPath = currentPath + directorySeparatorChar + "newFolder";
var betterWay = Path.Combine(currentPath, "newFolder");
var twoPaths = currentPath + pathSeparator + newPath;
$"DirectorySeparatorChar: {directorySeparatorChar}".
Dump(consoleColor);
$"PathSeparator: {pathSeparator}".Dump(consoleColor);
$"Current Path: {currentPath}".Dump(consoleColor);
$"newPath: {newPath}".Dump(consoleColor);
$"betterWay: {betterWay}".Dump(consoleColor);
$"twoPaths: {twoPaths}".Dump(consoleColor);
```

In this sample, I combine two parts of a path. You should never do that. I just wanted to show you what happens if you use DirectorySeparator. A better way to do this is to use Path.Combine(), as I also show in this code. That way, you can be sure to always get the right results.

> **A path separator versus a directory separator**
>
> I have shown you both a path separator and a directory separator in the sample. Many developers use path separators and directory separators interchangeably, but they are different things in this case. A directory separator is a character that separates different parts of an entire directory name. For instance, the c:\users\yourname\mydata path contains the three \ directory separators. A path separator is used if you need multiple directories in one string.
>
> A good example is the %PATH% environment variable, which shows all the directories that Windows uses to search for executables. They come in a long list separated by a path separator. In Windows and Linux, all these characters differ.

A similar thing happens with line endings. Windows uses two characters – return and line feed ('\r\n'). Linux uses line feed only – ('\n'). If you want to be sure your code works everywhere, use this code:

```
$"End of the output: {Environment.NewLine}".Dump(consoleColor);
```

That solves this problem for you.

Writing services for Linux

This book has mentioned background processes quite a lot. We've seen how to write them and how to deploy them. But how does that work on Linux? Let's find out!

A background service in Linux is called a **daemon**. This software runs in the background and doesn't immediately interact with a user. That sounds like something we, as system programmers, should recognize.

We can create a Worker Service in Visual Studio to write such software. Build it, then deploy it to a folder on your Linux distro.

The service description

Before you do that, add a new file to the project; this is the system description that Linux needs to register your services.

I called my file `crossplatformservice.service`. It looks like this:

```
[Unit]
Description=My .NET Core Worker Service
After=network.target
[Service]
WorkingDirectory=/home/dvroegop/service
ExecStart=/usr/bin/dotnet /home/dvroegop/service/14_
CrossPlatformService.dll
Restart=always
# Restart service after 10 seconds if the dotnet service crashes:
RestartSec=10
KillSignal=SIGINT
SyslogIdentifier=crossplatformservice
User=dvroegop
Environment=ASPNETCORE_ENVIRONMENT=Production
[Install]
WantedBy=multi-user.target
```

Obviously, you should make sure the paths in this file correspond to your paths. I doubt you have a folder called `dvroegop` on your machine. Let's investigate what this file does.

The `Unit` section contains metadata and the dependencies for the service. A `Description` is a human-readable description.

`After` specifies when the service should start. Here, we state that the service should start when the network has been initialized.

The `Service` section configures how the service should be run and managed. The parts of this section are explained in the following table:

Element	Description
`WorkingDirectory`	This is where the application will be executed. Can be used for relative path resolution.
`ExecStart`	This is the command used to start the service.
`Restart`	Defines the restart policy. `always` means it always restarts after a crash or unexpected stop.
`RestartSec`	This is the delay before restarting the service.
`KillSignal`	This defines the signal used to terminate the service. `SIGINT` is the most used one; we'll look into this later on.
`SyslogIdentifier`	Sets a name for the service's log entries.
`User`	Runs the service as a specified user.
`Environment`	Sets the environment variables needed for the service.

Table 14.7: The service elements for a service description

Finally, we have the `Install` section. This indicates how and when a service should be installed and started. The `WantedBy` element specifies the target to which this service should be linked. In our case, we used `multi-user.target`, which means it runs in a multi-user, non-graphical environment. This is typical for services such as ours.

Make sure you add this file to your deployment.

Installing the service

We can install the service once you have the binaries and the service description file on your Linux distro. In a Terminal, do the following.

Move the service description file to the correct directory. If you are in the publish directory on your distro, issue the following command:

```
sudo mv crossplatformservice.service /etc/systemd/system
```

You need to use `sudo`; a regular user has no right to access that folder.

Now, we have to restart the system manager configuration. Do that with this command:

```
sudo systemctl daemon-reload
```

Once the configuration is reloaded and has read our service description file, we can enable the service:

```
sudo systemctl enable crossplatformservice
```

The name `crossplatformservice` is the one that I used in the `SyslogIdentifier` setting in the description file.

If the Linux system restarts, our service will also start. But you don't have to reboot – you can also manually start the service to see whether everything works out fine. Do this with the following command:

```
sudo systemctl start crossplatformservice
```

The results are probably disappointing; you see nothing. But you can verify if it all worked out by using this command:

```
sudo systemctl status crossplatformservice
```

This command returns the status, confirming that everything works as expected.

If you want more information, you can look in the log files. All logs are collected by Linux, and acquiring them is done with this command:

```
sudo journalctl -u crossplatformservice
```

This command shows the last entries in the logs. Since many applications use the log, we can filter the results to only show the ones belonging to our service. That is what the -u parameter does.

You should get the expected data on your screen to confirm that the service works!

Uninstalling the service

You might want to get rid of the service on your development machine. That's not too difficult; just reverse the steps we just took.

1. First, stop the service:

    ```
    sudo systemctl stop crossplatformservice
    ```

2. Then, disable the service:

    ```
    sudo systemctl disable crossplatformservice
    ```

3. Remove the service description file:

    ```
    sudo rm /etc/systemd/system/crossplatformservice.Service
    ```

4. After that, reload the daemon configuration:

   ```
   sudo systemctl daemon-reload
   ```

5. And that's it. To verify that the service really is deleted, use this command:

   ```
   sudo systemctl status crossplatformservice
   ```

That last command should return an error, as our service no longer exists.

Handling signals

In the service description file, we told the system that our application could be stopped with the `SIGINT` signal. But that was not really true, as we haven't done anything to process signals.

> **What are signals?**
>
> A signal can be compared to events on a Windows machine, or, if you remember from earlier chapters, instances of Windows messages. In other words, they are messages that are sent to your application. Some are predefined, while others are user-defined, meaning you can also use them to communicate between programs. In this case, we are talking about the two most used messages in Linux. That's all there is to it.

Signals are ways for the operating system to send messages to your application or service. Two of the most used signals are `SIGINT` and `SIGTERM`. The first one, `SIGINT`, requests an interrupt – the OS wants to stop the service. The second, `SIGTERM`, is meant to stop the application immediately. I agree that it is hard to see the difference between these two, but there is logic here – `SIGINT` is usually a response to a user doing something, such as pressing *Ctrl + C*. You could say that a user is responsible for sending `SIGINT`. The `SIGTERM` signal is from the OS or other services if they think our service needs to be terminated.

We must write code to handle these signals and make our application behave nicely.

To do that, we must import a NuGet package. In this case, we need `Mono.Posix.NETStandard`.

Once you have done that, go to the `Worker` class and add the following method to that class:

```
private void RegisterSignalHandlers()
{
    // This is the default behavior for SIGTERM
    AppDomain.CurrentDomain.ProcessExit +=
        (sender, eventArgs) => $"Process exit".Dump();

    // Handle the signals
    UnixSignal[] signals =
    {
```

```
            new(Signum.SIGINT),
            new(Signum.SIGTERM)
        };
        var signalThread = new Thread(() =>
        {
            while (true)
            {
                var index = UnixSignal.WaitAny(signals);
                SignalHandler(signals[index].Signum);
            }
        })
        {
            IsBackground = true
        };
        signalThread.Start();
    }
```

This method does two things. First, it registers eventhandler for the "normal" ProcessExit event. This event is called when a process needs to terminate and is part of the .NET Runtime. In Linux, this is called when SIGTERM is used.

Next, we tell the system to listen to the SIGINT and SIGTERM signals. We create an array with these values and start a new background thread. All that the thread does is wait for those signals to arrive. When they do, it calls the SignalHandler() method. This method looks like this:

```
private void SignalHandler(Signum signal)
{
    switch (signal)
    {
        case Signum.SIGINT:
            _logger.LogInformation("Received SIGINT");
            break;
        case Signum.SIGTERM:
            _logger.LogInformation("Received SIGTERM");
            break;
        default:
            _logger.LogInformation($"Received signal {(int)signal}");
            break;
    }
    Environment.Exit(0);
}
```

This method is simple enough – we write to the log that we received and then terminate the program.

In the constructor of the `Worker` class, we add the call to `RegisterSignalHandlers()`, and then we are good to go.

Run the program from Linux (not as a service, but as a regular program), press *Ctrl + C*, and note the messages telling you that we managed to capture the signal. Cool, isn't it?

Summing up

Now, you should have all the knowledge to start working on Linux programs. Linux is the platform of choice for many services. Services, of course, are something we as system programmers work with all the time. Although a great platform, Linux has a steep learning curve. Many things are similar to what you are used to in Windows but differ slightly, whereas other things are entirely new or unique to the platform.

It takes time to learn it well. But with what we've discussed in this chapter, you are well on your way to feeling at home with Linux. We explored the history of the platform, and we discussed some of its most used commands. We discussed development and looked at how to write daemons for Linux.

Let's recap

Sit back. Take a deep breath. You've made it. You've reached the end of the book. And I hope you learned a thing or two.

Don't underestimate what we've done. We've answered so many questions:

- What is systems programming?
- How do we use low-level APIs?
- How do we use the Win32 API?
- How can we make our software run faster?
- How can we make our software memory efficient?
- What is I/O and how do we use it?
- What is the best way to have systems communicate over a network?
- How do we monitor and log what our systems are doing?
- What is the ultimate way to debug these low-level systems?
- How do we even deploy it all?
- How do we work with Linux?

That's a lot of information! But you have taken the challenge. You can call yourself a specialist in writing fast-performing, memory-efficient, network-aware, secure, and cross-platform low-level system software. That's a long title, but you deserve it!

And don't forget – these newfound skills made you a better developer. These skills can be applied to all sorts of projects, not only systems programming. The basic principles stand and are applicable everywhere. I look forward to hearing from you and discovering what you are going to do with what you have learned. The best way to learn new techniques is to try them out. So, I urge you to try the samples and write awesome system software. I have faith in you!

Index

A

action breakpoints 318
active breakpoints 318
Address Resolution Protocol (ARP) 179
admin-level scenarios 365
   filesystem operations 365
   network configuration 365
   registry operations 365
   service management 365
   system monitoring and diagnostics 365
Advanced Encryption Standard (AES) 159
ahead-of-time (AOT) compilation 384
algorithms
   selecting 58
anonymous pipes 176-178
ANTS Performance Profiler 346
AppDomain 5
application
   deploying, to Linux 426, 427
   publishing 381
   publishing, with CLI 384-386
   publishing, with Visual Studio 382-384
   running, in WSL 424-426
application performance
   profiling 337, 338

applications monitoring 296
   application logs 307
   application-specific metrics 307
   basic health monitoring 306
   dependency health 308
   errors 307
   exceptions 307
   performance counters 298-300
   tools 305, 306
   with Prometheus 300-305
   with Seq 296-298
AQtime 347
Arduino IDE 258
   device 258, 259
   software 260-262
arrays 58
asymmetric algorithm 156
Async all the way to the top rule 113
async/await pattern 110-115
asynchronous I/O 152
   BufferedStream class 155, 156
   CancellationTokens, using 153, 154
   naïve approach 152
Azure
   deploying to 386

438   Index

Azure DevOps
   continuous integration, enabling 392-395
   publish profile, building for 387-392
Azure Key Vault
   using 360, 361

B

Base Class Library (BCL) 27, 28
Basic Input/Output System (BIOS) 195
baud 253
benchmarking 337, 341
   solutions 341-344
Binary serialization 166-168
blocking code 237
Bourne Again Shell (Bash) 414
boxing 54, 55, 88
breakpoints 315
   code hitting, example 315, 316
   features 317-320

C

CancellationToken 275
certificate authorities (CAs) 371
ciphertext 157
circuit breaker pattern 248
cleartext 157
CLI
   used, for publishing application 384-386
code debugging issues, low-level APIs 39
   community support 43
   compatibility 43
   debugging tools 42
   documentation 43
   error handling 39
   interoperability 40-42
   portability 43

Common Language Runtime (CLR) 25, 26, 72
   features 26, 27
Common Language Specification (CLS) 50
Common Type System (CTS) 49
   classes 50
   floating-point numbers 51
   reference types 50
   reference type, versus value type 52
   stack, versus heap 52, 53
   structs 50
   value types 50
Communication Ports (COMs) 253
compiler optimizations 68
   aggressive optimization 68
   optimize flag 69
components, Linux
   daemons 414
   system libraries 414
   system utilities 414
COM ports 263
concurrency 97, 98
   Interrupt Request (IRQ) 99
concurrent collections, in .NET 127-130
conditional breakpoints 318
console application 354
console window 203
continuous integration and continuous deployment (CI/CD) 386
continuous integration (CI)
   enabling, from GitHub 395, 396
   enabling, in Azure DevOps 392-394
cooperative cancellation 120
cooperative multitasking 100
cross-platform code
   building 427
   paths and directories 428, 429
   running 428
   using 428

D

daemon 430
data structures
  selecting 58
deadlocks 332
  debugging 332, 333
  debugging, with Parallel Stacks 334
  debugging, with Threads window 334, 335
Debug builds
  versus Release builds 314
debugging 311-313
debugging tools 345
  Debug Diagnostic Tool (DebugDiag) 345
  GNU Debugger (GDB) 345
  LLVM Debugger (LLDB) 345
  Managed Debugger (MDbg) 345
  Microsoft Performance Tools (PerfView) 345
  ProcDump 345
  Remote Debugging Tools 345
  Son of Strike (SOS) Debugging Extension 345
  Strace 346
  Valgrind 345
  Visual Studio Code Debugger 345
  Visual Studio Debugger 345
  WinDbg 345
  Windows Performance Recorder (WPR) 345
debug windows 321
  Autos window 321-323
  Breakpoints window 321
  Locals window 321, 323
  Watch window 323
default logger, .NET 279, 280
  EventId, using 283, 284
  log levels 280, 281
  Settings file, using 282, 283
  Type information, using 284

dependent breakpoint 319, 320
development environment
  setting up 16
Diagnostic Tools window 324-326
Dictionary 60, 61
Directory class 144
  methods and properties 145, 146
DirectoryInfo class 146
  methods and properties 146, 147
directory operations 142
  Directory class 144-146
  DirectoryInfo class 146, 147
  Path class 143
directory separator
  versus path separator 429
distributed systems 2
Docker
  images, deploying 405, 406
  Production-ready Docker repository 407
  support, adding to background worker 404, 405
  using 404
Domain Name System (DNS) 236
Dynamic Link Library (DLL) 27, 28

E

elevated privileges 420, 421
email protocols 230
  email, sending 230, 231
  HTML messages, sending 231, 232
  IMAP 230
  MIME 230
  POP3 230
  SMTP 230
embedded systems 2
environment variables
  using 362

environment variable scopes 362
  machine scope (or system scope) 362-364
  process scope 362, 363
  session scope 362
  user scope 362, 363
  volatile environment variables 362

F

features, breakpoints 317, 320
  action breakpoints 318
  active breakpoints 318
  conditional breakpoints 318
  dependent breakpoint 319
  inactive breakpoints 318
  one-time breakpoint 319
  tracepoints 318
file compression 162
  data, compressing 162, 163
  data, decompressing 163, 164
file reading basics 140
  binary data reading 141, 142
FileStream 135-137
file system monitoring 147-151
  NotifyFilters options 149
file system security 156
  asymmetric decryption 160, 161
  asymmetric encryption 160, 161
  encryption basics 156, 157
  symmetric decryption 158-160
  symmetric encryption 158-160
File Transfer Protocol (FTP) 224, 228, 229
file writing basics 134, 135
  FileStream 135-137
  Win32 approach 138, 139
finalizer 78
  implications 79
first in, first out (FIFO) 59

foolproof system
  CancellationToken, using 275
  code, hardening 274
  creating 273
  failure reasons 273, 274
  logging and monitoring 276
  resource management 275
  robust connection loop, implementing 275
  thread safety, ensuring 275
  Try…Catch, using 275
ForEach 62

G

garbage collector (GC) 72
  finalizers 77-79
  generations 72-75
  IDisposable pattern 79-80, 81-87
  large object heap (LOH) 76
GlowCode 347
Gnu C Compiler (GCC) 421
GNU Debugger (GDB) 345
Google Performance Tools (gperftools) 346
Google remote procedure call (gRPC)
  NuGet packages, for client 192, 193
  NuGet packages, for server 189-192
  overview 189
  versus JSON RPC 193

H

HashSet 60
hidden boxing 56, 57
hidden unboxing 56-58
HTTPClient class 244-246
Hypertext Transfer Protocol (HTTP) 226, 227
Hyper Text Transport Protocol Secure (HTTPS) 369

Index

I

IDisposable pattern 79-86
inactive breakpoints 318
INI files 196
Initialization Vector (IV) 159
Input and Output (I/O) 133
installers 396
   building, with Visual Studio 396
   Custom Action, incorporating in setup 402, 403
   Custom Action, writing 399-402
   simple installer, building 397-399
integer
   selecting 47-49
interface
   hardware interface 20
   software interface 20
Intermediate Language (IL) code 82
Internet Control Message Protocol (ICMP) 179
Internet Message Access Protocol (IMAP) 230
Internet Protocol (IP) 179
interprocess communication (IPC) 169
   data format and serialization 170
   deadlocks 171
   documentation and maintainability 171
   error handling 171
   importance in modern computing 170
   language, selecting 170
   overview 170
   performance and scalability 171
   platform and environment constraints 171
   security 170
   synchronization 171
Interrupt Request (IRQ) 99

J

JetBrains dotTrace 346
JSON RPC 186-189
   versus gRPC 193
JSON serialization 164-166
just-in-time (JIT) compiler 47

K

kernel mode 9
key management 360
   Azure Key Vault, using 360, 361
   environment variable scopes 362
   environment variables, reading in code 364
   environment variables, setting 363
   environment variables, using 362

L

large object heap (LOH) 76
last in, first out (LIFO) 59
lazy initialization 88
LinkedList 59
Linux 411-413
   basic commands 418
   components 414
   development for 421
   distributions 414-416
   history 412, 413
   .NET background worker, running 424
   .NET, installing 421
   software 414
   using 416
Linux commands
   basic navigation and file management 418
   file viewing and editing 418

network commands 419
package management 420
system information and processes 419
Linux kernel 413
responsibilities 413
List<Tuple> 61
Lists 59
LLVM Debugger (LLDB) 345
local JSON files 203
logging frameworks 279
comparing 294, 295
default logger, in .NET 279, 280
NLog 285
Serilog 291
logical CPU 9
Long Term Support (LTS) 14
low-level APIs 20
calling 21-23
calling, with P/Invoke 29-34
debugging code challenges 39
errors handling 34-39
versus, high-level APIs 20

M

Managed Debugger (MDbg) 345
memory management 72
memory pressure 87
reducing 87-90
memory-saving tips 87
Microsoft Performance Tools (PerfView) 345
Multipurpose Internet Mail Extension (MIME) protocol 230
multithreaded code 327

N

named pipe 174, 175
.NET 12, 13
advantages 10-12
.NET background worker
running, on Linux 424
.NET Core 12-14
.NET Core runtime components 24
BCL 27
CLR 24-27
.NET Framework 14
.NET installation, on Linux
.NET Runtime, installing 422
performing 421
SDK, installing 423
.NET Memory Profiler 346
.NET SDK 422
.NET Standard 14
.NET threads 105-107
suspended thread 106
unstarted thread 106
network data transmission
certificates and certificate authorities 370, 371
development certificate, creating 372, 373
HTTPS 368-370
performing securely 368
TCP streams, securing 373-378
networking 101 178
networking applications
asynchronous calls, making 237, 238
networking errors and time-outs 244
non-blocking networking 237

Index 443

networking errors and time-outs
  circuit breaker pattern 248
  HTTPClient class, using 244-246
  monitoring and logging 249
  network availability, validating 248, 249
  retries, implementing with Polly 246, 247
networking performance 239
  caching 243
  compression 244
  connection pooling 239-243
  keep-alive connections 244
  serialization 244
Network Time Protocol (NTP) 235
NLog 285
  additional settings 291
  asynchronous logging 290, 291
  log levels 287
  rules 289, 290
  setting up 285, 286
  targets 288, 289
non-blocking networking 237

O

one-time breakpoint 319
Open Systems Interconnection (OSI) 178
  layers 179, 224, 225
operating systems 2
optimize flag 69
OutOfMemoryException error
  handling 76

P

page fault 104
Parallel Stacks
  deadlock, debugging 334
Parallel Watch window 327, 328
  adding 329
  Freeze option 330, 331
  Switch To Frame option 329
  Thaw option 330, 331
Path class 143
  methods and properties 143, 144
path separator
  versus directory separator 429
Perf 347
Perfino 347
PerfView 17, 346
pipes 174
  anonymous pipe 174-178
  named pipe 174, 175
  working with 174
Platform Invocation (P/Invoke) 29
  example 30
  used, for calling low-level APIs 29-34
  working 29
PL/I programming language 8
pointers
  using 91-94
Polly 246
  installing 246, 247
Post Operation Protocol (POP3) 230
preemptive multitasking 100
privilege level
  admin-level scenarios 365
  impersonating, as an admin 365-368
  using 364
ProcDump 345
profiling 313, 336, 337
  in Visual Studio 338-341
profiling tools 346
  ANTS Performance Profiler 346
  AQtime 347
  GlowCode 347
  Google Performance Tools (gperftools) 346

JetBrains dotTrace 346
.NET Memory Profiler 346
Perf 347
Perfino 347
PerfView 346
Valgrind 346
Visual Studio Profiler 346
VTune Profiler 346
Windows Performance Analyzer (WPA) 346
WPR 346
YourKit Profiler 347

Programming Language One 8
programming languages
  selecting 15
Prometheus
  URL 301
  used, for application monitoring 301-305
Protocol Buffers (Protobufs) 189
publish profile
  building, for Azure DevOps 387-392

Q

queues 59

R

Release builds
  versus Debug builds 314
Remote Debugging Tools 345
remote procedure call (RPC)
  JSON RPC 186-189
  overview 186
  using, for IPC 186
RESTFul services
  versus RPC 186
Rivest, Shamir, and Adleman (RSA) class 160

S

SecureStrings
  using 358-360
security 349
  for system programmers 350
  protection 352, 353
  vulnerability management 350-352
Seq 296
  used, for application monitoring 296-298
serial device
  faking 271, 272
serialization 164
  Binary serialization 166, 167
  JSON serialization 164-166
serial ports
  Arduino 257
  connecting to 252
  data size 256
  data sizes 255
  hardware 252-254
  parity 255, 256
  precautions 254
  serial data, receiving with .NET 262-266
  speed 255
  stop hits 255, 257
  working 269-271
  wrapping 266-268
Serilog 291
  log levels 294
  sinks 292
  standard logging 292, 293
service 204
services, for Linux
  description 430, 431
  installing 431
  signals, handling 433, 434
  uninstalling 432
  writing 430

Index 445

shared memory 184
  using, for data exchange between processes 184, 185
Simple Mail Transfer Protocol (SMTP) 230
sockets 178
  using, to establish network-based IPC 178
software
  software facing software 3
  user-facing software 2
Son of Strike (SOS) Debugging Extension 345
SortedDictionary 60
SortedList 60
stacks 59
stage setup 46
  accessibility 46
  energy usage 47
  hosting costs 47
  planned obsolescence 47
Standard Term Support (STS) 14
stop bits 257
Strace 346
streams 133
strings 62, 63
  comparison 64, 65
  disclosing, in your application 357, 358
  encrypted data, reading 356
  handling, in memory 357
  interning 63
  keys, locating 356
  SecureStrings, using 358-360
  settings, protecting 353-356
  StringBuilder, preallocating 66
  StringBuilder, using for concatenation 63
  String.Concat, using 64
  String.Join, using 64
  working with 353
su command 420

sudo command 420
symmetric algorithm 156
system
  definition 1
  distributed systems 2
  embedded systems 2
  operating systems 2
  software systems 2
system mode 9
System.Net namespace 226
  email protocols 230
  FTP 227-229
  HTTP/HTTPS 226, 227
System.Net.Sockets namespace
  IPv4 and IPv6 234
  sockets, working with 233
  time servers 235-237
  working with 232, 233
Systems Programming
  C#, using 8
  definition 1
  higher level languages 8
  .NET, using 8

T

Task Parallel Library (TPL) 108-110
Task.Result 115
Task.Wait() 115
TCP-based chat app 179-183
threading 97, 98
threads 100
  and breakpoints 316, 317
  canceling 120-123
  .NET threads 105-107
  principle 100, 101
  Win32 threads 101-104
thread-safe collections 129

Index

thread-safe programming techniques 124
  lock() 125
  records, creating 126
  static members and classes, avoiding 126
  volatile keyword, using 127
Threads window
  deadlock, debugging 334, 335
thread synchronization 116-119
  with async/await 119, 120
tracepoints 318
Transmission Control Protocol (TCP) connection 171
Try...Catch
  using 275

U

unboxing 54, 55
Unicode standard 62
unsafe code
  using 91-94
  writing 66, 67
User Datagram Protocol (UDP) 179, 183
  versus TCP 183
user-facing software
  identifying 3-6
user mode 9

V

Valgrind 345, 346
Visual Studio 2022 Enterprise 16
Visual Studio Code Debugger 345
Visual Studio Debugger 42, 345
Visual Studio Profiler 346
Visual Studio (VS) 314, 344, 363
  used, for publishing application 382-384
VTune Profiler 346

W

Win32 approach
  for file writing 138, 139
Win32 threads 101-104
WinDbg tool 17, 345, 357
Windows Management Instrumentation (WMI) 210, 211, 217, 263
  BIOS, reading 213, 214
  CPU temperature, reading 212
  risks, managing 219-222
  USB devices, watching 215, 216
  using 211, 212
  Windows Update service, controlling 214, 215
Windows Messages 172
  parameters 172, 173
  sample 173, 174
Windows NT kernel 414
Windows Performance Analyzer (WPA) 346
Windows Performance Recorder (WPR) 345, 346
Windows Registry 196-198
  binary data 197
  current settings, backing up 218
  data, accessing 199
  data, storing 199-201
  data types 198, 199
  error handling 218
  features 202
  loggings 218
  proper tools 218
  risks, managing 217, 218
  testing in isolated environment 219
  top-level keys 198
  versus JSON settings files 202
WMI Query Language (WQL) 219
worker process 5

Worker Services 203
  dissecting 206-208
  Docker support 205, 206
  lifetime, controlling 208, 209
  running 205
  wrapping up 210

Y

YourKit Profiler 347

<packt>

packtpub.com

Subscribe to our online digital library for full access to over 7,000 books and videos, as well as industry leading tools to help you plan your personal development and advance your career. For more information, please visit our website.

Why subscribe?

- Spend less time learning and more time coding with practical eBooks and Videos from over 4,000 industry professionals
- Improve your learning with Skill Plans built especially for you
- Get a free eBook or video every month
- Fully searchable for easy access to vital information
- Copy and paste, print, and bookmark content

Did you know that Packt offers eBook versions of every book published, with PDF and ePub files available? You can upgrade to the eBook version at packtpub.com and as a print book customer, you are entitled to a discount on the eBook copy. Get in touch with us at customercare@packtpub.com for more details.

At www.packtpub.com, you can also read a collection of free technical articles, sign up for a range of free newsletters, and receive exclusive discounts and offers on Packt books and eBooks.

Other Books You May Enjoy

If you enjoyed this book, you may be interested in these other books by Packt:

Pragmatic Microservices with C# and Azure

Christian Nagel

ISBN: 978-1-83508-829-6

- Understand microservices architecture benefits
- Utilize the cloud-ready .NET Aspire stack along with its associated tools and libraries
- Develop REST APIs with ASP.NET Core minimal APIs
- Implement database integration with relational and NoSQL databases
- Containerize microservices using Docker
- Deploy microservices to the Azure Container Apps environment and Kubernetes
- Configure logging, monitoring, and tracing for microservices
- Use advanced communication patterns with SignalR, gRPC, queues, and events

Refactoring with C#

Matt Eland

ISBN: 978-1-83508-998-9

- Understand technical debt, its causes and effects, and ways to prevent it
- Explore different ways of refactoring classes, methods, and lines of code
- Discover how to write effective unit tests supported by libraries such as Moq
- Understand SOLID principles and factors that lead to maintainable code
- Use AI to analyze, improve, and test code with the GitHub Copilot Chat
- Apply code analysis and custom Roslyn analyzers to ensure that code stays clean
- Communicate tech debt and code standards successfully in agile teams

Packt is searching for authors like you

If you're interested in becoming an author for Packt, please visit `authors.packtpub.com` and apply today. We have worked with thousands of developers and tech professionals, just like you, to help them share their insight with the global tech community. You can make a general application, apply for a specific hot topic that we are recruiting an author for, or submit your own idea.

Share Your Thoughts

Now you've finished *Systems Programming with C# and .NET*, we'd love to hear your thoughts! Scan the QR code below to go straight to the Amazon review page for this book and share your feedback or leave a review on the site that you purchased it from.

`https://packt.link/r/1-835-08268-8`

Your review is important to us and the tech community and will help us make sure we're delivering excellent quality content.

Download a free PDF copy of this book

Thanks for purchasing this book!

Do you like to read on the go but are unable to carry your print books everywhere?

Is your eBook purchase not compatible with the device of your choice?

Don't worry, now with every Packt book you get a DRM-free PDF version of that book at no cost.

Read anywhere, any place, on any device. Search, copy, and paste code from your favorite technical books directly into your application.

The perks don't stop there, you can get exclusive access to discounts, newsletters, and great free content in your inbox daily

Follow these simple steps to get the benefits:

1. Scan the QR code or visit the link below

   `https://packt.link/free-ebook/978-1-83508-268-3`

2. Submit your proof of purchase
3. That's it! We'll send your free PDF and other benefits to your email directly

Made in United States
North Haven, CT
08 February 2025